294583

DATE DUE

NOV 27 1991 BIRD			
		DEC 7 1991 RET	

Demco, Inc. 38-293

TWENTIETH CENTURY:
THE GREAT ISSUES

TWENTIETH CENTURY:
THE GREAT ISSUES

Edited by
William R. Hitchcock
University of California, Santa Cruz

Wadsworth Publishing Company, Inc.
Belmont, California

L. C. Cat. Card No.: 68–55792
Printed in the United States of America

PREFACE

A volume concentrating on the twentieth century is a relative rarity, in contrast to the number of books available on Western civilization or American culture. It certainly does seem simpler to draw up an anthology of classical Greek writings than to compile one from the mysterious present with which we are still involved. Fearless in this respect, the present collection aims at making available unfamiliar and unusual selections covering a wide spectrum of contemporary experience. The results are by no means definitive: I do not pretend to cover everything in the present century. Nor have I sought to effect a gathering of great writers or great ideas. An obscure writer may make the point as well as a celebrated author, and may help us see society as something other than a collection of geniuses busily "influencing" one another.

To stimulate discussion and individual thought, I have sought to include examples that express a clearly defined point of view and then have, whenever possible, juxtaposed some equally cogent expression of an opposite opinion. Certainly a provocative example of this approach is Churchill, young and radical, followed by Churchill, old and conservative (Chapter 9).

The reader, then, is about to discover not merely the convenience of a number of sources in one handy reference, but an interpretation of our experiences. In Charles A. Beard's phrase, here is "an interpretation of history past and in the making."

H

Particular thanks are due Mr. Leonard Freedman for editorial counsel plus innumerable suggestions, and Mrs. Phyllis Halpin for tireless secretarial efforts.

CONTENTS

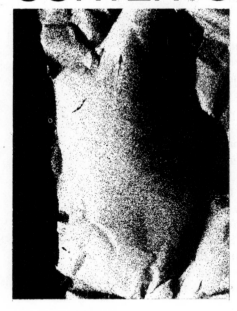

INTRODUCTION

Unlike some preceding ages, the twentieth century still has no identifying and presumably descriptive label, such as the "Renaissance" or the "Enlightenment." Various titles, ranging from critical to morbid, have been suggested—"Age of Anxiety," "Age of Aspirin," "Age of the Bomb." Older readers may recall the "contest" to select a fitting name for the most recent world war. Alas, it has remained World War II, a part of the twentieth century (not something like the "War of Liberation," a part of the "Age of the Common Man"). So we have no easy stereotypes to serve as boosters in the launching phase of our journey through the twentieth century. This is a blessing perhaps, since these stereotypes, unlike auxiliary rockets, do not always fall away in the second stage.

Accordingly, selecting characteristic readings from this period involves some definition of it. Instead of gathering those items illustrating what others have pointed out as the dominant characteristics of the period, the editor must, through the process of selectivity, advance his own thesis about the nature of the twentieth century.

The editor is aware that expressions appearing significant and revealing to him may say nothing to readers. This book seeks the identity of the century, but risks the presumption that this identity is the correct one and will seem so in decades to come. It is little comfort to recall critics and editors of the past who have hailed the ephemeral and dismissed the eternal!

A book of readings, of whatever century, implies a book of authors. Such a book tends to emphasize individuals, particularly those gifted with talents of expression. And the expressions of individuals inevitably predominate over statistical tables, for even the activities of crowds are described by acute individual observers. However, two of the commonest labels associated with the twentieth century have to do with the suppression of the individual: the "Mass Society" and the "Punch-card Age." It is also stylish to see our times as Franz Kafka viewed the world —with men as faceless automatons trapped in a no-man's-land and bombarded by an unseen, mysterious enemy. Our "search for identity" is made impossible, we are told, by "failure of communication." Yet this book contains extremely precise communication by many individuals. Or are these merely precise notions about the imprecise, carefully reasoned investigations of irrationalism?

If the individual still plays an important role, we should seek out those who particularly understand and speak for the century. Can Winston Churchill still be applauded as "the man of the twentieth century"? Should Bernard Shaw be relegated to the category of "last of the Victorians"? What better irony can be found than Shaw's earliest writing for the Fabian Society in 1884: "We had rather face a civil war than such another century of suffering as the present one has been"? Yet what a strange note of affirmation he gives in his evolutionary eulogy to human intelligence, *Man and Superman,* in 1903, a faith confirmed and put in scientific terms by the noted biologist P. B. Medawar in 1959 (Chapter 10).

Irony or affirmation? Since the former may seem particularly apropos, should we rather say, in twentieth century terms, "irony and/or affirmation"? To use its own jargon, the twentieth century is involved in a crisis of identity. Hopefully the present volume will contribute to the process of this century's finding itself.

1
Revolt Against the Old Order

We often refer to 1914 as the great dividing line between a golden age ("after plumbing and before taxes") and the endless horrors of the present century. Yet it is a commonplace of historical discussion to minimize the conflicts of one's own day by pointing to similar controversies in more distant periods.

Looking back on our own century we can see that whatever the importance of 1914, the "Twentieth Century" was taking a different turn by the time of World War I. The nineties of the previous century had been turbulent years of change, and thinking had been revolutionary in many areas, especially in the fields of art and women's rights. Holbrook Jackson's classic description of the eighteen nineties (written in 1913) suggests many parallels with our day and tempts us to approach the twentieth century as merely another of the endless variations in human folly. Yet, the last decade of the nineteenth century should not present a false analogy and obscure the distinct and peculiar outlines of the twentieth century. To understand ourselves and our era, to be aware of broad historical similarities and yet to beware of false analogies, we need to examine the early years of this century.

"In 1900, all was stable," ruefully asserts Spanish historian Salvador de Madariaga, looking back from 1954. But a closer examination of the old order reveals just how shaky were its foundations. American historian Charles A. Beard describes the rise of the world monetary system and its complete breakdown in the Great Depression of the nineteen thirties. That able critic George Bernard Shaw, middle-aged by the opening years of the twentieth century, was on the verge of conquering the theater in the hope of "using art to provoke thought." He poked at the apathy of the masses and the ineptness of the political aristocracy. Historian R. J. Sontag points out the unrest in Europe, where countries were struggling to maintain a balance of military power in order to forestall any one country from becoming all-powerful.

But with the war of 1914, "the twentieth century burst into history," tells Madariaga. "Gone the formal frames of the nineteenth." Mankind entered into a period of struggle and instability from which it has yet to emerge.

Holbrook Jackson
FIN DE SIÈCLE

In the year 1895 Max Beerbohm announced, how whimsically and how ironically it is not necessary to consider, that he felt himself a trifle out-moded. 'I belong to the Beardsley period,' he said. The Eighteen Nineties were then at their meridian; but it was already the afternoon of the Beardsley period. That very year Aubrey Beardsley's strange black and white masses and strong delicate lines disappeared from *The Yellow Book,* and he contributed only to the first few numbers of *The Savoy,* which began in 1896. Fatal disease was overtaking him, and remorse. Aubrey Beardsley actually abandoned his period in the evening of its brief day, and when he died, in 1898, the Beardsley period had almost become a memory. But after all, Aubrey Beardsley was but an incident of the Eighteen Nineties, and only relatively a significant incident. He was

From *The Eighteen Nineties* by Holbrook Jackson, pp. 15, 16–20, 21–22, 24–27, 28–30, published by Jonathan Cape Ltd. Reprinted by permission of the Executors of the Holbrook Jackson Estate.

Holbrook Jackson (1874–1948) was a British journalist and author of many books about books.

but one expression of *fin de siècle* daring, of a bizarre and often exotic courage, prevalent at the time and connected but indirectly, and often negatively, with some of the most vital movements of a decade which was singularly rich in ideas, personal genius and social will. Aubrey Beardsley crowded the vision of the period by the pecularity of his art rather than by any need there was of that art to make the period complete. He was, therefore, not a necessity of the Eighteen Nineties, although his appearance in the decade was inevitable; indeed he was so essentially *fin de siècle* that one can say of him with more confidence than of any other artist of the decade that his appearance at any other time would have been inopportune. . . .

Max Nordau, the Jeremiah of the period, linked up his famous attack on what were called '*fin de siècle* tendencies' with certain traditional beliefs in the evil destiny of the closure of centuries. 'The disposition of the times is curiously confused,' he said; 'a compound of feverish restlessness and blunted discouragement, of fearful presage and hang-dog renunciation. The prevalent feeling is that of imminent perdition and extinction. *Fin de siècle* is at once a confession and a complaint. The old northern faith contained the fearsome doctrine of the Dusk of the Gods. In our days there have arisen in more highly developed minds vague qualms of the Dusk of the Nations, in which all suns and all stars are gradually waning, and mankind with all its institutions and creation is perishing in the midst of a dying world.' All of which sounds very hectic and hysterical now, nearly twenty years after it was first written, when many of the writers and artists he condemned have become harmless classics, and some almost forgotten. But it is interesting to remember Nordau's words, because they are an example of the very liveliness of a period which was equally lively in making or marring itself. The Eighteen Nineties, however, were not entirely decadent and hopeless; and even their decadence was often decadence only in name, for much of the genius denounced by Max Nordau as degeneration was a sane and healthy expression of a vitality which, as it is not difficult to show, would have been better named regeneration.

At the same time the fact must not be overlooked that much of the vitality of the period, much even of its effective vitality, was destructive of ideas and conventions which we had come to look upon as more or less permanent; and one cannot help feeling, at this distance, that not a little of *fin de siècle* attractiveness was the result of abandonment due to internal chaos. But this is no cause for condemnation on our part, still less for self-complacency; for, as we have been told by Friedrich Nietzsche, himself a half-felt motive force, in this country at least, behind the tendencies of the times: 'Unless you have chaos within you cannot give birth to a dancing star.' More than one dancing star swam into our ken in the last decade of the nineteenth century, and the proof of the regenerative powers of the period is to be found most obviously, but perhaps even more certainly, if not quite so plainly, in the fact that those who were most allied with its moods and whims were not only conscious of the fact, but in some cases capable of looking at themselves and laughing. *Fin de siècle* was a pose as well as a fact, a point not realised by Nordau. John Davidson, among others, was able to smile at its extravagances, and in *Earl Lavender,* his burlesque novel of the decadence, one of the characters, a garrulous Cockney dame with a smattering of French, reveals the existence of power to cast what Meredith would have called 'the oblique ray' upon the doings of the time. 'It's *fang-de-seeaycle* that does it, my dear,' says this lady, 'and education, and reading French.'

It is obvious, then, that people felt they were living amid changes and struggles, intellectual, social and spiritual, and the interpreters of the hour—the publicists, journalists and popular purveyors of ideas of all kinds—did not fail to make a sort of traffic in the spirit of the times. Anything strange or uncanny, anything which savoured of freak and perversity, was swiftly labelled *fin de siècle,* and given a certain topical prominence. The term became a fashion, and writers vied one with another as to which should apply it most aptly. At least one writer emphasised the phrase in an attempt to stigmatise it. 'Observe,' wrote Max Beerbohm, 'that I write no fool's prattle about *la fin de siècle.'* And Max Nordau gives a useful list illustrating the manner in which the term was used in the country of its birth. A King who abdicates but retains by agreement certain political rights, which he afterwards sells to his country to provide means for the liquidation of debts contracted by play in Paris, is a *fin de siècle* king. The police official who removes a piece of the skin of the murderer Pranzini after execution and has it tanned and made into a cigar-case, is a *fin de siècle* official. An American wedding ceremony held in a gasworks and the subsequent honeymoon in a balloon is a *fin de siècle* wedding. A schoolboy who, on passing the gaol where his father is imprisoned for embezzlement, remarks to a chum: 'Look, that's the governor's school,' is a *fin de siècle* son. These are only a few from among innumerable examples illustrating the liveliness of the people of the Nineties to their hour and its characteristics. A further indication of the way in which the phrase permeated the mind of the period is found in its frequent occurrence in the books and essays of the day. It appears fittingly enough in Oscar Wilde's *The Picture of Dorian Gray,* that typical book of the period, as a reflection upon an epigram afterwards used in *A Woman of No Importance.* Lady Narborough is saying:

> "If we women did not love you for your defects, where would you all be? Not one of you would ever be married. You would be a set of unfortunate bachelors. Not, however, that that would alter you much.

Nowadays all the married men live like bachelors and all the bachelors like married men!"

"*Fin de siècle*," murmured Sir Henry.

"*Fin du globe*," answered his hostess.

"I wish it were *fin du globe*," said Dorian, with a sigh. "Life is a great disappointment."

But side by side with the prevailing use of the phrase, and running its popularity very close, came the adjective 'new'; it was applied in much the same way to indicate extreme modernity. Like *fin de siècle*, it hailed from France, and, after its original application in the phrase *l'art nouveau* had done considerable service in this country as a prefix to modern pictures, dresses and designs, our publicists discovered that other things were equally worthy of the useful adjective. Grant Allen wrote of the 'New Hedonism'; H. D. Traill, of the 'New Fiction', opening his essay with the words: 'Not to be *new* is, in these days, to be nothing.' In August 1892 William Sharp designed and produced one number, and one only, of *The Pagan Review*, which was written entirely by himself under various pseudonyms, to promote the 'New Paganism', described as 'a potent leaven in the yeast of the "younger generation", and which was concerned only with the *new* presentment of things.' And again, in the famous attack on *The Picture of Dorian Gray*, in the *St James's Gazette*, on the first appearance of the novel in the pages of *Lippincott's Monthly Magazine* for July 1890, reference is made to 'The New Voluptuousness' which 'always leads up to bloodshedding.' Oscar Wilde himself wrote on 'The New Remorse', in *The Spirit Lamp*, in 1892. The range of the adjective gradually spread until it embraced the ideas of the whole period, and we find innumerable references to the 'New Spirit', the 'New Humour', the 'New Realism', the 'New Hedonism', the 'New Drama', the 'New Unionism', the 'New Party', and the 'New Woman'. . . .

The period was as certainly a period of decadence as it was a period of renaissance. The decadence was to be seen in a perverse and finicking glorification of the fine arts and mere artistic virtuosity on the one hand, and a militant commercial movement on the other. The one produced *The Yellow Book* and the literature and art of 'fine shades', with their persistent search for the 'unique word' and the 'brilliant' expression; the other produced the 'Yellow Press', the boom in 'Kaffirs', the Jameson Raid, the Boer War and the enthronement of the South African plutocrat in Park Lane. But this decadent side of the Nineties must not be looked upon as wholly evil. Its separation from a movement obviously ascendant in spirit is not altogether admissible. The two tendencies worked together, and it is only for the sake of historical analysis that I adopt the method of segregation. Taken thus the decadence reveals qualities which, even if nothing more than 'the soul of goodness in things evil', are at times surprisingly excellent. The decadent vision of an Aubrey Beardsley introduced a new sense of rhythm into black-and-white art, just as the, on the whole, trivial masters of 'fine shades', with their peacock phrases, helped us towards a newer, more sensitive and more elastic prose form. The 'Yellow Press', with all its extravagances, was at least alive to the desires of the crowd, and the reverse of dull in the presentment of its views; and if it gave Demos the superficial ideas he liked, it was equally prepared to supply a better article when the demand arose. And, withal, a wider publicity was given to thought-provoking ideas and imaginative themes, although adjusted, and often very much adjusted, to the average taste, than had hitherto been possible. As for the 'New Park Lane' and 'New' aristocracy, they in their garish abandonment helped us to apply the abstract science of economics to life, thus probably preparing the path for the Super-tax and other so-called 'Socialistic' legislation of to-day. But apologies for the decadent side of the period do not complete the story of the renaissance of the Nineties. This latter was more real than the much advertised decadence, and as time goes on it will prove itself to have been more enduring. The atmosphere of the Eighteen Nineties was alert with new ideas which sought to find expression in the average national life. If luxury had its art and its traffic, so had a saner and more balanced social consciousness. If the one demanded freedom for an individual expression tending towards degeneration and perversion, the other demanded a freedom which should give the common man opportunities for the redemption of himself and his kind. Side by side with the *poseur* worked the reformer, urged on by the revolutionist. There were demands for culture and social redemption. A wave of transcendentalism swept the country, drawing with it the brighter intelligences of all classes; but it was not remote, it was of the earth and of the common life and hour, seeking the immediate regeneration of society by the abolition of such social evils as poverty and overwork, and the meanness, ugliness, ill-health and commercial rapacity which characterised so much of modern life. The vitality of this awakening of the social consciousness is proved by its extravagances. In the main it worked persistently, cheerfully and with that spirit of compromise dear to the English temperament. . . .

But the chief characteristics of the Eighteen Nineties proper, although dovetailed into the preceding decade, may be indicated roughly under three heads. These were the so-called Decadence; the introduction of a Sense of Fact into literature and art; and the development of a Transcendental View of Social Life. But again, it must not be assumed that these characteristics were always separate. To a very considerable extent they overlapped, even where they were not necessarily interdependent. Oscar Wilde, for instance, bridged the chasm between the self-contained individualism of the decadents and the communal aspirations of the more advanced social revolutionaries. His essay, *The Soul of Man under Socialism,* has been acclaimed by recognised upholders of Socialism. And even his earlier aestheticism (which belonged to the Eighties) was an attempt to apply the idea of art to mundane affairs. Bernard Shaw, rationalist and anti-romantic apostle of the sense of fact, openly used art to provoke thought and to give it a social, as distinct from an individualist, aim; just as other and more direct literary realists, such as Emile Zola and Henrik Ibsen, had done before him, either avowedly or by implication. The more typical realists of the Nineties, George Gissing and George Moore, seem to be devoid of deliberate social purpose, but the prevalent didacticism of the period is strikingly pronounced in the work of H. G. Wells, who has contrived better than any other writer of his time to introduce reality into his novels without jeopardising romance, to hammer home a theory of morality without delimiting his art. But apart from such obvious resemblances between types of *fin de siècle* genius, the popular idea of the period looked upon one phase of its thought as no less characteristic than another. The adjective 'new', as an indicator of popular consciousness of what was happening, was, as we have seen, applied indifferently to all kinds of human activity, from art and morals to humour and Trade Unionism.

There is no clearer example of the intimate relationship between what might have been called the degenerate notions of the period and those which are admittedly regenerate, than a comparison of the Epicurean ideas in such strikingly different works as Oscar Wilde's *The Picture of Dorian Gray* and Grant Allen's essay on 'The New Hedonism', which appeared in *The Fortnightly Review* of March 1894. Oscar Wilde says:

> Yes: there was to be, as Lord Henry had prophesied, a new Hedonism that was to recreate life, and to save it from that harsh, uncomely Puritanism that is having, in our own day, its curious revival. It was to have its service of the intellect, certainly; yet it was never to accept any theory or system that would involve the sacrifice of any mode of passionate experience. Its aim, indeed, was to be experience itself, and not the fruits of experience, sweet or bitter as they might be. Of the asceticism that deadens the senses, as of the vulgar profligacy that dulls them, it was to know nothing. But it was to teach man to concentrate himself upon the moments of a life that is itself but a moment.

Here we have a kind of self-culture by the constant variation of experiences, mostly passionate, with little if any reference to the rest of humanity. In a sense it is not a new Hedonism at all, but a Hedonism which had existed from time immemorial, although it found its way into

Oscar Wilde's novel by the aid of two modern books. One of these, the *A Rebours* of Joris Karl Huysmans, may be said to contain the apotheosis of the *fin de siècle* spirit; the other, *The Renaissance*, by Walter Pater, containing a famous passage which became the precious gospel of the Aesthetic Movement of the Seventies and Eighties. It was new, however, in so far as it reacted against the 'Nonconformist conscience' of the moment. But that it was not the only 'New' Hedonism may be realised by reference to Grant Allen's essay, which is little more than a veiled piece of Socialist propaganda. The central idea of this sociological Hedonism is shown in the following extract:

> Self-development, on the contrary, is an aim for all—an aim which will make all stronger, and saner, and wiser, and better. To be sound in wind and limb; to be healthy of body and mind; to be educated, to be emancipated, to be free, to be beautiful—these things are ends towards which all should strain, and by attaining which all are happier in themselves, and more useful to others. That is the central idea of the new hedonism. We see clearly that it is good for every man among us that he and every other man should be as tall, as strong, as well knit, as supple, as wholesome, as effective, as free from vice or defect as possible. We see clearly that it is his first duty to make his own muscles, his own organs, his own bodily functions, as perfect as he can make them, and to transmit them in like perfection, unspoiled, to his descendants. We see clearly that it is good for every woman among us that she and every other woman should be as physically developed and as finely equipped for her place as mother as it is possible to make herself. We see that it is good for every woman that there should be such men, and for every man that there should be such women. We see it is good for every child that it should be born of such a father and such a mother. We see that to prepare ourselves for the duties of paternity and maternity, by making ourselves as vigorous and healthful as we can be, is a duty we all owe to our children unborn and to one another. We see that to sacrifice ourselves, and inferentially them, is not a thing good in itself, but rather a thing to be avoided where practicable and only to be recommended in the last resort as an unsatisfactory means of escape from graver evils. We see that each man and each woman holds his virility and her femininity in trust for humanity, and that to play fast and loose with either, at the bidding of priests or the behest of Puritans, is a bad thing in itself, and is fraught with danger for the State and for future generations. . . .

It was an era of hope and action. People thought anything might happen; and, for the young, any happening sufficiently new was good. Little of the older sentimentalism survived among the modernists; those who were of the period desired to be in the movement, and not mere spectators. It was a time of experiment. Dissatisfied with the long ages of convention and action which arose out of precedent, many set about testing life for themselves. The new man wished to be himself, the new woman threatened to live her own life. The snapping of apron-strings caused consternation in many a decent household, as young men and maidens were suddenly inspired to develop their own souls and personalities. Never, indeed, was there a time when the young were so young or the old so old. No family, were its record for solid British respectability established on no matter how secure a basis, was immune from new ideas; and if the bourgeoisie of the Eighteen Eighties were inspired to throw their maghogany into the streets, as we have been assured by Max Beerbohm they were, their successors of the Eighteen Nineties were barely constrained from doing the same with their most cherished principles. Decadent minor poets sprang up in the most unexpected places. The staidest of Nonconformist circles begot strange, pale youths with abundant hair, whose abandoned thoughts expressed themselves in 'purple patches' of prose, and whose sole aim in life was to live 'passionately' in a succession of 'scarlet moments.' Life-tasting was the fashion, and the rising generation felt as though it were stepping out of the cages of convention and custom into a freedom full of tremendous possibilities.

There were misgivings in more directions than one, but these had small effect upon the spirit of the first half of the decade. The experimental life went on in a swirl of song and dialectics. Ideas were in the air. Things were not what they seemed, and there were visions about. The Eighteen Nineties were the decade of a thousand 'movements.' People said it was a 'period of transition', and they were convinced that they were passing not only from one social system to another, but from one morality to another, from one culture to another, and from one religion to a dozen or none! But as a matter of fact there was no concerted action. Everybody, mentally and emotionally, was running about in a hundred different directions. There was so much to think about, so much to discuss, so much to see. 'A New Spirit of Pleasure is abroad amongst us,' observed Richard Le Gallienne, 'and one that blows from no mere coteries of hedonistic philosophers, but comes on the four winds.' The old sobriety of mind had left our shores, and we changed from a stolid into a volatile nation. At this time the provinces saw the birth of a new type of music-hall, the 'Palace of Varieties', with two performances a night, and we began to amuse ourselves.

Our new-found freedom seemed to find just the expression it needed in the abandoned nonsense chorus of *Ta-ra-ra-boom-de-ay!* which, lit at the red skirts of Lottie Collins, spread like a dancing flame through the land, obsessing the minds of young and old, gay and sedate, until it became a veritable song-pest, provoking satires even upon itself in the music-halls of its origin. No other song ever took a people in quite the same way; from 1892 to 1896 it affected the country like an epidemic; and during those years it would seem to have been the absurd *Ça ira* of a generation bent upon kicking over the traces. Even to this day one can hear the song in the streets of Boulogne and Dieppe, where the urchins croak it for the benefit of the English visitor, under the firm conviction that it is the British National Anthem, and in hopes that the patriotic Britishers will reward their efforts with *petits sous*.

The old dim and dowdy chop-houses and taverns also changed with our new mood, and they were replaced by larger and brighter restaurants and 'tea shops', daintier food and orchestras, and we extended the habit of dining out, and mixing afternoon tea with shopping.

The 'safety' bicycle was invented, and it took its place as an instrument of the 'new' freedom as we glided forth in our thousands into the country, accompanied by our sisters and sweethearts and wives, who sometimes abandoned skirts for neat knickerbocker suits. 'The world is divided into two classes,' said a wit of the period, 'those who ride bicycles and those who don't.'

Salvador de Madariaga
END OF THE ELITE

When, from our troubled days, we turn our thoughts back to the beginning of our century, our first impression is one of dismay. Far from advancing along that "road" which for most nineteenth-century men symbolized "progress", the world seems to have receded into an almost barbarous age. When we tell the young that until 1914 Europeans travelled about Europe without a passport, and that five European nations (France, Belgium, Italy, Greece, and Switzerland) shared their currencies, they open wide incredulous eyes. To-day, in more than half of Europe, man is at the mercy of the police; in 1900, even the most conservative and reactionary Prussian Junker would have been unable to imagine, let alone approve, that a citizen could be arrested and kept in prison at the pleasure of the Government. When we seem on the brink of realizing the World State, frontiers become more impassable than ever; and the world that had dreamt of universal peace awaits with bated breath the day when two powers, mightier than any history saw, hurl at each other weapons loaded with planet-shattering ammunition.

From *Essays with a Purpose* by Salvador de Madariaga. Reprinted by permission of Collins-Knowlton-Wing, Inc., and A. P. Watt & Sons.

Salvador de Madariaga (1886–   ) is a Spanish essayist and historian.

The chief contrast between then and now is that between stability and instability. In 1900, all was stable. The merchant drew his contracts for months or for years, knowing that though prices might change, currencies were as fixed as the stars, revolving faithfully in their prescribed orbits round the sun of the gold standard. Values, standards, habits were solid, *bourgeois*, respectable; shirts were white, starched, and hard; meals were square, formal, and punctual. The frock-coat and the top hat kept men straight as the pillars of society; the corset held women firmly bound within the socially correct mould. The steady structure which Europe achieved then was the masterpiece of her *bourgeoisie*. The *Ancien Régime* had fallen at the advent of the nineteenth century dragging with it an obsolete aristocracy overgrown with oddities, gnarled with illogicalities, disguised with wigs. When this old curiosity shop crashed to the ground, the liberal burgesses of Europe breathed. At last, order and reason! Though a ruthless revolutionist, Robespierre adequately ushered in the new era by crowning the Goddess Reason in Notre Dame. Reason and Liberty were to be the deities of the century; science, its religion; and its motto: "Liberty, Equality, Fraternity."

The new era was one of the most creative mankind has ever seen. In the realm of applied science, it saw man's conquest of steam, of electricity and of the internal combustion engine; in that of exploration, the study and survey of practically the whole planet; in population, the spectacular growth of the Western world to unknown proportions, notably in the United States; in production and trade, a prodigious increase; in general wealth, a rise of comfort greater than in any other period of history. The criminal excesses of unlimited capitalistic liberty had soon been checked thanks to the unlimited liberty of the press; and, though far from satisfactory yet, the worker's standard of living in the whole White World had risen incomparably. On the whole, the men of 1900 could look forward with confidence to an era of ever ascending progress under the guidance of reason in a world of liberty.

Reason and liberty are precisely the two martyrs of our age. Can that be a mere coincidence? Hardly. What we are witnessing is in the main a reaction of human nature against the exacting claims made upon it by reason and by liberty during the nineteenth century.

It is characteristic of this century of ours that it "begins" or at any rate manifests itself, in 1914, with the wholly unreasonable, indeed anti-reasonable war declared on Europe by the second German Reich. By 1900 it had become plain that Germany was bound to acquire an undisputed preponderance over Europe. Her outstanding technical ability made of her Europe's natural leader in a technical age. All she had to do was to work on in peace. By 1930, Germany would have become the paramount power in Europe, and safely established Europe, perhaps for all time, as the paramount continent in the world.

All this was within Germany's easy, indeed almost inevitable, reach; and all this would have proved a boon to the rest of Europe. But all this presupposed one essential condition: that Germany remained faithful to the two deities of the nineteenth century: reason and liberty.

That was precisely the condition Germany could not fulfil. Her spirit, too heavy with fluid emotions, evades the definite structures of reason; and draws on the collective forces of the people for most of her inspiration. Germany's representative man is not Goethe but Luther. And who waxes more eloquent, indeed more "unprintable" than Luther against reason, and who was more nationalistic? In 1914 Germany was on her way to conquer Europe by peace, liberty, and reason. That is why she made war.

With that war the twentieth century burst into History. Gone the formal frames of the nineteenth. Classes, families, style of dress, of language, of behaviour, everything undergoes a revolution. Honest women paint their faces and smoke and show their legs, as only professional women dared in the previous generation. Gone the stays, gone the top hat and the frock-coat, gone the hard starched shirt. Clothes serve the limbs, and the body is happy in its new freedom. It all looks at first as if the century were drunk with liberty. Art joins in the general riot. Musicians break all the rules; painters all the perspectives; poets all the measures. This general onslaught, having crashed through the frames of form, soon attacks the frames of references within. Above all, no objectivity. The musician, the painter, the poet is no longer concerned with *das Ding an sich;* but with an esoteric mystery arising out of the thing, which no mere imitation of it can convey. Man claims mastery over nature. This "anthropocentric" stand was in all times typically Spanish (hence the myth of Don Juan); and so the leader of the art of the century had to be a Spaniard. Picasso, not merely by his invention of cubism, but by his revolutionary experiments in divorcing colour from line, opens new avenues to the plastic arts, and sets free new sensibilities in the men and women of our day.

At first it looks as if one of the deities of the nineteenth century—liberty—were to kill the other—reason. For all this vigour and even this violence of the new century is animated by a curious antagonism against reason. It all happened as if the new men turned their blind fury against the temple of Athene for having allowed itself to be destroyed by the earthquake of the war. "What were you the temple of the Goddess of Reason for?"—they seemed to think in secret, while blaspheming against reason in their loud words.

The war, of course, was but one of the forms the human revolution was taking; and in fact most of the seeds of the twentieth century had been planted in the nineteenth. Both "reason" and "liberty" as understood in the nineteenth century had been severely shaken by the first in date of the three great Jewish prophets of our day before the other two came to complete the work. Marx, Freud and Einstein are the three prophets of the gospel of the nineteenth century. Between them, they have radically altered world views on the three vastest domains of man: collective life, personal life, cosmic life.

Marx's attack goes to the heart of the matter. For him, human life is conditioned by his economic and social environment. Liberty and reason are shorn of their absolute crowns and universal mantles, and conditioned as "bourgeois" or "proletarian" as the case may be. Marx thus begins the era of relativity in which we swim—a strange paradox; for, in contrast with this powerful push into the sea of relativism which he inflicts on the once solid values of his time, Marx erects the most solid dogma and church the world has seen outside Rome. His action is two-fold. By a powerful and mostly correct criticism of society, he drives the bourgeoisie into doubt, disorder, and confusion; and by an equally powerful but less correct set of assertions, he erects a dogma and a doctrine and opens a vista of redemption for the working classes. His success is due to the fact that his tactics were so admirably fitted to the classes—doubt and criticism for the bourgeois; dogma and redemption for the people.

When the middle classes felt their ethics thus deprived of their absolute social value, they took refuge in the self. They bethought themselves of the famous Kantian phrase about the moral principle within and the stars without. Here, no matter how relative social conditions might be, here were indeed two absolutes. Alas! behind Marx, there came Freud and Einstein.

Moral principle? Just fear of your grumpy father, says Freud, unless it be, in your case, some obscure incestuous attachment to your mother. All this network of activities which covers behaviour and mis-behaviour, talk and slips of the tongue, wit and stupidity, faith and blasphemy, memory and absent-mindedness, is, indeed, says Freud, ruled by laws, but not the laws of ethics and religion you have fondly imagined as the reflection within of the fixity of the stars. They are the laws of a new psychology which your body-soul-mind obeys as blindly as the planets do those of Euler.

For the second time, a value once absolute is made relative. What else? The stars remain, the stars, on which the deist Voltaire founded his churchless faith.

> Quant a moi, plus j'y pense et moins je puis songer
> Que cette horloge existe et n'ait point d'Horloger.

Horloge?—asks Einstein. Do not put your faith in such things. Nothing less reliable than a clock. It is wholly subjective—indeed, so subjective that there is no way whatever of saying whether two events are simultaneous or not, in fact there is no sense in the idea of simultaneity. So that we mortals are not in a position to define the present, and hardly know the hour in which we live—or die.

Now, of course, competent men grappled with the problems raised by the three great prophets of our day, and set them within the framework of general knowledge. But in the world-wide seas of public opinion, the accumulated effect of their three gospels was a general loosening of all notions and faiths. "It all depends"; "Everything is relative"; such became, not so much the slogans as the attitudes of the day. This general and untutored relativism has been disastrous for both reason and liberty. Though the three founders of the modern Church were masters in the use of reason, the general effect of their doctrine has dangerously lowered the prestige of reason in the world; and, since the true foundation of liberty is an almost religious respect for man, for every man, the Freudian reduction of the human soul to the level of an ordinary organism ruled by objective laws led also to contempt for liberty.

The scene was thus set for an onslaught on man's reason and liberty by arousing against them the Boig—the mass. This was to be done soon and in several lands. The totalitarian movements of Russia, Italy, Germany, and Spain were but episodes of this rising of the blind mass against the two wings of individual life—reason and liberty. The struggle is still with us. It has brought to the surface abominable monsters that lay asleep—some of us thought, dead—in the depths of man. But though in what remains of the century we may still perish in the grip of these monsters of cruelty and inhumanity, we, men of the twentieth century, can look at Destiny in the face—for no century ever fought with cleaner weapons nor with more open eyes on a clearer future.

The struggle in which we live cuts deeper than a mere stress of the balance of power, a mere conflict of opinion on the structure of society. The onslaught from the mass, led by mass-leaders with mass-slogans against defenceless individuals, is due to causes that transcend the shallow level of politics.

When the leaders of the French Revolution coined the motto of the century—Liberty, Equality, Fraternity—they scarcely knew to what an extent they remained confined within the individualistic pole of the spirit of man. Liberty, Equality, and Fraternity, three virtues admirable in themselves, are in fact ideals and norms of the individual as such. Now, the individual as such is a pure abstraction. Nature does not provide it. Nature produces only societies of men; so that man may be conceived only as a bipolar being, an individual-in-society, whose existence can only be understood in terms of both its inseparable terms.

The scion of an eighteenth century dominated by French thought and, therefore, prone to take abstractions for realities, the nineteenth century endeavoured to live up to its individualistic motto. There is a French political satire from the Right to the effect that the famous motto must be read giving due emphasis (and a twisted meaning) to the stops after its three words, thus: *Liberté point, Egalité point, Fraternité point.* Witty but not correct. The failure of the motto did come from its three full stops; not, however, in the sense French reactionaries claim, by denying the substantives, but by separating them, by making of them three different aims to be considered seriatim, instead of just three aspects of one and the same organic whole.

The eighteenth century had completed the disintegration of the organic whole of Christendom which Luther had begun from within and Marco Polo and Columbus from without. Within this organic whole, liberty, equality, and fraternity were duly integrated, and men adequately provided for, since the social pole in them rested on the solid frame of the Church. Of this, nothing is left in the nineteenth century.

To this circumstance, more perhaps than to the inevitable failings of human nature, must be attributed the fact that the century, despite its remarkable achievements, proved unable to assimilate any of its three ideals without disastrous consequences for the whole.

Liberty was the first to fail. Unable to realize that the self-balancing virtues of liberty only can work within an organic society in whose service all so-called free moves operate, the nineteenth-century liberals attributed such virtues to liberty itself. The outcome of this naïve faith was twofold: in home affairs the criminal exploitation of workers and their children in the early nineteenth century; in international affairs, the excesses of unlimited sovereignty and war.

Equality gave vent to even worse evils. The disregard of the social pole of man which is typical of the century, led to a material, inorganic, and quantitative, instead of a spiritual, organic, and qualitative, conception of equality. This, in its turn, through equating men and women, disintegrated the family, forced women into factories (thereby doubling the proletariat and destroying domestic culture), and forced the State to shoulder duties which only the family can perform, such as the care of the very young and the very old. Finally, this inorganic conception of equality led to confusing the notions of *people* and *nation,* and so to universal and direct suffrage.

Fraternity is not a political value. It was inscribed over the portal of the century as a kind of "Holy Ghost" to the Father-Liberty and the Son-Equality already written; for the Trinity had sunk too deep into the soul of Europe to be uprooted by a mere Revolution; and so fraternity remained throughout the century a Ghost, no doubt most Holy, whom everyone took his hat off to and forgot about in actual business. Nevertheless, in so far as it lived, it led to one of the finest, if not always beneficent, social phenomena of the nineteenth century: the migration of many middle-class intellectuals to the leadership of the working classes. Less admirable to-day, when the working classes are powerful, it was in the nineteenth century a truly *fraternal* move. It led, however, also to aberrations of political "equality" on which more anon.

Then came the Machine. You know, of course: coal, steam, Watt, and all that. But the machine appears on the stage precisely when the social pole of man is at a loose end. The axle wants a bearing on which to rest. Man's liberty seeks a butt, a resistance. Such are the deeper motives. Nearer to the surface, man, emancipated from his old masters, kings and bishops, dreaming himself a king, seeks a truly obedient slave, whom he can drive with a clean conscience—the Machine.

But the new slave gradually enslaves his master, and forces him to comply with his laws.

It may begin anywhere you like; for instance, when, in the seventeenth century, Pascal invented the omnibus. Before then, this or that man went to this or that place in this or that way at this or that time. After then, everybody went from point A to point B at given times. Life had been mechanized. Men had been sunk into the mass.

This process spurts forward in the nineteenth century at a breath-taking speed; and it absorbs hundreds, thousands, millions of one-time peasants, who, forsaking the live earth and the company of plants and animals, go to live on dead cement and in the company of repetitive metals. This emigration of man from nature to factory will, with the passing of the years, sap both liberty and equality, further draining them of their spiritual contents and making them even more inorganic, mineral and quantitative. As the machine conquers vaster and vaster fields—transport—printing—film—radio—men degenerate to the status and function of pegs in a huge kind of factory that tends to supersede the State and Society itself. More and more, one reads of the "machinery of the State". And, indeed, truly; for more and more the State becomes also a machine and works with the same objective soullessness if not always with the same efficiency. This stress on "machinery" conditions most of the attempts at international "organization" made of late—UNO, UNESCO, COUNCIL of EUROPE, and other agencies active nowadays in Europe and America. Though under the aegis of "organization", these institutions are rather machines in that the central impulse, the living *kernel* is lacking that would give them life. The LEAGUE of NATIONS, for instance, was never more than a Co-operative of separate Sovereign-ties. UNO is not even that, since it cannot achieve co-operation. Thus Society tends to imitate machinery. The individual-in-society of old gradually evolves towards some monstrous "individual-in-machine".

Is mankind to evolve towards the hive or the ant-heap or towards a harmonious society of free men? The answer does not merely depend on a simple choice between Moscow and Washington, nor even (as some conceited Europeans fancy) on a choice between Moscow or Washington on the one hand and London or Paris on the other. No. The fact is that the whole world, East and West, North and South, faces the same dilemma, runs the same danger, and, though in an unequal degree, is unarmed, almost defenceless before it.

The conflict is one between an organic and qualitative, and an inorganic and quantitative conception of life. And our defencelessness against the evil choice comes from the fact that both the East and West are the slaves of a quantitative tradition in politics. This grave defect of our modern "ethos" may well have a twofold origin: a mistrust, historically well founded, of all political oligarchies, and a confusion between ends and means.

Since our modern political structure was not built on clear ground, but on a site strewn over with the *débris* of the old régime, it was but natural that its architects should have been chary of using a material so recently found wanting as the oligarchy that led the old régime to its doom. The representative institutions of the modern world were to be exclusively popular—i.e. quantitative, exclusively representative of the individual, with no thought whatever for his *social* pole. The few experiments to give a representation to the *élite* were so awkward and ill conceived—i.e. the very idea of *élite* was so inadequately understood— that the quantitative tendency triumphed in the end the more easily.

Nothing honours mankind less than the actual working of the institution of direct universal suffrage to which this triumph has led. The market-fair vulgarity, the noise, the confusion, the deceit, the flattery, the auction-like promises of material benefits, the debasement of candidates, the "showing of the wounds" which made Coriolanus angry—all that repugnant sight justifies the view that the civilized world must have the courage to think out afresh its basic political rules and standards.

For at present they rest on a deplorable confusion between the end of democracy which is to ensure that *tomorrow* all citizens are able and competent to advise on how to govern the State—and the means, which is to ensure that the State is well governed *to-day*.

The interplay of these two prejudices—mistrust of the *élite* and anticipation of the ability and competence of the masses—leads to quantitative or mass democracy. The claims of society as such—i.e. as an organism or paraorganism, endowed with differentiated organs, tissues, and cells—are not heeded. The Machine and the mass usurp the social pole of man. And so while Mr. Wallace waxes eloquent about this century being the century of the common man, we are threatened with the gradual destruction of that which is and always will be the salt of the earth—the man out of the common.

This danger of moral destruction (as instant as and perhaps more real than that of physical destruction by the self-murderous use of nuclear energy) lends to our day a gravity and an earnestness which our West had not known since the earliest days of Christendom. So far, mankind had been drawn forward by a historical urge, an inner feeling of "marching forward", probably borrowed from the myth of the Promised Land. "Some day, we shall get there"—seemed to say the inner voice of mankind; and so it flowed forward, with ever resurging hope. The theory of evolution came to consecrate this urge, born of the old religion, with the blessing of the new religion—science. But all this time, what went forward was mankind as a whole—men in their multitudes, and the whole spirit of man. It was, again, despite appearances, a predominantly individualistic 'conception, which visualized mankind as the sum arithmetic of all the men past, present, and future.

The idea of mankind as a complex congeries of organic societies and civilizations brings a new dimension into the picture. Time is no longer the paramount factor in the continuum of events. The relations between the parts of what in reality is an organic whole assert themselves, indeed, define our issue and our conflict. The present takes on a dramatic tension from which the future of mankind depends. Angels or beasts? The challenge is immediate. We can no longer dream the one or fear the other at a comfortable distance beyond the hills of the day, the month, the year. We must choose—now.

George Bernard Shaw
BREEDING POLITICAL CAPACITY

When we two were born, this country was still dominated by a selected class bred by political marriages. The commercial class had not then completed the first twenty-five years of its new share of political

From *Man and Superman* by George Bernard Shaw (Penguin Books, 1960; pp. xxiii–xxvi; 152–153; 171–174). Reprinted with the permission of The Public Trustee and The Society of Authors.

George Bernard Shaw (1856–1950) was a British playwright and member of the Fabian Society, a group of British socialists.

power; and it was itself selected by money qualification, and bred, if not by political marriage, at least by a pretty rigorous class marriage. Aristocracy and plutocracy still furnish the figureheads of politics; but they are now dependent on the votes of the promiscuously bred masses. And this, if you please, at the very moment when the political problem, having suddenly ceased to mean a very limited and occasional interference, mostly by way of jobbing public appointments, in the mismanagement of a tight but parochial little island, with occasional meaningless prosecution of dynastic wars, has become the industrial reorganization of Britain, the construction of a practically international Commonwealth, and the partition of the whole of Africa and perhaps the whole of Asia by the civilized Powers. Can you believe that the people whose conceptions of society and conduct, whose power of attention and scope of interest, are measured by the British theatre as you know it today, can either handle this colossal task themselves, or understand and support the sort of mind and character that is (at least comparatively) capable of handling it? For remember: what our voters are in the pit and gallery they are also in the polling booth. We are all now under what Burke called "the hoofs of the swinish multitude." Burke's language gave great offence because the implied exceptions to its universal application made it a class insult; and it certainly was not for the pot to call the kettle black. The aristocracy he defended, in spite of the political marriages by which it tried to secure breeding for itself, had its mind undertrained by silly schoolmasters and governesses, its character corrupted by gratuitous luxury, its self-respect adulterated to complete spuriousness by flattery and flunkeyism. It is no better today and never will be any better: our very peasants have something morally hardier in them that culminates occasionally in a Bunyan, a Burns, or a Carlyle. But observe, this aristocracy, which was overpowered from 1832 to 1885 by the middle class, has come back to power by the votes of "the swinish multitude." Tom Paine has triumphed over Edmund Burke; and the swine are now courted electors. How many of their own class have these electors sent to parliament? Hardly a dozen out of 670, and these only under the persuasion of conspicuous personal qualifications and popular eloquence. The multitude thus pronounces judgment on its own units: it admits itself unfit to govern, and will vote only for a man morphologically and generically transfigured by palatial residence and equipage, by transcendent tailoring, by the glamor of aristocratic kinship. Well, we two know these transfigured persons, these college passmen, these well groomed monocular Algys and Bobbies, these cricketers to whom age brings golf instead of wisdom, these plutocratic products of "the nail and sarspan business as he got his money by." Do you know whether to laugh or cry at the notion that they, poor devils! will drive a team of continents as they drive a four-in-hand; turn a jostling anarchy of casual trade and speculation into an ordered productivity; and federate our colonies into a world Power of the first magnitude? Give these people the most perfect political constitution and the soundest political program that benevolent omniscience can devise for them, and they will interpret it into mere fashionable folly or canting charity as infallibly as a savage converts the philosophical theology of a Scotch missionary into crude African idolatry.

I do not know whether you have any illusions left on the subject of education, progress, and so forth. I have none. Any pamphleteer can shew the way to better things; but when there is no will there is no way. My nurse was fond of remarking that you cannot make a silk purse out of a sow's ear; and the more I see of the efforts of our churches and universities and literary sages to raise the mass above its own level, the more convinced I am that my nurse was right. Progress can do nothing but make the most of us all as we are, and that most would clearly not be enough even if those who are already raised out of the lowest abysses would allow the others a chance. The bubble of Heredity has been pricked: the certainty that acquirements are negligible as elements in practical heredity has demolished the hopes of the educationists as well as the terrors of the degeneracy mongers; and we know now that there is no hereditary "governing class" any more than a hereditary hooliganism. We must either breed political capacity or be ruined by Democracy, which was forced on us by the failure of the older alternatives. Yet if Despotism failed only for want of a capable benevolent despot, what chance has Democracy, which requires a whole population of capable voters: that is, of political critics who, if they cannot govern in person for lack of spare energy or specific talent for administration, can at least recognize and appreciate capacity and benevolence in others, and so govern through capably benevolent representatives? Where are such voters to be found today? Nowhere. Plutocratic inbreeding has produced a weakness of character that is too timid to face the full stringency of a thoroughly competitive struggle for existence and too lazy and petty to organize the commonwealth co-operatively. Being cowards, we defeat natural selection under cover of philanthropy: being sluggards, we neglect artificial selection under cover of delicacy and morality.

Yet we must get an electorate of capable critics or collapse as Rome and Egypt collapsed. At this moment the Roman decadent phase of *panem et circenses* is being inaugurated under our eyes. Our newspapers and melodramas are blustering about our imperial destiny; but our eyes and hearts turn eagerly to the American millionaire. As his hand goes down to his pocket, our fingers go up to the brims of our hats by instinct. Our ideal prosperity is not the prosperity of the industrial north, but the prosperity of the Isle of Wight, of Folkestone and Ramsgate, of

Nice and Monte Carlo. That is the only prosperity you see on the stage, where the workers are all footmen, parlormaids, comic lodging-letters, and fashionable professional men, whilst the heroes and heroines are miraculously provided with unlimited dividends and eat gratuitously, like the knights in Don Quixote's books of chivalry. The city papers prate of the competition of Bombay with Manchester and the like. The real competition is the competition of Regent Street with the Rue de Rivoli, of Brighton and the south coast with the Riviera, for the spending money of the American Trusts. What is all this growing love of pageantry, this effusive loyalty, this officious rising and uncovering at a wave from a flag or a blast from a brass band? Imperialism? Not a bit of it. Obsequiousness, servility, cupidity roused by the prevailing smell of money. When Mr. Carnegie rattled his millions in his pockets all England became one rapacious cringe. Only, when Rhodes (who had probably been reading my Socialism for Millionaires) left word that no idler was to inherit his estate, the bent backs straightened mistrustfully for a moment. Could it be that the Diamond King was no gentleman after all? However, it was easy to ignore a rich man's solecism. The ungentlemanly clause was not mentioned again; and the backs soon bowed themselves back into their natural shape.

Charles A. Beard
THE TRANSFORMATION OF CAPITALISM

Monetary Developments

The period of 1875–1933 opened with the classical conception of the world monetary system approaching the peak of a long development that was soon to close with its complete overthrow. The pinnacle was reached in the years around 1900 with the almost universal acceptance of the international gold standard. It had taken more than a century for the chief nations to come to such an agreement, but the system collapsed in less than thirty years.

Quoted by permission from Charles A. Beard and George H. E. Smith, *The Old Deal and the New*, copyright, 1940, by The Macmillan Company.

Charles A. Beard (1874–1948) has been one of the most influential of twentieth century American historians.

At the culmination of the classical system, monetary control rested securely in the hands of representatives of private banking systems. Great central banks, privately owned, were the primary agencies of control. In each country they enjoyed the status of public agencies and were powerful in dictating monetary policies, but remained more or less independent of the political government. They held the power to create money and control credit on the theory that the political government could not be freely trusted with such important functions. They exercised these powers chiefly through the workings of the gold standard, dealings in foreign exchange, manipulation of capital movements, and control over the domestic discount rate.

Within thirty-five years after 1900, the gold standard collapsed and political governments nearly everywhere took the power of monetary control out of the hands of private bankers.

The World War delivered the first smashing blow to the orthodox system. In war time governments are dictatorial; no private interest can stand in the way of the public need in the "national emergency." The warring nations had to have more money and had to get it faster than private bankers could create it under the orthodox rules of private finance. Governments got the money in several ways. They simply printed what they needed and issued it—inflation. They engineered forced loans and gave out government certificates of indebtedness, piling up huge public debts. They took over the control of gold, the foreign exchanges, and capital movements. These acts shook the monetary system to its foundations and although the private bankers resented them and feared the consequences, they were helpless in the circumstances; *c'est la guerre.*

After the war was over bankers sought to regain control over the monetary system. Their movement toward independent central banking gained considerable headway after 1922, but they were never able to restore the pre-war system in its entirety. Some of the war shocks left permanent effects. Chief among these was the dilution of the gold standard caused by inflation. The deflation of national currencies engineered by the bankers during the 1920's counteracted the wartime inflation only in part and was itself partly offset by the new currency issues that had to be set up for the countries created by the peace treaties. In consequence gold had to support a much larger superstructure of paper currency and credit than the calculations of the pre-war monetary system allowed. Bankers met the situation by devising the gold *exchange* standard and by placing gold movements on a bullion basis. Thus, in place of a full cover of gold, most of the new countries of central Europe used paper exchange on straight gold standard countries. The relation was no longer the simple one of gold to paper, but paper to paper to gold. The metal itself was progressively withdrawn from circulation and could be had only in bullion lots of approximately five thousand dollars value. This was the first great rift in the gold standard.

Moreover, private bankers never succeeded in throwing off all of the government wartime controls over money and credit. Working in close collaboration, Montague Norman of the Bank of England, Hjalmar Schacht of the Reichsbank, and Benjamin Strong of the New York Federal Reserve Bank, virtually dictated monetary policies at home and abroad, but it was a dictatorship unwilling and unable to keep its fingers out of political affairs. Interallied debt settlements, reparation payments, financing in central Europe, and the operation of a complex and sensitive exchange standard compelled private bankers to take an active part in national policy, and consequently to trim their sails to the capricious winds of political forces.

The monetary system of the 1920's thus rested upon a weakened gold standard, the steady withdrawal of gold from actual circulation, and an unstable interaction between politics and private finance. Banker-manipulated fiscal policies and huge international loans and investments helped to keep the precarious system afloat for a time.

The world depression dealt the second and finishing blow to the international monetary system. Loans fell off and trade melted away. Long-term loans froze, and a scramble set in to liquidate and repatriate short-term funds. Strains on the slender gold supply produced crisis after crisis. In rapid succession, prop after prop fell out from under the exchanges as the artificial stability of 1924–1929 disintegrated in the fierce heat of depression reality. In the fall of 1931 a general abandonment of the gold standard heralded the collapse of the system. Out of the utter confusion and chaos that followed came fierce trade wars and competitive exchange depreciation. "By the middle of 1932, it was obvious that the international trading mechanism was in real danger of being smashed as completely as the international monetary system had been."

Widespread defaults on international loans, gold embargoes, foreign exchange controls and clearing systems, trade controls and restrictions appeared on the heels of the depression as it raced from country to country. To the cries of anguish coming from the starved and the dispossessed were added the wails of those whose falling dividends and shrunken stocks caused acute pains in the pursestrings, so that demands for government aid no longer met with resistance in the historic style. The way was opened and by one device or another governments moved in to occupy the remaining strongholds of private finance in the international monetary system, including the domestic money and banking structures. Political authorities, in response to appeals from private interests, brushed aside private rights and set up their own controls over banks, currency, and credit, bending fiscal policy to the service of other ends than those traditional with the orthodox gold standard and with the interests of private bankers as formerly conceived. Gold was even more diluted by "recovery" financing and more completely withdrawn from circulation. New devices for currency and credit regulation were established. In the six years from 1929 to 1935, what remained of the international monetary system of classical economy, and its supporting financial structure in each nation, was almost finished off. Politics was openly joined to finance and economics and the myth of their separate spheres, so long perpetuated by private bankers and business men, vanished into the thin air from which it had come. For good or evil, managed money, managed by public authorities in what was called the public interest, displaced private management whose criteria had failed, despite its pretensions, to serve the general welfare. If private bankers are ever again to possess and control money and credit, it will have to be on some other authority than the mere assumption of their exclusive wisdom respecting the mysteries of finance.

The Organization of Private Group Interests and the Growth of Government Regulation

A society featured by individual initiative and enterprise, and possessing unlimited frontiers for land settlement and the exploitation of natural resources, is one with little organization and great freedom from the restraining hands of authority. By its open and fluid nature, such a society has natural safety valves for the conflicts and tensions which arise from the forces within it. Where there are people, there is always organization of some sort, but in frontier societies the organization is extremely simple. With the exception of Europe and some parts of Asia, where crowded populations had knocked elbows in limited space for a long time, most of the world in the century from 1775 to 1875 enjoyed the frontier features of individual independence, little organization, and relative freedom from political authority. What little organization there was came from other characteristics of pioneer society—the transference of traditional customs from the old country to the new and the voluntary drawing together for mutual aid against the loneliness and hazards of the new environment.

But, with the rapid growth of population, the increasing spread of fixed land settlement, the reduction of natural resources to exclusive possession, and the cohesive effects of technology, the fluid, frontier character of the society began to change. Increasing contact and the steadily narrowing limits of physical environment and of opportunity to get at land raised the tensions of conflicts and enlarged the area of their operation. All this was clearly apparent by 1890 and it gave added impetus to the organizing tendencies of the people. . . .

Competing Theories of Social Organization and Development

The cluster of revolutionary events and the forces operating in every distinctive epoch or period provide materials for competing theories as to the deeper meanings, values, and objects of the age—old and new theories. These theories, composed of many subordinate ideas lending themselves to logical unity, are classed as systems and acquire labels expressive of their dominant themes. In retrospect, historical thought tends to come to agreement upon a single system as dominating an age, such as the Feudal System. In the perspective of time, all the competing theories within the age either become reconciled to form the system or are destroyed in the competition or become lost in the waste-thought of the age. History tends to draw the age to its climax and to stamp it with its prevailing theme. "That was the age of Feudalism" is a judgment of the present—a present conception of the past. The past itself, in its own living present, came to no such conclusion.

As history comes nearer the present, agreement on the dominant theme becomes more difficult, if not impossible. Crystallization is only in progress; it is not yet completed. And so instead of a system to mark the immediate past and the present, there are only competing systems, schemes, and theories drawn from the revolutionary events and forces of the times. This is the complexity of the century preceding 1875, although a vast literature appears to be distilling the system of "Capitalism" out of the competing theories of the times.

No such determinateness marks the period from 1875 to the present. A cluster of disturbing events and a development of revolutionary forces are clearly discernible, but their precise nature, their deeper meanings, the values they establish, and the ends toward which they are driving the world are still obscure. They furnish only the raw materials for philosophic speculation, for competing concepts; but no finished products. Thus the present age is peculiarly a period of competing ideas and theories constructed out of politics, economics, race, culture, social relations, and the various combinations they permit. Even the labels attached to these theories do not yet express correctly the ideas they pretend to embrace. Men are extraordinarily ingenious and prolific in giving names to things which serve to disturb their interests and in using those names for their own ends. Democracy competes with dictatorship;

the peace-lovers with the aggressors; liberalism with authoritarianism; capitalism with socialism and communism; individualism with collectivism. The swarm of "isms" let loose upon the modern world is as voluminous, as varied, and as productive of conflict and distress as the things that came out of Pandora's box.

Historians of the future who seek to simplify and "order" things will doubtless note the finished products of the present epoch. Perhaps for them too the myriad conflicts and theories of these times will become blurred as have those of the Feudal period for historians of today. And as in the past, only the dominant theme of this age will stand out in relief against the vast waste-thought of the times. And then it may be said that the present *was* the age of the X System. But for the people of today there is no such certainty. There is only the reality of the thought, the conditions, the institutions, and the vested interests that is the heritage of the past; there is the cluster of the revolutionary events and forces; there are the endless controversies and conflicts over interests, means, and ends; and there are these vague competing theories and systems into which men weave their interests, their beliefs, and convictions, their aims, hopes, ideals and aspirations. These are observable trends—realities not to be lost sight of in the "background" of the Great Depression and the New Deal.

American Trends 1875 to 1930

All these revolutionary events and developments of the modern world were especially in evidence in American experience. Many of them originated or acquired their initial momentum in the United States. In many cases their influences and effects were deeper, more widespread, and more intense in the United States than in any other area of the world.

Certainly this is true of the new technology and its accompanying revolutionary inventions which reached its highest peaks in the United States in the years before the Great Depression. Here too, the population increased enormously—far beyond the world trend—and then commenced to taper off in the direction of a stationary or declining population. Migration likewise first rose to unprecedented heights, as the waves of immigrants from Europe poured into the country, and then was reduced to a trickle as successive legislation from the Chinese Exclusion Act to the quota laws shut off the flow.

As a nation the United States pushed its boundaries first until they approached continental limits and then on to embrace overseas territories as distant as the Philippines adjacent to the coast of Asia. Within the country every acre of land (with the exception of relatively small government preserves) and practically all the country's vast mines, fields, forest resources, and water utilities were reduced to private, exclusive possession. The tendency toward exclusive possession did not stop with control over the land and natural resources of the nation. It extended to almost every opportunity, privilege, advantage, process, operation, device, and contrivance in production, trade, and finance, that could be calculated to yield a private profit and was capable of being clothed with the right and power of exclusive ownership and enjoyment. Every agency at work in the American society—constitutions, the legislative process, the laws, courts, and enforcement bodies, the frontier conditions and pioneer customs and methods, the agriculture, manufacturing, trade and banking institutions—tipped the scales in that direction under a political and economic philosophy that proclaimed individual freedom of enterprise and the full protection of its fruits.

At the same time exclusive ownership itself passed over from extensive application by the many to the greater refinement of concentration—ownership or control—in the hands of the few. Whether it was the logical consequence of free competition or of the working of some mysterious force, the trend was everywhere evident—in land and natural resources, in manufacturing, trade, and finance, in transportation and communication. The primary business unit steadily grew larger in terms of the money capital accumulated, the land and resources controlled, the labor commanded, the share of the market it enjoyed, and consequently the influence it exercised over political and economic policy. An ever-increasing wage and salary class of people emerged, and became dependent for a livelihood upon the property ownership or control of a relatively small number of people and the business units through which they operated.

Every process of the whole economy became enormously complex and the business units through which it was carried on developed into fantastic shapes and forms. Giant corporations and combines, huge industrial empires, with consequent advantages and disadvantages, dominated the national economy. Industrialization completely overshadowed agriculture, drawing people from farms and rural areas to cities and urban centers. The drive for ever-increasing quantities of goods, agricultural and industrial, reached the highest peak in intensity and results in all the history of civilization, and the potentialities for even greater quantitative production faced few barriers other than those which the will, the prevailing ideas, and institutions prescribed. It was not without considerable justification in fact that leaders in the United States began to speak of the conquest of poverty and the provision of abundance, for saturation points in the production and use of goods began to appear; and even if these long-sought-for goals were not universally achieved in fact, the possibility of attaining them appeared to be open and clear for the first time in the history of the nation.

The world's monetary developments likewise pervaded the American economy. In the United States the classical conception of the gold standard and of the ordering of currency and credit was carried close to perfection in substance, before the combined effects of the World War, the dislocation of the 1920's, and the onset of the Great Depression destroyed the gold standard and developed the conditions for a reconstruction of the banking and the monetary system. Chiefly in connection with the World War, in the period between the triumph of the gold standard and its collapse, the United States changed its financial status from a heavy debtor nation to one which shared with Great Britain the position of a great creditor nation.

As the industrial system grew to giant stature, it reached out to the ends of the earth for the raw materials which were required in ever-increasing tonnages to feed it. Exports, likewise, mounted to ever-larger quantities in exchange for the imported raw materials and finished products of other countries, in consequence of huge financial loans and transactions, and in response to many other stimuli exerted by the prevailing economy. But in the United States as elsewhere, even during the period when trade with the rest of the world was reaching higher and higher totals, forces tending to limit the relative growth of trade were steadily at work. Up until the Great Depression, when the sum total of restrictive forces within and outside the nation drastically cut down the volume of trade, the tariff remained the chief domestic instrument for this purpose, although its influence in that direction was considerably exaggerated in the partisan debates it occasioned. . . .

In the narrower field of government, likewise, the tendency toward more complete and complex organization was plainly evident. As the circle of its operations widened, government not only penetrated other activities with measures of supervision, regulation, and control; but it also became a distinct segment of the economy in its own right, like industry, agriculture, and the private professions. Careers in government had always been open to individuals in Europe, chiefly to the titled and the well-to-do, but never so open to the commonality or on such a scale as developed in the United States in the years after 1875. And as government expanded, it intensified old problems and raised up entirely new ones of the utmost gravity—problems concerning jurisdiction, organization, functions, intergovernmental relations, and the bearing of government upon private business and upon the individual.

The clash of economic ideas, political theories, and social philosophies that began a new cycle in the world after 1875 was late in coming to prominence in the United States. There were occasions, to be sure, when controversies of this nature agitated the whole citizenry; but usually they centered about narrow issues and ran a quick course. There was a tariff issue here and a monetary issue there. The basic foundations of the whole society never became the stakes of public debate, as they had in 1783–1889. But the World War with its slogans of the fight for democracy and the Communist triumph in Russia, coupled with the rapidly changing conditions in American life, helped to lift broad social issues from obscurity and thrust them into the field of practical affairs. For a while during the 1920's they remained just below the surface of general public debate, cropping out only here and there. But the Great Depression created conditions which facilitated bringing these issues into the open, and, for the first time since the Civil War, an ideological crisis involving the very foundations of American government and economy was precipitated. . . .

Only an arbitrary act of will, falsifying and distorting, can, therefore reduce the state of affairs existing just prior to the Great Depression to an "order" or "system" which was subject merely to a temporary disarrangement and could be "recovered" or "restored" by measures of legislation, executive decrees, political speeches or banquet addresses. Established knowledge of history forbids any such conclusion. The fateful year 1929 was a mere time point on which converged powerful dynamic activities that had been tearing up traditions and inherited institutions for more than half a century. The Great Depression was not an arbitrary break in history; it was a manifestation of history.

Raymond James Sontag
THE DOOM OF EUROPE

During the early years of the twentieth century the will to peace was stronger and more nearly universal than ever before in modern history. Never before had the foundations of European civilization

From *European Diplomatic History: 1871–1932* by Raymond James Sontag. (Pp. 144–149.) Copyright, 1933, by The Century Co. Reprinted by permission of Appleton-Century-Crofts.

Raymond James Sontag (1897–   ) is Emeritus Professor of History, University of California, Berkeley, California, and an authority on European diplomatic history.

seemed so unstable. The defeat of Russia by Oriental Japan sent a tremor of hope through "backward" countries. From Morocco to China opposition to European domination became more determined. Was the revolt only transitory, or had the tide of imperialism definitely turned? In Europe itself things were not well. "Three hundred men, all acquainted with each other, control the economic destiny of the Continent," wrote a German industrialist in 1907. These 300, plus a few thousand others, realized that the great mechanism of finance, commerce, and industry was both unwieldy and delicate, hard to control even in times of tranquillity, reacting violently to the slightest political disturbance. Closely connected with economic instability was political and social instability. The shadow of revolution hung over Russia and Austria. Liberals in the west looked forward to these revolutions as the logical and too long-delayed conclusion of the great nineteenth century liberal movement. More discerning observers were fearful. They knew nineteenth century liberalism was bankrupt. The middle classes, the leaders of liberalism, had largely attained their ends in the western countries, and desired nothing better than the *status quo*, which gave them political power and wealth. The old liberal catchwords were still used, but they no longer enthralled the workers. Increasingly, the proletariat complained that the prizes in the political battles which they had helped to win had gone to the middle class. Discontent found expression in the rapid growth of Marxian socialism and in the increasing number and violence of labor disputes. The shadow of revolution was creeping westward. Imperialism was under attack; the European social and political order was under attack; credit, the heart of capitalistic enterprise, was notoriously subject to panic. Here was instability indeed! War would change instability into chaos. War would plunge Europe into the throes of revolution.

The doom which threatened Europe was seen more or less clearly by statesmen in every country. It was seen most clearly in England because England had the greatest imperial domain, the most highly developed industrial system, and the most active and powerful laboring class. It was seen by the ruling element of Russia, although the insatiable expansionist instincts of Russia fought hard against the moderation inspired by fear of revolution. In Germany, industry, commerce, and finance counseled moderation, but here too the desire for expansion was strong and untempered by weakness. Austria was coming to believe that even war might be better than slow disintegration. Italy was, as always, restless, restrained only by consciousness of weakness. In France the older philosophy still dominated. There was little fear of revolution. The proletariat was violent, but it was small and was more than counter-balanced by the great mass of conservative peasant proprietors. Neither industry nor foreign trade played a dominant part in the national economy. French finance made huge investments abroad, but the banks and the Bourse were more completely under governmental control than in any other European country. France wanted peace, but her rulers did not dread war with the same intensity as the rulers of England, Germany, and Russia, because the disruptive elements in French national life were less strong.

Despite the fact that Europe was filled with dread of war, the organization of European international life still presupposed the acceptance of war as the final, decisive argument in disputes between states. Since on all important questions each state wished its own will to prevail, and since the interests of states were divergent, conflicts of interest were inevitable. In each conflict, victory went to the state which could mass the greatest force on its side. Armies, navies, and allies were instruments of national policy, instruments by which a state could make its will prevail against the will of other states. Armed forces were not intended primarily for use in war; they were to bring victory without war by forcing rival states to give way without an armed encounter. Only if both antagonists thought the issue vital, and only if the discrepancy of power was not overwhelming, did both stand firm. Then there was war. The ideal was power so great that other states would, unless desperate, invariably give way rather than fight. No state had ever attained that peak of strength. Occasionally Europe had been threatened by the hegemony of one state. Then the rest of Europe combined in opposition. For centuries the ideal of a "balance of power" had tempered the rule of force in Europe; but it had not prevented war, as the bloody history of Europe showed. A perfect balance of power, while theoretically possible, was actually unattainable. Inevitably, each country wished the balance weighted in favor of its own interests, since those interests seemed natural and just.

Englishmen, for instance, regarded their country as the traditional defender of the balance of power. They did not deny that their policy resulted from selfish interest. If any one state dominated the Continent, that state could concentrate on the building of a fleet to conquer England. At the same time, Englishmen felt that their policy furthered the cause of European liberty by preventing the growth of a single despotic state. British interest and European progress were alike served when England nerved the Continent against Louis XIV and Napoleon, or when England shielded the smaller states, like Holland and Belgium, from more powerful neighbors. Further, English sea power could only protect, and never menace, European liberty. England had no army with which to fight the huge Continental forces. Therefore, in insisting on naval supremacy, the British felt they were protecting a claim which no one but a potential world despot could protest. There was much in the English claim so long as the Continental states were preoccupied almost exclusively with European affairs, although England had certainly exploited her rôle of balance-wheel to acquire a rich colonial domain. In the twentieth century Englishmen still used the traditional arguments to justify their naval hegemony, but the new imperialism had demolished the premises upon which these arguments rested. Overseas colonies and overseas trade were now of major importance to the Continental states. So long as England was undisputed master of the seas, the colonies and trade of other countries were at her mercy. Furthermore, the increasing dependence of Continental states on non-European countries for products vital in wartime made the blockade a deadly weapon which England could use to enforce her will. The setting for international politics was now not Europe but the world. On that larger stage sea power provided opportunities for despotic rule such as Napoleon never enjoyed.

The Germans were quick to sense the situation. They realized that in every quarrel with England, German colonies and trade were, as Sir Edward Grey said, hostages for England to take. How could the bargaining power of England and Germany be made more nearly equal? Directly by building up the German fleet; indirectly by securing allies. William II tried both methods. His objective was not the destruction of England; it was the creation of a balance of power on the sea. His plan to unite the Continent failed, partly because England made timely concessions to French and Russian land hunger, but chiefly because France and Russia felt German hegemony on the Continent to be more dangerous to their interests than British maritime hegemony. Here again, self-interest had prevented understanding of the interests of other states. Blinded by his own satisfaction with the Continental *status quo,* and by his desire to change the *status quo* outside Europe, William II drove France and Russia to a decision which they had been reluctant to make. Despite his failure to win the Dual Alliance, the Kaiser was confident that Germany could, unaided, establish a balance of power on the sea. The navy scare of 1909 brought fear of Germany home to the English people for the first time. They ignored the justifiable elements in the German fleet argument. They forgot that the British fleet could seize and blockade. They saw only that Germany, the greatest military power, was challenging their naval supremacy, their bulwark against starvation and Europe's bulwark against despotism.

It was not only in Berlin and London that passion clouded reason. France had forgotten Delcassé's sins but remembered Germany's efforts to browbeat her into surrender. France watched for another insult, and prepared to meet it by strengthening her army. Russia could not understand Austria's fear of Serbia. Austria was desperate with fear of Pan-Slavism. In this atmosphere peace had but a poor chance of survival. Each side feared that the balance was turning in favor of the other. Each side piled more arms into the scales. So long as faith in arms as instruments of policy continued, the race must also continue until ended by war or revolution. The imagination of Europe recoiled from these alternatives. Statesmen labored to find some other solution, but they were afraid to abandon the weapon of force. They wanted no war, but what if war came and they were unprepared? To be sure, the masses everywhere were desirous of peace, but experience showed how weak a prop this sentiment was: desire for peace could change into bellicose fervor almost overnight. To be sure, the peace movement was growing, but only in England did the pacifists possess appreciable political influence. Even there, while the overburdened taxpayer might for a time heed the pacifists' plan for reduction of armaments, reaction followed. English pacifists held down ship-building for three years; the advocates of preparedness became strident in their warnings; in 1909 came the naval scare, and eight dreadnaughts. There were trouble-makers in every country: Russians who plotted dangerously in the Balkans; Austrians who preached war against Serbia; Pan-Germans intoxicated with dreams of conquest; Frenchmen who hoped to use Morocco as a means of stirring the embers of *revanche;* Englishmen who would block German expansion completely, who would sink the German fleet without warning. Every country had its firebrands. If they controlled one government, they could embroil all Europe. If any state felt confident of victory, would it not be tempted to heed aggressive counselors? The times were too dangerous for new and untried experiments. Force and the balance of power were dangerous guardians for peace, but they were the best Europe knew.

2
Getting into War

History seems to show that war is endemic; yet the influence of war has varied over the ages. In the twentieth century it has dominated human experience, and thus the subject makes a fitting opening to a study of the century, since nothing would have been the same without the two world wars. Twentieth century man appears to have recognized this fact, for he has engaged in endless discussion of how wars start, hoping thereby to avoid future wars.

The 1907 memorandum of Sir Eyre Crowe, an influential civil servant in the British foreign office, provides a classic example of a familiar line of reasoning. The enemy will respect a tough line, said Crowe; weakness invites aggression. Paul Johnson, a left-wing Laborite, today regards this reasoning as based upon false analogies and, hence, as self-defeating. According to Johnson, "Political leaders should not substitute analogy for thought: they should judge each situation on its merits."

A more fundamental and moral analysis of the whole system of international affairs appeared in the doctrines of Woodrow Wilson, but Wilson's diplomacy of peace brought appalling disillusionment for such followers as Harold Nicolson. After World War I, Nicolson, a British diplomat and member of Parliament, poured out his bitterness in his book,

Peacemaking 1919. The American journalist Vincent Sheean went even further and rejected the whole dream of the League of Nations as an outmoded legacy of the nineteenth century.

The strong-line views of Sir Eyre Crowe underwent an important revival in the light of the appeasement era prior to World War II when many concessions were made to Nazi Germany. And while the challenge to the appeasement policy, as posed by A. J. P. Taylor, has been taken up by stalwarts like Hugh Trevor-Roper, there is no debate over the matter in today's world of practical politics. Sir Eyre Crowe and Thomas K. Finletter bracket the age, with the tough-line approach prevailing.

Here in the nineteen sixties we may feel we are witnessing the same old story in trying to draw a hard line on Vietnam. The present conflict in Southeast Asia has employed all the traditional concepts and analogies, from Crowe to Finletter, and to do it justice would require a separate volume. Perhaps the war in Vietnam has no new lessons, only an old warning against false or misleading comparisons of one bit of history with another.

Sir Eyre Crowe
THE STRONG LINE

Memorandum on the Present State of British Relations with France and Germany

If it be considered necessary to formulate and accept a theory that will fit the ascertained facts of German foreign policy, the choice must lie between the two hypotheses here presented:

Either Germany is definitely aiming at a general political hegemony and maritime ascendency, threatening the independence of her neighbours and ultimately the existence of England;

Or Germany, free from any such clear-cut ambition, and thinking for the present merely of using her legitimate position and influence as one of the leading Powers in the council of nations, is seeking to promote her foreign commerce, spread the benefits of German culture, extend the scope of her national energies, and create fresh German interests all over

From G. P. Gooch and Harold Temperley (eds.), *British Documents on the Origins of the War, 1898–1914* (London, 1926–1938), III, pp. 397–420.
Sir Eyre Crowe (1864–1925) was an important civil servant in the British Foreign Office.

the world wherever and whenever a peaceful opportunity offers, leaving it to an uncertain future to decide whether the occurrence of great changes in the world may not some day assign to Germany a larger share of direct political action over regions not now a part of her dominions, without that violation of the established rights of other countries which would be involved in any such action under existing political conditions.

In either case Germany would clearly be wise to build as powerful a navy as she can afford.

The above alternatives seem to exhaust the possibilities of explaining the given facts. The choice offered is a narrow one, nor easy to make with any close approach to certainty. It will, however, be seen, on reflection, that there is no actual necessity for a British Government to determine definitely which of the two theories of German policy it will accept. For it is clear that the second scheme (of semi-independent evolution, not entirely unaided by statecraft) may at any stage merge into the first, or conscious-design scheme. Moreover, if ever the evolution scheme should come to be realized, the position thereby accruing to Germany would obviously constitute as formidable a menace to the rest of the world as would be presented by any deliberate conquest of a similar position by "malice aforethought."

So long as England remains faithful to the general principle of the preservation of the balance of power, her interests would not be served by Germany being reduced to the rank of a weak Power, as this might easily lead to a Franco-Russian predominance equally, if not more, formidable to the British Empire. There are no existing German rights, territorial or other, which this country could wish to see diminished. Therefore, so long as Germany's action does not overstep the line of legitimate protection of existing rights she can always count upon the sympathy and good-will, and even the moral support, of England.

It would be of real advantage if the determination not to bar Germany's legitimate and peaceful expansion, nor her schemes of naval development, were made as patent and pronounced as authoritatively as possible, provided care were taken at the same time to make it quite clear that this benevolent attitude will give way to determined opposition at the first sign of British or allied interests being adversely affected. This alone would probably do more to bring about lastingly satisfactory relations with Germany than any other course.

There is no suggestion more untrue or more unjust than that England has on any recent occasion shown, or is likely to show in future, a *parti pris* against Germany or German proposals as such, or displayed any unfairness in dealing strictly on their own merits with any questions having a bearing on her relations with Germany. This accusation has been freely made. It is the stock-in-trade of all the inspired tirades against the British Government which emanate directly or indirectly from the Berlin Press Bureau. But no one has ever been able to bring forward a tittle of evidence in its support that will bear examination. The fact, of course, is that, as Mr. Balfour felt impelled to remark to the German Ambassador on a certain occasion, German communications to the British Government have not generally been of a very agreeable character, and, unless that character is a good deal modified, it is more than likely that such communications will in future receive unpalatable answers. For there is one road which, if past experience is any guide to the future, will most certainly not lead to any permanent improvement of relations with any Power, least of all Germany, and which must therefore be abandoned: that is the road paved with graceful British concessions— concessions made without any conviction either of their justice or of their being set off by equivalent counter-services. The vain hopes that in this manner Germany can be "conciliated" and made more friendly must be definitely given up. It may be that such hopes are still honestly cherished by irresponsible people, ignorant, perhaps necessarily ignorant, of the history of Anglo-German relations during the last twenty years, which cannot be better described than as the history of a systematic policy of gratuitous concessions, a policy which has led to the highly disappointing result disclosed by the almost perpetual state of tension existing between the two countries. Men in responsible positions, whose business it is to inform themselves and to see things as they really are, cannot conscientiously retain any illusions on this subject.

Here, again, however, it would be wrong to suppose that any discrimination is intended to Germany's disadvantage. On the contrary, the same rule will naturally impose itself in the case of all other Powers. It may, indeed, be useful to cast back a glance on British relations with France before and after 1898. A reference to the official records will show that ever since 1882 England had met a growing number of French demands and infringements of British rights in the same spirit of ready accommodation which inspired her dealings with Germany. The not unnatural result was that every successive French Government embarked on a policy of "squeezing" England, until the crisis came in the year of Fashoda, when the stake at issue was the maintenance of the British position on the Upper Nile. The French Minister for Foreign Affairs of that day argued, like his predecessors, that England's apparent opposition was only half-hearted, and would collapse before the persistent threat of French displeasure. Nothing would persuade him that England could in a question of this kind assume an attitude of unbending resistance. It was this erroneous impression, justified in the eyes of the French Cabinet by their deductions from British political practice, that brought the two countries to the verge of war. When the Fashoda chapter had ended with the just discomfiture of France, she remained for a time very sullen, and the enemies of England rejoiced, because they believed that an impassable gulf had now been fixed between the two nations. As a matter of fact, the events at Fashoda proved to be the opening of a new chapter of Anglo-French relations. These, after remaining for some years rather formal, have not since been disturbed by any disagreeable incidents. France behaved more correctly and seemed less suspicious and inconsiderate than had been her wont, and no fresh obstacle arose in the way which ultimately led to the Agreement of 1904.

Although Germany has not been exposed to such a rebuff as France encountered in 1898, the events connected with the Algeciras Conference appear to have had on the German Government the effect of an unexpected revelation, clearly showing indications of a new spirit in which England proposes to regulate her own conduct towards France on the one hand and to Germany on the other. That the result was a very serious disappointment to Germany has been made abundantly manifest by the turmoil which the signature of the Algeciras Act has created in the country, the official, semi-official, and unofficial classes vying with each other in giving expression to their astonished discontent. The time which has since elapsed has, no doubt, been short. But during that time it may be observed that our relations with Germany, if not exactly cordial, have at least been practically free from all symptoms of direct friction, and there is an impression that Germany will think twice before she now gives rise to any fresh disagreement. In this attitude she will be encouraged if she meets on England's part with unvarying courtesy and consideration in all matters of common concern, but also with a prompt and firm refusal to enter into any one-sided bargains or arrangements, and the most unbending determination to uphold British rights and interests in every part of the globe. There will be no surer or quicker way to win the respect of the German Government and of the German nation.

Paul Johnson
THE POLITICS OF ANALOGY

The theory that the way to 'contain' communism is to reverse the Appeasement policies of the Thirties has always seemed to me to compound a mistaken assumption the Appeasers themselves made—namely,

Reprinted from the *New Statesman* (February 26, 1966, p. 252) by permission of the *New Statesman,* London.
Paul Johnson (1928–   ) is editor of the London *New Statesman.*

that history repeats itself. What our Cold Warriors forget is that the hard line was tried before 1914. In 1907 Sir Eyre Crowe produced his famous memorandum about the containment of Germany. He argued that, by a policy of firmness, we had converted France from an enemy into an ally, and that we could do the same with Germany by providing 'ocular evidence' of our military might and will to resist. Crowe's theory (itself based on false historical analogy) became government gospel: far from preventing war, it merely ensured that Britain became involved in it. The Appeasers had this very much in mind when they reversed the policy in the Thirties—with the same disastrous results. Now we are urged, in effect, to go back to Crowe. The truth is that history has no such simple lessons. A little history is a dangerous thing. Political leaders should not use analogy as a substitute for thought: they should judge each situation on its merits. If Mr. Rusk doubts this, let him remember the scorn with which Washington rightly greeted Eden's use of the same analogy in 1956, when he compared Nasser to Hitler.

Harold Nicolson
THE DIDACTICISM OF PRINCETON

By the end of 1918 the teaching of Woodrow Wilson had resolved itself into three main categories in my mind. There were his major articles of faith, simple and withal mystic. There was the application of these beliefs to the great problem of American neutrality. There were, as a corollary to his proposition, the 'Fourteen Points,' the 'Four Principles' and the 'Five Particulars.'

In the main tenets of his political philosophy I believed with fervent credulity. In spite of bitter disillusionment I believe in them today. I believed, with him, that the standard of political and international conduct should be as high, as sensitive, as the standard of personal conduct. I believed, and I still believe, that the only true patriotism is an active desire that one's own tribe or country should in every particular minister to that ideal. I shared with him a hatred of violence in any form, and a loathing of despotism in any form. I conceived, as he conceived,

From *Peacemaking 1919* by Harold Nicolson, pp. 36–42, 43. Reprinted by permission of Harcourt, Brace & World, Inc.

Harold Nicolson (1886–   ) a British diplomat, member of Parliament, and author of novels, biographies and historical studies.

that this hatred was common to the great mass of humanity, and that in the new world this dumb force of popular sentiment could be rendered the controlling power in human destiny. 'The new things in the world,' proclaimed President Wilson on June 5, 1914, 'are the things that are divorced from force. They are the moral compulsions of the human conscience.' 'No man,' he said, 'can turn away from these things without turning away from the hope of all the world.'

I admitted, of course, that in the weeks which followed upon this utterance the 'moral compulsions of the human conscience' had not proved themselves very compelling. I admitted also that Wilson, as a prophet, was a very American prophet—that his philosophy was in practice applicable only to the proportions of power obtaining in the Western Hemisphere. I was conscious, moreover, that there was in his pronouncements a slight tinge of revivalism, a touch of methodist arrogance, more than a touch of presbyterian vanity. Yet I was not deterred by these disadvantages. 'The United States,' I read, 'have not the distinction of being masters of the world'—(Mr. Wilson was speaking in 1914)—'but the distinction of carrying certain lights for the world that the world has never so distinctly seen before, certain guiding lights of liberty, and principle, and justice.' I was disconcerted neither by the biblical, nor yet by the Princeton savour of these words.

I like to think also that, with nerves frayed by the duration of the war, I still retained my faith in Wilson as a prophet of human reasonableness. My faith was revived, from time to time, by the privilege of converse with Walter Page. 'There is such a thing,' I read in May of 1915, 'as a man being too proud to fight. There is such a thing as a nation being so right that it does not need to convince others by force that it is right.' I did not, as did the majority of my countrymen, regard this as an irritating remark: I regarded it as consistent, courageous, sane. Nor was I very deeply estranged, in January of 1917, by the dictatorial, the almost theocratic, tone which from that date began to encroach upon the didacticism of Princeton. 'There are,' I read, 'American principles, American policies. We stand for no others. They are the principles of mankind and must prevail.' This statement, I felt, might have been more tactfully worded: yet as a statement it was sound enough. I agreed with it. Nine days later the Germans in their blindness published their decision regarding unrestricted submarine warfare. On April 4 the United States entered the war. From that moment I was not in a minority in my faith in Woodrow Wilson.

And then, on January 8, 1918, came the Fourteen Points.

Much casuistry, and some wit, has been expended upon these historic pronouncements. President Wilson himself referred to them in 1919 as 'certain clearly defined principles which should set up a new order of right and justice.' On the very same day we find Mr. Balfour writing of them as 'certain admirable but very abstract principles.' Yet were they so very abstract? Considering the date at which they were first issued, the Fourteen Points are precise to the point of recklessness. It may be well to summarise them as follows:

Speech of January 8, 1918

'The programme of the world's peace, therefore, is our programme, and that programme, the only possible programme, as we see it, is this:

1. 'Open covenants of peace openly arrived at, after which there shall be no private understandings of any kind, but diplomacy shall proceed always frankly and in the public view.

2. 'Absolute freedom of navigation upon the seas outside territorial waters alike in peace and in war. . . .

3. 'The removal, as far as possible, of all economic barriers. . . .

4. 'Adequate guarantees given and taken that national armaments will be reduced to the lowest point consistent with domestic safety.

5. 'A free, open-minded and absolutely impartial adjustment of colonial claims based upon a strict observance of the principle that in determining all such questions of sovereignty the interests of the populations concerned must have equal weight with the equitable claims of the Government whose title is to be determined.

6. 'The evacuation of all Russian territory. . . . Russia to be given unhampered and unembarrassed opportunity for the independent determination of her own political development and national policy.' Russia to be welcome, 'and more than welcome' in the League of Nations 'under institutions of her own choosing' and to be given every form of assistance.

7. Belgium to be evacuated and restored.

8. France to be evacuated, the invaded portions 'restored' and Alsace-Lorraine returned to her.

9. 'A readjustment of the frontiers of Italy should be effected along clearly recognisable lines of nationality.

10. 'The peoples of Austria Hungary . . . to be accorded the freest opportunity for autonomous development.' (N.B.—This point was subsequently modified to provide for complete independence in lieu of autonomy.)

11. Rumania, Serbia and Montenegro to be evacuated, occupied territories to be 'restored.' Serbia to be given free access to the sea.

12. Turkish portions of Ottoman Empire to be assured 'a secure sovereignty.' Subject nationalities to be assured security and 'absolutely unmolested opportunity of autonomous development.' Freedom of the Straits to be guaranteed.

13. Independent Polish State to be erected 'which should include territories inhabited by indisputably Polish populations, which should be assured a free and secure access to the sea.

14. A general association of nations to be formed under specific covenants 'for the purpose of affording mutual guarantees of political independence and territorial integrity to great and small States alike.'

To the Fourteen Points themselves must be added the 'Four Principles' and the 'Five Particulars.' The former were contained in an address of February 11, 1918, and were prefaced by a statement that the eventual Peace should contain 'no annexations, no contributions, no punitive damages.' The Principles themselves can be summarised as follows:

1. Each part of the final settlement must be based upon the essential justice of that particular case.
2. Peoples and provinces must not be bartered about from sovereignty to sovereignty as if they were chattels or pawns in a game.
3. Every territorial settlement must be in the interests of the populations concerned; and not as a part of any mere adjustment or compromise of claims among rival states.
4. All well-defined national elements shall be accorded the utmost satisfaction that can be accorded them without introducing new, or perpetuating old, elements of discord and antagonism.

The 'Five Particulars' figure in an address of September 27, 1918. They are less illuminating. The first insisted on justice to friends and enemy alike. The second denounced all 'separate interests.' The third provided that there should be no alliances within the body of the League and the fourth forbade all economic combinations between League members. The fifth 'Particular' reaffirmed the prohibition against secret Treaties.

Not only did I believe profoundly in these principles, I took it for granted that on them alone would the Treaties of Peace be based. Apart from their inherent moral compulsion, apart from the fact that they formed the sole agreed basis of our negotiation, I knew that the President possessed unlimited physical power to enforce his views. We were all, at that date, dependent upon America, not only for the sinews of war, but for the sinews of peace. Our food supplies, our finances, were entirely subservient to the dictates of Washington. The force of compulsion possessed by Woodrow Wilson in those early months of 1919 was overwhelming. It never occurred to us that, if need arose, he would hesitate to use it. 'Never,' writes Mr. Keynes, 'had a philosopher held such weapons wherewith to bind the Princes of the world.'

He did not use these weapons. He was not (and the slow realisation of this was painful to us) a philosopher. He was only a prophet. . . .

Let me contrast the principles enunciated by the Fourteen Points with the extent to which those principles were embodied in the eventual Treaties of Peace.

Our covenants of Peace were not openly arrived at: seldom has such secrecy been maintained in any diplomatic gathering. The Freedom of the seas was not secured. So far from Free Trade being established in Europe, a set of tariff-walls were erected, higher and more numerous than any known before. National armaments were not reduced. The German Colonies were distributed among the victors in a manner which was neither free, nor open-minded, nor impartial. The wishes, to say nothing of the interests, of the populations were (as in the Saar, Shantung and Syria) flagrantly disregarded. Russia was not welcomed into the Society of Nations, nor was she accorded unhampered freedom to develop her own institutions. The frontiers of Italy were not adjusted along the lines of nationality. The Turkish portions of the Ottoman Empire were not assured a secure sovereignty. The territories of Poland include many people who are indisputably not Polish. The League of Nations has not, in practice, been able to assure political independence to Great and Small Nations alike. Provinces and peoples were, in fact, treated as pawns and chattels in a game. The territorial settlements, in almost every case, were based on mere adjustments and compromises between the claims of rival States. Elements of discord and antagonism were in fact perpetuated. Even the old system of Secret Treaties was not entirely and universally destroyed.

Vincent Sheean
TO DIE IN BEAUTY—THE LEAGUE

Everything had been going along very nicely. Speeches galore had been made; commissions and subcommissions had met, discussed, reported. Geneva was somnolent, with the beatific, happy drowsiness the League used to know how to bestow. All was for the best in the best of all possible worlds, and before long a fine new peace promise was going to be signed by fifty-odd nations beneath the purring benediction of Mr. MacDonald and M. Herriot.

At this juncture, in the midst of a warm, lazy afternoon, Baron Adatci got up in open meeting and moved an amendment to the clause of

From *Personal History* by Vincent Sheean, pp. 86–89. Reprinted by permission of Curtis Brown, Ltd. Copyright © 1934–35–36 by Vincent Sheean. Copyright renewed 1962 by Vincent Sheean.
Vincent Sheean (1900–   ) is an American journalist.

the new protocol that defined the arbitrable causes of war. His amendment provided that disputes likely to cause war should be arbitrable,
even though one party to the dispute might claim that the question at
issue was one of internal jurisdiction.

The phrases meant little to me at first: I was sleepy; but I could
see the astonishment and agitation that suddenly broke out in the quiet
corridors of the Palais des Nations. Lord Parmoor and M. Briand, who
had succeeded MacDonald and Herriot at the head of the British and
French delegations, went off in a hurry, beset by questions; the Prime
Minister of New Zealand, Sir James Craig, was a thundercloud. I went
along to the Japanese delegation, obtained a copy of the amendment, and
read it over stupidly. A Japanese correspondent—the representative of
the Osaka *Asahi*—saw, apparently, that here was an example of the invincible ignorance of the Yankee. He leaned towards me gently and said
one word: "Immigration."

Light broke; and with it something of a small thrill. Here was the
first word of sense I had heard at Geneva since my arrival; here was, at
last, one definite reference to a dispute that might bring on war. Moreover, here was a great "story" for America: a warning, polite but as clear
as a clap of thunder, of the storm the Japanese were not afraid to expect.

Geneva became almost hysterical for two or three days. The
Australians and New Zealanders were up in arms, and even if the gentle,
easy-going, absent-minded Lord Parmoor had been unable to see the
dangers of the situation they would have opened his eyes. Briand—the
old fox—seemed almost happy: for once the villain of the piece was not
France. He would come into the room at the Beau Rivage where he
received us, his head sunk in his wing collar, his marvellous, magical
voice emerging gaily in the accents of a taxi-driver.

"B'en, messieurs! Ça va? Quoi de nouveau?"

And with a twinkle in his eyes, at an awkward question:

"Ah, ça—! Ah, ça—! Faut demander, vous· savez, aux Japonais."

The Japanese amendment was, of course, nothing new in history.
Exactly the same thing had been proposed by Viscount Ishii at Versailles
and defeated by Wilson. The Japanese had always maintained that immigration laws in any country discriminating specifically against them were
an offence to their national honour. It had to be conceded by any reasonable person that they were right. The Americans (like the Australians,
New Zealanders, and Canadians) were also right in wishing to prevent a
flood of Japanese immigration; but the Americans, in particular, had
taken the most offensive way possible to achieve their aims. Instead of
continuing the quiet little agreement Lansing had made with Ishii,
whereby the Japanese government itself kept its subjects from moving to
America, the Congress at Washington had recently taken it into its head

to pass a Japanese Exclusion Act—a wholly unnecessary insult to a susceptible people. There had been disorders in Tokyo, suicides; one man had committed hara-kiri in front of the American Embassy as a protest; and here, in the calm backwaters of Geneva, we were presented with the results.

For some days the thought of war—the actual thought of a real war, not a rhetorical one—agitated the minds that had grown fat on toothsome words. The Japanese amendment, stripped bare, meant just this: some day Japan might very likely see fit to fight in defence of the national honour attacked in the Exclusion Act passed by the American Congress; when that happened the Americans would say that the question was one of their own internal jurisdiction; where, then, did the League stand? Was Japan to be judged an aggressor in that war? Or would the League compel the Americans to arbitrate the dispute?

The League, of course, driven into a corner, forced to consider such a terrible question, was paralyzed with fright. It was impossible to offend the Japanese; it was impossible to offend the Australians and New Zealanders; it would have been almost worst of all to offend the Americans, who were not members of the League and would certainly never become members if this amendment entered the constitution of Geneva. The Australians wanted the amendment rejected at once, and the Japanese wanted it accepted. The League did what the League has always done in such cases: referred the problem to committees and adjourned. The protocol was never ratified; the question was never settled.

So this poor League—broken, shattered by Corfu—was again, just a year later, despised and rejected of men; it was nerveless, without power and without will, the shadow of a dream. True, the dream had been a grandiose one. It had been the best dream of middle-class idealism in its dying years—the perfect dream flower of a culture that had always preferred to disguise ugly reality with pleasant appearance. What prettier thought had the nineteenth century, lingering on in its elder statesmen and college professors until 1919, brought forth in all its history? It wanted, that world—the world of Gladstone, Napoleon III, Mazzini; of social democracy and imperialism, antimacassars and the "white man's burden," Mr. Asquith and Mr. Wilson—to die in beauty. It hoped at the last to decorate its realities, so hideously exposed from 1914 to 1918, with something gentle, noble and persuasive. A league of nations—a Tennysonian super-parliament among the buttercups, settling the bitter quarrels of mankind by sweet reasonableness . . .

That was the dream—pleasant enough, if superficial. And the shadow?

The things I was to remember best about Geneva that year were trivial, with scarcely more relation to causes than had the League itself. I remember Lord Parmoor, the gentle old Quaker who had joined the Labour party, referring to the British government, in an open meeting of the Council, as "Her Majesty's government." Lorelei, the smiling barmaid at the Victoria, was an optimist: "Sie werden sehen," she would say, "everything s'arrangera." The baccarat room at the Casino was open all night for delegates and accredited press correspondents, although the citizens of Switzerland were forbidden to gamble. The blue lake was particularly brilliant, and M. Briand's voice, that violoncello without an equal, was at its best. The whole thing was a large, pleasant, mixed house party, from which the grim suggestions of a world of struggle and death were automatically, as by the most ordinary politeness, excluded. Into this charming salon the Japanese, deplorably blunt, obtruded their awkward question; the party broke up in a flurry and scurry of dismay.

A. J. P. Taylor
REEXAMINING APPEASEMENT

Neville Chamberlain seeks peace in Europe

Chamberlain took a practical line in foreign policy as in everything else. He had long groaned under Baldwin's drift and delay. He was impatient with words and phrases, whether those of the Labour party, or all that structure of pacts and treaties, on which the French relied. He disliked pretence and uncertainty. He had been the first minister to advocate the abandonment of sanctions against Italy, when they had obviously failed, just as he had been the most rigorous in pressing Edward VIII. He had led every step towards rearmament and, indeed, more than any other man, laid the foundations for British fighting power during the Second World War. On the other hand, he resented the money wasted on armaments and resented, too, the way in which foreign affairs distracted him and his government from their projects of domestic reform. He believed that the European dictators, Hitler and Mussolini, were rational

From *English History 1914–1945* by A. J. P. Taylor, pp. 414–420, by permission of the Clarendon Press, Oxford.
    A. J. P. Taylor (1906–   ) is a Fellow of Magdalen College, Oxford, and the most provocative of contemporary British historians.

statesmen like himself, or at any rate must be treated as such, and that their discontents could be appeased by rational discussion. He was therefore eager to start this discussion and to get Europe resettled on new lines.

Chamberlain's asset was his sharp rationalism. He beat down critics with the question: what is the alternative? Hardly anyone now believed that the League of Nations could be effective in its existing form, though many shrank from admitting it—Germany, Italy, and Japan outside the League; sanctions shattered by the failure over Abyssinia. Churchill tended to talk as though Great Britain and France could still lay down the law to Europe; some members of the foreign office thought that Hitler should be 'hit on the head'. Chamberlain had no faith in this policy. Though he regarded France as secure from invasion behind the Maginot line and Great Britain as equally so behind the shield of sea power, he believed that Germany was also secure on her side. At least, she could be tamed only by a great war, lasting for years and tearing Europe to pieces. Such a war he and nearly all Englishmen wished to avoid.[1] The few who suggested that Hitler was bluffing could be answered by the estimates of the service chiefs—or, for that matter, of Churchill himself. Nor did Chamberlain regret the decline of Anglo-French influence in eastern Europe. This was precisely what British statesmen, including his own brother Austen, had advocated ever since the end of the first World war.

It was, of course, obvious to him, as to everyone else, that Germany would become the predominant power in eastern Europe and the Balkans; there was no escape from this, once she was acknowledged as a Great Power at all. Did Chamberlain go further and look forward to a war between Germany and Soviet Russia as a way of getting the British empire out of all its troubles? This sophisticated explanation was put forward, to Chamberlain's discredit, by a few extreme socialists at the

[1] The opponents of appeasement and, for that matter, its supporters often failed to distinguish between 'stopping' Hitler and defeating him in a great war. Hitler could be stopped only in areas directly accessible to Anglo-French forces, particularly to the French army (assuming, as was not in fact the case, that it was capable of offensive action). For instance, Hitler's reoccupation of the Rhineland could have been stopped theoretically by the French army. German and Italian intervention in Spain could have been stopped by the British and French navies. Hitler's annexation of Austria could have been stopped by the French and Italian armies, if Mussolini had still been on the side of the Western Powers. Austria was the last occasion when direct opposition was possible. Great Britain and France could not have stopped a German invasion of Czechoslovakia. They could only threaten to attack Germany's frontiers, which they believed, rightly or wrongly, to be heavily defended. Similarly, they could not stop the German invasion of Poland. They could only begin a general war which brought no aid to the Poles. There were thus two different questions. At first: shall we go to the aid of this country or that? Later: shall we start a general war for the overthrow of Germany as a Great Power? In practice, of course, the two questions were always mixed up.

time, and has occasionally been put forward, to his credit, later. There is little evidence for it. Chamberlain lived in the present. He wanted to settle immediate problems and did not much peer beyond. No doubt he hoped that Germany and Soviet Russia would balance out and hold each other in check. A war between them would be a catastrophe also for Great Britain, if it ended in a decisive victory for either. On this subject, Chamberlain kept his fingers crossed, if he thought about it at all.

It is possible to speculate whether Chamberlain ever envisaged an alliance with Germany against Soviet Russia. It is certain that he abhorred alliance with Soviet Russia against Germany. This was the favourite idea of the extreme Left—of the Left Book Club, of the un-avowed Popular Front, and of those who were fighting for the Spanish republic. The bulk of the Labour party shuffled towards it more reluctantly. It is a reasonable surmise that most English people came to regard Communist Russia as less wicked than Nazi Germany only late in the day, perhaps not until Hitler's attack on Russia. Besides, there were in 1937 and the years immediately after it practical objections. Russia was in the midst of Stalin's great purge, and it was difficult to take her seriously as a military power when all her principal military leaders had just been shot. The British service chiefs rated Russia's power very low, and their opinion carried weight even if it sprang as much from political prejudice as from knowledge. Again, Soviet Russia could not act effectively against Germany even if she had the power, so long as the *cordon sanitaire* of eastern European states was in existence—and anti-Russian. The settlement of Europe had to be revised one way or the other. It was plausible to argue that a revision to suit Germany would be less drastic than one to suit Russia, and the outcome less painful. Russia would want to communize Europe. Germany sought the redress of her national grievances and would then settle down to a happy partnership in prosperity with the Western Powers.

These were more or less rational calculations which Chamberlain made to himself. The great debate over British foreign policy did not revolve round them. It was conducted in moral terms. Most English people still assumed that Great Britain was a power of the first rank, despite the deficiencies in her armaments. Hence she was free to choose the moral course, and, if she did so, this course would inevitably triumph. English people were in fact more concerned to be on the side of God than to keep their powder dry. One moral argument told strongly in Germany's favour: the argument which had been pressed, particularly by the Left, ever since the end of the first World war. The treaty of Versailles had been presented as unjust, punitive, and unworkable. Germany was entitled to equality in armaments and everything else. The Germans of Austria, Czechoslovakia, and Poland were entitled, like other nationalities, to self-determination, even if this meant an increase in German power. More broadly, Germany was entitled to a place in Europe and in the world commensurate with her greatness in population, economic resources, and civilization. This doctrine had long been the stock-in-trade of Labour foreign policy. Labour was still solid for it when Hitler reoccupied the Rhineland. Even later, Labour men could not bring themselves to renounce it altogether. They felt, with a puzzled embarrassment, that Germany's demands were just, even though Hitler was not entitled to make them.

Conservatives took up Germany's moral claims just as Labour was backing away from them. The Conservatives of the nineteen-thirties were no longer the fire-eating imperialists of the first World war. They, too, had been gradually educated by Keynes in his denunciation of the peace settlement. The first World war, it seemed, had shaken Great Britain's position both at home and abroad.   No sensible man wanted another. Again, there had always been something strained and artificial in the *entente cordiale* with France. Some army men of the type who always dislike their allies, were accustomed to say that Great Britain had fought on the wrong side. Businessmen preferred the hard-working Germans to the unreliable French. They admired Hitler for his economic achievements, just as earlier they had been impressed when Mussolini allegedly made Italian trains run on time. There was, of course, apprehension of Germany's power and of her economic competition. But meeting her just grievances seemed the most sensible way of taming her—certainly much more sensible than a great war. Guilty conscience was undoubtedly the strongest factor: a desire to atone for the mistakes of the past and a hope that this atonement would settle things. Geoffrey Dawson, editor of *The Times,* was a striking example. Like most of Milner's kindergarten in South Africa long ago, he had always tended to sympathize with the Germans—this was why Northcliffe had dismissed him as editor in 1919.[2] Dawson was superbly confident in his own righteousness. He had been implacable against Edward VIII. He was now equally ruthless for reconciliation with Germany. He turned *The Times* into a propaganda sheet and did not hesitate to suppress, or to pervert, the reports of his own correspondents. ·

For there was also a strong moral argument on the other side: the character of the German government. Germany ceased to be a democratic country after Hitler became chancellor in January 1933. She was, in the contemporary phrase, a totalitarian state. All political parties,

[2] Northcliffe said: 'Dawson is naturally pro-German. He just can't help it.' The first act of Astor and Walter was to restore Dawson as editor when they acquired *The Times* after Northcliffe's death. Lord Lothian (formerly, as Philip Kerr, one of Lloyd George's private secretaries) and Lionel Curtis were also members of Milner's kindergarten who now supported appeasement.

other than the National Socialist, were suppressed. Political opponents were sent without trial to labour camps—called by the Nazis, in wicked echo of British practice during the Boer war, concentration camps. Religion was hampered. General elections became artificial plebiscites for a single party. British and American reporters did full, and perhaps more than full, justice to what was happening in Germany. The Nazi dictatorship was no worse than that in some other countries, particularly that in Soviet Russia, with whom, all the same, the Left were advocating an alliance. But events in Germany were reported much more fully. Besides, Germany had once been democratic and law-abiding; Russia had not. It was Germany's lapse from her high estate which constituted her special crime.

The Labour Left, spurred on by the Communists, had denounced German fascism from the first day. Few of them openly preached a crusade or war of liberation. But they came near to it. Just as they had exaggerated the effect of economic sanctions against Italy, so they seemed to imagine that moral disapproval and economic boycott would bring down German fascism. In any case, most of them accepted the current Marxist doctrine that fascism inevitably led to war, thus finding themselves in unwelcome agreement with the service chiefs, who regarded war as inevitable on other grounds. There was not much difference in practice between regarding war as inevitable and advocating it. This anti-Fascist crusade deepened the cleavage between Labour and the supporters of the government. Conservatives had no desire to be taken for an ideological ride. They reacted by finding apologies for Hitler and were the more provoked to do so, when socialists discovered 'fascism' even in the policy of the National government. Most Englishmen had no desire to interfere in the affairs of other countries and held that what went on in Germany was 'no business of ours'.

This aloofness broke down at one point. Englishmen of all classes and of all parties were offended by the Nazi treatment of the Jews. Here again, Jews were treated as badly in other countries, and often worse—in Poland, for example, with whom, nevertheless, Great Britain remained on friendly terms. For that matter, there was a good deal of quiet anti-semitism in England. Jews were kept out of many social organizations such as golf clubs, and some of the most famous public schools exercised a *numerus clausus* against them. Indeed, until Hitler's time Germany had probably been an easier country than most for Jews to rise high in industry and the professions. Once more, it was the reversion to barbarism almost as much as the barbarism itself which made Nazi Germany peculiarly hateful, and some English people were no doubt the more annoyed at having to repudiate the anti-semitism which they had secretly cherished.

Besides, the German Jews were not poor people, like most Jews in Poland or Rumania. They were famous authors, musicians, bankers, and scientists. There was now a planned exclusion of them from public life. Many left Germany—particularly those who could afford to do so. They received a warm welcome in England. As early as 1933, a fund was opened to place academic refugees in English universities. Some refugees set up their own businesses, to British advantage. Some became journalists and writers. Every refugee was walking propaganda against the Nazis, even if he never opened his mouth—propaganda which often reached people remote from the Left. The most non-political professor was moved by the sufferings of those who were now his colleagues. Even city bankers became champions of freedom when a Rothschild was imprisoned in Vienna. After the incorporation of Austria into Germany, Sigmund Freud, founder of psychoanalysis, was admitted into England with none of the usual formalities, and, against all the rules,[3] was made a British citizen the next day. The membership roll of the Royal Society, which had never left the Society's premises before, was taken to Freud's house for his signature. Baldwin's only speech on the radio after his retirement was in aid of a fund for resettling the Jews. Nazi treatment of the Jews did more than anything else to turn English moral feeling against Germany, and this moral feeling in turn made English people less reluctant to go to war.

Chamberlain shared this feeling. But he rarely allowed emotion to determine his policy. In any case he believed that appeasement was the best way of bringing Germany back to civilized behaviour. It is a fair guess that his outlook was shared by the great majority of English people outside the Labour party, and Labour was ruled out of court by its seeming advocacy of collective security, unsupported by arms. Chamberlain was further sustained by the representatives of the Dominions, when an Imperial conference was held in May 1937 during the coronation. They were unanimously for appeasement of the European dictators. Australia and New Zealand were especially anxious to see Europe settled, so that more British power could be built up against Japan in the Far East, and their anxiety grew greater in July 1937 when fighting was renewed between China and Japan. It is not surprising that the son of Joseph Chamberlain responded to this prompting. Chamberlain also received strong support from the leading members of his own cabinet; nothing could be further from the truth than the idea that his policy was a one-man affair. The two former foreign secretaries in the cabinet, Simon and Hoare, worked closely with him; they were joined by Halifax, now

---

[3] Legally naturalization was granted at the unfettered discretion of the home secretary. The invariable practice was to require five years' residence and evidence of good character.

lord president of the council, who had learnt the virtue of appeasement during his long negotiations with Gandhi. Eden, the actual foreign secretary, stood practically alone against this formidable combination, with some feeble support occasionally from junior members of the government. . . .

An Examination of Hitler's Hossbach Memorandum*

The watershed between the two World wars extended over precisely two years. Post-war ended when Germany reoccupied the Rhineland on 7 March 1936; pre-war began when she annexed Austria on 13 March 1938. From that moment, change and upheaval went on almost without interruption until the representatives of the Powers, victorious in the Second World War, met at Potsdam in July 1945. Who first raised the storm and launched the march of events? The accepted answer is clear: it was Hitler. The moment of his doing so is also accepted: it was on 5 November, 1937. We have a record of the statements which he made that day. It is called "the Hossbach memorandum", after the man who made it. This record is supposed to reveal Hitler's plans. Much play was made with it at Nuremberg; and the editors of the *Documents on German Foreign Policy* say that "it provides a summary of German foreign policy in 1937–38".[4] It is therefore worth looking at in detail. Perhaps we shall find in it the explanation of the Second World War; or perhaps we shall find only the source of a legend.

That afternoon Hitler called a conference at the Chancellery. It was attended by Blomberg, the minister of war; Neurath, the foreign minister; Fritsch, commander-in-chief of the army; Raeder, commander-in-chief of the navy; and Goering, commander-in-chief of the air force. Hitler did most of the talking. He began with a general disquisition on Germany's need for *Lebensraum*. He did not specify where this was to be found—probably in Europe, though he also discussed colonial gains. But gains there must be. "Germany had to reckon with two hate-inspired antagonists, Britain and France. . . . Germany's problem could only be solved by means of force and this was never without attendant risk." When and how was there to be this resort to force? Hitler discussed three "cases". The first "case" was "period 1943–1945". After that the situation could only change for the worse; 1943 must be the moment for action. Case 2 was civil war in France; if that happened, "the time for action against the Czechs had come". Case 3 was war between France and Italy. This might well occur in 1938; then "our objective must be to overthrow

* Here to end of article from *The Origins of the Second World War* by A. J. P. Taylor. Copyright © 1961 by A. J. P. Taylor, Hamish Hamilton, London.
4 *Documents on German Foreign Policy*, series D. i., footnote on p. 29.

Czechoslovakia and Austria simultaneously". None of these "cases" came true; clearly therefore they do not provide the blueprint for German policy. Nor did Hitler dwell on them. He went on to demonstrate that Germany would gain her aims without a great war; "force" apparently meant to him the threat of war, not necessarily war itself. The Western Powers would be too hampered and too timid to intervene. "Britain almost certainly, and probably France as well, had written off the Czechs and were reconciled to the fact that this question of Germany would be cleared up in due course". No other Power would intervene. "Poland—with Russia in her rear—will have little inclination to engage in war against a victorious Germany." Russia would be held in check by Japan.

Hitler's exposition was in large part day-dreaming, unrelated to what followed in real life. Even if seriously meant, it was not a call to action, at any rate not to the action of a great war; it was a demonstration that a great war would not be necessary. Despite the preliminary talk about 1943–1945, its solid core was the examination of the chances for peaceful triumphs in 1938, when France would be preoccupied elsewhere. Hitler's listeners remained doubtful. The generals insisted that the French army would be superior to the German even if engaged against Italy as well. Neurath doubted whether a Mediterranean conflict between France and Italy were imminent. Hitler waved these doubts aside: "he was convinced of Britain's non-participation, and therefore he did not believe in the probability of belligerent action by France against Germany". There is only one safe conclusion to be drawn from this rambling disquisition: Hitler was gambling on some twist of fortune which would present him with success in foreign affairs, just as a miracle had made him Chancellor in 1933. There was here no concrete plan, no directive for German policy in 1937 and 1938. Or if there were a directive, it was to wait upon events.[5]

Why then did Hitler hold this conference? This question was not asked at Nuremburg; it has not been asked by historians. Yet surely it is an elementary part of historical discipline to ask of a document not only what is in it, but why it came into existence. The conference of 5 November 1937 was a curious gathering. Only Goering was a Nazi. The others were old-style Conservatives who had remained in office to keep Hitler under control; all of them except Raeder were to be dismissed from their posts within three months. Hitler knew that all except Goering were his opponents; and he did not trust Goering much. Why did he reveal his inmost thoughts to men whom he distrusted and whom he was shortly to discharge? This question has an easy answer: he did not reveal his inmost thoughts. There was no crisis in foreign policy to provoke a broad discussion or sweeping decisions. The conference was a manoeuvre

[5] Memorandum by Hossbach, 10 Nov. 1937. *German Foreign Policy*, series D. i. No. 19.

in domestic affairs. Here a storm was brewing. The financial genius of Schacht had made rearmament and full employment possible; but now Schacht was jibbing at further expansion of the armament programme. Hitler feared Schacht and could not answer his financial arguments. He knew only that they were wrong: the Nazi régime could not relax its momentum. Hitler aimed to isolate Schacht from the other Conservatives; and he had therefore to win them for a programme of increased armaments. His geopolitical exposition had no other purpose. The Hossbach memorandum itself provides evidence of this. Its last paragraph reads: "The second part of the conference was concerned with questions of armament". This, no doubt, was why it had been called.

The participants themselves drew this conclusion. After Hitler had left, Raeder complained that the German navy would be in no strength to face war for years ahead. Blomberg and Goering pulled him into a corner, where they explained that the sole object of the conference was to prod Fritsch into demanding a larger arms programme. Neurath made no comment at the time. He is said to have grasped the full import of Hitler's wickedness some days later, and then to have suffered "several severe heart attacks". These attacks were first revealed in 1945 when Neurath was being tried as a war criminal; he showed no sign of ill-health in 1937 or for years afterwards. Fritsch prepared a memorandum, insisting that the German army must not be exposed to the risk of war against France, and took this to Hitler on 9 November. Hitler replied that there was no real risk and that, in any case, Fritsch would do better to speed up rearmament instead of dabbling in political questions. Despite this rebuke, Hitler's manoeuvre had succeeded: henceforward Fritsch, Blomberg, and Raeder had no sympathy with Schacht's financial scruples. Otherwise, none of the men who attended the meeting on 5 November gave it another thought until Goering found the record produced against him at Nuremberg as evidence of his war guilt. From that moment it has haunted the corridors of historical research. It is the basis for the view that there is nothing to be discovered about the origins of the second World war. Hitler, it is claimed, decided on war, and planned it in detail on 5 November 1937. Yet the Hossbach memorandum contains no plans of the kind, and would never have been supposed to do so, unless it had been displayed at Nuremberg. The memorandum tells us, what we knew already, that Hitler (like every other German statesman) intended Germany to become the dominant Power in Europe. It also tells us that he speculated how this might happen. His speculations were mistaken. They bear hardly any relation to the actual outbreak of war in 1939. A racing tipster who only reached Hitler's level of accuracy would not do well for his clients.

The speculations were irrelevant as well as mistaken. Hitler did not make plans—for world conquest or for anything else. He assumed that others would provide opportunities, and that he would seize them. The opportunities which he envisaged on 5 November 1937 were not provided. Others were. We must therefore look elsewhere for the man who provided an opportunity which Hitler could take and who thus gave the first push towards war.

Hugh Trevor-Roper
REASSERTING ORTHODOXY

It is over twenty years since the war began. A generation has grown up which never knew the 1930's, never shared its passions and doubts, was never excited by the Spanish civil war, never boiled with indignation against the "appeasers," never lived in suspense from Nuremberg Rally to Nuremberg Rally, awaiting the next hysterical outburst, the next clatter of arms, from the megalomaniac in Berlin. Those of us who knew those days and who try to teach this new generation are constantly made aware of this great gulf between us. How can we communicate across such a gulf the emotional content of those years, the mounting indignation which finally convinced even the "appeasers" themselves that there could be no peace with Hitler, and caused the British people, united in pacifism in 1936, to go, in 1939, united into war? For it was not the differing shades of justice in Germany's claims upon the Rhineland, Austria, the Sudetenland, Prague, and Danzig which caused men who had swallowed the first of these annexations to be increasingly exasperated by those which followed and take up arms against the last. It was a changing mood, a growing conviction that all such claims were but pretexts under which Hitler pursued not justice or self-determination for Germany but world-conquest, and that, now or never, he must be stopped. And even across the gulf such a mood must be conveyed by those who teach history to those who learn it: for it is an element in history no less important than the mere facts.

From *Encounter,* July 1961. By permission of H. R. Trevor-Roper and Encounter.

Hugh Trevor-Roper (1914–   ) is Regius Professor of Modern History at Oxford.

Or is it? Mr. A. J. P. Taylor, it seems, does not think so.[1] He sees the gulf all right, and he wishes to speak to those on the other side of it; but in order to do so, he has decided to lighten the weight he must carry with him. Stripping himself of all personal memories, and thus making himself, in this respect, as naked as they are, he has jumped nimbly across the gulf and now presents himself to them as the first enlightened historian of the future, capable of interpreting the politics of the 1920's and 1930's without any reference to the emotions they engendered, even in himself. Their sole guide, he tells them, must be the documents, which he will select and interpret for them; and indeed, by selection and interpretation, he presents them with a new thesis, illustrated (we need hardly say) with all his old resources of learning, paradox, and *gaminerie*.

The thesis is perfectly clear. According to Mr. Taylor, Hitler was an ordinary German statesman in the tradition of Stresemann and Brüning, differing from them not in methods (he was made Chancellor for "solidly democratic reasons") nor in ideas (he had no ideas) but only in the greater patience and stronger nerves with which he took advantage of the objective situation in Europe. His policy, in so far as he had a policy, was no different from that of his predecessors. He sought neither war nor annexation of territory. He merely sought to restore Germany's "natural" position in Europe, which had been artificially altered by the Treaty of Versailles: a treaty which, for that reason, "lacked moral validity from the start." Such a restoration might involve the recovery of lost German territory like Danzig, but it did not entail the direct government even of Austria or the Sudetenland, let alone Bohemia. Ideally, all that Hitler required was that Austria, Czechoslovakia, and other small Central European states, while remaining independent, should become political satellites of Germany.

Of course it did not work out thus. But that, we are assured, was not Hitler's fault. For Hitler, according to Mr. Taylor, never took the initiative in politics. He "did not make plans—for world-conquest or anything else. He assumed that others would provide opportunities and that he would seize them." And that is what happened. The Austrian crisis of March 1938, we are told, "was provoked by Schuschnigg, not by Hitler." Hitler was positively embarrassed by it: "he was Austrian enough to find the complete disappearance of Austria inconceivable until it happened." Similarly we learn that the Sudeten crisis of 1938 was created by the Sudeten Nazis, who "built up the tension gradually, without guidance from Hitler": Hitler himself "merely took advantage of it." Having taken

[1] *The Origins of the Second World War.* By A. J. P. TAYLOR. Hamish Hamilton, 25s.

advantage of it at Munich, he had no intention of going on and annexing the Czech lands: "he merely doubted whether the settlement would work . . . [he] believed, without sinister intention, that independent Czechoslovakia could not survive when deprived of her natural frontiers and with Czech prestige broken." So, within six months, as "the unforeseen by-product of developments in Slovakia," he felt obliged to tear up the settlement and occupy Prague; but there was "nothing sinister or premeditated" in that. It was an unfortunate necessity forced upon him by the unskilful President Hacha. The Polish crisis of 1939 was similarly forced upon him by Beck. "The destruction of Poland," we are told, "had been no part of his original project. On the contrary, he wished to solve the question of Danzig so that Germany and Poland could remain on good terms." The last thing he wanted was war. The war of nerves was "the only war he understood and liked." Germany "was not equipped to conquer Europe."

> The state of German rearmament in 1939 gives the decisive proof that Hitler was not contemplating general war, and probably not contemplating war at all.

Even on August 23rd, 1939, when the Nazi-Soviet Pact was signed, "both Hitler and Stalin imagined that they had prevented war, not brought it on." What rational person could have supposed that this pact, instead of discouraging the British, would determine them to stand by their commitments? The war, "far from being premeditated, was a mistake, the result on both sides of diplomatic blunders."

Hitler's own share of these diplomatic blunders was, it seems, very small. He "became involved in war," we are told, "through launching on August 29th a diplomatic manœuvre which he ought to have launched on August 28th." The blunders of the Western statesmen were far more fundamental. For what ought the Western statesmen to have done when faced by Hitler's modest demands? According to Mr. Taylor, they should have conceded them all. They should not have conceded anything to Mussolini, for Mussolini's demands were essentially different from Hitler's. Mussolini was "a vain, blustering boaster" whose government, unlike the "solidly democratic" rule of Hitler, "lived in a state of illegality," and whose demands, since they did not correspond with "reality," were "a fraud." Western statesmen, says Mr. Taylor, lost all claim to respect by recognising such a man. But Hitler was a statesman who merely sought to reassert Germany's "natural weight," and they would therefore have gained respect by recognising him. Accordingly Mr. Taylor's heroes among Western statesmen are those who recognised German claims: Ramsay MacDonald and Neville Chamberlain. Winston Churchill believed in the balance of power and would have maintained frontiers designed on principles of security, not nationality. Intolerable cynicism! How much nobler was that "triumph for British policy," the Munich settlement!

> It was a triumph for all that was best and most enlightened in British life; a triumph for those who had preached equal justice between peoples; a triumph for those who had courageously denounced the harshness and shortsightedness of Versailles.

Munich, according to Mr. Taylor, "atoned" for all the previous weakness of British policy; it was a victory for "morality" (which is his word for political realism); and he praises Chamberlain's "skill and persistence" in bringing "first the French and then the Czechs to follow the moral line." If only Chamberlain had not lost his nerve in 1939! If only he had shown equal "skill and persistence" in enabling Hitler to detach Danzig and the Polish Corridor, how happy we should all be! Germany would have recovered its "natural" position, "morality" would have triumphed, and everyone would be happy in the best of possible worlds.

Such, in brief, is Mr. Taylor's thesis. It is not surprising that it has been hailed with cries of delight in neo-Nazi or semi-Nazi circles in Germany. It is more surprising that the book has been greeted by the fashionable Grub Street of England as the highest achievement of British historiography. Mr. Taylor has been compared with Gibbon and Macaulay; his failure to secure worthy promotion has caused astonishment. The anonymous oracle of the *Times Literary Supplement* has predicted finality for the result of his "methodical and impeccable logic." In the *Observer*, Mr. Sebastian Haffner (who recently published a panegyric of that "greatest Roman of them all," Dr. Goebbels) has declared the book "an almost faultless masterpiece" in which "fairness reigns supreme"; and his cosy, middlebrow colleagues in rival papers, hypnotised by a reputation which they are unqualified to test, have obediently jollied their readers along in harmony with the blurb. However, let us not all be hypnotised. Before hurling ourselves down the Gadarene slope, let us ask of Mr. Taylor's thesis, not, Is it brilliant? Is it plausible? but, Is it true? By what rules of evidence, by what philosophy of interpretation is it reached? . . .

Take the inconvenient fact of Hitler's avowed programme of a great Eastern land-empire. In spite of some casual admission, Mr. Taylor effectively denies that Hitler had any such programme. Hitler, he says, "was always the man of daring improvisations: he made lightning decisions and then presented them as the result of long-term policy." Hitler's *Table Talk*, he says airily (as if this were the only evidence for such a programme), "was delivered far in occupied territory during the campaign against Soviet Russia, and *then* Hitler dreamed of some fantastic empire which would rationalise his career of conquest." [My italics here, and in all quotations below.] But why does Mr. Taylor believe, or rather pretend, that it was only in 1942, after his Russian conquests, that Hitler dreamed of an Eastern Empire? His programme had been stated, as clearly as possible, in 1924, in *Mein Kampf,* and on numerous other occasions since. Mr. Taylor hardly ever refers to *Mein Kampf* and never to the other occasions. In 1939, he admits, some people "attributed" to Hitler "grandiose plans which *they claimed* to have discovered by reading *Mein Kampf* in the original (Hitler forbade its publication in English)." The implication is that such plans are not to be found in *Mein Kampf* and that those who "claimed to have discovered" them had not really read, or been able to read, an untranslated work. But the fact is that those plans are unmistakably stated in *Mein Kampf* and that all the evidence of the 1930's showed that Hitler still intended to carry them out. I may add (since Mr. Taylor includes me among those who have ascribed to Hitler "preconceived plans" which he never pursued) that I myself read *Mein Kampf* in the original in 1938, and that I read it under the impact of Munich and of the remarkable prophecies of Sir Robert Ensor, who had read it and who insisted that Hitler meant what he said. By absolutely refusing to face this evidence, and contemptuously dismissing those who have faced it, Mr. Taylor contrives to reach the preposterous conclusion that men like Ensor, who correctly forecast Hitler's future programme from the evidence, were really wrong, and that men like Chamberlain, who did not read the evidence and were proved totally wrong by events, were really right. His sole justification of this paradox is that he has accepted as an axiom a characterisation of Hitler as a "traditional" statesman pursuing limited aims. Mr. Taylor's Hitler cannot have held such views, and therefore the inconvenient fact that the real Hitler uttered such views with remarkable consistency for twenty years and actually put them into practice, is simply puffed aside. When Hitler, in 1941, finally launched that conquest of Russia which, as he himself said, was "the be-all and end-all of Nazism," Mr. Taylor easily explains it away. "By 1941," he says, "Hitler had lost his old gift of patience": he "gratuitously" deviated from his former course; and at the mere thought of such an unaccountable fall from grace, Mr. Taylor promptly ends his book.

Nor is this the only perversion of evidence to which Mr. Taylor has to resort, in order to represent Hitler as a "traditional" statesman. The traditional statesmen *did not seek,* as Hitler did, to incorporate the Sudeten Germans in the Reich. Traditional statesmen demanded the frontiers of 1914; but Hitler, again and again, repudiated the frontiers of

1914 as a contemptible ambition. They looked back, at most, to the war-aims of 1914; he repudiated those war-aims. Even the "natural" position of January 1918, after the huge gains of Brest-Litovsk, was insufficient for Hitler. The treaty of Brest-Litovsk gave Germany the Ukraine as a colony of exploitation, a capitalist colony. But Hitler always made it quite clear that he spurned such a colony: he wanted the Ukraine as a colony of settlement. "I should deem it a crime," he said, "if I sacrificed the blood of a quarter of a million men merely for the conquest of natural riches to be exploited in a capitalist way. The goal of the *Ostpolitik* is to open up an area of settlement for a hundred million Germans." All this is pushed aside by Mr. Taylor with the remark,

> when Hitler lamented, "If only we had a Ukraine . . ." he seemed to suppose there were no Ukrainians. Did he propose to exploit, or exterminate them? *Apparently he never considered the question.*

As if Hitler had not made his answer perfectly plain! As if he had any scruples about transporting or even exterminating populations! What about the European Jews? But that episode is conveniently forgotten by Mr. Taylor. It does not fit the character of a traditional German states-man who "in principle and doctrine, was no more wicked and unscrupu-lous than many other contemporary statesmen." . . .

Now let us take a few instances. On November 5th, 1937, Hitler summoned his war-leaders to the Chancellery and made a speech which, he said, in the event of his death was to be regarded as his "last will and testament." That suggests that he was not talking irresponsibly. The official record of this speech is the so-called "Hossbach Memorandum" which was used at Nuremberg as evidence of Hitler's plans for the gradual conquest of Europe. In it Hitler declared that the aim of German policy must be the conquest of *Lebensraum* in Europe, "but we will not copy liberal capitalist policies which rely on exploiting colonies. It is not a case of conquering people but of conquering agriculturally useful space." That seems clear enough. Then Hitler went on to consider the means of making such conquests. "German politics," he said, "must reckon with two hateful enemies, England and France, to whom a strong German colossus in the centre of Europe would be intolerable." Moreover, he admitted, these two hateful enemies would probably, at some stage, resist him by force: "the German question can only be solved by way of force, and this is never without risk." He then proceeded to discuss hypothetical possibilities. Since the hypothetical circumstances did not in fact arise, we need not dwell on them. The essential points are that the risk of Euro-pean war must be faced by 1943–5, for "after that we can only expect a change for the worse," and that "our *first* aim" must be, at the first convenient opportunity, "to conquer Czechoslovakia and Austria simultaneously." This first conquest he hoped to achieve without war, for "in all probability England and perhaps also France have already silently written off Czechoslovakia." It could and should therefore be attempted as soon as circumstances make it possible in order that the later, more real risk could be faced before 1943–5. But there was to be no doubt about the nature of the conquest. It was not to be (as Mr. Taylor always maintains) the reduction of Austria and Czechoslovakia to the role of satellites: it was to be, in Hitler's own words, "the annexation of the two states to Germany, militarily and politically." The idea of satellite states in Eastern Europe, Hitler said in a secret speech delivered only a fortnight later, was one of the futile notions of "traditional" German politicians, and he dismissed it as "idiotic" (*wahnsinnig*). Finally, it is clear that conquered Austria and Czechoslovakia cannot themselves have consituted the *Lebensraum* which was the ultimate objective. Austria and Czechoslovakia were to be stepping-stones, "in all probability" secured without war, towards larger conquests which would entail a greater risk.

Such was Hitler's "testament" of November 1937. Its content is clear and logical and it has been taken seriously by all historians—until Mr. Taylor comes along and tells us that we have all been hoodwinked. For was not this document produced at Nuremberg? All documents produced at Nuremberg, he says, are "loaded," and "anyone who relies on them finds it almost impossible to escape from the load with which they are charged." So Mr. Taylor gives us a sample of his method of using such documents. Why, he asks, was the speech made? "The historian," he observes, "must push through the *cloud of phrases*" (so much for Hitler's perfectly clear statements) "to the *realities* beneath." The speech, he notes, was not made to Nazis but to generals and admirals, and its purpose was clearly to demand greater rearmament. With this we can agree. But Mr. Taylor does not stop there. In order to persuade these "conservative" war-leaders of the necessity of further rearmament, Hitler (he says) had to overcome the economic opposition of Dr. Schacht. His speech therefore "*had no other purpose*" than "to isolate Schacht from the other conservatives"; the dates 1943–5 (to which Hitler consistently kept) "*like all such figures, really meant* this year, next year, sometime . . .'" and the content of a speech which Hitler himself described as his political testament (but Mr. Taylor does not quote that description) is dismissed as "daydreaming unrelated to what followed in real life." Why Hitler should be expected to speak more "realistically" on military matters to Nazis at a froth-blowers' meeting than to hardheaded war-leaders who would have to organise and carry out his programme is not clear. Presumably it is "an elementary part of historical discipline" to assume that. . . .

Thomas K. Finletter
MASSIVE RETALIATION

The most important new emphasis on the Far East has been in Southeast Asia. After the Korean armistice in July 1953 the Chinese Communists turned their attention to Indo-China and, to counter it, the United States Government made some very strong statements about its determination to keep the area out of the hands of the Communists. For a long time these statements were unilateral. The United States alone, without consulting the UN or concerting its policy with its main NATO Allies, warned the Chinese Communists not to move into Indo-China.

President Eisenhower gave the lead to this policy in singling out Southeast Asia and Indo-China as the key point in the line of the Gray Areas which had to be defended. In his speech to the Conference of Governors on August 4, 1953, the President, defending the increase in United States appropriations to help the French in the war against the Viet-Minh, said that the Communists' expansion into Southeast Asia just had to be blocked and that Indo-China was the place to block it. Indo-China was the key, the President said, to the defense not only of Southeast Asia, including Indonesia, Burma and Malaya as well as Indo-China and Thailand, but of India as well. The $400 million additional aid to help the French in Indo-China was the cheapest way, the President said, to prevent the occurrence of something that would be of a most terrible significance to the United States of America and our security.[1]

Several important statements of US policy preceded and followed this statement of the President, all pointing up the interest of the United States in Southeast Asia, our determination to take risks, even the risk of general war, to hold it, and to do this alone if necessary.

The Korean War and the fighting in Indo-China were identified as never before as part of one single front. In March 1953, in a Joint Communiqué with the French, the United States announced that if the Chinese Communists took advantage of an armistice in Korea to pursue aggressive war elsewhere in the Far East, such action would "have the most serious consequences for the efforts to bring about peace in the

From *Power and Policy*, copyright, 1954, by Thomas Finletter, pp. 94–103. Reprinted by permission of Harcourt, Brace & World, Inc.

Thomas K. Finletter (1893–   ), was Secretary of the Air Force from 1950 to 1953.

[1] Talk by President Eisenhower at the 45th Annual Governors' Conference, August 4, 1953.

world and would conflict directly with the understanding on which any armistice in Korea would rest."[2] The United States, that is, warned the Red Chinese that they should not use the Chinese armies that would be released by the armistice in Korea to attack Indo-China and that if they did there would be "the most serious consequences."

Already the warning by the sixteen UN countries which had been fighting in Korea, combined with the US bilateral treaty of guaranty with the Republic of Korea, had warned the Chinese that they would be at war with the United States and the other fifteen UN countries, if they attacked the Korean Republic. The Joint US-French Communiqué now covered the possibility of an attack in Indo-China.

A most serious warning to the Chinese Communist regime was yet to come. In September of 1953 Secretary of State Dulles told the American Legion that "there is the risk that, as in Korea, Red China might send its own army into Indo-China. The Chinese Communist regime should realize that such a second aggression could not occur without grave consequences which might not be confined to Indo-China. I say this soberly in the interest of peace and in the hope of preventing another aggressor miscalculation."

This is strong language. When the American Secretary of State tells the hostile Communist government of China that the United States is so interested in Indo-China that if Peiping repeats in Indo-China what it did in Korea there will be "grave consequences which might not be confined to Indo-China," this can mean only that the United States will fight the Chinese if necessary to hold Indo-China—not just by helping the French, but by using United States military forces to do the fighting. And it would not be a localized war as in Korea; it would extend to the Chinese homeland. How is not stated, whether by aerial bombing only, or by all-out war with ground troops too.

The Dulles speech is remarkable too in other respects. It announces an important new precept for the conduct of foreign affairs by the United States—one that had been forecast in Mr. Dulles' statements for some time and now comes out as flat US policy. We have learned from the Korean War a lesson, the Secretary of State said,

which we expect to apply in the interests of future peace. The lesson is this: if events are likely which will in fact lead us to fight, let us make clear our intention in advance; then we shall probably not have to fight. Big wars usually come about by mistake, not by design. Aggressive despots think they can make a grab unopposed, or opposed but feebly. So, they grab. And to their surprise they find themselves involved in unexpected opposition which means major war.

2 Joint U.S.-French Communiqué, Washington, March 28, 1953.

Many believe that neither the First World War nor the Second World War would have occurred if the aggressor had known what the United States would do. It is even more probable that the Korean War would not have occurred if the aggressor had known what the United States would do. The Communists thought, and had reason to think, that they would not be opposed except by the then small and ill-equipped forces of the Republic of Korea. They did not expect what actually happened.

> There is in this a profound lesson. . . .
> Peace requires anticipating what it is that tempts an aggressor and letting him know in advance that, if he does not exercise self-control, he may face a hard fight, perhaps a losing fight.
> The Korean War—the third such war in our generation—should finally have taught us that if we can foresee aggression which will cause us to fight, we should let this be known, so that the potential aggressor will take this into his calculations.

This vigorous warning was followed up by President Eisenhower when he announced in December 1953 that United States ground forces in Korea would be progressively reduced and that as an initial step two US Army divisions would soon be withdrawn and returned to the United States. The President repeated the warning to China that the sixteen nations had given at the time the armistice was signed. If the Chinese Communists were to take advantage of the weakening of our ground forces in Korea and to attack the United Nations army "the consequences of such a breach of the armistice would be so grave that, in all probability, it would not be possible to confine hostilities within the frontiers of Korea." And Secretary Dulles soon afterward gave an even more pointed warning, advising China not to attack in Korea or anywhere else, and warning them of atomic war if they did. In his January, 1954 speech before the Council on Foreign Relations, the Secretary told China, and Russia too, that if they attacked in places where they could not be held by local resistance, the United States, in accordance with a "basic policy decision" taken by the President on the advice of the National Security Council, would rely, to hold the Communists in check, on its "great capacity to retaliate instantly by means and at places of our choosing." This was a serious warning, made with a bluntness rare in international affairs.

The evolution of this tough line about Indo-China and the Far East generally has been a *crescendo,* moving step by step from the first multilateral and plainly necessary warning of the sixteen United Nations in Korea in July 1953 to the climax of the unilateral, go-it-alone massive retaliation warning in the Council of Foreign Relations Speech of the

Secretary of State in January 1954. The sixteen-nation warning to the Chinese in July 1953 not to start up the fighting again in Korea was unavoidable; we could not have done otherwise with due regard to the safety of our troops in Korea. The 1953 armistice had greatly strengthened the Communist military position. It stopped the UN Air from hammering North Korea, enabled the Communists to build airfields in North Korea, and gave them a striking power in the air which they would not have had if the fighting had not stopped. The threat to give up the limited war, which had been kept limited with such tenacity by the United States and the other UN countries, could not now be avoided. If it turned out that the Communists had trapped the United Nations into an armistice merely to improve their military position, that would be too much for us to put up with. We would have no alternative but to give up our efforts to keep the war limited to Korea.

The policy announced in the American Legion Speech (September, 1953) was quite different. It was not at all orthodox; it was not forced on us by circumstances. It was a new and daring line. It established the threat of "grave consequences" which might not be confined to the area in question as the technique which would be used generally in the Gray Areas to stop the Chinese Communists from moving their frontier forward.

The Council on Foreign Relations Speech went another step in advance. It told the Chinese and the world what the "grave consequences" would consist of; they would include instant and massive retaliation, which could only mean atom bombs.

And in all the statements after the initial Korean Declaration of July 1953, it is the United States alone which speaks. All the warnings to the Chinese, starting with the Joint US-French Communiqué through the American Legion and Council on Foreign Relations speeches and various statements to the press, are unilateral, by the United States alone.

This was new policy. Until this series of warnings was made the United States had been trying stubbornly to avoid general war with China. We now were prepared to risk it, and risk it alone. But could we go it alone this way, as a military matter? Could we make this instant retaliation on our own and without using bases in NATO and other sovereign countries? And what about the right of the US Congress to declare war? And what would a go-it-alone policy do to the solidarity of NATO on which the safety of the United States homeland depends?

Nor was it possible to discount these warnings of Secretary Dulles because they referred only to open armed attacks by the Chinese Red armies, to orthodox invasions such as the North Koreans made when their armies went over the 38th Parallel in June 1950. In fact, the Russo-Chinese gave no signs of making another orthodox invasion as in Korea.

Indirect aggression was now the technique they relied on—feeding in war matériel and technical advice to the Communist side of a civil war.

Indirect aggression works for the Russo-Chinese better than direct aggression. They have learned from their experience in Korea that direct military attack even when carried out by a subsidiary puppet irritates the free states and makes them fight. The free states on the other hand have not found a formula to combat indirect aggressions where Russian military equipment, Russian and Chinese technicians and, if necessary, Chinese "volunteers" are fed in to a local Communist-run civil war. The odds are strongly in favor of the Communists in the new indirect technique which they started in the Korean War and developed further in Indo-China. The Communists can step up the pressure when they want to and to the level they want to. They can keep it going indefinitely. The initiative is theirs. And it is easy for the Communists to paralyze the Western democracies who depend on their public opinion by not giving that public opinion a sensational brutality—such as the North Korean attack over the 38th Parallel—on which to feed. It is significant that when the Viet Minh armies started to move against Laos in a frank invasion they were quickly called off. Why give up a winning formula and go back to the old one which had aroused the Free World to fight?

Mr. Dulles' warnings did not refer to the indirect form of aggression. But the Chinese could not possibly rely on this technical distinction. If the United States felt so strongly about holding Indo-China that it would be willing to make war on the Chinese mainland, and do it alone, if the Red Chinese armies were to go over the boundary of Indo-China, the Chinese cannot have been sure that we would not feel equally strongly if they took over Indo-China by the indirect method—by feeding in enough supplies and technicians to the Viet Minh to enable them to win.

In any case, this point has now been clarified. In a speech to the Overseas Press Club in March 1954, Mr. Dulles announced that "the imposition in Southeast Asia of the political system of Communist Russia and its Chinese Communist ally, *by whatever means* would be a grave threat to the whole free community [italics added],"[3] and would, presumably, bring down on the Chinese the various sanctions with which they had been threatened.

The Overseas Press Club speech completed a cycle of warnings to the Russo-Chinese. They amounted to this: (1) the warnings were now universal for all the Gray Areas; they covered any attack by the Russians or Chinese anywhere; (2) the warnings now applied to indirect aggressions of the Viet Minh or Tudeh variety, as well as to an orthodox

[3] Speech to the Overseas Press Club, March 29, 1954.

rolling-over-the-frontier invasion such as the North Koreans made in 1950; (3) the warnings had become increasingly clear about the use of atom bombs, and we had now made the flat statement that we will rely primarily on atomic power to stop any further advances in the Gray Areas by the Russo-Chinese; (4) the warnings had evolved from the multi-lateral, juridically sound UN statement at the time of the armistice in Korea into a number of unilateral warnings by the United States alone which our principal Allies have not joined and probably would not support if the Russo-Chinese were to take up our challenge; (5) we had moved more and more in the direction of an ultimatum to Russia that we will hold her, the main source of Communist power, responsible for further Communist aggressions by anyone anywhere in the Gray Areas. In one respect only has there been a withdrawal from this increasingly strong go-it-alone line toward the Russo-Chinese. The Overseas Press Club Speech of the Secretary of State introduced for the first time, in his series of warnings to the Chinese, the idea of united action, united that is with our major Western Allies. But as yet, at this writing, the political arrangements to unify Western policies in Southeast Asia have not been set up.

3
Getting out of War

Neither appeasement nor the hard line has prevented two world wars in half a century. If the wars were caused by such mistaken theories, were they not prolonged by similar errors? George Kennan, an American with a background in both diplomacy and historical research, denounces the tendency of democratic countries to wage crusades to "make the world safe for democracy." Kennan expresses deep sympathy for the idea that World War I should have been ended before the collapse of the Central Powers in 1918.

The most famous example of the argument for ending World War I short of total victory was that of Lord Lansdowne, a former British Foreign Secretary. Such a view was completely at odds with the policy of the Prime Minister and of Lloyd George, soon to be Prime Minister, who favored complete defeat of Germany. Lloyd George used the expression "knock-out blow" in a famous newspaper interview during September of 1916.

In the Second World War, the policy of total victory was represented by Franklin D. Roosevelt's phrase "unconditional surrender." This policy came under violent attack after the dropping of the atomic bomb and raised a host of questions, both strategic and moral. Of relevance in recent years has been the contention expressed by Chester Wilmot, an Australian journalist, that diplomacy based upon "unconditional surrender" facilitated the expansion of Russia in the Cold War. The leadership vacuum left by Germany in Europe allowed Russia open entry into Eastern Europe. The further complexity of this theme is developed by a clergyman, Robert C. Batchelder, who analyzes the many motives driving the men who actually made the decision to use the bomb. He points out that it was a decision of doubtful merit on purely ethical grounds.

The concept of complete surrender remains a matter of urgent concern, though actual experience has not yet offered conclusive evidence to support or discredit it. The Cuban crisis of 1962 with its provision for graceful retreat by Russia illustrated almost complete, but not complete surrender to U.S. demands.

George F. Kennan
HOLY WAR

In the Western countries . . . war fervor had by 1917 attained a terrific intensity. The Western democracies had by this time convinced themselves, as embattled democracies have a tendency to do, that the entire future of civilization depended on the outcome of the military struggle.

There is, let me assure you, nothing in nature more egocentrical than the embattled democracy. It soon becomes the victim of its own war propaganda. It then tends to attach to its own cause an absolute value which distorts its own vision on everything else. *Its* enemy becomes the embodiment of all evil. *Its* own side, on the other hand, is the center of all virtue. The contest comes to be viewed as having a final, apocalyptic quality. If *we* lose, all is lost; life will no longer be worth living; there will be nothing to be salvaged. If we win, then everything will be possible; all problems will become soluble; the one great source of evil—*our* enemy—will have been crushed; the forces of good will then sweep forward unimpeded; all worthy aspirations will be satisfied.

From *Russia and the West under Lenin and Stalin* by George F. Kennan, pp. 5–9, 47–48, by permission of Atlantic-Little, Brown and Co. Copyright © 1960, 1961 by James K. Hotchkiss, Trustee.

George F. Kennan (1904–   ) is an American diplomat and historian. He has written many books on Russia and modern international affairs.

It will readily be seen that people who have got themselves into this frame of mind have little understanding for the issues of any contest other than the one in which they are involved. The idea of people wasting time and substance on any *other* issue seems to them preposterous. This explains why Allied statesmen were simply unable to comprehend how people in Russia could be interested in an internal Russian political crisis when there was a war on in the West. Did the Russians not realize, it was asked in Paris and London, that everything depended on the defeat of the Germans, that if Germany was successful, no one could ever conceivably be happy again, whereas if Germany lost, everyone would somehow or other receive what he wanted?

You saw this well illustrated in the first reaction of President Woodrow Wilson to the news of the seizure of power in Russia by the Communists, in November 1917. "It is amazing to me"—he said—

> . . . that any group of persons should be so ill-informed as to suppose, as some groups in Russia apparently suppose, that any reforms planned in the interests of the people can live in the presence of a Germany powerful enough to undermine or overthrow them by intrigue or force. . . .

There was, of course, an important substantive difference between the issue that interested the early Bolsheviki and that which interested the warring powers in the West. The first was ideological, with universal social and political implications. The Bolsheviki believed that questions of social organization—in particular the question of ownership of the means of production—had an importance transcending all international rivalries. Such rivalries were, in their eyes, simply the product of social relationships. This is why they attached so little importance to the military outcome of the struggle in the West.

The conflict in which the Western peoples were interested was, on the contrary, overwhelmingly a national one. It was almost devoid of ideological overtones. It had begun in large part as a struggle between the Russian and Austro-Hungarian empires for succession to the declining power of Turkey in the Balkans. By 1917 this issue had been largely fought to death, in the sense that both of these empires had now weakened themselves so seriously by the military exertion that they were beyond the point of caring much about the original points of difference. With their exhaustion, the center of gravity of the war had moved northward, and had settled on the German problem. To the extent that a real issue was still involved during the last two years of the war, as distinct from the emotional states into which people had now worked themselves, it was simply the question of the position Germany was to occupy in the future Europe and on the trade routes of the world.

There was, to be sure, an effort on the Allied side, increasing as that war ran its course, to portray the contest as one of political ideology: as a struggle between democracy and autocracy. To this, I think, we Americans were particularly prone. The effort was, in retrospect, unconvincing. Wilhelminian Germany at its worst was much closer to Western parliamentarianism and to Western concepts of justice than was the Tsarist Russia whose collaboration the Western Allies so gladly accepted in the early stages of the war. The truth is that the war was being waged against Germany, not because of the ideology of her government but because of her national aspirations. The ideological issue was an afterthought.

We can see, today, that in the overriding significance they attributed to their respective conflicts, both Allies and Bolsheviki were largely wrong. Both were pursuing illusions which time was destined to correct.

The Bolsheviki were right, of course, in believing that their victory would have far-reaching international effects. But the nature of this impact was destined to be quite different from what they anticipated. The future was to reveal that the socialist revolution to which they so fervently aspired would not take place in the major industrialized countries of the West, where they confidently expected it. The success of their diplomacy toward the West in the coming decades would be derived, as time would show, not from the strength of their ideas: not from the workings of the laws they conceived Marx to have discovered, not from the economic rivalries among the Western countries to which the Marxists looked as the guarantee of the collapse of the capitalist system. It would be derived from the weaknesses of the Western community itself: from the social and spiritual exhaustion of the Western peoples by the two great wars of this century, from the deficiencies of the Versailles settlement, from the failure to find an answer to the German problem, from the disintegration of Europe's overseas relationships.

But even these weaknesses, while giving valuable opportunities to Soviet diplomacy and eventually placing half of Europe under Russian Communist power, would not produce the European revolution for which the Russian Communists hoped. In so far as their political impulses had an exciting, important future, this would not be with direct relation to the highly industrialized countries of the West to which Marx's calculations were supposed to be relevant but, rather, with relation to the awakening peoples of Asia and Africa. And even here, the power of Communist inspiration would prove to reside not in anything essential to the structure of Marxist thought, but in the infectious example of a political movement successfully contemptuous and defiant of old Europe; in the identification of the Marxist slogan of imperialism with the national and racial resentments of peoples emerging from colonialism in many parts of the world; in the political fascination inevitably radiated by any effective despotism in an age of change and uncertainty; in the inacceptability, to many ruling groups, of the liberal freedoms of the West; and, finally, in a pervasive illusion that the devices of Communist dictatorship in Russia represented a short cut, available to any people, to the glories of industrial and military power. These were to prove the real sources of future Russian Communist strength in the world arena; and precious little any of them had to do with Marxism.

As for the Western peoples and their passionate preoccupation with the issues of World War I, I would not wish to wander too far into the realm of controversy. What is at issue here is, of course, the soundness of the Allied cause in the latter stages of that war, as the Allied peoples and governments then conceived it. There can of course be many views about this. No one would wish to belittle the huge fund of idealism, courage, and good faith that was invested in the war on the Allied side in those final months. Nor would I wish to suggest that the German problem was not an important problem in its own right. It was then; it still is today.

But I wonder whether anyone can read today the literature emanating from the Western countries in the final year of World War I without feeling that he is in the presence of a political hysteria so violent that the real outlines of right and wrong, in so far as they may ever have existed at all, are largely lost in the turmoil. In the bewilderment that accompanied this hysteria, two mistakes were made. First, the significance of the German problem was inflated out of all semblance of reality. The Germans were a problem in Europe—yes; but they were not as awful a problem as all this: their guilt for the outbreak of the war was not *so* great, their victory would not have been quite *such* a catastrophe, nor would *so* many problems be solved by their defeat. But an even more serious error was the failure to recognize the limitations of modern war generally as a means to an end—the failure to realize to what extent prolonged warfare in the industrial age, with its fearful expenditure of blood and substance, was bound to be self-defeating.

The things people thought they were trying to achieve by the long and terrible military exertion in Europe were simply not to be achieved by this means. The indirect effects of that war—its genetic and spiritual effects—were far more serious than people realized at the time. We can see, today, that these effects penalized victor and vanquished in roughly equal measure, and that the damage they inflicted, even on those who were nominally the victors, was greater than anything at stake in the issues of the war itself. In other words, it did not take the atom to make warfare with modern weapons a fruitless and self-defeating exercise. This was already a reality in 1918; and the recognition of this offers, in my opinion, the key to the understanding of a great deal of the subsequent history of the Western peoples. . . .

[On November 28, 1917, Lord Lansdowne's letter to the *Daily Telegraph* urged modification of Allied peace aims. "Prolongation (of the war) will spell ruin for the civilized world." On October 20, Russia asked her Allies to accept the principle of "no annexations and no indemnities" —without success. In November the Bolsheviki seized power and repeated the appeal, again without success. In December Russia signed an armistice with Germany. . . .]

The official Communist thesis is that the Bolsheviki, immediately on their assumption of power in Russia, offered to all the warring powers a general peace on a decent basis; that the Allied governments, intent on their various imperialistic designs, selfishly rejected this offer, caused the slaughter to endure for another year, and abandoned Russia to plunder and oppression at the hands of the Germans.

I should like to make my own position clear. I hold the first World War to have been *the* great catastrophe of Western civilization in the present century. I think it an endless pity that it did not cease in November 1917, when the Bolsheviki called for its termination. It was just at this time that Lord Lansdowne published his well-known letter, pleading for an early end of the war on the basis of compromise with the Germans rather than unconditional surrender. Lansdowne was a man whose patriotism was unchallengeable, who had suffered keenly from the war in the personal sense, and who wrote from great depths of sadness and reflection. His letter has always seemed to me one of the most moving and penetrating documents of the time; and I consider that the Western governments would have done well to be guided by it instead of rejecting it out of hand, as they did.

But to say that this war ought to have ended in 1917 is not to say that the Soviet Decree on Peace was a proper or feasible basis for its termination. The Russian Communists, determined as they were to tear the social structure of old Europe stone from stone in the name of a doctrine whose actual relevance to the development of Western society was even then on the wane, were not the people under whose auspices Europe was suitably to be rescued from the madness in which it was then engaged. If Allied statesmanship was at fault in the autumn of 1917, it was at fault in its failure to see the tragedy and futility of the war itself and to bring the struggle to an end by its own efforts, on a basis of compromise. It was not at fault in its failure to accept the political initiative of Communist Petrograd, which viewed Western society through an ideological lens as distorted as any men have ever used, which had no understanding for the deeper values of Western civilization as most of us see them, and the motive of which, in calling for a cessation of hostilities in the war, was not to end violence and bloodshed but only to transfer them from the arena of formal international conflict to that of civil strife within the warring countries.

David Lloyd George
THE KNOCK-OUT BLOW

The first serious peace movements in Europe started immediately after the termination of the sanguinary battle of 1916. The horrible and futile carnage of the Somme following on the ghastly losses of Verdun had sent a thrill of horror through all the belligerent lands and there was a distinct movement for an interchange of views as to the possibility of a settlement.

In the middle of November Lord Lansdowne startled the Cabinet by a memorandum which he circulated amongst members with the consent of the Prime Minister. It was written the day before Mr. Asquith and I left England for the Paris Conference and was in the hands of members of the Cabinet on our return. This bold document frankly suggested doubts as to the possibility of victory. It was at least courageous, and proved that he, at any rate, was quite alive to the perils of the Allied situation. It was clear that Lord Lansdowne thought a condition of stalemate had been reached and that there was no prospect of any improvement.

The text of this memorandum was as follows:

Memorandum by Lord Lansdowne Respecting Peace Settlement

The members of the War Committee were asked by the Prime Minister some weeks ago to express their views as to the terms upon which peace might be concluded. I do not know whether there has

From *War Memoirs of David Lloyd George: 1915–1916*, Vol. II, pp. 288–289, 291–292, 292–293, 295–296, 310–311, 314–316; by permission of The Beaverbrook Foundations.
David Lloyd George (1863–1945) was Prime Minister of England from 1916 to 1922.

been a general response to this invitation, but the only reply which I have seen is one written last month by the First Lord of the Admiralty, in which he deals at some length with the problems which might have to be discussed at any Peace Conference. Mr. Balfour observes truly that these questions cannot be profitably examined except upon an agreed hypothesis as to the military position of the combatants at the end of the war, and he proceeds to assume, though merely for the sake of argument, that the Central Powers, either through defeat or exhaustion, have to accept the terms imposed upon them by the Allies.

I venture to suggest that the attention of the War Committee might with advantage be directed to a somewhat different problem, and that they should be invited to give us their opinion as to our present prospects of being able to "dictate" the kind of terms which we should all like to impose upon our enemies if we were in a position to do so.

We are agreed as to the goal, but we do not know how far we have really travelled towards it, or how much nearer to it we are likely to find ourselves even if the war be prolonged for, say, another year. What will that year have cost us? How much better will our position be at the end of it? Shall we even then be strong enough to "dictate" terms?

It seems to me almost impossible to overrate the importance of these considerations, because it is clear that our diplomacy must be governed by an accurate appreciation of them.

We have obtained within the last few days from the different Departments of the Government a good deal of information as to the situation, naval, military and economic. It is far from reassuring. . . .

It will be replied, and no doubt truly, that the Central Powers are feeling the pressure of the war not less acutely than we feel it, and I hope we shall also be told that our staying powers are greater than theirs; but, even if this be so, it is none the less our duty to consider, after a careful review of the facts, what our plight and the plight of the civilised world will be after another year, or, as we are sometimes told, two or three more years of a struggle as exhausting as that in which we are engaged. No one for a moment believes that we are going to lose the war; but what is our chance of winning it in such a manner, and within such limits of time, as will enable us to beat our enemy to the ground and impose upon him the kind of terms which we so freely discuss?

I do not suppose for an instant that there is any weakening in the spirit of the people of this country, and I should hope, although I do not feel absolute confidence on the subject, that the same might be said of our Allies; but neither in their interests nor in ours can it be desirable that the war should be prolonged, unless it can be shown that we can bring it to an effectual conclusion within a reasonable space of time.

What does the prolongation of the war mean?

Our own casualties already amount to over 1,100,000. We have had 15,000 officers killed, not including those who are missing. There is no reason to suppose that, as the force at the front in the different theatres of war increases, the casualties will increase at a slower rate. We are slowly but surely killing off the best of the male population of these islands. The figures representing the casualties of our Allies are not before me. The total must be appalling.

The financial burden which we have already accumulated is almost incalculable. We are adding to it at the rate of over £5,000,000 per day. Generations will have to come and go before the country recovers from the loss which it has sustained in human beings, and from the financial ruin and the destruction of the means of production which are taking place.

All this it is no doubt our duty to bear, but only if it can be shown that the sacrifice will have its reward. If it is to be made in vain, if the additional year, or two years, or three years, finds us still unable to dictate terms, the war with its nameless horrors will have been needlessly prolonged, and the responsibility of those who needlessly prolong such a war is not less than that of those who needlessly provoke it. . . .

Many of us, however, must of late have asked ourselves how this war is ever to be brought to an end. If we are told that the deliberate conclusion of the Government is that it must be fought until Germany has been beaten to the ground and sues for peace on any terms which we are pleased to accord to her, my only observation would be that we ought to know something of the data upon which this conclusion has been reached. To many of us it seems as if the prospect of a "knockout" was, to say the least of it, remote. Our forces and those of France have shown a splendid gallantry on the Western Front, and have made substantial advances; but is it believed that these, any more than those made in 1915 with equally high hopes and accompanied by not less cruel losses, will really enable us to "break through"? Can we afford to go on paying the same sort of price for the same sort of gains? . . .

As to peace terms, I hope we shall adhere steadfastly to the main principle laid down by the Prime Minister in the speech which he summed up by a declaration that we could agree to no peace which did not afford adequate reparation for the past and adequate security for the future, but the outline was broadly sketched and might be filled up in many different ways. The same may be said of the not less admirable statement which he has just made at the Guildhall, and of the temperate speeches which the Secretary of State for Foreign Affairs has from time to time delivered.

But it is unfortunate that, in spite of these utterances, it should be possible to represent us and our Allies as committed to a policy partly vindictive and partly selfish, and so irreconcilably committed to that policy that we should regard as unfriendly any attempt, however sincere, to extricate us from the *impasse*. The interview given by the Secretary of State for War in September last to an American correspondent has produced an impression which it will not be easy to efface. There may have been circumstances of which I am unaware, connected perhaps with the Presidential election, which made it necessary to announce that at the particular moment any intervention, however well meant, would be distasteful to us or inopportune. He said, indeed, that "the world must know that there can be no outside

interference *at this stage"*—a very momentous limitation. For surely it
cannot be our intention, no matter how long the war lasts, no matter
what the strain on our resources, to maintain this attitude, or to
declare, as M. Briand declared about the same time, that for us, too,
"the word peace is a sacrilege." Let our naval, military and economic
advisers tell us frankly whether they are satisfied that the knock-out
blow can and will be delivered. The Secretary of State's formula holds
the field, and will do so until something else is put in its place.
Whether it is to hold the field, and, if not, what that something else
should be, ought surely to depend upon their answer, and that again
upon the result of the careful stocktaking, domestic and international,
which, I hope, is already taking place.

I have given a fairly exhaustive account of the Lansdowne
episode because I am anxious to demonstrate that the governments that
conducted the war never lost sight of the importance of seizing any
favourable opportunity that might offer itself to make an honourable
peace. The Lansdowne discussions have also their special value because
they are the first occasion on which any of the belligerent governments
courageously faced the possibility that peace might have to be considered
without victory. The Asquith Government examined the whole position
with great care and came to the unanimous conclusion that to enter into
peace negotiatons with Germany before inflicting a complete defeat
upon her armies would be disastrous. The principle of President Wilson's
subsequent dictum in favour of peace without victory was carefully
studied and emphatically repudiated in advance by the Asquith Government. What is more to the point, when one considers the kind of criticism
levelled at the Government of 1917, is the conclusion come to by the
Asquith Administration that without acknowledgment of defeat on the
part of the Central Powers, overtures of peace should not be encouraged,
as they would settle none of the issues raised by this colossal struggle and
might and probably would be dangerous to the *morale* and solidarity of
the Allies.

Mr. Asquith himself gave no countenance to a timorous or
defeatist attitude. A fortnight after my "knock-out blow" interview had
been published, he delivered, on October 11th, 1916, a speech in the
House of Commons, in the course of which he said:

> The strain which the war imposes on ourselves and our Allies, the
> hardships which we freely admit it involves on some of those who are
> not directly concerned in the struggle, the upheaval of trade, the
> devastation of territory, the loss of irreplaceable lives—this long and
> sombre procession of cruelty and suffering, lighted up as it is by
> deathless examples of heroism and chivalry, cannot be allowed to end
> in some patched-up, precarious, dishonouring compromise, masquerad-
> ing under the name of Peace. No one desires to prolong for a single

unnecessary day the tragic spectacle of bloodshed and destruction, but we owe it to those who have given their lives for us, the flower of our youth, the hope and promise of our future, that their supreme sacrifice shall not have been in vain. The ends of the Allies are well known; they have been frequently and precisely stated. They are not selfish ends, they are not vindictive ends, but they require that there shall be adequate reparation for the past and adequate security for the future. On their achievement, we in this country honestly believe depend the best hopes of humanity.

Here we had a fine and firm resolve expressed in the splendid eloquence of which Mr. Asquith was a master. The fact that his eldest son, Mr. Raymond Asquith, a young man of great brilliance and promise, had fallen in action a few weeks before the delivery of this speech, gave tragic force to this passage. . . .

It is often said now by men who are seeking busily to find fault with those who shouldered the terrible responsibilities of decision in the war, that no harm would have been done had the Allies taken the initiative in approaching the Central Powers with a view to the Convocation of a Peace Conference in 1916, even if such a conference failed. It is urged that if Germany and Austria made unreasonable conditions the Allied populations would have firmly supported their representatives in rejecting these terms and would then have continued the fight with renewed zeal and conviction. Would they? If Germany had offered to withdraw all her forces from Northern France and from Belgium, merely imposing certain conditions in the case of Belgium as to the uses of the ports of Belgium and as to the dismantlement of her frontier fortresses, could the Allied Governments have roused once more the spirit of 1914 to the pitch of facing for more than two years the horrible losses of the preceding two and one-half years, merely in order to restore Alsace-Lorraine to France or to hand back Courland and other conquered territories to the incompetent hands of Russian autocracy? The inhabitants of these lands are no more Russian than they are German. Once the carnage of war had stopped, would Britain have consented to renew it and send her sons to fight other bloody battles like the Somme in order to restore the useless fortifications of Belgrade or to rescue some obscure vilayat in Macedonia from the clutches of the Bulgarian king? At any rate, the risk that nations would have accepted any humiliations inflicted upon foreigners, rather than send millions more of their own kinsmen to the wholesale slaughter of modern warfare, were too great for those who looked forward to the permanent triumph of international right, justice and peace as a result of the sacrifices of this generation. We should have met at the Congress a Germany which had victoriously held up Europe for two and one-half years, shattered completely the power of three of her enemies, Russia,

Roumania and Serbia, and was still in occupation of the territory of two more, and had successfully defied every effort to dislodge her hold on her conquests. The best that could be hoped for would be a completely liberated France and Belgium, with a Germany swollen through its eastern conquests by scores of thousands of square miles and tens of millions of population. With a war so ended we should have been confronted with a triumphant Prussian militarism which had demonstrated its invincibility in the field against overwhelming odds in numbers, material and wealth. Mr. Asquith and his Cabinet were emphatically right in refusing to assent to the Lansdowne proposition. Had they done so, even if they had secured the adhesion of France, it could not have ended in a great and workable peace. France would not have agreed readily to make any overtures, because no peace possible at that time would have satisfied her essential conditions—the restoration of her lost provinces and reparation for her damaged towns and villages. Italy would have been fooled, for she had banked on Allied success for the redemption of the Italian valleys in the Austrian Empire, and notwithstanding her heavy losses she would have had nothing out of any peace settlement which was attainable in 1916. It would have been said that Britain was anxious for peace and was prepared to sell her Allies to attain it. Such an impression would have had a shattering effect on Allied *morale*—east and west. The failure to make peace or a refusal by France to follow a peace initiative from Britain would have distracted and divided opinion in America, at the moment when opinion in that great country was being driven rapidly in our direction by the reckless and indiscriminate methods of the submarine campaign.

Chester Wilmot
UNCONDITIONAL SURRENDER

Although the military discussions at Casablanca left many questions unanswered, there was one issue on which the Allied leaders committed themselves unreservedly and publicly. At a Press conference on the final day, January 24th, the President made an announcement which,

From *The Struggle for Europe* by Chester Wilmot, pp. 121–123. Copyright, 1952, by Chester Wilmot. Reprinted by permission of Harper & Row, Publishers.
Chester Wilmot (1911–1954) was an Australian journalist.

for good or ill, was to have a profound influence on the war and, therefore, on the character of the post-war world. Roosevelt told the correspondents that the Allies were determined to demand the 'Unconditional
Surrender' of Germany, Italy and Japan, and added, says the correspondent of *The Times*, "as if it were a happy thought that had just entered
his mind, that we might call this the 'Unconditional Surrender' Meeting."

The President himself subsequently intimated to Hopkins that
this phrase had 'popped into his mind' while he was talking and that he
had used it on the spur of the moment. This casual explanation is not
accepted by Hopkins's biographer, Robert Sherwood, himself a member
of Roosevelt's personal staff. Sherwood says, "This announcement of
Unconditional Surrender was very deeply deliberated," and he insists
that the President "had his eyes wide open when he made it." This is
undoubtedly true. In Washington, a week before the start of the Casablanca Conference, the American Chiefs of Staff discussed and approved
"the President's Unconditional Surrender formula." On the third day at
Casablanca Roosevelt brought out the phrase while lunching with
Churchill and Hopkins. The Prime Minister immediately expressed his
approval and on the following day (January 19th) cabled to the War
Cabinet: "We propose to draw up a statement of the work of the conference for communication to the Press at the proper time. I should be glad
to know what the War Cabinet would think of our including in this
statement a declaration of the firm intention of the United States and the
British Empire to continue the war relentlessly until we have brought
about the 'unconditional surrender' of Germany and Japan." He suggested that in order to speed Mussolini's downfall the formula should not
be applied to Italy, but in their answer the War Cabinet said it was
"unanimously of opinion that the balance of advantage lay against excluding Italy," and it endorsed the general proposal.

After receiving this reply, it appears that the Prime Minister did
not discuss the matter again with the President and, when the official
communiqué was being drafted by members of their staffs, no reference
to 'Unconditional Surrender' was included. Roosevelt evidently assumed,
however, that his proposal had been fully approved, and before the Press
conference he drafted the following notes:

> The President and the Prime Minister, after a complete survey of
> the world situation, are more than ever determined that peace can
> come to the world only by a total elimination of German and Japanese
> war power. This involves the simple formula of placing the objective
> of this war in terms of an unconditional surrender by Germany, Italy
> and Japan.

The President had these notes in his hand when he spoke to the correspondents and he reminded them that in the American Civil War General Ulysses S. Grant had become known as 'Unconditional Surrender' Grant—a nickname he had earned through demanding the 'Unconditional Surrender' of the beleaguered garrison of Fort Donelson in Tennessee. This formula may have been appropriate in the case of an isolated fortress in a domestic conflict, but to apply it *carte blanche* to the contestants of a world struggle—contestants so varied in national character and martial ardour as Germany, Italy and Japan—seems to have been both illogical and dangerous. Yet it appears that little consideration was given to the effect of this demand on enemy resistance. Certainly there was no preliminary examination by experts in psychological warfare of the probable impact of these two ominous words upon the German armed forces or the German people. The slogan was looked upon at the time as a vote of self-confidence, as a clarion call to the United Nations to rally for victory, and, above all, as an assurance to Stalin that the inability to open a Second Front in 1943 did not indicate any weakening in the resolution of the Western Allies. The effect upon post-war Europe of a fight to the finish seems to have been overlooked.

The Anglo-American decision to make this demand was the outward expression of new-found faith in their own strength and of their determination to ensure that never again would Germany threaten the peace of the world. Before Casablanca the British Government was publicly committed—by the Anglo-Soviet Agreement of July 1941—to make no separate peace with Germany, and Eden had then declared that Britain was "not in any circumstances prepared to negotiate with Hitler at any time on any subject."

This stand had subsequently been endorsed by the Americans, who were as determined as the British that this time they would carry the war into the heart of the German homeland. There would be no compromise with the devil nor would the German people escape unscathed and untaught, as in 1918. They would not give the Germans the chance to charge them with breaches of this war's 'Fourteen Points.' They would offer Germany no points at all. To those whose minds ran along these lines, 'Unconditional Surrender' seemed to be the appropriate demand to make of an enemy who waged 'Total War.' This point of view was not unreasonable in the light of past experience, but it was one thing to form this resolve in secret for ultimate enforcement; it was quite another to proclaim it to the enemy in advance.

By doing this, the Anglo-Saxon powers denied themselves any freedom of diplomatic manoeuvre and denied the German people any avenue of escape from Hitler. Ten months before Casablanca Goebbels had written in his diary, "The more the English prophesy a disgraceful peace for Germany, the easier it is for me to toughen and harden German resistance." After Casablanca Goebbels had delivered into his hands a propaganda weapon of incalculable power. The Nazis were now able to command conviction when they said to the Nation, "It is you, as well as we, that they want to destroy."

Robert C. Batchelder
TOTAL WAR AND ETHICAL FAILURE

A theme frequently encountered in churchly criticisms of the bombing of Hiroshima and Nagasaki is that Japan was already defeated, and therefore that the atomic bomb was unnecessary for winning the war. Churchmen citing these grounds varied from calling the bombing "unwise and unjust" to denouncing the bomb's "reckless and irresponsible employment against an already beaten foe." Churchmen found support in the criticisms of scientists and military men. Albert Einstein wrote, "The war could have been won without it." Admiral Leahy, Chief of Staff to the President, wrote following the war, "It is my opinion that the use of this barbarous weapon at Hiroshima and Nagasaki was of no material assistance in our war against Japan. The Japanese were already defeated and ready to surrender . . ."

Evidence cited above demonstrates that Japan was indeed essentially defeated in mid-1945, although her defending armies were still intact. But the evidence also indicates that Japan's military leaders, who dominated the government and controlled policy up to August 6, insisted upon defying the facts and definitely were not ready to surrender—and in fact maintained this position even *after* the atomic attacks. Therefore, the simple allegation that Japan was already defeated does not overthrow the main argument of Truman and Stimson. The recommendation implicit in this level of criticism is that the war should have been allowed to take its natural course. The war could certainly have been won by con-

From *The Irreversible Decision* by Robert C. Batchelder, pp. 190–201, 204–205, 208–209, 210–212, 221–222. Reprinted by permission of Houghton Mifflin Company.

Robert C. Batchelder is a graduate of Yale Divinity School, and an ordained minister.

ventional means without the atomic bomb, but the cost in human suffering would have been greater than the cost of Hiroshima and Nagasaki,
even had Japan surrendered prior to invasion.

Moreover, the evidence suggests the ironical conclusion that in
the absence of the atomic bomb the invasion, although unnecessary,
would have been inevitable. General MacArthur and General Marshall
insisted that the invasion was necessary to bring Japan to surrender. No
major power in the history of the world had capitulated and allowed
enemy occupation of its homeland in the absence of an invading army;
our military strategists could not conceive of Japan's doing so. Even
General Arnold of the Air Force, although believing that bombing alone
could bring Japan to surrender, wanted to invade Kyushu to obtain more
and closer air bases. The Army view had prevailed among the Joint
Chiefs of Staff, despite Navy misgivings. Preparations for the invasion
were being pushed ahead; had not the atomic bomb precipitated Japan's
surrender, it is very likely that these plans would have come to fruition in
an assault on the Kyushu beaches.

In Japan, in the meantime, Army leaders were determined to
hold out until they could meet the invader on the beaches and, it was
hoped, inflict upon him severe damage. That Japan was already essentially defeated, with dwindling stocks of fuel and ammunition, was
irrelevant to this stubborn determination. Japan's soldiers had shown
themselves upon many earlier occasions to be capable of fierce resistance
to the last man, even in the face of certain defeat. The strength of this
determination in Japan's military leaders is indicated by the fact that it
did not crack even after the dropping of two atomic bombs.

Thus, what was in reality unnecessary for the defeat of Japan
was psychologically necessary for the Army leaders, both American and
Japanese. The former were determined to invade, and the latter were
determined to fight the invader on the beaches. Had the atomic bomb not
cut short the war, the world might well have witnessed the disaster of
two armies, each directed by its own shortsighted military prejudice,
drawn irresistibly into a death grapple tragic for both.

Another group criticized the atomic bombing of Japan as unnecessary on deeper grounds. These critics pointed out that Japan was
already known to be seeking peace by negotiation; had we skillfully
capitalized on this knowledge, we could have achieved surrender by
diplomatic means, thus eliminating the need for dropping the bomb.

A British historian of World War II wrote that by June 1945 only
the obstacle of "unconditional surrender" prevented bringing the war to
an end highly advantageous to Britain and the United States. Had the
Allied leaders been truly interested in saving lives, then "all President
Truman and Mr. Churchill need have done was to remove the obstacle of

unconditional surrender, when the war could have been brought to an immediate end." Had the Potsdam Declaration stated clearly that the Emperor's status would be preserved, "there can be no doubt whatsoever. that the ultimatum would have been accepted, in which case there would be no need to use the atomic bomb."

Hanson W. Baldwin made essentially the same point:

> But, in fact, our only warning to a Japan already militarily defeated, and in a hopeless situation, was the Potsdam demand for unconditional surrender issued on July 26, when we knew Japanese surrender attempts had started. Yet when the Japanese surrender was negotiated about two weeks later, after the bomb was dropped, our unconditional surrender demand was made conditional and we agreed, as Stimson had originally proposed we should do, to continuation of the Emperor upon his imperial throne.
>
> We were, therefore, twice guilty. We dropped the bomb at a time when Japan already was negotiating for an end of the war, but before these negotiations could come to fruition. We demanded unconditional surrender, then dropped the bomb and accepted conditional surrender, a sequence which indicates pretty clearly that the Japanese would have surrendered, even if the bomb had not been dropped, had the Potsdam Declaration included our promise to permit the Emperor to remain on his imperial throne.

Is it true that Japan was seeking peace as early as May or June 1945, as some have stated? There were two independent moves in the direction of peace by Japanese attachés in Europe during the spring of 1945, but the initiative in these moves was undertaken by persons who had no authority to speak for the Japanese *government,* and all were ordered by Tokyo to cease their activities. Meanwhile, in Japan, War Minister Anami had four hundred persons thrown into prison for harboring antiwar sentiments. It was clearly not the official policy of the Japanese government to seek peace, until at the imperial conference of June 22 it was decided that overtures should be made to Moscow for the purpose of obtaining a negotiated peace. This change of policy (not known to the United States until the interception of the messages sent to Moscow beginning on July 12) meant only that negotiations should be sought, but did not determine the terms upon which a peace settlement would be acceptable to Japan's military leaders.

The minimum that Japan's military leaders were willing to settle for (retention of the Emperor, plus three further conditions) was much more than Washington was willing to grant. Foreign Minister Togo recognized that the most Japan could hope for was capitulation barely short of unconditional surrender—and Prince Konoye understood that the purpose of his journey to Moscow was to get Japan out of the war on any basis whatever, so long as the Emperor was preserved. In short, even during July the Japanese government, although agreed upon a policy of seeking a negotiated peace, was not agreed upon the peace terms to be sought. An Allied statement indicating that the Emperor might be preserved would have been reassuring, but would not have resolved the disagreement.

Meanwhile the United States government was having similar difficulty in reaching agreement upon the terms of surrender. The disagreement centered upon the proper interpretation of the formula "unconditional surrender." This formula was announced by President Roosevelt at a press conference at the conclusion of the Casablanca Conference in January 1943—although the official joint communiqué from the conference contained no mention of unconditional surrender. Did Allied adherence to this rather informally adopted formula prolong the war unnecessarily? In the case of Japan, the question turns upon the one condition essential for the Japanese, and upon which both the war and peace parties were in complete agreement: namely, the preservation of the Emperor and the imperial system.

The one condition that the Japanese agreed was most crucial was the very one upon which the Americans were unable to agree. United States officials had been wrestling with the problem of the Emperor for months. In response to inquiries from the War Department, which was to have responsibility for occupying and administering a defeated Japan, the Department of State prepared in May 1944 a report setting forth its policy recommendations on the postwar treatment of Japan. This report dealt at some length with the question of the Emperor and concluded that the United States should refrain from committing itself in advance regarding the Emperor's future status. Secretary of State Hull summed up the State Department's position in these words:

> In general, we felt we should not make advance commitments which would prejudice the situation in favor of the Emperor institution, or against it. We did not want to come out against the institution lest this give the Japanese militarists live coals to blow upon and bring up a flame of last-man resistance. Nor did we wish to come out for the institution lest this discourage whatever popular movement there might be in Japan to erase it.

Hull resigned in November of 1944 because of ill health, but his noncommittal policy continued to have influence.

When the final defeat of Germany became imminent, thoughts began to turn toward the surrender of Japan. In some quarters, it was felt (and, as we have seen, rightly so) that the unconditional-surrender formula was too vague; without more detailed specification of what unconditional surrender would mean for Japan, those in Tokyo favoring surrender would have great difficulty in countering the arguments of the military that unconditional surrender would mean—as Premier Suzuki put it—the "destruction" of the national polity and the "ruin" of the Japanese race. Accordingly Captain Ellis Zacharias, of the Office of Naval Intelligence, drafted a presidential statement clarifying what unconditional surrender would mean for the Japanese people; Mr. Truman issued the statement on May 8, the same day that he officially announced the surrender of Germany:

> Nazi Germany has been defeated.
> The Japanese people have felt the weight of our land, air, and naval attacks. So long as their leaders and the armed forces continue the war, the striking power and intensity of our blows will steadily increase and will bring utter destruction to Japan's industrial production, to its shipping, and to everything that supports its military activity.
> The longer the war lasts, the greater will be the suffering and hardships which the people of Japan will undergo—all in vain. Our blows will not cease until the Japanese military and naval forces lay down their arms in *unconditional surrender*.
> Just what does the unconditional surrender of the armed forces mean for the Japanese people?
> It means the end of the war.
> It means the termination of the influence of the military leaders who have brought Japan to the present brink of disaster.
> It means provision for the return of soldiers and sailors to their families, their farms, their jobs.
> It means not prolonging the present agony and suffering of the Japanese in the vain hope of victory.
> UNCONDITIONAL SURRENDER DOES NOT MEAN THE EXTERMINATION OR ENSLAVEMENT OF THE JAPANESE PEOPLE.

It will be noted that the President's statement narrowed the unconditional surrender of Japan to "the unconditional surrender *of the armed forces*" (italics added). Zacharias, speaking as the "official spokesman" of the United States government, delivered a series of broadcasts to Japan emphasizing that "unconditional surrender is a military term, meaning the cessation of resistance and the yielding of arms. It does not entail enslavement. It does not entail the extermination of the Japanese people." These propaganda broadcasts were designed to allay the fears of the Japanese people, undercut the arguments of the military clique, and provide "ammunition" for the end-the-war party.

Although he was aware that the question of the preservation of the Emperor was crucial for his Japanese hearers, Zacharias could not get authorization from his superiors to include in his broadcasts an assurance on this subject. He therefore resorted to the strategem of arranging for an anonymous letter to appear in the Washington *Post* in July which he felt sure the Japanese authorities would recognize as an unofficial expression of United States policy. The letter stated that the term "unconditional surrender" referred not to the content of the surrender terms but only to "the manner in which the war is terminated . . . namely, the acceptance of terms without qualifying counterarguments." As for the content of America's terms, they have already been explicitly stated in the Atlantic Charter, the Cairo Declaration, and President Truman's May 8 declaration. With regard to the concern of the Japanese people over their Emperor,

> If . . . their chief concern is over Japan's future national structure (Kokutai), including the Emperor's status after surrender, the way to find out is to ask. Contrary to a widespread belief, such a question can be answered quickly and satisfactorily to all those who are concerned over the future peace of the Orient and the world.

Meanwhile, Joseph C. Grew (who had served as Ambassador to Japan from 1932 until Pearl Harbor, as Under-Secretary of State under Stettinius, and then as Acting Secretary of State), having originally agreed with Hull's noncommittal policy, became convinced that the time had come to speak out more clearly. To give Japan a definite and official assurance on the Emperor, he felt, would aid those in Japan who were struggling to facilitate surrender. On May 28, 1945 Grew, on his own initiative as Acting Secretary of State, went to President Truman and urged upon him the importance of reassuring the Japanese on this point. Grew proposed issuing a proclamation calling on Japan to surrender, but also stating that the United States was open to retention of the Emperor as Head of State. Truman considered this proposal "a sound idea" but asked Grew to sound out the opinions of our military leaders. The next day Grew presented his idea to Secretary of War Stimson, Secretary of the Navy Forrestal, and General Marshall, the Chief of Staff. They agreed that such a statement should be issued, but recommended delay on the grounds that immediate proclamation (while the outcome of the battle for Okinawa was still in doubt) might be interpreted by the Japanese military as a sign of weakness on our part. When Grew brought the matter up with the President a second time on June 18, Mr. Truman said that he had decided the proclamation should be issued at the forthcoming conference of the Allies at Potsdam in July.

Other forces were at work, however. Grew was denounced as an appeaser by those who felt that the imperial system was the root of Japanese militarism. Admiral William F. Halsey is reported to have recommended the bombing of Shinto shrines, because of the evils of Shintoism, in which the Emperor is regarded not only as the head of the state but also as divine. The present writer clearly remembers the wartime atmosphere in which Emperor Hirohito was considered on the same level as Hitler and Mussolini, as one of the three Axis leaders who must be overthrown. Many who did not subscribe to the proposed abolition of the Emperor were nevertheless hesitant to give Japan a public assurance of the continuance of the Emperor, because of the frequent—and sometimes extreme—denunciations of the Emperor made by U.S. officials during the war. Admiral Halsey had vowed to add humiliation to defeat by riding the Emperor's white horse through the streets of Tokyo. Such statements had created a climate of opinion within the United States, many feared, which would lead people to cry shame if our government reversed its field and guaranteed to preserve the man we had been denouncing as a war criminal.[1]

Stimson's original memorandum of July 2 stated that Japan would be more likely to accept the ultimatum if we gave some assurance regarding the Emperor. Stimson continued at Potsdam to press for inclusion of such an assurance in the forthcoming warning to Japan. The Joint Chiefs of Staff also urged that the Emperor be retained, on the ground that only the authority of the Emperor could insure the prompt surrender of the hundreds of thousands of Japanese troops scattered throughout Asia and the Pacific islands. Nevertheless, when the Potsdam Declaration was issued on July 26 it contained no reference to the Emperor. The decision must have been made by Byrnes and Truman— but neither in his memoirs specifies the reasons for the omission.

Would the Japanese have accepted the Potsdam Declaration had an assurance regarding the Emperor been included? Certainly the silence of the Potsdam Declaration on this point aided the militarists and handicapped Togo's group; the latter could only argue on the basis of their *hope* that the United States would respond favorably *if asked* about the Emperor. A clear assurance on this point would have given Togo a formidable weapon with which to beat down the objections of the war party. Even so, it remains questionable whether such an assurance in the Potsdam Declaration would have produced surrender. As it was, Anami and his party insisted either upon adding further conditions or fighting to the death—even after the shock of the atomic bomb, Russia's entry into the war, and the receipt of Byrnes's message implying the retention of the Emperor. Only the Emperor's intervention a *second* time broke the deadlock and brought the Cabinet to acceptance of surrender. It is not obvious, to say the least, that the military extremists would have capitulated at the mere statement of Allied willingness to retain the Emperor— in the absence of the sense of emergency created by the atomic bomb and

---

[1] This incident suggests the degree to which a government, seeking to be reasonable and flexible in negotiations toward viable objectives, may be hampered by a total and unrestrained propaganda war of its own making.

the Russian intervention which allowed the full weight of the Emperor's authority and influence to be thrown into the scales on the side of surrender.

Another factor remains to be considered. As events actually worked out, the influence of the Emperor was barely able to thwart a military coup, following the final imperial conference's decision to accept surrender. At midnight on August 14 a group of Army fanatics attempted to take over the Imperial Palace Guards; after a fruitless search for the phonograph record of the imperial rescript (which His Majesty had just cut) scheduled to be broadcast the next day, the attempted coup disintegrated. Groups of would-be assassins raided the homes of Premier Suzuki and Privy Seal Kido, but failed to find their victims. Navy planes flew over Tokyo dropping leaflets denying the validity of the imperial rescript and calling for continued resistance. It was only with difficulty that a group of *kamikaze* fliers were prevented from carrying out their plan of diving their suicide planes into the U.S.S. *Missouri* as it entered Tokyo Bay to accept Japan's surrender. The Emperor had to dispatch his brother in order to pacify a group of malcontents at Atsugi airfield (where MacArthur subsequently landed) who wanted to re-engage the Americans when they approached Tokyo.

That these various attempts were quelled, and better organized attempts prevented altogether, was due to the unique influence of the throne, and to the fact that the Emperor had *personally* announced his desire for surrender at two imperial conferences and in the imperial rescript. This put the fanatics in an awkward position: "To have acted against the express wishes of an Emperor whom they had unceasingly extolled as sacred and inviolable and around whom they had woven a fabric of individual loyalty and national unity would have been to destroy the very polity in perpetuation of which they had persistently declared they were fighting . . ." Had Foreign Minister Togo been able to persuade the Cabinet to accept a Potsdam Declaration (expanded to include an assurance on the Emperor) an extremist coup would have been quite probable. In the absence of the direct personal intervention of the Emperor (which would not have come about had the Cabinet reached its own decision), the coup might easily have succeeded, leaving the fate of Japan entirely in the hands of a fanatical clique determined to fight on for the "preservation of the Emperor" and the "glory of Japan." It was the crisis precipitated by the atomic bomb that rendered a successful military coup impossible.

In short, it is not self-evident, as claimed by the critics under consideration, that the inclusion in the Potsdam Declaration of an assurance promising the retention of the Emperor would have resulted automatically in Japan's surrender.

The "political failure" criticism may be made on a deeper level still: the Japanese cables intercepted on July 13 gave a clear indication of Japan's desperate desire to end the war—but our leaders failed to capitalize on this first-rate piece of intelligence. Could not a sensitive study of the cables and an imaginative diplomatic initiative have brought Japan to surrender and rendered use of the atomic bomb unnecessary? . . .

It may be possible to explain America's failure to seize the diplomatic initiative partly in terms of the inexperience of her leaders. With a new President (in office only three hectic months) and a new Secretary of State (in office less than a month and without previous responsibility in diplomacy or foreign affairs), both pressed with momentous events and involved in their first international conference, it would be understandable if the interceptions of the cables received less attention than they might have received in other circumstances.

But the root of the political failure reaches deeper. The handling of the Japanese surrender is related to a larger pattern of other events in which United States leaders tended to emphasize purely military means and purely military ends to the neglect of political means and political ends. A few significant examples will suffice to trace this pattern.

American leaders tended strongly to view the primary *aim* of the war purely in terms of military victory, and to ignore, or subordinate, the political objectives for the sake of which the war was being fought. President Truman reported that the political and economic matters discussed at Potsdam were subordinate in the minds of the American delegation to "one strictly military matter . . . the winning of the war against Japan. On our program that was the most important item."

Stimson agreed. For him, "the dominant fact of 1945 was war, and . . . therefore, necessarily, the dominant objective was victory. . . . Surrender was a goal sufficient in itself, wholly transcending the use or nonuse of the bomb." . . .

The tendency to overemphasize the military aspects of the war and to overlook the nonmilitary was also reflected in a shift in attitude toward the atomic bomb as the war progressed. In the beginning the scientists had looked upon the development of the atomic bomb as insurance against its being used—by Hitler. The bomb was not looked upon as "just another weapon"; paradoxically, it was being developed precisely so that it would not be used. As the war progressed, however, the paradox was lost, and the bomb came to be regarded as merely a new weapon, "as legitimate as any other of the deadly explosive weapons of modern war," and the question of the use of the bomb came to be subordinated to the question of military victory. Stimson writes that the "entire purpose" of the atomic project was "the production of a military weapon"; he emphasizes that "it was our common objective, throughout the war, to be the first to produce an atomic weapon *and use it*" (italics added). Truman reports that he "regarded the bomb as a military weapon and never had any doubt that it should be used."

So it was that the question of the use of the atomic bomb came to be subordinated to the achieving of victory by military means. By the spring of 1945 the question was for all practical purposes settled: the atomic bomb, created under the auspices of a military organization, was essentially a bigger and better weapon, and should be used to secure victory by applying such overwhelming physical power to the enemy as to force him to surrender. Arthur Compton reports that in the discussions of the Interim Committee it appeared to be "a foregone conclusion" that the bomb would be used. Ralph Bard reports that as a member of the Interim Committee he came to the crucial May 31 meeting with no special preparation for making a momentous decision; he felt that the committee was merely giving formal approval to a decision already made. Had the identification of the atomic bomb simply as a military weapon still been open to debate, had the 1939 sense of paradox persisted until 1945, then serious and imaginative exploration of the possibilities of the new instrument might have led to employment less crude and more creative. . . .

At a whole series of points, a military way of thinking shaped decisions affecting the later decision about the use of the first atomic bomb. It cannot be proved that a less military and a more political way of thinking, resulting in modifications all along this series, actually would have ended the war without the atomic bomb. What the military way of thinking undeniably did, however, was to close the door on a whole series of opportunities, any one of which *might* have made a difference, and which, taken all together, probably would have resulted in an outcome different from that which actually occurred—the killing of more than 100,000 people, and the crossing of the barrier into the dangerous world where a precedent exists for the military use of atomic energy.

The decision to use the atomic bomb took place within a historical situation with a peculiar political-military configuration. This context shaped the way in which policymakers thought about the bomb and its relation to the war, and heavily influenced the outcome of the decision itself. In particular, the gradual acceptance of obliteration bombing as a military necessity, until the mass-bombing of Japanese cities was regarded as standard procedure, largely determined that the atomic bomb —once it was decided to use it—would be dropped on the center of a large city, despite the professed concern of our leaders to avoid the killing of undefended civilians.

This particular decision took place within a larger context, a significant characteristic of which was the tendency on the part of American leaders (both military and civilian) to think of the war in purely military rather than in political terms. As a result, the goal of the war was military victory; the way to victory was the military defeat of the enemy armed forces; since the major decisions to be made were of a military character, policy formation was delegated to military men. The result was a whole series of decisions: to treat the atomic bomb as a bigger and better military weapon, to exclude civilian leaders from the highest war councils of the nation, to accept the judgment of generals that obliteration bombing was necessary for victory, to try a political method to end the war only as an afterthought, to ignore vital intelligence because it did not indicate that the enemy was ready to accept total surrender, to let a military commander decide on purely tactical grounds how much time the Japanese government should have to decide to surrender after the first atomic bomb—a series of decisions which tended to mold events in such a way that the atomic bomb would finally be used in a total and unrestrained military manner. Any one of these decisions, had the emphasis lain on the political rather than on the military way of thinking, *might* have precluded or tempered our use of the atomic bomb; the cumulative effect of making all these decisions on political rather than on military grounds could well have resulted in termination of the war by diplomatic means, and prevented the destruction of Hiroshima and Nagasaki.

Focusing more narrowly upon the specific decision to drop the atomic bomb—and taking as given the political failure and the war situation as it stood in mid-1945—one cannot escape the conclusion that the atomic bombing of Hiroshima and Nagasaki caused less loss of life (and general human suffering and chaos) than would have come about had the new weapon been withheld and the war been allowed to continue by conventional means, with or without invasion of the Japanese home islands. Within this narrow context Truman and Stimson were right: the atomic bomb did cut short the war and save thousands of lives. Nevertheless, even within the situation as it had developed by August 1945, alternatives were still open—such as a demonstration of the atomic bomb against a large military installation in Japan, followed by a stern warning—which probably would have brought about Japan's surrender without the great toll of civilian lives resulting from atomic attacks upon two large cities. . . .

While it is important to recognize the ethical failures in the making of a particular crucial decision, it is even more important to be aware of the ethical failures implicit in the unquestioned assumptions about the nature of war that were shared in 1945 by American leaders and people alike. The assumptions that war is primarily a military matter, that war is now total, that the purpose of fighting a war is to achieve military victory, and that war can end in victory only if the enemy is forced to surrender unconditionally—these came to be accepted as self-evident and unquestionable truths by the vast majority of the American people, despite the fact that such axioms stand in direct contradiction to the main stream of Christian ethical thought about war. Such general assumptions about modern war were at least as important—if not more so—in the shaping of the decision to drop the atomic bomb as were the ethical considerations consciously brought to bear upon that particular choice. What is required for the future is not only that proper ethical thinking be applied to the making of each particular policy decision affecting nuclear weapons. It is even more important that our whole style of thinking about war be such that these particular decisions are not—as in 1945—morally compromised before they are reached.

4
Violence versus Law and Order

The wars of the twentieth century have led to accomplishments as well as senseless destruction. They have revolutionized the way of life at home and abroad. New governments have appeared, old trade patterns have been altered, minority groups have gone to work in factories— we are still unable to catalogue all the results.

Do such changes wrought by war suggest· that violence has its positive aspect, that direct action is the method of social change? The totalitarian movements of our age, communism and fascism, have been well-known theorists and practitioners of this belief. Others, however, have strongly rejected the idea. British playwright George Bernard Shaw expressed the Fabians' belief in gradual and intelligent change. If only the Tsar had allowed Fabian societies in Russia, lamented Shaw, socialism might have survived there. Contemporary British historian Alec Nove, after a study of the Stalinist era, declares that he cannot justify violence as part of a program of rapid industrialization.

Americans tend to feel that the horrors of the Stalinist era could not happen in the U.S.A. The semi-industrialized nature of Russian society in 1917 or the instability of the new African nations might support the notion that violence is endemic in underdeveloped countries; but the Nazis in Germany showed what could happen in a fully developed industrial nation as well. Albert Grzesinski, police president of Berlin during the civil wars in post-World War I Germany (1930–1932), gives a vivid account of how the democratic Weimar Republic was rendered helpless by endless threats from the Nazis and Communists.

It is certain that violence breaks out in respectable Anglo-American areas, though the present outcry over civil-rights activities shows that most people have forgotten the outrages perpetrated by the suffragettes and the panic created by industrial strikes. Violence could hardly be more contemporary, and analogies readily come to mind. Margaret Cole, an active participant in the British general strike of 1926, and Felix Riesenberg, Jr., a journalist covering the San Francisco waterfront in the nineteen thirties, recorded these events with some sympathy. Economic historian George Soule reminds us that it was almost fashionable to talk about a revolution in America during the depression.

Revolutions have eventually taken place in the U.S.A., but, thus far, they have been on a limited scale. The Negro revolution, described by American journalist Harry Golden, has been steadily gaining momentum since the late nineteen thirties. Least foreseen, the student revolution, a real threat to universities and to the whole democratic order as defined by University of California faculty members Seymour Martin Lipset and Paul Seabury. Not all will accept the thesis of a Berkeley revolution which, like all other revolutions or violent protests, must in time face the question: "How much was actually changed?"

George Bernard Shaw
DIRECT ACTION POLITICS

You must first grasp the difference between revolutions and social changes. A revolution transfers political power from one party to another, or one class to another, or even one individual to another, just as a conquest transfers it from one nation or race to another. It can be and

From George Bernard Shaw's "Intelligent Woman's Guide to Socialism and Capitalism" by permission of The Public Trustee and The Society of Authors.

George Bernard Shaw (1856–1950) was a British playwright and member of the Fabian Society, a group of British socialists.

often is effected by violence or the threat of violence. Of our two revolutions in the seventeenth century, by which political power in England was transferred from the throne to the House of Commons, the first cost a civil war; and the second was bloodless only because the King ran away. A threat of violence was sufficient to carry the nineteenth century revolution of 1832, by which the political power was transferred from the great agricultural landowners to the industrial urban employers. The South American revolutions which substitute one party or one President for another are general elections decided by shooting instead of by voting.

Now the transfer of political power from our capitalists to our proletariat, without which Socialist propaganda would be suppressed by the Government as sedition, and Socialist legislation would be impossible, has already taken place in form. The proletarians can outvote the capitalists overwhelmingly whenever they choose to do so. If on the issue of Socialism versus Capitalism all the proletarians were for Socialism and all the capitalists for Capitalism, Capitalism would have had to capitulate to overwhelming numbers long ago. But the proletarians who live upon the incomes of the capitalists as their servants, their tradesmen, their employees in the luxury trades, their lawyers and doctors and so on, not to mention the troops raised, equipped, and paid by them to defend their property (in America there are private armies of this kind) are more violently Conservative than the capitalists themselves, many of whom, like Robert Owen and William Morris, not to mention myself, have been and are ardent Socialists. The Countess of Warwick is a noted Socialist; so you have seen a Socialist Countess (or at least her picture); but have you ever seen a countess's dressmaker who was a Socialist? If the capitalists refused to accept a parliamentary decision against them, and took to arms, like Charles I, they would have in many places a majority of the proletariat on their side.

If you are shocked by the suggestion that our capitalists would act so unconstitutionally, consider the case of Ireland, in which after thirty years of parliamentary action, and an apparently final settlement of the Home Rule question by Act of Parliament, the establishment of the Irish Free State was effected by fire and slaughter, the winning side being that which succeeded in burning the larger number of the houses of its opponents.

Parliamentary constitutionalism holds good up to a certain point: the point at which the people who are outvoted in Parliament will accept their defeat. But on many questions people feel so strongly, or have such big interests at stake, that they leave the decision to Parliament only as long as they think they will win there. If Parliament decides against them, and they see any chance of a successful resistance, they throw Parliament over and fight it out. During the thirty years of the parliamentary campaign for Irish Home Rule there were always Direct Action men who said "It is usless to go to the English Parliament: the Unionists will never give up their grip of Ireland until they are forced to; and you may as well fight it out first as last". And these men, though denounced as wanton incendiaries, turned out to be right. The French had to cut off the heads of both king and queen because the king could not control the queen, and the queen would not accept a constitutional revolution, nor stop trying to induce the other kings of Europe to march their armies into France and slaughter the Liberals for her. In England we beheaded our king because he would not keep faith with the Liberal Parliament even after he had fought it and lost. In Spain at this moment the King and the army have suppressed Parliament, and are ruling by force of arms on the basis of divine right, which is exactly what Cromwell did in England after he had cut off King Charles's head for trying to do the same. Signor Mussolini, a Socialist, has overridden parliament in Italy, his followers having established what is called a reign of terror by frank violence.

These repudiations of constitutionalism in Spain and Italy have been made, not to effect any definite social change, but because the Spanish and Italian governments had become so unbearably inefficient that the handiest way to restore public order was for some sufficiently energetic individuals to take the law into their own hands and just break people's heads if they would not behave themselves. And it may quite possibly happen that even if the most perfect set of Fabian Acts of Parliament for the constitutional completion of Socialism in this country be passed through Parliament by duly elected representatives of the people; swallowed with wry faces by the House of Lords; and finally assented to by the King and placed on the statute book, the capitalists may, like Signor Mussolini, denounce Parliament as unpatriotic, pernicious, and corrupt, and try to prevent by force the execution of the Fabian Acts. We should then have a state of civil war, with, no doubt, the Capitalist forces burning the co-operative stores, and the proletarians burning the country houses, as in Ireland, in addition to the usual war routine of devastation and slaughter.

But no matter how the government of the country may pass from the hands of the capitalists into those of the Socialist proletarians, whether by peaceful parliamentary procedure or the bloodiest conceivable civil war, at the end of it the survivors will be just where they were at the beginning as far as practical Communism is concerned. Returning a majority of Socialists to Parliament will not by itself reconstruct the whole economic system of the country in such a way as to produce equality of income. Still less will burning and destroying buildings or killing several of the opponents of Socialism, and getting several Socialists killed in doing so. You cannot wave a wand over the country and say "Let there be Socialism": at least nothing will happen if you do.

The case of Russia illustrates this. After the great political revolution of 1917 in that country, the Marxist Communists were so completely victorious that they were able to form a Government far more powerful than the Tsar had ever really been. But as the Tsar had not allowed Fabian Societies to be formed in Russia to reduce Socialism to a system of law, this new Russian Government did not know what to do, and, after trying all sorts of amateur experiments which came to nothing more than pretending that there was Communism where there was nothing but the wreck of Capitalism, and giving the land to the peasants, who immediately insisted on making private property of it over again, had to climb down hastily and leave the industry of the country to private employers very much as the great ground landlords of our cities leave the work of the shops to their tenants, besides allowing the peasant farmers to hold their lands and sell their produce just as French peasant proprietors or English farmers do.

This does not mean that the Russian Revolution has been a failure. In Russia it is now established that capital was made for Man, and not Man for Capitalism. The children are taught the Christian morality of Communism instead of the Mammonist morality of Capitalism. The palaces and pleasure seats of the plutocrats are used for the recreation of workers instead of for the enervation of extravagant wasters. Idle ladies and gentlemen are treated with salutary contempt, whilst the worker's blouse is duly honored. The treasures of art, respected and preserved with a cultural conscientiousness which puts to shame our own lootings in China, and our iconoclasms and vandalisms at home, are accessible to everyone. The Greek Church is tolerated (the Bolsheviks forbore to cut off their Archbishop's head as we cut off Archbishop Laud's); but it is not, as the Church of England is, allowed without contradiction to tell little children lies about the Bible under pretence of giving them religious instruction, nor to teach them to reverence the merely rich as their betters. That sort of doctrine is officially and very properly disavowed as Dope.

All this seems to us too good to be true. It places the Soviet Government in the forefront of cultural civilization as far a good intention goes. But it is not Socialism. It still involves sufficient inequality of income to undo in the long run enough of its achievements to degrade the Communist Republic to the level of the old Capitalist Republics of France and America. In short, though it has made one of those transfers of political power which are the object of revolutions, and are forced through by simple slaughter and terror, and though this political transfer has increased Russian self-respect and changed the moral attitude of the Russian State from pro-Capitalist to anti-Capitalist, it has not yet established as much actual Communism as we have in England, nor even raised Russian wages to the English level.

The explanation of this is that Communism can spread only as Capitalism spread: that is, as a development of existing economic civilization and not by a sudden wholesale overthrow of it. What it proposes is not a destruction of the material utilities inherited from Capitalism, but a new way of managing them and distributing the wealth they produce. Now this development of Capitalism into a condition of ripeness for Socialization had not been reached in Russia; consequently the victorious Communist Bolsheviks in 1917 found themselves without any highly organized Capitalistic industry to build upon. They had on their hands an enormous agricultural country with a population of uncivilized peasants, ignorant, illiterate, superstitious, cruel, and land-hungry. The cities, few and far between, with their relatively insignificant industries, often managed by foreigners, and their city proletariats living on family wages of five and threepence a week, were certainly in revolt against the mis-distribution of wealth and leisure; but they were so far from being organized to begin Socialism that it was only in a very limited sense that they could be said to have begun urban civilization. There were no Port Sunlights and Bournvilles, no Ford factories in which workmen earn £9 in a five-day week and have their own motor cars, no industrial trusts of national dimensions, no public libraries, no great public departments manned by picked and tested civil servants, no crowds of men skilled in industrial management and secretarial business looking for employment, no nationalized and municipalized services with numerous and competent official staffs, no national insurance, no great Trade Union organization representing many millions of workmen and able to extort subsidies from Capitalist governments by threatening to stop the railways and cut off the coal supply, no fifty years of compulsory schooling supplemented by forty years of incessant propaganda of political science by Fabian and other lecturers, no overwhelming predominance of organized industry over individualist agriculture, no obvious breakdown of Capitalism under the strain of the war, no triumphant rescue by Socialism demonstrating that even those public departments that were bywords for incompetence and red tape were far more efficient than the commercial adventurers who derided them. Well may Mr. Trotsky say that the secret of the completeness of the victory of the Russian Proletarian Revolution over Russian Capitalist civilization was that there was virtually no Capitalist civilization to triumph over, and that the Russian people had been saved from the corruption of bourgeois ideas, not by the famous metaphysical dialectic inherited by Marx from the philosopher Hegel, but by the fact that they are still primitive enough to be incapable of middle class ideas. In England, when Socialism is consummated it will plant the red flag on the summit of an already constructed pyramid; but the Russians have to build right up from the sand. We must build up Capitalism before we can turn it into Socialism. But meanwhile we must learn how to control it instead of letting it demoralize us, slaughter us, and half ruin us, as we have hitherto done in our ignorance.

Thus the fact that the Soviet has had to resort to controlled Capitalism and bourgeois enterprise, after denouncing them so fiercely under the Tsardom in the phrases used by Marx to denounce English Capitalism, does not mean that we shall have to recant in the same way when we complete our transfer of political power from the proprietary classes and their retainers to the Socialist proletariat. The Capitalism which the Russian Government is not only tolerating but encouraging would be for us, even now under Capitalism, an attempt to set back the clock. We could not get back to it if we tried, except by smashing our machinery, breaking up our industrial organization, burning all the plans and documents from which it could be reconstructed, and substituting an eighteenth for a twentieth century population.

The moral of all this is that though a political revolution may be necessary to break the power of the opponents of Socialism if they refuse to accept it as a Parliamentary reform, and resist it violently either by organizing what is now called Fascism or a *coup d'état* to establish a Dictatorship of the Capitalists, yet neither a violent revolution nor a peacefully accepted series of parliamentary reforms can by themselves create Socialism, which is neither a battle cry nor an election catchword, but an elaborate arrangement of our production and distribution of wealth in such a manner that all our incomes shall be equal. This is why Socialists who understand their business are always against bloodshed. They are no milder than other people; but they know that bloodshed cannot do what they want, and that the indiscriminate destruction inseparable from civil war will retard it. Mr. Sidney Webb's much quoted and in some quarters much derided "inevitability of gradualness" is an inexorable fact. It does not, unfortunately, imply inevitability of peacefulness. We can fight over every step of the gradual process if we are foolish enough. We shall come to an armed struggle for political power between the parasitic proletariat and the Socialist proletariat if the Capitalist leaders of the parasitic proletariat throw Parliament and the Constitution over, and declare for a blood and iron settlement instead of a settlement by votes. But at the end of the fighting we shall all be the poorer, none the wiser, and some of us the deader. If the Socialists win, the road to Socialism may be cleared; but the pavement will be torn up and the goal as far off as ever.

Alec Nove
INDUSTRIALIZATION IN A HURRY

Stalin has suffered a dramatic post-mortem demotion, and a monument to his victims is to be erected in Moscow. The present Soviet leadership is thus disassociating itself publicly from many of the highly disagreeable features of Stalin's rule, while claiming for the Party and the Soviet system the credit for making Russia a great economic and military power. Is this a logically consistent standpoint? How far was Stalin, or Stalinism, an integral, unavoidable, "necessary" part of the achievements of the period? How much of the evil associated with the Stalin system is attributable to the peculiar character of the late dictator, and how much was the consequence of the policies adopted by the large majority of the Bolshevik party, or of the effort of a small and dedicated minority to impose very rapid industrialisation on a peasant country? . . .

What were the practical alternatives before the Bolsheviks in the late 'twenties, which contributed to the creation of the Stalinist régime, or, if one prefers a different formulation, gave the opportunity to ambitious men to achieve so high a degree of absolutism?

The key problem before the Bolsheviks concerned the linked questions of industrialisation and political power. They felt they had to industrialise for several reasons, some of which they shared with non-Bolshevik predecessors. Thus the Tsarist minister, Count Witte, as well as Stalin, believed that to achieve national strength and maintain independence, Russia needed a modern industry, especially heavy industry. The national-defence argument, re-labelled "defence of the revolution," was greatly strengthened by the belief that the Russian revolution was in constant danger from a hostile capitalist environment, militarily and technically far stronger than the U.S.S.R. . Then there was the belief that the building of socialism or communism involved industrialisation, and, more immediately, that a "proletarian dictatorship" was insecure so long as it ruled in an overwhelmingly petty-bourgeois, peasant, environment. There had to be a large increase in the number and importance of the proletariat, while the rise of a rich "kulak" class in the villages was regarded as a dangerous (or potentially dangerous) resurgence of capi-

Reprinted from "Was Stalin Really Necessary?" by Alec Nove (*Encounter,* April 1962) by permission of Encounter and Alec Nove.

Alec Nove is a British historian and reader in Russian studies at the University of London.

talism. It was clear, by 1927, that it was useless to wait for "world revolution" to solve these problems. These propositions were common to the
protagonists of the various platforms of the middle 'twenties.

Until about 1927, a rapid rise in industrial production resulted
from (or, "was a result of") the reactivation of pre-revolutionary productive capacity, which fell into disuse and disrepair in the civil war period.
However, it now became urgent to find material and financial means to
expand the industrial base. This at once brought the peasant problem to
the fore. The revolution had distributed land to 25 million families, most
of whom were able or willing to provide only small marketable surpluses.
Supplies of food to the towns and for export fell, peasant consumption
rose. Yet the off-farm surplus must grow rapidly to sustain industrialisation, especially where large-scale loans from abroad could scarcely be
expected. As the "left" opposition vigorously pointed out, the peasant, the
bulk of the population, had somehow to be made to contribute produce
and money, to provide the bulk of "primitive Socialist accumulation."

The arguments around these problems were inextricably en-
tangled in the political factional struggles of the 'twenties.[1] The moderate wing, led by Bukharin, believed that it was possible to advance
slowly towards industrialisation "at the pace of a tortoise,"[2] a pace
severely limited by what the peasant was willing to do voluntarily. This
was sometimes described as "riding towards socialism on a peasant nag."
The logic of this policy demanded priority for developing consumers'
goods industries, to make more cloth to encourage the peasants to sell
more food. At first, Stalin sided with the moderates.

The case against the Bukharin line was of several different kinds.
Firstly, free trade with the peasants could only provide adequate surpluses if the better-off peasants (i.e., those known as kulaks) were
allowed to expand, since they were the most efficient producers and
provided a large part of the marketable produce. Yet all the Bolshevik
leaders (including, despite momentary aberrations, Bukharin himself)
found this ideologically and politically unacceptable. A strong group of
independent, rich peasants was Stolypin's dream as a basis for Tsardom.
It was the Bolshevik's nightmare, as totally inconsistent in the long run
with their rule or with a socialist transformation of "petty-bourgeois"
Russia. But this made the Bukharin approach of doubtful internal
consistency.

A second reason concerned the pace of the tortoise. The Bolshe-

---

[1] See A. Erlich: *The Soviet Industrialisation Debate* (Harvard, 1960) for a
most valuable account of the interaction between the debates and the economic
realities of the period. The account given here is necessarily oversimplified.

[2] Paper read at a plenum of the Agricultural Economics Research Institute,
Moscow, 1927.

viks were in a hurry. They saw themselves threatened by "imperialist interventionists." Even though some war scares were manufactured for factional reasons, the Party as a whole believed that war against them would come before very long. This argued not merely for speed, but also for priority to *heavy* and not light industry, since it provided a basis for an arms industry. Still another reason was a less tangible but still very real one: the necessity of maintaining political *élan*, of not appearing to accept for an indefinite period a policy of gradualism based on the peasant, which would have demoralised the Party and so gravely weakened the régime. It was widely felt, in and out of Russia, that by 1927 the régime had reached a *cul-de-sac*.

Stalin at this point swung over towards the left, and his policy of all-out industrialisation and collectivisation was a means of breaking out of the *cul-de-sac*, of mobilising the Party to smash peasant resistance, to make possible the acquisition of farm surpluses without having to pay the price which any free peasants or free peasant associations would have demanded. He may well have felt he had little choice.

It does not matter in the present context whether Stalin made this shift through personal conviction of its necessity, or because this seemed to him to be a clever power-manœuvre. The cleverness in any case largely consisted in knowing that he would thus strengthen his position by becoming the spokesman of the view which was widely popular among Party activists. The "leftists," destroyed organisationally by Stalin in earlier years, had a considerable following. Stalin's left-turn brought many of them to his support—though this did not save them from being shot in due course on Stalin's orders. It is probably the case that he had at this time genuine majority support within the Party for his policy, though many had reservations about certain excesses, of which more will be said. But if this be so, the policy as such cannot be attributed to Stalin personally, and therefore the consequences which flowed from its adoption must be a matter of more than personal responsibility.

Let us examine some of these consequences. Collectivisation could not be voluntary. Rapid industrialisation, especially with priority for heavy industry, meant a reduction in living standards, despite contrary promises in the first five-year plans. This meant a sharp increase in the degree of coercion, in the powers of the police, in the unpopularity of the régime. The aims of the bulk of the people were bound to be in conflict with the aims of the Party. It should be added that this conflict is probably bound to arise in some form wherever *the state* is responsible for financing rapid industrialisation; the sacrifices are then imposed by political authority, and the masses of "small" people do not and cannot provide voluntarily the necessary savings, since in the nature of things their present abstinence cannot be linked with a future return which they as individuals can identify. However, this possibly unavoidable unpopularity was greatly increased in the U.S.S.R. by the sheer pace of the advance and by the attack on peasant property, and, as we shall see, both these factors reacted adversely on production of consumers' goods and so led to still further hardships and even greater unpopularity. The strains and priorities involved in a rapid move forward required a high degree of economic centralisation, to prevent resources from being diverted to satisfy needs which were urgent but of a non-priority character. In this situation, the Party was the one body capable of carrying out enormous changes and resisting social and economic pressures in a hostile environment; this was bound to affect its structure. For a number of years it had already been in process of transformation from a political into a power machine. The problems involved in the "revolution from above" intensified the process of turning it into an obedient instrument for changing, suppressing, controlling.

This, in turn, required hierarchical subordination, in suppression of discussion; therefore there had to be an unquestioned commander-in-chief. Below him, toughness in executing unpopular orders became the highest qualification for Party office. The emergence of Stalin, and of Stalin-type bullying officials of the sergeant-major species, was accompanied by the decline in the importance of the cosmopolitan journalist intellectual type of party leader who had played so prominent a role earlier.

But Stalin's personal responsibility goes far beyond his being the voice and leader of a party majority in a given historical situation. For one cannot possibly argue that all the immense evils of the Stalin era flowed inescapably from the policy decisions of 1928-29. In assessing Stalin's personal role in bringing these evils about, it is useful to approach the facts from two angles. There was, first, the category of evils which sprang from policy choices which Stalin made and which he need not have made; in other words we are here concerned with consequences (perhaps necessary) of unnecessary decisions. The other category consists of evil actions which can reasonably be attributed to Stalin and which are his direct responsibility.

Of course, these categories shade into one another, as do murder and manslaughter. In the first case, the evils were in a sense situation-determined, but Stalin had a large hand in determining the situation. In the second, his guilt is as clear as a politician's guilt can be.

The most obvious examples of the first category are: the brutality of collectivisation and the madly excessive pace of industrial development. In each case, we are dealing with *"excessive excesses,"* since we have already noted that collectivisation without coercion was impossible, and rapid industrialisation was bound to cause stresses and strains.

But we must now come to Stalin's more direct contribution to the brutality and terrorism of the Stalin era.

There was, firstly, his needless cruelty which showed itself already in the methods used to impose collectivisation. The great purges were surely not "objectively necessary." To explain them one has to take into account Stalin's thirst for supreme power, his intense pathological suspiciousness, *i.e.*, matters pertaining to Stalin's personal position and character. These led him to massacre the majority of the "Stalinist" central committee elected in 1934, who had supported or at the very least tolerated Stalin's policies up to that date. The facts suggest that they believed that relaxation was possible and desirable; many of them seem to have died for the crime of saying so. Nor was there any "police logic" for the scale and drastic nature of the purges. Indeed, the police chiefs figured prominently among the victims. True, there was a kind of "snowballing" of arrests, which might have got out of control in 1938, but this was due largely to the effect of the terror on the police, who had to show zeal or go under. Nor can any "necessity" explain the post-war repressions, the death of Voznesensky, the so-called "Leningrad affair," the shooting of the Jewish intellectuals, the "doctors' plot." Stalin played so prominently a personal role in establishing a reign of terror in the Party and the country that he must bear direct responsibility even where executions were the result of false information supplied to him by his subordinates for reasons of their own.

The atmosphere of terror had, of course, far-reaching consequences in every sphere of Soviet life. It became particularly grotesque and purposeless in the last years of Stalin, when the social and economic developments, plus victory in war, provided the Soviet régime with a much firmer base among the people, so that a considerable part of the discontent was the result, rather than the cause, of repressive measures. Many obviously overdue reforms had to await his death. As did Tsar Nicholas I, a century earlier, Stalin was able to delay "necessary" changes.

Many other examples can be given of the personal role of Stalin. On the economic front, the miserable state of the peasants in 1953 was due largely to Stalin's obstinate refusal to face the facts and listen to serious advice. He contributed greatly to wasteful and grandiose schemes to "transform nature," and to a wasteful and grandiose style of architecture. In the military field, history will, I think, support Khrushchev's accusation that Stalin's inability to see the signs of a German attack, his unwillingness to allow preparations, his massacre of the best Soviet officers, all made a personal contribution to the Russian disasters of 1941. Stalin personally insisted on his own deification, the rewriting of history, the creation of myths. Some myths were based on lies which he himself publicly uttered. For instance, in 1935 he announced: "We have had no poor for two or three years now"—and this when bread had reached the highest price, in relation to wages, that it had ever attained in Soviet history. Or equally ridiculous was his claim, in 1947, that Moscow "had completely abolished slums." In this personal way he made impossible all serious discussion either of living standards or the housing problem, just as his wildly false assertions about "Bukharin and Trotsky, agents of Hitler and the Mikado," made the writing of Soviet history impossible in Russia. One could argue that the myth about "voluntary collectivisation" was an objectively necessary lie, in the sense of transcending Stalin's personality; indeed, this lie figures in the Party programme adopted by the 22nd Congress last November. But Stalin's lies went very much beyond this, and beyond the distortions and myths which can be ascribed to other politicians in other countries.

Throughout Russia, officials at all levels modelled themselves on Stalin, and each succeeded in imposing more unnecessary misery on more subordinates, stultifying initiative, penalising intelligence, discouraging originality. The price of all this is still being paid.

The urgent need to prepare for war has often been advanced as an excuse for Stalin's industrial "tempos" and for the terror. This can hardly be accepted. In the worst years of social coercion and over-ambitious plan, i.e., 1929–33, Hitler was only just climbing to power, and Comintern policy showed that he was not then regarded as the main enemy. It is possible that Stalin was liquidating all potential opponents in the Purges of 1936–38 as a precaution in case war broke out, though this seems doubtful for a variety of reasons. But it is quite false to use the result of the war as ex-post-factum justification of Stalinism. Perhaps, with less harsh policies, the greater degree of loyalty in 1941 would have offset a smaller industrial base? In any event the Purges not only led to the slaughter of the best military officers but also halted the growth of heavy industry.

The attentive reader will have noticed that this analysis has some features in common with Khrushchev's. Before 1934, Stalin had been carrying out policies which commanded the assent of a majority of the Party and which, like collectivisation, had been accepted as necessary and irreversible by the bulk of Party members, whatever their reservations about particular mistakes and acts of brutality. However, after that date he took more and more personal, arbitrary measures, massacred much of the Party, behaved like an oriental despot. It is true that he was also arbitrary before 1934, and that he took some wise decisions after that date; but there is a case for placing a qualitative change around then.

But this is by no means the end of the matter. It is not only a question of making some obvious remarks concerning Khrushchev's own role during the terror. Of much more general significance is the fact that the events prior to 1934, including the building-up of Stalin into an all-powerful and infallible dictator (by men many of whom he afterwards massacred), cannot be disassociated with what followed; at the very least they provided Stalin with his opportunity. This is where the historian must avoid the twin and opposite pitfalls of regarding what happened as inevitable, and regarding it as a chapter of "personalised" accidents. At each stage there are choices to be made, though the range of possible choices is generally much narrower than people suppose. In 1928 any practicable Bolshevik programme would have been harsh and unpopular. It might not have been *so* harsh and unpopular but for choices which need not necessarily have been made. If before 1934, *i.e.*, in the very period of maximum social coercion, Stalin truly represented the will of the Party, and Khrushchev argues that he did, some totalitarian consequences logically follow. One of these, as already suggested, is the semi-militarised party led by a *Fuehrer*, a dictator, because without an unquestioned leader the consequences of the policies adopted could not be faced.

But, even if it is true that the triumph of a dictator may be explained by objective circumstances which certainly existed in the Soviet situation, the acts of a dictator once he has "arrived" involve a considerable (though of course not infinite) degree of personal choice. Those who gave him the opportunity to act in an arbitrary and cruel way, who adopted policies which involved arbitrariness and coercion on a big scale, cannot ascribe subsequent events to the wickedness of one man or his immediate associates and claim that their hands are clean, even indeed if they were shot themselves on Stalin's orders. The whole-hog Stalin, in other words, was not "necessary," but the possibility of a Stalin was a necessary consequence of the effort of a minority group to keep power and to carry out a vast social-economic revolution in a very short time. And *some* elements of Stalinism were, in those circumstances, scarcely avoidable.

The serious problem for us is to see how far certain elements of Stalinism, in the sense of purposefully-applied social coercion, imposed by a party in the name of an ideology, are likely or liable to accompany rapid economic development even in non-Communist countries.

For it is surely true that many of the problems tackled by Stalin so brutally are present elsewhere, though events in the U.S.S.R. were, of course, deeply affected by peculiar features of Russia and of Bolshevism. The West should indeed emphasise the high cost in human and material terms of a Stalin, and show that the rise of such a man to supreme power in the Soviet Union was, to use the familiar Soviet-Marxist jargon phrase, "not accidental." Indeed, some Western historians who normally write "personalist" and empiricist history will begin to see the virtues of an approach they normally deride as "historicist"; they will analyse Soviet history to establish patterns, regularities, "necessities" which lead to Stalin. By contrast, an embarrassed Khrushchev will be—is being—forced to give an un-Marxist emphasis to personal and accidental factors.

But, of course, we must not confine our search for "necessities" in history only to instances which happen to serve a propagandist purpose. This would be a typically Soviet approach to historiography, only in reverse. It is particularly important to think very seriously about the inter-relationship of coercion and industrialisation, about the nature of the obstacles and vicious circles which drive men to think in totalitarian terms. Unless we realise how complex are the problems which develop-ment brings, how irrelevant are many of our ideas to the practical possi-bilities open to statesmen in these countries, we may unconsciously drive them towards the road which led to Stalin. They cannot be satisfied with "the pace of a tortoise."

Albert C. Grzesinski
PUTSCH VERSUS POLICE

Those who maintain that civil wars in post-war Germany oc-curred with clock-like regularity may be accused of exaggeration. But the young republic did have more than its share of violent and bloody struggles. On the left side stood the communists, determined to drive the revolution on—to where? The leaders in Moscow were still dreaming of world revolution and a Western Europe under Bolshevist rule. If a state-ment by Stalin in the *Pravda* of February, 1938, is to be believed, this hope is not even now a thing of the past.

All hopes of a communist world revolution hinged on Germany. Yet, aside from various inconsequential election victories, communism never gained a foothold in Germany. The growth or decline of commu-nism in Germany was determined solely by economic conditions. Com-munism was not a threat to the German Republic. The danger, nay the mortal enemy, stood at the right.

From the book *Inside Germany* by Albert C. Grzesinski, pp. 98–99, 101, 105–106, 106–107, 130–134. Copyright, 1939, renewal, © 1957 by E. P. Dutton & Co., Inc. Reprinted by permission of the publishers.
Albert Grzesinski (1879–   ) was Police President of Berlin during the years from 1925 to 1926 and 1930 to 1932.

The rightist menace drew its strength from the so-called *Frei-korps* and the reactionary old army commands. The latter were liquidated by me as Reich Commissioner on March 31, 1921. The *Freikorps* too had been repeatedly dissolved, but they had always found new opportunities to reorganize. They counted on the support of the Junkers and reactionary landowners who availed themselves of the services of these adventurers as strikebreakers and protective guards. The republic had granted the agricultural workers the right of coalition and collective bargaining. These workers had been the victims of brutal exploitation and unbelievably low wages and living conditions for so long that strikes were only natural and to be expected. The Junkers chose to overlook the plight of their men, and when the latter resorted to strikes, strike breakers in the person of military adventurers came in handy.

The Kapp *Putsch*, so-named after its leader, the agricultural director Dr. Kapp, occurred in March, 1920. This uprising was the answer of the plotting militarists to the government decree ordering the dissolution of the marine brigade under the command of Captain Ehrhardt. During the night of March 12th, the brigade, 5,000 men strong and heavily armed, marched from Doeberitz, where it had been in temporary quarters, to Berlin. They entered the city early in the morning without encountering resistance. The populace of Berlin was deeply shocked when it heard that the government had abandoned all thought of resistance and had fled the capital. . . .

At a secret meeting of Social Democratic and trade-union leaders, plans for a general strike and other measures against the rebels were discussed. The same morning a leaflet was distributed proclaiming the general strike and calling upon all workers to take their stand in defense of the constitutional government. The proclamation was signed by the Social Democratic members of the Reich cabinet and the Chairman of the Social Democratic Party, Otto Wels. The strike order met with enthusiastic approval of the workers, with the exception of the communists. The communist leadership immediately issued a vicious counterappeal captioned "Military Dictatorship or Proletarian Dictatorship?" which proclaimed, "The revolutionary proletariat will not lift a finger for the democratic republic which is only a thin mask for the bourgeois dictatorship. . . . At this moment the workers are unable to take action. We consider it our duty to make this clear . . ." Fortunately, the appeal was ignored by the workers who did not hide their disgust with the communist tactics.

The general strike, while proving fully effective, was not the greatest worry of Kapp, Luettwitz and their henchmen. Germany's economic life was at a standstill and a general strike could hardly make conditions worse. Moreover, the Kapp movement was not concerned with the plight of the people and would not have hesitated to crush active opposition by force. What happened was that the rebels failed to find active support from the leaders of the upper middle class and from the high bureaucracy which had remained in Berlin. Additional factors militating against the *Putsch* were the time chosen for the rebellion and the obvious personal motives behind it. . . .

It took a long time before the effects of the Kapp *Putsch* wore off. Clashes in Pomerania and Westphalia resembling real warfare occurred constantly. Central Germany, Schleswig-Holstein and Saxony reported serious clashes between Reichswehr troops and workers: 351 lives were lost; many thousands were wounded. Economic losses were considerable. The government announcement that the rebels would be severely punished and their property confiscated remained an empty threat. Nothing of consequence happened. Even Ehrhardt was permitted to draw his government pension.

A communist uprising similar to the one in the winter of 1918–19 occurred in Central Germany in the spring of 1921. It was heralded by bomb throwings in Berlin and various cities in Saxony. Moscow emissaries operating under cover in the heavily populated industrial districts of Central Germany instigated violent strikes. Armed gangs under the leadership of Max Hoelz, a former army corporal, did the rest. Hoelz's red troops fought numerous battles with the Prussian police. Losses on both sides were heavy. Not until the end of April were the heavily reinforced police forces able to gain the upper hand.

This uprising was openly supported by the Communist Party and its press. The appeals to the great masses of the German workers to join the revolt met with no response. German organized labor also ignored the communist plea for a general strike. Max Hoelz finally fell into the hands of the police and was sentenced to life imprisonment. He was later granted amnesty and went to Russia where he was applauded as Germany's revolutionary hero.

In October of 1923, the communists planned another uprising which, due to the economic crisis, had a fair chance of success. Conditions were desperate. French and Belgian troops had occupied the Ruhr district. The German currency was sliding rapidly downhill, one American dollar buying hundreds of millions of Reichsmark. Wages were incredibly low. Food was getting scarce and fetched sky-high prices. The communists' star seemed in ascent. With 500,000 rifles allegedly at their disposal, they decided to act. At the same time, they appealed to the German trade-unions for support.

The latter, however, bluntly refused to become a party to the communist scheme. They served notice that they would fight any attempt directed at the overthrow of constitutional government. The more moderate and experienced communist leaders hesitated after learning that not 500,000 rifles, as claimed, but only 50,000 would be available. The revolt was called off before it began. . . .

The occupation of the Ruhr district by the French and Belgian troops early in 1923 gave rise to another rightist revolt that was to rank high in history—the Hitler *Putsch* in November of the same year. This uprising was really planned as a government-inspired and organized state *Putsch*, that is, a *Putsch* of the State of Bavaria against the Reich. The Bavarian Prime Minister, von Kahr, was opposed to the Reich government and to Reich President Ebert. For various reasons, the Reichswehr stationed in Bavaria refused to recognize the authority of the Reichswehr Ministry and to obey orders of the Chief of Staff General von Seeckt. These maneuvers were also supported by the flourishing nationalist elements organized in so-called defense formations. The rebels were united only by their common hatred of the republic and the "November criminals," the men who had assumed revolutionary authority in 1918 and had saved Germany from the brink of the abyss. For the rest, they feared and mistrusted each other. . . .

Bloody clashes and violent street fighting between the members of the radical parties were on the increase. Nazi and communist propaganda was responsible for grave disorders. Ordinary brawls had given way to murderous attacks. Knives, blackjacks and revolvers had replaced political argument. Terror was rampant. Carefully prepared alibis helped the terrorists on both sides to escape conviction. In my efforts to deal with the incipient civil war, I availed myself of a law dating back as far as 1850 and authorizing the police to take disturbers of the peace into *Schutzhaft*—temporary custody. These measures were sharply criticized and denounced by the republican press. Their criticism did not deter me.

Rowdiness and political degeneracy had already reached appalling proportions. A surprise police raid of a secret radical meeting netted over fifty revolvers, daggers, brass knuckles and weapons of every description which I placed as visual demonstration before the Prussian Diet. One might have expected signs of disgust and revulsion on the part of the people's representatives, but this was not so. On the contrary, they laughed at the exhibition and showed their obvious incapacity to grasp the true meaning of portents.

The terrorist methods of both Nazis and communists were essentially the same. Communist terrorist groups, consisting of four men, operated in districts where they were unknown. The number of these groups never exceeded twenty, but despite a reward of 20,000 Reichsmark, approximately $5,000, the police were unable to make arrests. Numerous police officers were killed in these years. The most outrageous case was the murder of two police captains on August 9, 1931, near the

Karl Liebknechthouse, Communist Party headquarters, at the Buelow Square in East Berlin. The two were ambushed on the day the plebiscite on an early dissolution of the Prussian Diet was held. This plebiscite had been demanded by the Nationalists and the Nazis and was actively supported by the communists.

Beginning with August, 1931, there was no nook or cranny in communist headquarters and adjoining buildings that was not known to the police. Reports of secret passages and vaults were pure invention. These "vaults" were abandoned beer cellars (the house had formerly been a restaurant) and the subterranean passages were ordinary cellars such as may be found in any other house. Every scrap of material seized by the police during our ten-day search had been turned over to the offices of the state attorney. Communist headquarters could not possibly have contained new and incriminating material, as von Levetzow maintained. If the evidence allegedly discovered by the Nazis had been of real importance, the Hitler regime would not have hesitated to use it to the utmost extent. This was not done—another proof of Nazi lying. In December, 1931, the Communist Party dissociated itself from these outrages and condemned individual terror acts. The overwhelming majority of the German communists were by that time opposed to terror acts which, they rightly felt, would only discredit their movement.

In May of the same year a series of political murders was unloosed with the murder of the communist Heimburger by Nazis. Other assassinations followed in quick succession and within a short time the number had risen to twenty-nine. Twelve communists, six Nazis, one member of the Nationalist Stahlhelm, two Social Democrats, four police officers and four men with unknown party affiliations were killed. Thirteen murders had been committed by communists, nine by Nazis. Large stores of arms were found by the police in their periodical searches of radical hide-outs: 168 revolvers and 12,000 rounds of ammunition, not to speak of a motley collection of other weapons, were confiscated early in 1931.

The number of major political crimes was increasing so rapidly that I decided to go before the public. In a press interview, I made the facts known and insisted that the governments of the Reich and Prussia take strong measures to put an end to this state of affairs. In March, 1931, the long overdue emergency decree was passed. It provided the police authorities with new powers to strike at the political underworld. It came too late. These measures were only temporarily successful. The political crisis could no longer be solved by ordinary means. Public safety became more and more insecure. From June 1 to July 20, 1932, 416 political riots occurred in Prussia. Eighty-two persons were killed and 400 seriously wounded.

The Nazis, faithful to the communist example, met and conspired in beer taverns. These places served as training and conspiracy centers, and from there swift raids were undertaken. In February, 1932, the police raided one of these Nazi meeting halls and found two life-size effigies of Severing and myself, the heads of which were neatly punctured by bullet holes. They had proven a convenient target for the young soldiers of the Third Reich. This was the training and political education of the younger party members, ranging from seventeen to twenty years. Most of the Nazis arrested were youths under twenty years of age. I was appalled to realize the moral degradation of these youngsters. Killing a fellow man was nothing to get excited about, and as for repentance, there was none. They were no longer adherents of a political creed—just gangsters. They were already well schooled in the methods which were to find their culmination in concentration camps and prison dungeons of Hitler's Third Reich.

In October, 1931, a new decree authorized the police to close these political murder nests. New stringent penalties were imposed. Commendable as these efforts were, they did not, in my opinion, go far enough. They should have gone hand in hand with efficient counter-propaganda exposing the conspirators and presenting the enormous accomplishments of the republic to the people. Radio, motion pictures and other public means should have been exploited to the utmost. Unfortunately, the government did not realize the importance of a propagandistic counter-campaign. Today, when we look back on the events of the last few years, this official lethargy and lack of understanding seems incomprehensible. Another mortal threat to the democratic republic was the gigantic monopoly of Dr. Alfred Hugenberg, the leader of the German Nationalists, who by means of a far-flung chain of motion picture houses, press services, newspapers, etc., dominated public opinion throughout Germany. The Hugenberg trust also controlled the production of German motion pictures, which permitted him to influence public opinion abroad. There was one great opportunity to strike at the roots of German reaction —but nobody grasped it.

It is perhaps important in this connection to recall the experience of the German public with the American motion picture, *All Quiet on the Western Front,* based on the book of the same name by the German author Erich Maria Remarque. The picture was first shown in Berlin early in December, 1930. It met with an unprecedented success. After the second performance on December 10th, Nazis and Nationalists started serious disturbances in the theater, as well as outside. The rightist press clamored that further showings of the picture be forbidden because of its contents which was "insulting" to the German people. The military authorities, too, took exception to the manner in which German militarism was depicted.

I bluntly refused. The film had passed the censors and I felt that to give in to the demands of the right and their terrorists would further undermine public authority, safety and order. I made certain that the theater had proper police protection, and that the neighboring streets were closed to demonstrations. The picture continued to run without disturbances. If it had been up to me, *All Quiet on the Western Front* would have been shown for an indefinite period in Berlin and elsewhere, but the Reich government of Chancellor Bruening retreated before the increasing agitation of the right.

A disorderly Nazi protest meeting near the theater furnished the excuse. Before I was able to enforce a rigid ban on all demonstrations, the Reich government, taking advantage of legal loopholes, induced another board of censors to prohibit further showings of the picture. Reactionary elements were wild with joy. Another battle had been won. The failure of the government to enlist the state-owned radio in the struggle for the soul of the people was equally pathetic and ridiculous. Not once was a serious effort made to counteract reactionary and anti-democratic propaganda, and to break the stranglehold of the rightist pied pipers over the people. The occasional and all too rare radio addresses by republican spokesmen only served to emphasize the helplessness of the government.

Roy Jenkins
BATTLE OF THE SEXES

[One] threat of violence which hung over England in 1911 came from the suffragettes. "Militancy" had begun as long before as October, 1905, when Christabel Pankhurst and Annie Kenney succeeded in wrecking a meeting which Grey was addressing in Manchester. In the early years of the Liberal Government it grew gradually, and the methods employed became progressively more violent. In September, 1909, the permanent secretary to the Home Office sent Herbert Gladstone a Metropolitan Police report that women were practising pistol shooting at an address in Tottenham Court Road. "The annexed report," he commented,

Reprinted from *Asquith* by Roy Jenkins, pp. 245–247. By permission of Chilmark Press. Copyright Roy Jenkins, 1964.
Roy Jenkins (1920–   ) is a biographer and Labor member of Parliament. He wrote a biography of Herbert Henry Asquith, who served as Prime Minister of Great Britain from 1908 to 1916.

"seems to me to show that there is now definite ground for fearing the possibility of the P.M's being fired at by one of the pickets at the entrance of the House (of Commons)." He added, however, that he was against the pickets being removed as the police were confident that they could get a woman before she "damaged" the Prime Minister. Gladstone was nervous, but Asquith unhesitatingly pronounced against removal.

In fact the Prime Minister was never shot at, but numerous other assaults upon him were attempted. He emerged unharmed from them all, although others sometimes suffered on his behalf. Lord Weardale, when mistaken for him, was whipped at Euston. Augustine Birrell, when accompanying him in Whitehall, had his knee-cap damaged. And Redmond, sitting in the same carriage in Dublin, was wounded in the ear by a hatchet. At other times the intimidation was less vicarious. The Downing Street windows were occasionally smashed; and Asquith himself was often hectored and sometimes hustled by militant women. What he particularly disliked about the hectoring was that it tended to occur at evening parties and contrasted sharply with the form which he believed conversation between the sexes should take on such occasions. The hustling took a still more disagreeable form. On the golf links at Lossiemouth some militants tried to tear off his clothes, and were frustrated only by the presence and intervention of his daughter Violet. Thereafter a repetition of this form of attack was one of his principal fears, even when something more vicious was attempted. In November, 1913 when motoring to Stirling to unveil the Campbell-Bannerman memorial he was held up by women lying across the road. As the car slowed down others emerged from behind the hedgerows on either side of the road, jumping on the running boards, and proceeded to belabour him over the head with dog whips. His top hat provided a surprisingly adequate degree of protection.

All this and the other dramatic manifestations of the time—the slashing of the Rokeby Venus, Miss Wilding Davison's death fall in front of the King's horse at the 1913 Derby, the burning of pillar boxes, the destruction by acid of golf course greens—had no favourable effect upon Asquith. He found the whole performance both distasteful and mystifying. As Mr. Roger Fulford has written:

> The idea of converting a human being's reason by parades, marches and fighting the police was incomprehensible to him. The more the women marched, the less his reason marched with them. Therefore the work of the militants strengthened his opposition to the vote. The women pursued him with much shrill invective—some of which was not without its effect in damaging his standing in the country—but he remained like a rock, which by reason of its natural formation, repels the froth and fury swirling round it.

In part Asquith's attitude to the suffrage question was due to a failure of imagination. He simply could not understand why anyone, man or woman, should get so excited about the matter. It should be settled, not on the basis of abstract right, but by the practical test of whether or not a change would be likely to improve the system of government. He therefore always wanted to play the issue down. He was an effective controversialist on the subject, but, unlike some of the other anti-suffragists—Lewis Harcourt amongst the Liberals or F. E. Smith amongst the Tories—not a happy one. He would much rather that the subject had never been raised, and like other leaders confronted with a subject on which they did not wish to lead, he tried unsuccessfully to take the passion out of an essentially passionate controversy. He told the House of Commons in May, 1913:

> There are very few issues in politics upon which more exaggerated language is used both upon the one side and upon the other. I am sometimes tempted to think, as one listens to the arguments of supporters of woman suffrage, that there is nothing to be said for it, and I sometimes am tempted to think, when I listen to the arguments of the opponents of woman suffrage, that there is nothing to be said against it.

Margaret Cole
DIRECT INDUSTRIAL ACTION

The General Strike of 1926 was a tragedy; but it was an exciting and, in retrospect, an important and illuminating experience. It was the last throw of "insurrectionism," of "direct industrial action," belief in which had been for so long part of the cardinal faith of the "Left." Ever since, in 1920, the threat of direct action had stopped the Polish war, the Left had not ceased to believe that the *industrial* movement, if really united and determined, could make its will prevail, and further that some day the opportunity would come, and the shame of Black Friday (when the Unions, except the miners, were neither united nor determined) be avenged; and this belief was only strengthened in 1924–25, after Mac-

From *Growing Up into Revolution* by Margaret Cole, pp. 119–122, 125. Reprinted by permission of the author.
    Margaret Cole (1893–   ) is a prominent member of the British Labor Party, as was her late husband, Professor G. D. H. Cole.

Donald's first government had come to its inglorious end, while at the same time the period of post-war wage-cuts seemed to be over, trade was improving, and many groups of workers were making tentative forward moves. When the strike failed, in spite of the most impressive exhibition of working-class solidarity seen since the days of Chartism, and when, after much post-mortem discussion, it gradually became clear that it could not possibly have succeeded, the long dreams of Syndicalists, Direct-Actionists, and the rest of them withered and died. No Trade Union, since 1926, has seriously proposed to use withdrawal of its labour as a means of coercing Parliament or the Government on a large issue; nor does any Tory of any intelligence now attack the Trade Unions for presuming to give a lead to the nation. At the beginning of 1948, indeed, the Tories were actually abusing the Trades Union Congress for failing to give a lead—on wage policy, for example. But in 1926 Trade Unionists who tried to help the miners to resist slashing wage-cuts were traitors, striking against the Constitution, according to the present Viscount Simon, and according to Winston Churchill to be crushed at all costs.

I think there can be no doubt that the outbreak of May 1926 was deliberately provoked by the Government. By the summer of 1925, the Trades Union Congress was getting much too uppish, flirting with revolutionary ideas, forming, wicked creatures, an Anglo-Russian Trade Union Committee—and that at a time when the return to the gold standard made it desirable that wages should be lowered, not raised, if the price of British exports was to be kept down. But when the mineowners, always ready to lead on the downward path, proposed large reductions in miners' wages, they were promptly met by the announcement that the miners would strike, which they had expected, and that they would be supported by all the transport workers, which they had not. The other side was not ready for a big strike; there were no stocks of coal on hand; so the Government put off the showdown to a more convenient season, buying off the owners with a large temporary subsidy. There was much premature rejoicing in the Labour ranks and talk of "Red Thursday" wiping out "Black Friday"—and the leaders then sat back and did nothing whatever, so as to avoid "provocation." The Government and the employers, however, started to make serious preparations, piling up big stocks of coal in convenient places and creating, through Churchill's Organisation for the Maintenance of Supplies, the first, and only, avowedly strike-breaking force ever seen in this country. (Earlier strikes had been broken by the private recruitment of blacklegs, or, in extreme cases, by the use of soldiers and sailors; the O.M.S. was a general invitation to middle-class loyalists.)

The subsidy was to end in the spring; and in the spring the mineowners again presented their programme of lower wages and longer hours. The Miners' Executive, led by the stubby and obstinate Yorkshire-man, Herbert Smith,[1] and Arthur Cook, the fiery Communist orator from South Wales, responded with the slogan, *Not a penny, not a minute;* and called on the other Unions for help. On May Day—Labour Day—there was called a special meeting at the Memorial Hall in Farringdon Street, at which representative after representative went up to the table to hand in his Union's promise to come out with the miners. Over three and a half million workers were put at the disposal of the T. U. C. General Council; but it was still not certain that they would be called out. The leaders were deeply concerned to prevent the strike; they "grovelled," as J. H. Thomas said, in the attempt to get any concession at all which they could take to the miners. They got none; the Government had made up its mind, and when on the night of May 2nd the compositors of the *Daily Mail* refused to set up a leader violently abusing the miners, Baldwin, the Prime Minister, jumped at this convenient chance, called off all negotia-tions and went to bed while the negotiators were actually sitting in his house. Next morning the "front-line troops" came out—all rail and road transport workers, power station workers, iron and steel, metal and chemical workers, builders (except those building hospitals and houses) and printing workers. This last was a bad mistake, since it prevented the Unions from getting their case put publicly to anyone outside their own ranks, whereas the Government commanded the radio (B.B.C. employees were not organised and so could not have been called out, even if anyone had thought of it). Eight days later, the strike call came to the second line—engineers and shipyard workers; on the following morning, after the miners had refused even to discuss a compromise memorandum presented by Sir Herbert (now Lord) Samuel,[2] the T. U. C. announced that the limit of support had been reached, and ordered the solid ranks back to work. The miners stayed out according to their slogan, and fought on until *November,* only one coalfield breaking away; in Novem-ber they went back on the owners' terms.

Because the General Strike lasted so short a time and could not be reported in non-existent newspapers, the general public knew very little about it, either at the time or afterwards, except in so far as it affected them individually—*e.g.,* by making them walk to work. After it was over, they heaved a great sigh of relief—though they spared a little sympathy for the miners' wives and children—and promptly forgot all

---

[1] The same who in a previous wage dispute had given great pleasure by adjuring the Prime Minister (Lloyd George) with the words, "Ye silly old boogger, are ye daft?"

[2] This was not a "peace offer"; the Government never promised to take it even as a basis for discussion; if the miners' leaders had accepted, some small face-saving concessions might have been made. We shall never know; but if they had accepted, their constituents would certainly have turned them down.

about it. This was unfortunate, because it brought out some facts that were extremely interesting and which students of society ought to have studied for the future.

First, the solidarity of the working-class, which astonished their own leaders as much as anyone else. In town after town, including many—like Oxford—where the Labour movement was generally considered weak and unreliable, reports of nearly 100 per cent. response to the call was reported; during the whole nine days, even after Sir John Simon, speaking as a Liberal, had threatened all strike leaders with imprisonment, there were scarcely any breakaways; and, most impressive of all, when the men obeyed the orders to return and found that many of their employers were seizing the opportunity to do a little victimisation on their own, they promptly came out again until that attempt was squelched. A wise man might have guessed from this what account of themselves they might be able to render on other occasions when they had a chance—in 1940, say, or 1945.

Secondly, the extraordinarily peaceable character of the whole brief war. I cannot assert that no blackleg was ever maltreated; but I can say that the report of a local strike committee to its district headquarters to the effect "Found lorries labelled FOOD not carrying food; put in canal; hope correct," was regarded as a case of exceptionally vigorous action, although a safe conduct had been manifestly abused; that there was no bloodshed at all, and that in at least one town the police drafted to keep order played a football match with the strikers. This, I think, could have happened in no other country in the world; it certainly could not have happened in the United States; and the fact that it did happen here, with all the self-restraint and regard for public order that this implies, might have caused one to hope that, given reasonably favourable conditions, a good deal of fundamental change might be carried out in Britain without civil war.

The third fact, and the most important of all, though the least observed, was the quantity of organising ability that was disclosed among the rank-and-file Trade Unionists who manned the local Trades Councils and Strike Committees. They had a great deal of work to do, particularly since the national leaders had made no plans at all; as the orders were that food and health services were not to be interfered with they had the responsibility of issuing permits for the transport of food and where necessary of coal; they had further to organise meetings and pickets, occupation and amusement for those on strike, intelligence services and news services to fill the place of the vanished newspapers. For the most part they did it extremely well, showing plenty of initiative and decision—fully as much as was displayed by local civil defence groupings during the last war; even to-day we have not yet found out how in ordinary times to tap effectively the reserves of ability in ordinary people and use them in the public service. . . .

The Government had made up its mind that "direct action" must be scotched once and for all, and, that being so, the Unions had no choice between surrendering and going on to civil war and revolution, which was the last thing they had envisaged or desired. They surrendered, ingloriously, but with the ranks unbroken; and though the immediate outcome was, naturally, a falling-off of membership, and a good deal of angry recrimination, the absence of any real *revanche,* any sacking of the leaders who had so patently failed to lead, showed that the movement, when it had had time to think things over, realised that it had in effect made a challenge to the basis of British society which it was not prepared to see through and that, therefore, post-mortems on who was most to blame were unprofitable.

Felix Riesenberg, Jr.
SAN FRANCISCO'S GENERAL STRIKE

On the morning of May 9, 1934 the month of tension along the feverish waterfront was relieved by the screaming of police sirens as squad cars converged on a pier half-way up the north side of the Embarcadero. Five hundred angry men of the International Longshoremen's Association moved back sullenly when police lines formed outside the steel-rolling doors behind which Negroes were working a ship. Other squads were mobilizing at the Nippon Yusen Kaisha dock: there was danger of an outbreak on the arrival of the Japanese mail liner *Tatsuta Maru.* Along seventeen miles of waterfront, pickets had gathered around the sixty ships in port. The most complicated strike in the city's history had started with threatened violence.

When the "innocent bystander" was hauled from his automobile and given a severe beating, on the second day of the strike, the employers announced that they were going to make a fight of it. It would not be the short labor war which strike strategists had predicted. On May 11, advertisements appeared in San Francisco newspapers:

From *Golden Gate: The Story of San Francisco Harbor.* (1945)
Felix Riesenberg, Jr. (1913–   ) has been a seaman, author, and was a San Francisco journalist from 1936 to 1939.

LONGSHOREMEN WANTED
Experience Desirable
But Not Necessary
Apply Navy Landing Pier, Foot of
Howard Street, San Francisco
85¢ an Hour Straight Time
$1.25 an Hour Overtime
Strike Conditions Prevail
Waterfront Employers' Union
By W. J. Petersen

Soon more than one thousand strike-breakers were working on the docks, housed aboard the barrack-ship *Diana Dollar* and other vessels. Sunburned strikers crowded about the wire fences, watching the "scabs" at work, shouting threats. One hundred ships were tied up and docks had become dangerously congested, for the teamsters joined with the I.L.A., refusing to haul "hot cargo." Then strikers drove automobiles in front of Belt Line railroad engines or stood and lay on the tracks.

On May 15 the strike had spread north and south; for the first time in history not a freighter sailed from an American Pacific port. At San Francisco outbreaks became more frequent. Through the days riot squads of police were rushed to points along the waterfront where beatings had taken place, and the newspapers carried stories of injured men who suffered for hours awaiting ambulances whose drivers claimed to have been threatened with death if they answered calls.

Night found the Embarcadero flickering with sinister bonfires around which pickets huddled. Occasionally a spotlight stabbed the darkness, pointing toward some suspicious heap. Gangs lay in wait for scabs, terrifying screams came from empty lots in the warehouse district. San Francisco was in a state of civil war.

Assistant Secretary of Labor Edward F. McGrady, the Administration's "trouble-shooter," met with the men and employers. He was generally liked and trusted by the strikers until condemned by Lawyer Leo Gallagher, just arrived from Germany, where he had been defending Communists. Gallagher urged that the I.L.A. not submit to arbitration nor settle any differences until the demands of all striking unions were met. That stand was passed as a resolution, and another deadlock resulted. Secretary McGrady charged that radicals in the I.L.A. were "throwing a monkey wrench into the situation" and added that "San Francisco ought to be informed of the growth of the Red element."

Threats to "clean out the nest of Communists" were heard as the city began to feel the pinch of a strangled waterfront. Reactionaries declared the strike was "Moscow-made" and supported by "Red gold."

Bridges had the power of the men behind him when, on June 1, 1934, he flatly rejected an agreement signed for the men by Joseph P.

Ryan, heavy-set leader of the I.L.A. in New York. The men would return to work, said Harry, only if two thirds of the unions' entire Pacific Coast membership so voted. West-coast seaports followed San Francisco, where a meeting booed Ryan out of the hall and voted against the agreement because it failed to include unions that had meantime gone out in sympathy with the I.L.A. On the picket lines by that time were sailors, engineers, stewards, and masters and mates.

Further violence came with this attempt to terminate the month-old strike. A Communist, Ellain Black, was arrested on the waterfront, charged with making "inflammatory speeches"; everywhere assaults were increasing in number and viciousness. Steamship executives, employees, and strikers were under constant threat: bricks and milk bottles full of creosote flew through windows; beaten and mutilated bodies floated on the Bay.

Docks became so congested that strike-breakers could no longer work, and with more cargo diverted to the Golden Gate by the closing of Portland and Seattle, the problem of moving shipments demanded an immediate solution. The building of the great trans-Bay bridges was delayed; industries were closing; steamship lines announced that San Francisco was no longer a port, that their ships were being diverted to Los Angeles, then comparatively open by reason of its geographic features and union weakness. The Board of Health raised a cry when medical supplies were delayed, and newspapers aroused citizens with reports that tons of perishable food had rotted.

In one month the strike cost San Francisco three hundred million dollars!

Citizens were indignant over reported beatings of innocent persons, incendiary fires, and general disorder. There was talk of Vigilantes, and National Guard commanders had orders to be ready for mobilization. Finally merchants, paying seven hundred thousand dollars a day for the closed waterfront, were aroused to the point where talk of "opening the port" grew into demands for immediate action. The city was being choked.

On Thursday, July 5, before dawn, hundreds of pickets swarmed along the fog-chilled Embarcadero toward China Basin, armed with every sort of available weapon, even to guns, which would be heard before the end of that momentous day. Excited, swearing groups hustled past silent pier fronts, moving along like low-flying storm clouds. Men stopped to pick up loose bricks, and strike cars raced by, carrying strategists. An air of desperation had seized the pickets. This was to be the "show-down."

Down Spear, Main, Beale, and Frémont streets came stewards still in their white coats, sailors in dungarees, and newspaper reporters carrying gas masks. From the Southern Pacific depot at Third and Townsend and up out of the Potrero district, along Third Street, trudged other hundreds. A crowd of more than one thousand was packed around the south end of the Embarcadero by daylight.

"Ten more men wanted at the King Street warehouse!" a voice was croaking through a megaphone on one of the strike cars. "More of you fellows on the tracks there—go over to the pier." The strikers were getting set. Police whistles shrilled above the noise of people, cars, and loud-speakers. Cops forced the growing horde back across the tracks, into vacant lots near Japan, Gale, and Stanford streets. At old South Park and up the sides of Rincon Hill hundreds spread their coats to sit and watch. Errand boys, messengers, and men due to work half an hour earlier lingered, waiting.

Eyes were focused on the closed doors of Pier 38; faces were seen peering out from behind its dirty windows. A signal sounded. It was almost eight o'clock. Something was about to happen; a thrill ran through the spectators. Men in the strikers' ranks breathed hard, gripped their clubs, spanners, and rocks. Determined, scowling men heard the coughing engine being raced inside the pier.

The door came up; a heavily laden truck ground its gears and shot out, thundering down toward King Street. The driver shielded his face and crouched low over the wheel as rocks and stones pinged on the fenders and hood. Cops, not waiting this time, threw their tear-gas bombs and swung nightsticks. Defiant union men raised a tremendous shout and pitched in against the police.

Men went down before face-mashing blows, came up dripping blood, spluttered their curses, and swung furiously. A cop chased a striker to the tracks, got his head against the rail, and began pounding with a nightstick. Six longshoremen moved in on the fighters, grabbing the policeman, and hammered him. More cops came to the rescue, their sticks flaying the union members. On the corner of Federal and First streets a red-headed man came up from a blow on the head with part of his scalp ripped loose. Into the cops he tore, his arms working like pistons as he dodged from their blows. People swept down from the hills to get closer. Five men finally got the red-head down, then dragged him to an ambulance.

All morning the fighting waged while trucks rumbled through the clouds of dust and gas. Choking curses and prayers came from hundreds of bitter people. Gasping men, blinded by the tear fumes, held their arms over their heads and stumbled crazily to get away from more blows. Unconscious pickets were dragged from the fighting, into the ambulances that wailed down from the Ferry Building.

At noon a truce was called as if by agreement; rioting stopped. Leaders from the longshoremen's hall passed through the ranks giving encouragement; agitators ranted at the strikers. Bloody noses, black eyes, and bandaged heads on every side told the extent of the battle. News-papers had extras on the streets, screaming their headlines of new violence. The strike was coming to a climax. The noon respite was only a pause.

In the sullen afternoon pickets returned to the Embarcadero in knots of ten and twenty. The new strategy was to avoid large gatherings. "Then the gas won't be no good." Unshorn, excited radicals were trying to whip the men into a fervor near one o'clock. A woman with disheveled hair was shrilling near the foot of Mission Street. "The bloated scab-herders aren't here," she rasped. "No! Why should they be? They've got their paid beat-up gangs, *their* police. And why do we pay taxes? I'll tell you why. So that we can have police to beat us, to choke us with tear gas. That's why!"

A general strike had been mouthed by agitators for more than a month as the quick method of settling the waterfront deadlock. The Joint Maritime Strike Committee urged, in the strongest language, support of such action by the San Francisco Labor Council. It was the vote of the Teamsters' Union to strike, cutting off the city's transportation, that started the waves breaking. On the sweep of feeling engendered by the Bloody Thursday victims' funeral, other unions joined the movement.

Five hundred strikers and sympathizers were turning back trucks at highway entrances on July 12, virtually blockading the city. Panic gripped San Francisco.

Threatened shortage of gasoline sent motorists into long lines to await their turn at the pumps. Other citizens were laying in supplies of canned food, and the banks were stormed in the morning for cash. Anonymous calls flashed across telephone wires: threats, demands, and false orders. With more unions growing restless, a strike to paralyze the city was imminent. Police issued premonitory orders to pawnshops and sporting-goods stores to remove firearms from their windows. Merchan-dise and food began moving by parcel post. Restaurants were closed; small shop-proprietors were intimidated; trucks were turned upside-down, and roving bands of toughs entered private homes to threaten occupants. In its wildest days San Francisco had not been so unruly.

Sunday dawned on a dead city. The docks were idle, trains and trucks moved rarely, if at all, and taxis and street cars had stopped. People kept off the streets, fearful of some sudden wave of violence. There were threats of martial law by the Governor if the delivery of milk and other essentials were stopped. The eyes of the nation focused on the port by the Golden Gate. It was the eve of the country's first general strike in fifteen years, the second in United States history.

Reports that proprietors of a store were attempting to profiteer brought food rioting to open the great industrial crisis on Monday morn-ing, July 16. The National Guard moved on the state-owned wharves to quell disorder, and Mayor Rossi on the radio made a plea for calm, calling this the greatest emergency since the 1906 disaster. "Keep cool," nervous people were urged. There was no food shortage, they were assured. Convoys of armed trucks were converging on the peninsula from outlying counties. The strike would soon be over.

Small stores were closed and the nineteen restaurants left open were running short of food. Hotels served only their regular guests. Business had stopped and in homes people huddled around radios waiting for news flashes. Few automobiles were seen on the streets as motorists conserved their gasoline for an exit from the city if the strike continued.

Through the day many were hauled into court on charges of assault and battery, for beat-up gangs were cruising in cars to smash the plate-glass windows of stores still open. Pilferers lurked in alleys; newsboys were driven from the corners. Automobiles filled with self-appointed Vigilantes began racing through the streets, breaking into the premises of Communists and others suspected of being radicals. Stacks of alien literature were burned or torn up, furniture was wrecked, pictures smashed, and people beaten. Following in the wake of these Vigilantes came police, who arrested five hundred persons "said to be" Communists or sympathizers of the cause.

The transcontinental telephone wires between San Francisco and Washington were busy through three days. Sporadic violence continued; but people confined in their homes grew restless. In strong front-page editorials the newspapers stormed against the strike. San Francisco had isolated itself from the nation, was being throttled by the senseless strife.

Slowly public opinion swung. The municipal streetcar workers voted to return to work, for civil-service jobs were at stake. The general strike lost its sting with the return of the carmen and with the lifting of restrictions on food and gasoline. Shops opened. The panic was past. On July 19 the general strike committee, by a close vote, ordered the resumption of work.

Two days later teamsters decided to terminate their strike, and again the waterfront unions were alone. On July 21 the Waterfront Employers proffered a new set of proposals and along the Pacific Coast the unions voted to submit to arbitration. The end of the ten weeks' strike came on July 31, 1934. The unions lined up on the waterfront and in a show of solidarity marched across the weathered Embarcadero, back to work.

A six-hour day was awarded the longshoremen, together with wages of 95 cents an hour straight time and $1.40 an hour overtime. Hiring halls were to be jointly controlled. The International Longshoremen's Association, and Harry Bridges, claimed a victory.

San Francisco had left another passing point behind, emerging from what the *Nation* called "one of the most harrowing records of brutality to be found outside of Hitler's Third Reich." Repercussions from the Battle of Rincon Hill were to echo along the waterfront for four years to shake down poorly financed shipping structures, companies dying to the requiem of their "ghost port," for a deadly blow had been dealt to private enterprise.

Walter Lippmann
SOCIETY AND THE STRIKE

(July 17, 1934) Whatever the general public and the authorities may think of the shipping dispute, they are now confronted with a situation where it is impossible for them to be neutral. They are compelled by the general strike to take measures to defeat the general strike.[1]

The particular issues between management and men are immediately swallowed up in the urgent need of the people for food, for safety of movement, for the right to proceed with their own affairs. A general strike is in its very nature a strike not against certain employers or even against the whole class of employers but against the public and against public authority. It is bound to enlist against organized labor, however just may have been the original complaint, the force of that public opinion which ultimately wields the whole power of government.

When that happens, organized labor is bound to lose and to be the victim of a severe reaction.

The ordinary localized strike is deplored but tolerated in free states because it is recognized that there does not yet exist a satisfactory system of representative government for industry. It is a very difficult thing to devise a system which really works under all conditions, to bring management and labor into a legal relationship which is certain to do justice and to maintain efficiency. If such a system existed, the strike and the lockout would become obsolete and would be outlawed. That they are still a recognized form of industrial adjustment is a confession that their legal and moral equivalent has not been achieved.

Reprinted with permission of The Macmillan Company from *Interpretations: 1933–1935* by Walter Lippmann. Copyright 1936 by Walter Lippmann.
Walter Lippmann (1889–   ) is dean of American journalists and author.
[1] The San Francisco general strike grew out of the longshoremen's strike which had been in progress since early spring. It was brief, commencing June 16 and terminating June 19. General Hugh S. Johnson visited the scene and took a vigorous stand, in characteristically picturesque language, against the general strike.

Nevertheless, even the most democratic community in recognizing the right to strike will not recognize it as an unlimited and absolute right. As a matter of fact, in any severe test the right will be found to be limited. The state will permit the strikers to attack the profits of their employers; it will not permit them to starve a city or paralyze its whole economic life or shut down essential services on which depend the health and the security of the whole community. The state will tolerate strikes if they hit only particular groups of employers and shareholders; it will excuse inconvenience and some economic loss. But it will strike against a strike which is general, which is vital, which is broadly destructive.

A general strike is a wholly different thing from a local or particular strike. It is not merely a bigger strike. It is not a weapon for collective bargaining between capital and labor. A general strike affects the whole organized life of the community. Its impact is not upon the particular employers, who may be entitled to no sympathy, but upon the whole mass of the people, who have had no part in the dispute. The general strike is, therefore, a political weapon directed against the state rather than against special interests, and those who take up this weapon compel the state to act. Once a general strike is in effect, the strikers are no longer in direct and primary conflict with their employers; they are in conflict with the mass of people and with organized government.

That the general strike is a political weapon is well known to all experienced labor leaders. They know that it is suicidal folly to call a general strike to settle a specific dispute. A general strike is the last resort of labor when it is fighting, not particular employers, but the political power of the government. It is a weapon to be used against political tyranny or to promote a political revolution. In either case, the strikers mean to strike against the state. But if they do not mean to strike against the state, if they are not fighting political tyranny or engineering a revolution, if what they want is simply to remedy grievances or to improve their position within the existing order, then the general strike is a weapon which will cut the hands of those who wield it. There is reason to believe that the mass of unionists in San Francisco and most of their leaders think they are waging a purely industrial conflict. But they will soon find out that the general strike is not industrial but political. For by calling a general strike they force the government, which protects their right to strike against political employers and is neutral in their particular disputes, to abandon its neutrality and break the strike. The call for a general strike is a compulsion upon all the neutral, innocent forces of the community and upon the authority of the government to oppose the strike.

George Soule
ARE WE GOING TO HAVE A REVOLUTION?

If you want to hear discussions of the future revolution in the United States, do not go to the breadlines and the mill towns, but to Park Avenue and Wall Street, or to the gatherings of young literary men. Well-fed people will anxiously inquire when you think the revolution is coming. They will admit in a large way that profits must be abolished and that some form of Communism might be desirable. In the next breath they may express doubt whether the Democrats can muster enough votes to defeat Mr. Hoover for reelection, or they may oppose moderate reforms like unemployment insurance, or may support the sales tax, which transfers burdens from the rich to the poor. Nevertheless, they vaguely expect profound changes. But you will find that searching for actual flesh-and-blood revolutionary proletarians is a thankless task. Most of those who really suffer from the depression are, according to the best-informed reports, simply stricken dumb by it. Like the Republican administration, they are awaiting nothing more drastic than the return of prosperity.

The strange inertia of those who would benefit most by a revolution and, therefore, it is supposed, will create it, is a subject for frequent remark. When an economist heard that the son of a prominent banker had become a Communist he replied that he would be more impressed if the son of a prominent workman had become a Communist. As a matter of fact, if one can believe the reports of the party membership drives in the *Daily Worker,* converts are numbered by dozens or at most hundreds rather than by thousands or hundreds of thousands. There are a few strikes and riots, to be sure, but why are there not more? The unemployed number between eight and ten million.

This distressing lack of authentic bread riots may shortly be supplied when relief funds run out, as it is almost certain that they will. But bread riots do not necessarily mean revolution. People may smash windows because they are hungry without wanting a governmental overturn or knowing how to bring it about. . . .

"Are We Going to Have a Revolution?" by George Soule from *Harper's,* August 1932. Reprinted by permission of the author.

George Soule (1887–   ) is a prominent American writer on economic and social affairs.

The most solid recent gains of the revolutionary faith have taken place among the intellectuals. So marked has been the drift of writers toward the left that it has been discussed at length in the critical reviews. These persons, who are, with few exceptions, of middle-class origin and training, have identified themselves emotionally with the worker. Not, however, with the American worker as he actually is and thinks, in the great average, but as he ought to be and ought to think, according to revolutionary theory. The worker, in this sense, is not a concrete or representative person, but an abstraction, a Platonic ideal. The workers may not be conscious of the class struggle, but that makes no difference to these intellectuals; the class struggle is there just the same, and the workers are unconscious of it only because their minds have been poisoned by bourgeois ideology. Given the right leadership and education, they will respond. . . .

It would be easy . . . to dismiss the whole subject with a superior smirk, to join the humorous writers of the respectable press in kidding the parlor-pinks. But that is not, I think, either a just or a sound conclusion from these observations. The revolt of the intellectuals has a more valid meaning than it would have if one accepted all their phrases and assumptions at face value. Of course they are not proletarians, and cannot become proletarians. The revolution to which they look forward probably is not imminent. The class struggle does not at this moment threaten to split the American people and lead to a triumph of the downtrodden workers. But the mistake may not lie in the intellectuals' sense of the needs of modern society or its main drift. The mistake may reside in their beliefs as to the exact course which revolution is to take, and in their timing of the process. I believe that, in one sense of the word, we are veritably in the midst of a great social revolution. But a hard-boiled look at the facts indicates that the prevalent popular beliefs about what a revolution is and how it comes about are naïve and unscientific.

These popular beliefs—held, apparently, both by the literary radicals and by the Park Avenue conservatives—may be briefly summarized as follows:

1. Capitalism may soon come to an end by a final collapse.
2. A revolution is a violent overturn of political government.
3. Nothing is essentially changed, or can be changed, before this overturn; after it a brand new order is suddenly set up.
4. The revolution is brought about by rioting mobs who overrun the capital and loot and massacre; there are barricades in the streets, and the air is noisy with gunfire.
5. The riots and mobs result from the discontent of an oppressed class, whose misery is so profound that it is driven to revolt. Actual starvation is the usual motive for revolution.

Every one of these beliefs is almost completely unfounded. A mental picture of revolution based only on these assumptions is sure to be misleading.

First let us examine the collapse of capitalism. This is a vague term. Precisely what is meant by it? The closing of banks? The inability to get money with which to buy goods? Wholesale bankruptcies and defaults? Vanishing of capital values through the shrinking of trade and the disappearance of profits? Widespread unemployment? Starvation? There is not one of these phenomena which has not occurred in previous depressions. In 1907 all banks were closed for days and nobody could get a check cashed. We have had numerous financial panics in which, for a time, no new money at all was invested, and the rates for even collateral loans rose to prohibitive heights. Failures, shrinkage of trade, unemployment—these are the common marks of hard times. Our unsystematic system always fails to work when we have a crisis. Perhaps the difference is one of degree. The system may not be in danger when the curve of economic activity sinks 20 per cent or 30 per cent. But perhaps at, say, a decline of 47 per cent it will pitch over into the abyss. In order to make the argument conclusive, let us imagine that the drop of the curve will be 100 per cent. All businesses shut down, all railroads stop running, all banks are closed. All stocks and bonds, all deeds to real estate become worthless. Everybody is unemployed, nobody has a cent of income. What would happen?

What would happen would depend, not on exterior conditions, but upon what was in people's minds. If they were still imbued with habits of trading, of individualistic competition, of accumulation, they would immediately start to rebuild capitalism. . . .

Capitalism is not going to collapse. It *did* collaspe in the fall of 1929. It has collapsed many times before—1921, 1893, 1873, for instance. The point is that a collapse of capitalism does not necessarily lead to a revolutionary change. The revolution depends on what is in men's minds and habits. Capitalism fails, in some degree, every time we have a depression. It is rebuilt every time we come out of one. The whole building does not crash down in dust and splinters, to be sure, but parts of the roof give way, walls sag and crumble, foundations rot. Whether we replace them or abandon the old structure and erect a new building depends on something more profound than the chronic unworkability of individualism in production and distribution. Kreugers may commit suicide, railroad companies may go into receivership, banks may close. But that does not mean that new Kreugers, new railroad companies, and new banks may not eventually take their places, and carry on in essentially the same way.

Nor is it true that a revolution is a sudden, violent overturn of political government. That is, the kind of revolution the intellectuals really are talking about is not that. Governments are overturned by violence every few years, and all over the world, without bringing any change in the way people make their living, or in the relationship of classes, or in the ideals of rulers. . . .

The progress of a typical revolution may . . . be crudely divided into the following steps. These steps are not strictly successive; some go on simultaneously with others.

1. The development of wide disparities of wealth and power;
2. Blind, sporadic, and unsuccessful protests from the oppressed classes;
3. Stern and efficient repression of discontent;
4. A long process of widespread disillusionment;
5. A long process of criticism, ridicule, and reformulation of ideas by intellectuals;
6. Loss of faith in themselves and their institutions by many in the ruling classes;
7. Rise in welfare and power of the oppressed classes;
8. Reforms from above;
9. Accession to power of moderate revolutionaries;
10. Last of all, what is usually called revolution—violence and dictatorship by an extremist minority—perhaps to be followed by temporary reactions.

The final developments do not alway occur. They did not occur, for instance, in the American Revolution: the moderates remained in power and established a stable government. Minor revolutionary changes in English government have been made without any violent revolt by the extremists. A revolution need not reach the final stages if the moderates are sufficiently capable and resolute to make the necessary changes and to defeat the inevitable opposition from the reactionaries. But if they allow confusion to go on, and if the success of the revolution is endangered, the aroused activists among the people will almost inevitably support a radical dictatorship by the hundred per-centers.

If there is truth in this analysis, it is not strange that while the masses in the United States now appear to be inert and non-revolutionary, there are revolutionary fears in high places, and the chief vocal opposition to the existing regime comes from a few writers and technical experts. This is precisely what we should expect. Ideas of revolutionary implication are bound to arise first among the best educated and those near to power, not among those who are in the depths of penury and hopelessness.

Acknowledging that prediction in this field can have no pretension to scientific assurance, and that the unexpected may always occur, let us fancifully lay out—on the basis of what has usually happened in the past—the probable course of any future overturn of capitalism in this country. It will presumably take some such form as this.

First, there will in the course of time be many riots, strikes, and demonstrations, not for the most part revolutionary in purpose, but prompted by immediate conditions. These will be firmly suppressed by groups who have supreme faith in the traditional forms of "Americanism." They will not produce a revolution.

Meanwhile those who deal in ideas will increasingly express dislike of the existing culture and will expose and ridicule its outstanding figures. They will build up new conceptions of the right way to conduct affairs. Not all intellectuals will do this, but those who do will gain a larger and larger following. This process will be, as it has been in the past, spasmodic. It will grow rapidly at some times and will falter at others. But, over a long period, it will make headway. It will eventually provide a body of new ideas, sanctioned not solely or even mainly by insecure proletarians, but by a large body of cultivated, comparatively well-to-do Americans. The most efficient advocates of the new order will not be unwashed day laborers from the steel mills but white-collared citizens of Main Street. There will be general acknowledgment, except among a few capitalists, corporation presidents, politicians, members of patriotic societies, and the more densely ignorant strata, that a society governed by competition, unchecked private acquisition of wealth, and lack of intelligent foresight and planning, is injurious, ridiculous, and outmoded.

Reforms will be made which will increase the power and wealth of the potential governors of a new society and of the classes with which they are allied. The importance of the business executive (divorced from ownership and profits), of the technician, of the management engineer, of the practical social scientist will be greatly enhanced in industry, finance, and politics. Organized farmers and organized labor will achieve greater recognition than in the past, and in co-operation with active management will force the adoption of measures of planning and control which will improve their status. Their leaders will become really influential.

The result of these reforms will be, not to satisfy the rising classes and leaders, but to make them more radical and active. We had a taste of this development just after the War, when organized labor and the organized farmers had become more powerful than ever before, when unemployment had virtually disappeared, and the farmers were really making money, and when movements for government ownership of railways and other economic and political changes made real though temporary headway. The vigorous agitation for the Plumb Plan in 1919 was a result, not of the desperate condition of railway labor, but of its growing power.

Corruption and incompetence among the traditional powers of

government and finance will become more prevalent and injurious than ever. These powers will be sustained less than at present by faith in their legitimacy and necessity, and more by cynical clutching for immediate advantage, stupid assertion of outworn dogma, and ineffectual efforts at repression of the rising forces. Their elements of strength and intelligence will be drained away by the new movements.

Abuses and confusion will finally produce a crisis which will lead the newly powerful classes and leaders to move actively for more thorough-going changes than have previously been made. Almost nobody will believe that the old regime can or will do what is necessary. A shift in the governing powers will take place—probably by constitutional means. Then, and only then, will begin the critical period when the capacity of the more moderate reformers who have gained power will be tested, and when it will be decided whether the irreconcilable revolutionaries will gain the ascendancy.

On the basis of this prediction, it looks as if we had begun to float on a revolutionary tide but were still far from its flood. Prophecy of this sort, as I have already said, is extremely uncertain. Nobody can tell how rapidly the current may flow around the next headland. All one can do is to chart the course which it has generally followed in the past. But of one thing I am sure. As long as people wait for the downtrodden and the hopeless to produce a revolution, the revolution is far away. Revolutions are made, not by the weak, the unsuccessful, or the ignorant, but by the strong and the informed. They are processes, not merely of decay and destruction, but of advance and building. An old order does not disappear until a new order is ready to take its place.

Harry Golden
RACE RIOTS AND REVOLUTION

For thirty years Southern legislators and legislatures waged legal war against the Negro. They disfranchised him, denied him schools,

From *Mr. Kennedy and the Negroes* by Harry Golden, pp. 38–39, 47–50, 57–58. Copyright © 1964 by Harry Golden. Reprinted by permission of The World Publishing Company.

Harry Golden (1902–   ) is an American journalist and was editor of the *Carolina Israelite*.

hospitals, and access to tax-supported facilities and public accommodations. They refused to prosecute the men who lynched Negroes and refused to condemn the men who regularly defiled Negro women. The politicians of the South constantly boasted of their paternal love, knowing all the time that their strategy would help maintain the *status quo*. Nor were conditions much better in the North. Northerners penned the Negro into ghettos and kept him uneducated, unskilled, and consequently unemployed. It was a war of subjugation and I doubt seriously that the Negro was biding his time. He was humiliated and degraded, ruthlessly proscribed, pushed to the absolute conditions of survival. Yet he did not mutiny. Why?

The social revolution of the American Negro, as a matter of fact, comes at a time when those conditions of survival are appreciably better than they have ever been, considerably better than the conditions most of the rest of the world knows.

Why did the Negro wait? Why did he only begin to make his move in the late 1930s? Why did these moves become powerful only in the late 1950s and early 1960s? Roy Wilkins, head of the four hundred thousand members of the National Association for the Advancement of Colored People, has given his version:

> ". . . this new push? It's cumulative. It's the emergence of Africa. It's being hungry. It's the G.I. Bill. It's major-league baseball with Negroes. It's the eight thousand to ten thousand Negroes graduating from college each year. It's kids being impatient. . . ."[1]

World War I gave many Negroes the opportunity to see that there was not equal poverty and equal segregation everywhere. Negroes who served in France quickly realized that the taboos their Southern neighbors insisted upon were not at all natural. The French and the English cheered the Negro soldier just as they cheered the white doughboy. In addition, the Negro soldier was part of the morale and camaraderie of the whole army. It could not help but make a difference. And there were thousands of other Negro soldiers who left the South for the first time and were stationed in the ports of embarkation, in the training centers, and in the hospitals of America.

While studying the history of lynching, I was amazed at the incidence of lynchers burning and hanging Negroes after World War I, the sole reason being that the Negro was wearing an army uniform. This uniform had not only made the Negro the white man's equal at least for the duration and, more than that, it had put the Negro under the protec-

---

[1] *Time*, August 30, 1963, p. 14.

tion of the Federal Government. It was a symbolic protection just as it was a symbolic equality, but the symbolism was a portent which enraged the lynchers.

The real change World War I made in the Negro's condition was to create a demand by Northern war industries for hundreds of thousands of Southern Negroes for factory work. However cruel it was, the North offered better prospects and better opportunities than the South. The North kept him bottled up in ghettos, but it did not bar the way of his son from becoming a dental technician or lathe operator, if he could make it on his own. Negroes received wages comparable with the white man's. He got jobs heretofore solely the monopoly of whites. He sent his children to school.

More and more Negroes came. And right after the war, they showed no disposition to return to what they had had before. In fact, they fought for their new life. To see how times had changed, one has only to compare the race riot which exploded in Atlanta in 1906 with the one that broke out in Chicago in 1919.

In 1906 Georgia was in the process of making absolute and final its disfranchisement and segregation of the Negro. Part of this campaign was helped by an inflammatory press which kept reporting fictitious attacks on white women by illusory black rapists. On Saturday, September 22, the newspapers reported that the assaults had reached epidemic stage. Four white women had been raped. On Peachtree and Decatur streets a mob gathered, a Negrophobe harangued them, and the mob turned and lynched a colored bystander. The animal was loose.

A thousand men marched to a Negro skating rink, there to be turned back by police. They broke into a Negro barbershop and lynched the two barbers. As the mob swelled, it took to stopping trolleys and killing the Negro passengers. Firemen tried drowning the mob with hoses, but the men laughed and moved back out of range. Already downtown Atlanta was a shambles. On the outskirts of the city, police and other citizens were warning Negroes to go home. Negro saloons, pawnshops, and homes were burned and their occupants beaten. By Sunday morning the mayor had to summon the state militia.

By this time, however, the mob was armed, having stormed the sports shops and hardware stores for guns. An armed battle broke out in Brownsville, a Negro settlement two miles outside of Atlanta. One company of cavalry stormed the settlement, killing two Negroes and capturing two hundred and fifty-seven others, all of whom were sentenced to the chain gang for carrying weapons. The infantry finally quelled the disorder and for several weeks Atlanta lived under martial law. How many Negroes were killed has never been determined. The official estimate was fifty, but that figure was obviously forwarded by the Chamber of Commerce. That many innocent Negroes were dragged from trolleys and run down in the alleys in the first hour alone.

The riot had its inception in a long political war in which both sides seized upon the "Negro issue." The two contending newspapers had long since forgotten why they had joined the war, and were building immense circulation gains with sensational stories about the violation of Southern womanhood. Atlanta Negroes were helpless and the white power structure of the city indifferent until the mob began smashing up white stores and shooting down white policemen, ambushes later conveniently attributed to Negro "rapists."

The Chicago race riot was another story. On the last Sunday of July, 1919, a Negro boy at a Chicago beach swam over an imaginary segregation line. He was immediately stoned by white boys who knocked him from a raft into the water where he drowned. Colored people rushed to the policeman and asked him to arrest the stone-throwers. The policeman refused. As the body of the drowned boy was brought to shore more rocks were thrown on both sides. The policeman held to his refusal to make an arrest. Fighting broke out on the beach, then spread to all borders of the "black belt."

Three weeks before this riot began, the Chicago *Daily News* had assigned its poet and special reporter, Carl Sandburg, to do a series of articles on the booming Negro population. His articles had been running for two weeks and were on the verge of inspiring some sort of concerted community action when the stone-throwers, followed by the delinquents and then the hoodlums, took over. "Then," writes Sandburg, "as usual nearly everybody was more interested in the war than how it got loose." At the end of three days, twenty Negroes and fourteen white men were dead and a large number of Negro houses had been burned.

Grim as it was, the Chicago race riot was a break with the past. The riot was not inspired by claims of race supremacy nor by fears of Negro sexuality, nor was the nation indifferent. It is no oversimplification to say the Chicago race riot stated the problem we still labor to resolve. The virtue of Sandburg's story is that he understood these differences: that this riot came about not because menace and terror stalked the streets but because the Negro demanded equity, the freedom to use public accommodations as he sees fit.

Three new conditions attended this 1919 riot. During the war, the Black Belt population of Chicago had doubled from fifty thousand to one hundred thousand. No new houses had been built to accommodate these people. Large numbers of returning Negro soldiers had also settled in Chicago as had thousands of Negroes imported to the city to service its wartime industries. In addition, into Chicago yearly poured streams of Negroes fleeing the lynchings in Texas, Virginia, Alabama, Tennessee, and Mississippi.

None of these Negroes, however, was helpless. The Negroes of Chicago had political strength. A city administration had recently appointed some twenty Negro precinct officials. The mayor's opponents had failed to defeat him by calling him "nigger-lover."

The last and most significant development was that thousands of white men and Negroes stuck together during the riot. White and Negro officials of the Stockyards Labor Council asked the public to witness that they were shaking hands as "brothers" and could not be counted on for any share of the mob shouts and ravages.

A large body of mixed Americans—Poles, Negroes, Lithuanians, Italians, Irishmen, Germans, Slovaks, Russians, Mexicans, Yankees, Englishmen, Scotsmen—proclaimed their opposition to any violence to either white union men or Negro union men.

Sandburg prophesied in his little monograph, *The Chicago Race Riots,* that as the Negro drove for equality there would be fewer lynchings and more riots. For these riots would be provoked not because a large mass of illiterate, semiliterate, and unskilled workers moved in, but because the Negro would become more literate, more skilled, and more desirous of his fair share.[2] Ten years later, this same Chicago sent to the House of Representatives Oscar De Priest, the first Negro elected to national office since the Reconstruction. (Atlanta did not send a Negro to the state legislature until 1962.)

What the race riot of 1919 portended came to fruition with De Priest's election. After World War I, the Negro population of northern cities increased on an average of 500 per cent. This increase made sure that the racial problem was no longer a sectional one. In leaving the South, the Negro left a rural area where he was disfranchised for an urban area where he had the right to vote. In the cities he was concentrated, but it was by virtue of that concentration that he could force political action. . . .

Years ago no Southern merchant sought the Negro for a customer because the Negro was impoverished. Yet there were whites who even then found in him a source of profit. I have described in *Forgotten Pioneer* how the Jewish itinerant peddler found a role in the South by filling a great need of the Negro. The Jewish peddler supplied the rural Negroes with goods and necessities at a time when the midtown white

[2] Carl Sandburg, *The Chicago Race Riots* (New York, Harcourt, Brace & Howe, 1920), p. 16.

wanted no Negro business. The peddler extended credit which no other white man ever extended. It was from this peddler that the Negro bought mattresses, shoes, clocks, and clothes for his family. The Jewish peddler let the Negro try on the garment he might wish to purchase. In a midtown store, once a Negro touched a garment he had to buy it, whether it fit or not.

Much the same might be said of the Jewish storekeeper who set up in the Negro ghetto. In their way, the Jewish peddler and slum storekeeper conspired unwittingly to keep the Negro in check. They furnished those immediate needs which, while not making the Negro contented, made him less mutinous.

But sometime around the late 1930s and early 1940s the midtown storekeeper beckoned to the Negro. The midtown white was now openly competing for the Negro purchasing power. Twelve dollars a week to an unemployed white man might be a dole, but to an unemployed Negro it was a fortune. These stores offered easy credit (and still do) and they let Negroes take goods home with no down payment. Here, too, the Negro found better quality at cheaper prices. Soon enough, the midtown white storekeeper found the Negro business a bonanza.

Hundreds of Negroes who had had no occasion to leave their slum district began making the trip to midtown. They discovered how dismaying it was to sit in the back of the bus, how unfair to contribute to an entrepreneur's profit and not be allowed to use a rest-room while doing so, how uncomfortable not to be able to eat at the snack bar while spending money in the store.

In its way it is ironic that the Negro pressed his right to use such facilities, not in the courts but in the stores themselves. For the Negro knew the argument is not whether he shall be allowed into the store; he knows there is general agreement on that. It is how he shall be treated within. It is not whether he shall be allowed to spend his money but whether one of the clerks who takes it will be a Negro or not. So he won his point in the store by organizing sit-ins and boycotts, knowing that anything that interrupts trade panics the business community of the town. He gauged his opponent well. Throughout the South, the first segregationist to sell out is always the merchant. If the White Citizens Councils ask him to lose money while they win their fight, he simply deserts them and seeks refuge and repair in an anonymous citizens' report that urges that the store be integrated and the rest-rooms and water fountains made available to all.

The Negro revolt is *now*, in the 1960s, not only because the attitude of the whole country has changed, not only because the Negro's lot is appreciably better, as is the country's; not only because he, the Negro, is better educated and better informed; not only because he has had examples to sustain him; not only because the courts sustain his revolts; but also because the major overpowering institution of the country—business—is waving welcome whether it knows that it is waving or not.

Seymour Martin Lipsett
and
Paul Seabury

BERKELEY: A GENUINE REVOLUTION

Improbable as it may have seemed to outsiders, events at the Berkeley campus of the University of California during the last three months of 1964 constituted a small-scale but genuine revolution. Through continuous violation of university regulations, sit-ins, almost daily mass demonstrations, and finally a strike by students and teaching assistants, the authority of both the administration and the faculty had become virtually nonexistent at Berkeley by December.

The immediate cause was the withdrawal of a privilege. In mid-September, political groups and civil-rights organizations were barred from a twenty-six-foot-long strip of pavement at the entrance to the campus that traditionally had been used as a site for informal debate. More recently, it had been used for fund raising and recruiting for off-campus activities, both forbidden on university property.

Much of the intensity of student reaction to this ruling is directly attributable to a change of attitude on the part of young people all over the country—a change brought about by their participation in the civil-rights movement. Moreover, both students and faculty members at Berkeley, as at other large universities, are unhappy about changes taking place in American higher education today. In protesting the university administration's political restrictions, they were also voicing a discontent

From *The Reporter* (January 28, 1965). Copyright 1965 by The Reporter Magazine Company. Reprinted by permission of the authors and *The Reporter*.

Seymour Martin Lipset (1922–   ), a sociologist, and Paul Seabury (1923–   ), a political scientist, have been members of the University of California faculty at Berkeley, California.

with the nonpolitical aspects of university policy. American students today are more concerned with ultimate moral ends than with responsibility or consequences. The civil-rights movement has provided them with a moral cause, and the example of civil disobedience with a tactic.

In the last two or three years, a civil-rights movement emanating from colleges in the San Francisco Bay area has conducted sit-ins in hotels, restaurants, banks, supermarkets, and newspapers to demand the hiring of Negroes. Of the students arrested in these demonstrations, many were strongly influenced by various leftish groups that are currently stronger in the Bay area than anywhere else in the United States.

Steering Left

The campus protests crystallized in the organization of the Free Speech Movement (FSM) early in October, with Mario Savio, a twenty-two-year-old philosophy major, as its leading figure. Savio spent last summer in Mississippi and was arrested during a sit-in demonstration in San Francisco last spring. He is an emotional, effective speaker and calls himself a "democrat with a small *d.*" Membership in the FSM is open to any individual or organization that chooses to affiliate. Hard-core support is estimated at around five hundred; by December as many as three or four thousand students were committed to all-out support, and according to FSM claims three thousand nonstudents from the university community were supporting the movement. The executive committee is composed of delegates from affiliated groups, elected representatives of graduate-student organizations, unaffiliated students meeting in assembly, and elected spokesmen for the nonstudents in the university community. But the real leadership of the movement is provided by a steering committee (appointed by the executive committee) of less than a dozen members who are considerably to the left of the executive committee. The political convictions of the steering committee notwithstanding, the overwhelming majority of student followers of the FSM, including those who have engaged in the sit-ins, are moderates whose politics are limited to the civil-rights cause. A minority within the FSM—drifting in and out of affiliation —has attempted to restrain the more extreme elements and has included at various times two democratic socialist organizations, the Young Democrats, and a variety of conservative groups, including Youth for Goldwater.

The growth of FSM must be ascribed to a series of blunders caused to some degree by the fact that various crucial decisions have been made at different levels of the local campus administration as well as by the president, the regents, and the governor. Repeatedly, the university took an uncompromising position on a variety of matters, and then, under FSM pressure, backed down and accepted conditions it had previously rejected out of hand. Naturally, this behavior encouraged the FSM to increase its demands.

In mid-September, the students were demanding only the return of the "right" to carry on political activity on the twenty-six-foot strip; gradually this demand grew into an insistence on the elimination of all university restriction of political activity on campus. The FSM's position is that there should be no restrictions besides those imposed by the civil authority for any public place, and that the only enforcement agency should be the police—the reverse of the one usually taken by leftist student movements abroad and people concerned with academic freedom in this country. These groups have maintained that universities should govern their own affairs, and that public authority is a greater threat to academic freedom than university administration. Indeed, in much of Latin America, students are legally protected from arrest within university precincts. Some who oppose the FSM on this position point to the fact that the city and county police, summoned when a campus police car was held captive for thirty-six hours on October 1 and 2, were not sent into action against the students by President Kerr, who had authority over them. By the time of the second major sit-in on December 3, Governor Edmund G. "Pat" Brown took over control of law enforcement on campus and, against the explicit advice of the university administration, ordered police to arrest students sitting in at Sproul Hall.

The most important reason for the weak position of the university administration during the past four months has been that there were few on campus, among either students or faculty, who supported its original position on the political-rights issues: that a university has the authority to restrict the collection of funds for, or the advocacy of, off-campus political activities. The administration, in fact, modified its original position by early November and agreed to all the major student demands except the right to advocate and plan unlawful actions—chiefly the sit-ins. This position was ratified by the regents, and though the FSM continued to denounce university policy, it seemed at the time that it had lost the bulk of its support. The university returned the moral advantage and mass backing to the FSM by bringing charges over the Thanksgiving weekend against Savio and three other leaders for having organized the original sit-ins and capturing the campus police car almost two months earlier. To many, this seemed an implicit violation of the signed agreement between the university and the student leaders that had brought the police-car episode to an end. The December sit-in and strike were a result of this action.

Kerr as Prophet

The opposition to the FSM among faculty members and students was based on antagonism to the use of illegal means, such as campus sit-ins and deliberate violations of university regulations, to attain political ends that might have been gained through conventional channels of redress. But these critics, many of whom felt that the use of illegal tactics was part of a conscious effort by extremists to undermine faith in the democratic system, were constrained to silence by their belief that the university's position was morally indefensible.

The real meaning of these events cannot be understood by limiting the discussion to an analysis of the right of on-campus advocacy, or of the use of illegal and extremist methods. Despite the FSM's name, free speech has never been the central issue—Savio has admitted as much. The revolt is not just against the injustices of society at large but also against the university as a microcosm of that society. To fully understand the student and faculty response, one must recognize that the American university community is becoming increasingly restive as a result of changes in our system of higher education. Ironically, a vivid description of these changes can be found in *The Uses of the University*, by the president of the University of California, Clark Kerr.

Kerr warns that major universities have become predominantly research institutions; that teaching, particularly on the undergraduate level, holds little interest for many on the faculty; that administrators tend to become preoccupied with raising funds and gaining influence; that faculties have little institutional loyalty, with many professors choosing their universities on a careerist basis. These circumstances produce considerable resentment among students, and Kerr, in fact, predicted a sharp increase in tensions and conflicts between students and instructors.

The large degree of political free speech long enjoyed at Berkeley, the size and eminence of the university, and the high caliber of its students and teachers are the very reasons why a mass student uprising took place there. Berkeley students have always made more use of their political rights to meet and speak freely on campus than American students elsewhere. Every sort of extreme-left group is represented—the DuBois Club (Communist), the Young Socialist Alliance (Trotskyist), the Independent Socialist Club (Revolutionary Marxist Socialist), and the Progressive Labor Council (Maoist)—and so are various rightist groups. Even the American Nazi Party has been presenting speakers on campus and has announced that it will open headquarters nearby. The new student revolt began precisely where students were most free to organize.

For years, Berkeley has been evolving into a research center perched precariously on a mountain of somewhat neglected undergraduates. These students feel remote from the internationally renowned on the faculty. To them, Berkeley is a big, impersonal place, and their restlessness has found an outlet in the strikingly fervid support the FSM obtained even from students with little interest in politics. These young people and many on the faculty cherish the notion that the revolt will help to establish better contact between students and faculty and to increase autonomy of the Berkeley campus within the vast machinery of the "multiversity"—nine campuses of the statewide university system geared into a cumbersome synchronization.

Though the ideology of the movement has been directed mainly against the university, the idea of alienation has become the intellectual rallying point for a rejection of all power centers. The tragedy is that many within the university community who have diverse grievances against aspects of the university have been drawn into support of a movement whose leaders have seen every crisis as an opportunity to humiliate the university administration and to demonstrate the hollowness of authority.

Following the arrest on December 3 of about eight hundred students for occupying the university administration building, Sproul Hall, many faculty members who had previously ignored the struggle came to the support of the few professors who had defended the FSM, in principle at least, almost from the start. Graduate students and teaching assistants went on strike. Growing faculty support for the FSM resulted not only in the passage of resolutions backing much of the FSM position by the Berkeley Academic Senate (assistant professors and above), but also in the emergence of a variety of faculty grievances against the multiversity system. This accumulation of grievances naturally gravitated to the aggressive leadership of the FSM protest. In early December, dozens of new student organizations, closely linked to the FSM leadership, sprang up to advance special causes.

The strike, which closed down at least half the university, convinced many that peace was worth any price. A number of conservatives on the faculty who disagree in principle with the FSM reluctantly agree that the university has to give up its power to regulate political activities on campus, and on December 8 voted in the Academic Senate for a motion that incorporated almost all FSM demands. While many voted on principle, others voted for it as a strike settlement by the weaker party.

The faculty voted for the right of free speech on all issues and the right to organize for off-campus political action, including civil-rights demonstrations. The regents accepted all but two points. First, they refused to yield to a committee of the Academic Senate their authority over matters of student discipline for infractions of rules governing political matters. (They did provide, however, that the faculty could take part in local campus administration judgment of such infractions.) Second, while affirming the rights of students and their organizations to advocate anything on campus that is lawful under the provisions of the First and Fourteenth Amendments, the regents continued to insist on the university's right to prohibit *organized* efforts to prepare illegal off-campus activities—a restriction aimed primarily at the organization of civil-rights sit-ins. A special emergency faculty committee, which had been elected on December 14 to represent the Academic Senate and which had discussed these issues with the regents before they met, concluded that the new regulations promised by the regents for early this year will grant almost all that the faculty and the FSM have demanded in the area of free speech.

The new year brought an uneasy truce. During the holidays, the faculty emergency committee worked hard to obtain a broad consensus for reasonable regulations governing "time, place, and manner" of political activity acceptable to faculty, students, and regents. On January 2, just before classes resumed, the regents appointed a new acting chancellor, Martin Meyerson, the forty-two-year-old dean of the School of Environmental Design. Meyerson already has shown strength and sophistication in dealing with the crisis, and he commands wide support from all major groups within what had been a badly divided Academic Senate.

This truce has been welcomed by the great majority of the students. For most of them, the events of the past fall were emotionally shattering. In delaying a resumption of civil disobedience, the FSM leadership has shown awareness of this changed mood. The imminence of final exams in late January has introduced a note of realism into the picture, even among the FSM supporters. Noon rallies on the steps of Sproul Hall do not attract the throngs of the pre-Christmas period. Within the faculty, there is now a general satisfaction with the promised reforms and a feeling that any further acts of civil disobedience by the FSM cannot be tolerated.

The Berkeley revolt is not just another California curiosity. This new style of campus political action may affect other campuses, and eventually our national political life. The new student generation is brilliant and aggressively serious. The number of graduate students who spend years at a university increases steadily. And the frustrations so eloquently described by Clark Kerr in *The Uses of the University* occur everywhere. The student leftist movements are growing and probably will continue to grow. Student groups at many colleges have already voted support of the FSM, and Mario Savio has addressed students at several universities, including Columbia and Harvard. The indifference to legality shown by serious and dedicated students threatens the foundations of democratic order. Extremism in the pursuit of liberty was quite recently a favorite slogan of the radical Right. Berkeley has shown that anyone can play this game. But while the game goes on, this great university is in danger of losing its stature and its independence.

5
East and West

The results of the world wars of the twentieth century have been particularly clear in the realms of imperialism and colonialism. The wars ended Europe's hegemony in the world at large, in part by the sheer physical destruction of the old colonial powers. K. N. Panikkar, former Indian ambassador to China, explains from an Asiatic point of view the effects of World War I upon the relations between East and West. As a result of the breakdown of colonialism, there is now much discussion of the future role and importance of Asia and an increasing interest in the civilization of the more "scrutable" East.

Can there be a "meeting of East and West" culturally? American philosopher F. S. C. Northrop conceives of two essential components in culture: the "aesthetic," represented by the East; and the "theoretic," represented by the West. He feels that these two components are compatible in the ideal society. Edward Conze, British authority on Buddhism, feels a meeting of East and West might be based on the anticipations of Western thought which he sees in Buddhism. Buddhists view the world as such a place of suffering that it must be renounced to be endured. "The discoveries that philosophers and psychologists have made in recent years about the central importance of anxiety at the very core of our being, have quite a Buddhist ring about them," says Conze.

In this new climate of opinion, Europeans, with the notable exception of Winston Churchill, hesitate to defend their imperialistic record, though they may attempt, like John Strachey, a Laborite in the British parliament, to be as accurate as possible about the actual nature of colonial exploitation. European guilt about the imperialist past is not always convincing, at least to the intellectuals of the emerging nations, although the "neo-colonialist United States" has largely replaced European colonialism as a target.

Americans naturally resent and repudiate colonialist charges, but the inaccuracy or injustice of the cry "neo-colonialism" is actually that it exaggerates the power of the West. It is now clear that the twentieth century is no longer one of Western domination; Western emphasis, including even the events stressed in the study of history, is over in every respect. The true impact of the East is being felt.

Meantime, East and West meet technologically and industrially. Despite the passions aroused by colonialism or neo-colonialism, Asiatics want the benefits of Westernization. The Chinese novelist Lau Shaw is a Chinese intellectual who supported the Communists against the Nationalist regime in the hope of achieving greater progress along Western lines. His story *Grandma Takes Charge* points up the urgent need for Westernization in the East.

Winston S. Churchill
EAST OF SUEZ

1899: The Ruin and Rescue of the Sudan

In the summer of 1886, when all the troops had retreated to Wady Halfa and all the Soudan garrisons had been massacred, the British people averted their eyes in shame and vexation from the valley of Nile. A long succession of disasters had reached their disgraceful culmi-

From *The River War* by Winston Churchill (New York: Universal Publishing and Distributing Corporation, 1964).

Winston S. Churchill (1874–1965) was Prime Minister of England (1940–1945, 1951–1955) and wrote many historical works.

nation. The dramatic features added much to the bitterness and nothing to the grandeur of the tragedy. The cost was heavy. Besides the pain produced by the death of General Gordon, the heavy losses in officers and men, and the serious expenditure of public money, the nation smarted under failure and disappointment, and were, moreover, deeply sensible that they had been humiliated before the whole world. The situation in Egypt was scarcely more pleasing. The reforms initiated by the British Administrators had as yet only caused unpopularity. Baring's interference galled the Khedive and his Ministers. Vincent's parsimony excited contempt. Moncrieff's energy had convulsed the Irrigation Department. Wood's army was the laughing-stock of Europe. Among and beneath the rotten weeds and garbage of old systems and abuses the new seed was being sown. But England saw no signs of the crop; saw only the stubborn husbandmen begrimed with the dust and dirt, and herself hopelessly involved in the Egyptian muddle: and so in utter weariness and disgust, stopping her ears to the gibes and cat-calls of the Powers, she turned towards other lands and other matters.

When the attention of the nation was again directed to Egypt the scene was transformed. It was as though at the touch of an angel the dark morasses of the Slough of Despond had been changed to the breezy slopes of the Delectable Mountains. The Khedive and his Ministers lay quiet and docile in the firm grasp of the Consul-General. The bankrupt State was spending surpluses upon internal improvement. The disturbed Irrigation Department was vivifying the land. The derided army held the frontier against all comers. Astonishment gave place to satisfaction, and satisfaction grew into delight. The haunting nightmare of Egyptian politics ended. Another dream began—a bright if vague vision of Imperial power, of trans-continental railways, of African Viceroys, of conquest and commerce. The interest of the British people in the work of regeneration grew continually. Each new reform was hailed with applause. Each annual Budget was scrutinised with pride. England exulted in the triumph of failure turned into success. There was a general wish to know more about Egypt and the men who had done these great things. In 1893 this desire was satisfied and yet stimulated by the publication of Sir Alfred Milner's 'England in Egypt.' His skilful pen displayed what had been overcome, no less than what was accomplished. By explaining the difficulties he enhanced the achievement. He showed how, while Great Britain was occupied elsewhere, her brilliant, persevering sons had repeated on a lesser scale in Egypt the marvellous evolution which is working out in India. Smaller systems circulate more rapidly. The administrators were guided by experience. The movement had been far swifter, and the results were more surprising. Such was the wonderful story, and it was told in a happy moment. The audience were eager and sympathetic.

The subject was enthralling. The story-teller had a wit and a style that might have brightened the dullest theme. In these propitious circumstances the book was more than a book. The words rang like the trumpet-call which rallies the soldiers after the parapets are stormed, and summons them to complete the victory.

1964: The Destiny of Britain in the Orient

I have always been in favour of preserving both the British relation with Egypt and the Egyptian relation with the Sudan. I trust both British and Egyptian statesmen and administrators will work together with goodwill and for the common advantage for centuries to come. These views are, however, highly controversial. A generation has grown up which knows little of why we were in Egypt and the Sudan, and what our work there was. Uninstructed and ignorant impressions colour the decisions not only of Parliaments but of Cabinets. It is my hope that the story which these pages contain may be some help and encouragement to those young men and women who have still confidence in the destiny of Britain in the Orient. They may learn from it how much harder it is to build up and acquire, than to squander and cast away.

John Strachey
IMPERIALISM AND ECONOMICS

The British conquest of India had momentous economic and political consequences for Britain. . . .

In order to consider the economic consequences we shall have to return to the last decades of the eighteenth century, and trace, if we can, the effect upon the development of the British economy of the unequal trade which the East India Company was carrying on with India. For it was during these decades that the British economy went through that hitherto unprecedented transformation which we now call primary industrialisation.

From *The End of Empire* by John Strachey, pp. 60–68, 188–194. Reprinted by permission of the publisher, Frederick A. Praeger, Inc.

John Strachey (1901–1963) was a British writer and Labor member of Parliament.

Indian historians, following Romesh Chandra Dutt in *Economic History of India Under British Rule* (1902), a school of American and British historians, such as Brook Adams, in his work, *The Law of Civilisation and Decay* (New York, 1910) and William Digby in *Prosperous British India* (1901), as also Marxist analysts, such as R. P. Dutt in his *India To-day*, have taken the view that the fruits of the pillage of India in the late eighteenth century played a major part in providing the initial capital for the contemporary industrial revolution in Britain. This is one aspect of the theory of "the drain", as it is often called, which has played a major part in Indian nationalist propaganda. We must attempt to assess what really happened. For it will appear that this whole issue of whether, or to what extent, one country can get fat by battening upon another: or, conversely, of whether, or to what extent, one country can help another over the critical period in its development, is of the highest present-day political importance. It is certainly a natural assumption that a "drain" of unrequited value, extorted from India (and the West Indies) by Britain not only had dire consequences for the former but also greatly helped the latter to industrialise. The question is a quantitative one. How big a part of that precious initial store of capital, command over which alone enables a nation to begin to industrialise, was provided by the British imperial conquests?

In order to answer such a question we shall have to look at the amount of wealth transferred, unrequited, to Britain, and then attempt to analyse what that wealth really was. In some cases of conquest the amount of wealth forcibly transferred to the conqueror can be estimated without undue difficulty. The treasure which Spain drew from South and Central America in the sixteenth and seventeenth centuries is fairly well known, for example. This is partly because it took the direct and simple form of the importation of gold and silver. But it is partly also because the Spanish system was so highly centralised that the whole of this treasure came, officially at any rate, through the hands of the Casa de Contratación at Seville. A recent historian of imperial Spain, Mr. R. T. Davies, in his book, *The Golden Century of Spain 1501–1621* (Macmillan, 1937), is, for example, able to print as an appendix a table of the total gold and silver imports into Spain from the Americas from 1503 to 1660. At their peak these imports (1591–5) were running at some £4 million a year, to which, we are told, must be added "from 10%–50%" for smuggled imports. Perhaps £5 million to £6 million a year would be the order of magnitude of the sum transferred to Spain. And, since the metals were mined by slaves who were fed and maintained out of American resources not much was probably transferred in the opposite direction, from Spain to the Americas.

No such simple calculation can be made in the case of the East

India Company's trade with India. In the first place, far from importing bullion or precious metals into Britain, the Company was, even after the conquest, hard put to it to avoid exporting them both to India. What it imported from India were above all textiles. Up to the conquest these were paid for in gold and silver. After the conquest of Bengal, as we [have already noted], the Company attempted not to pay for them at all, but to raise the money for their purchase by taxation in the province, and in other provinces too as the conquest extended. This ideal of the Company's ships going out empty and returning laden with free goods was never quite achieved. But it was approached.

Professor Holden Furber in his *John Company at Work* (Harvard University Press, 1948), a leading American authority on this matter, gives us the figures. During the decade 1783-93 only £721,914 in gold were sent to India from Britain. A rate of under £100,000 a year means that the flow of gold had been reduced to a trickle. For the scale of the transactions between the two countries was quite large. For example, in this decade over £23 million of goods from India were imported. On the face of it, it looks as if during this decade, Britain only paid for about £7¼ million worth of the £23 million worth of her imports from India. In fact, the discrepancy was not as extreme as that. For some actual goods, as well as gold, were exported by Britain. In order to illustrate and exemplify the sort of thing that was happening, Professor Furber has given us a detailed account of the cargoes on both the outward and the homeward voyages of the *Berrington,* the ship in which Warren Hastings returned to England in 1785. The *Berrington* had carried out to India various goods, namely lead, copper, steel, woollen clothes and naval stores, to the value of £27,300. She brought back from India cotton piece goods, cotton yarn, indigo, redwood, silk and saltpetre to the value of £119,304. If her voyage was typical, as Professor Furber implies that it was, she was evidently transferring an unrequited value to Britain, on this voyage, of about £90,000. The Indian produced goods were promptly sold at auction in London, to both British and European buyers, and the profit credited to the Company. It is not particularly relevant to our purpose that at this date little of the profit so realised found its way into the pockets of the holders of East India Company stock. For the Company, largely in order to finance Clive's "military transactions", had borrowed extensively in India, above all from its own servants.

What, typically, happened was something like this. Some Company's servant made, say, £20,000 on a contract for supplying bullocks for the baggage train of one of the Company's armies. Or still more frequently such a sum was made in "the country trade", *i.e.,* in trade, either internal or sea-borne, between different places in India, or between India and some other part of Asia, a trade in which, as we saw, the Company's servants engaged at an immense advantage over their Indian competitors. What the lucky man wanted to do was to transfer the money he had made to England for his future use and enjoyment. Accordingly he lent it to the Company in India, which gave him a promise to pay him the amount, with interest, on a certain date in England. At least this is what he did if he did not have much to conceal as to how he had made the money. If he had a good deal to conceal he lent the money, on the contrary, to one of the other East India companies, the Dutch, the Danish, the French, the Ostend, or the Trieste companies, which were still operating in India more or less on British sufferance. If he had still more to conceal he bought diamonds in India and sent them back to England either by ship or overland, through Bagdad, Constantinople and Vienna. Or, yet again, he might speculate again in another trading venture either in the East, or in a voyage back to Europe, which, if successful, would leave his money there on call.

Professor Furber makes a gallant effort to estimate what this jungle of transactions really meant in terms of a transfer of wealth to Britain from India. After complex calculations, involving much guesswork, he comes to the conclusion that during the decade 1783–93, on which he concentrates his researches, something under £2 million a year was being transferred unrequited. This is a surprisingly modest sum. For example, William Digby, in his *Prosperous British India* (1901) calculated that "the drain", or "the tribute", as it was often called, of unrequited value exacted from India averaged £18 million a year during the whole period from Plassey (1757) to Waterloo (1815). But it may be that Professor Furber is nearer the mark. He is a recent and American investigator with no motive for minimising the figure. At any rate, before challenging it, it would be necessary to conduct researches into the original documents, bills of lading and labyrinthine accounts of the East India Company comparable to those undertaken by the professor. Moreover, on consideration, several factors may incline us to suppose that the amount may have been of this order of magnitude. First, applying our multiplier of 10, this would be equivalent to an annual transfer of £20 million in 1959 money. Second, we must remember that Britain was then a country of some 8 or 10 million inhabitants, say a fifth of its present population. Therefore, per capita the transfer would be equivalent to one of £100 million a year to-day. So the amount was modest, though not insignificant.

The explanation of why the devastation of Bengal seems to have resulted in such relatively modest gains for Britain is, surely, that pillage is an almost incredibly wasteful process. Clive's salt monopoly and the virtual monopolising of trade by the Company's servants and their agents produced the famine of 1770 and reduced much of Bengal, in Cornwallis' phrase, to "a jungle inhabited only by wild beasts". But that did not mean that it enriched Britain to any remotely comparable degree. By far the greater part of the values taken from Bengal were simply lost to both countries. Only a minor part was successfully brought to England.

Nevertheless, the inflow to Britain of unrequited value on the above scale, while not very great, may still have been significant for the economy. And this brings us to the question of what it was that was being transferred from India to Britain. It is only too easy to become bewildered by the maze of transactions involved. Not only the above described elaborate transactions between the Company and its own servants are involved, but also the web of exchanges which began to be woven as soon as an Indian cargo reached London. Let us return to the example of the *Berrington*'s cargo, worth £119,000, which reached London in 1885. Let us suppose that a particular "lot" of calicoes, cambrics or silks, was sold at the Company's auctions to an Austrian buyer for, say, £10,000. Let us further suppose that this £10,000 enabled the Company to pay part of its debt to the *Berrington*'s most distinguished passenger, Warren Hastings, the Company's retiring Governor-General. During his period of office the Governor-General had made, in one way or another, considerable sums which he had then lent, in Bengal, to the Company. These debts had now to be repaid to him out of the sales of the Company's goods. Thus the £10,000 now passed to him.

Now let us consider what Hastings did with the money and with all the other sums so paid to him. One thing which he did was to buy back his ancestral manor of Daylesford in Worcestershire and re-equip the estate. And in this he was typical of many of the Nawobs. The theme of repurchasing or redeeming run-down or mortgaged family estates runs through the histories of early "Indians". This, for example, was Clive's own first action. And this was the result of my ancestor, Sir Henry Strachey's, first voyage to India. Imprudent management had so heavily mortgaged the family estate in Somerset that it would have been lost within a few months of the time when Clive engaged the young Strachey as his Secretary for his third and last voyage to India. When Clive discovered this situation he, with characteristic magnificence, lent Strachey £10,000 to be duly repaid when Strachey got his share out of the system of better-regulated pillage which, as we noticed, Clive went out to establish in Bengal. Again Scotland contains many an estate, the land of which was originally drained or the farm improved, by returning "Indians", who owed their places and opportunities to Dundas. For in the seventeen-eighties and 'nineties Dundas, as the younger Pitt's political manager in such matters, was busily staffing India with his compatriots. The significance of this for our purpose is that many of the Nawobs appear to have used their fortunes *productively* when they came home. They invested in improving their estates or in buying new ones. They took part in the revolution in agricultural technique which was going on throughout the eighteenth century and which underlay and made possible the industrial revolution.

In order to trace the significance of this, let us return to our imaginary example of the £10,000 "lot" of textiles sold to an Austrian buyer out of the *Berrington's* cargo. Since the textiles had been taken from Bengal without any equivalent value being sent there, the transaction meant that Britain could now import £10,000 of corn, or anything else, without having to make and export anything in return. If, on the other hand, the silks in the cargo were sold to an English buyer[1] the transaction meant that the wealthier classes in Britain could satisfy their desire for fine textiles, again without any British labour being used up for that purpose. In general the acquisition of this amount of unrequited imports meant that the existing standards of life of the British people could be maintained with less British labour. An amount of labour which would have been needed to produce £10,000 worth of goods had been freed for other purposes. Therefore this quantity—let us say for argument 500 man-years—of British labour, were now available for such purposes as improving the productivity of the Nawob's estates, or more dramatically, for building Mr. Boulton's and Mr. Watt's new steam engines in Birmingham.

This argument is only valid, however, upon the hypothesis that the available supply of British labour was fully employed. For if it was not then there was no need to "free" a part of it in order to improve estates or build steam engines. There are no such things as eighteenth-century employment statistics. But for the sake of simplicity let us assume full employment for the moment, and continue to trace the effect of the receipt of the unrequited value from India on that assumption. We will withdraw the assumption in due course.

Workers could now be spared for the above purposes without anyone being the poorer during the time before their work on the estates or the steam engines had resulted in any more consumers' goods being available. That is the point to be observed. If it had not been for the unrequited import of the £10,000 worth of goods, the diversion of 500 man-years of labour to investment must have reduced the supply of goods for immediate consumption correspondingly. It is only by means of the advent of some outside, adventitious, aid that a community, already fully employed on sustaining its own standard of life, can divert some of its resources to producing new capital goods, without reducing its standards. Of course, as soon as the initial job has been done the *further* production of capital goods becomes far easier. In our example, as soon

[1] In order to protect the home cotton trade, the cottons had to be exported.

as the first Nawobs' estates had been improved and were producing more food with less labour, or as soon as the new steam engines had been sent to Lancashire and were turning the spindles and driving the shuttles, so that more shirts were being made by fewer workers, the thing became self-perpetuating. More and more workers were each year freed to produce more machines which, in turn, freed more workers. It is that first agonising pull off the dead centre of an undeveloped and unchanging technique of production which is the trouble. At that juncture an import of even quite a modest amount of unrequited value can be important. The present-day importance of getting this basic economic consideration clear will emerge. For to-day the position as between not only India and Britain, but the under-developed and the highly developed worlds in general, is just the opposite to the eighteenth-century situation. Then it was Britain which was in the throes of the first critical stage of industrialisation. And she managed to lay her hands on some unrequited value from abroad to help her through it. To-day it is India and the other undeveloped nations which face that same crisis. And dire will be the consequences unless they are enabled to borrow, or are given, some unrequited value in their turn.

When we have once realised this vital fact, however, we must not exaggerate the part which the import of unrequited value from India played in the British industrial revolution. Other major influences were at work. For example, if Duplieux instead of Clive had conquered India; if the spoils had flowed to Paris, not London, would the Industrial Revolution have first taken place in France instead of Britain? Imperialist gains did not, in my view, play anything like so decisive a part as that. There were more important sources for the accumulation of the primary capital which made possible the industrial revolution in Britain. Much the largest of them, was the agricultural revolution, marked by the enclosures, which had been going on, not only since the beginning of the eighteenth century (with its great technical achievements), but since before 1500. Every decade the food necessary to sustain the British population at a given standard of life, and the wool to clothe them, were being produced by a slightly smaller number of workers. This freed a slowly but steadily expanding number of workers for making the steam engines and, still more important, for building the roads and digging the canals of eighteenth-century Britain. The process of "freeing" the former peasants from not only their food-producing labour, but also, and particularly, from their hereditary holdings, was a savage business: but this was the way in which productivity in agriculture rose and so provided the basis of all subsequent development. This internal process resulted, at certain times and places, in a terrible initial fall in the peasants' standard of life, but it provided resources which were probably many times as important as the unrequited imports of the East India Company and the other imperial spoils such as the slave-produced sugar of the West Indies.

We must now withdraw the assumption that there was full employment in Britain when the unrequited Indian imports began to arrive. On the contrary the enclosures and the associated rise in agricultural techniques had for long been continually freeing labour from food production. Thus at any given moment there already existed a pool of unemployed labour. Accordingly if we take the shortest possible view it may be suggested that neither unrequited imports nor the agricultural revolution were necessary to free labour for accumulation. For there was unemployed labour available already. And this is what certain economists, brought up in the Keynesian tradition, are in fact apt to suggest. But the suggestion only shows the superficiality of the Keynesian analysis if it is applied to long periods and to major historic developments. For, of course, the pools of unemployed labour which such commentators notice had only come into existence as a result of a *previous* change in agriculture. If mediaeval agriculture had been left untouched with its huge, under-employed but unavailable labour force, securely "bound" to its peasant holdings, there would have been nobody to use for the vast work of the Industrial Revolution. On the contrary what the unrequited imports did was to add to the stream of unemployed labour which was becoming available for capital accumulation—and by so doing no doubt helped to keep wages down to a subsistence level.

It is true that all this labour might have been freed from its previous employment and then not re-employed on capital accumulation. It might simply have rotted and perished unused. And some of it did. But in eighteenth-century Britain, almost uniquely up to that time, much at least of this freed labour (though after immense suffering) actually found new employment in capital accumulation—in what we now call development. That was the remarkable thing: that is what has to be accounted for. Naturally, the major explanation is the break through in technique (the greatest since the invention of the wheel) associated with the steam engine which was occurring at the same time and place. Nevertheless it is precisely in this respect that the receipt of unrequited value from India may have played an important role. It provided a basis for the liquid funds—capital in readily disposable form—which is so hard to accumulate and which plays a major role in the actual application of new techniques. That the "enterprisers" of the early industrial revolution were able to find banks and finance houses able and willing to finance them may have been partly due to the unrequited gains of the unequal trade of the East India Company and its imitators.

We should therefore conclude that though the notorious "drain" from India was by no means the largest factor in Britain's pioneer accomplishment of primary industrialisation, it played a very real part. That process was, in comparison with present-day developments, a slow one, stretching over more than, one century. Nevertheless, at the critical moment, in the mid-eighteenth century, it received the impetus of un-requited imports. . . . In the middle of the twentieth century the question is: how can the undeveloped countries of the world, which are largely the ex-colonies of the empires, be provided with an external contribution to capital accumulation? For, even though such a contribution may be quite minor in amount, in comparison to the vast sums which they must somehow raise from their own peoples, it may yet be indispensable to getting the whole process fairly under way. The thing has been aptly compared to the "assisted take-off" whereby a modern fighter aircraft may be shoved off the ground by a rocket mechanism which can be easily dispensed with once it is flying. We should not forget that we in Britain benefited from "an assisted take-off" in our pioneer industrial revolution two hundred years ago. To-day not merely Britain but the whole of the West must on pain of catastrophe to themselves help forward the industrialisation of the undeveloped three-quarters of the world. We must do so both in our own interests and in the interests of the human race as a whole. But we should also remember that we are repaying a debt. . . .

[But if the profits from the Indian empire did help the Industrial Revolution, what will be the economic loss to England in relinquishing her Empire?]

It seems probable, therefore, that any economic loss which the British people may suffer as they relinquish their residual ability to exploit their ex-colonies, will be far less than is usually supposed. The main remaining potential loss is oil profits. This would be some £323 million gross, if it is assumed that non-imperialist policies would result in us losing the whole of our oil profits. But this is a wholly unrealistic assumption. The most that would be likely to happen is that those profits of £323 million gross or £93 million net, as Shonfield estimates them, would gradually diminish. Thus we might think of the total potential loss as of the order of a per cent or so at the very most of the gross national income (£18,000 million in 1957). This, let it be reiterated, would be the *gross* loss. To set against it are the expenses entailed in attempting to maintain British power over peoples which have reached, or are reaching, the stage at which they are determined to make the attempt to govern themselves; these are very considerable. It is difficult to distinguish this element in our defence budget of £1,400 million. But Mr. Shonfield (op. cit.) makes an attempt to do so. He calculates that we are spending about £160 million a year on defence overseas. To this sum he adds £40 million for subsidies of one kind or another paid to colonies, dependencies and satellites. This gives a direct drain of some £200 million a year, and this is a drain not only upon our resources in general but upon our earnings of foreign currency. Mr. Schonfield seems to imply that we could save the whole of this £200 million a year. This is no doubt an exaggeration. But it is clear from these figures that, quite contrary to what is almost universally supposed, it is by no means certain that there will be any net loss at all to the British people in forgoing their remaining opportunities for imperialist exploitation. In other words, it is probable that the remaining elements of British imperialism no longer pay even on the narrowest bookkeeping view of the matter.

All this may cause us to speculate as to whether Hobson's foreboding of a totally imperialist world, was not always a mere nightmare. Even, if for example the European powers, or later Japan, had conquered China, as they so nearly did, would they not have given up the enterprise when they found that it did not pay? But the fact that imperialism can be shown to be no longer bringing any gains to the mass of the populations of the possessing countries (if it ever did) is not really a refutation of the possibility that a "total imperialism" might have been established by the conquest of China. What we have shown is that for purposes of *trade* between countries imperialism is often unnecessary or even harmful. But we have also shown that such trade, by becoming first, trade in capital goods, and then investment, tends to pass over into the direct exploitation of the wage-earners and peasants of a colony. And no one can deny that such direct exploitation of, for example, the labour of 600 million Chinese *could* have provided unearned incomes for considerable sections of the populations of the West. What Hobson, and Lenin too I believe, had not fully realised was the profound change in the structure, and therefore the nature, of capitalism which such total imperialism would have involved. After all the first effects of harnessing the labour of 600 million Chinese to the task, as Hobson suggests, of supplying all the products of the basic industries of the West, would have been to ruin those industries. Theoretically no doubt the wage-earners, salary-earners and capitalists in those industries could have been pensioned off out of the gigantic profits made out of exploitation in China. In the end large sections of the Western population could have lived in idleness. Something like the later Roman social pattern of limitless unearned wealth for patricians and bread and circuses for the plebs could have been reproduced. But to do this would have meant so radical a reconstruction of capitalism that there would have been little of the system left. Experience suggests, therefore, that imperialism, if it had not destroyed itself in its internecine struggles, would have had to abolish capitalist relations of production as such, and substitute for them some sort of industrial feudalism, with a much more fixed and rigid social system. (The Nazis and the Japanese militarists might have done it.)

I do not, therefore, think that there is a contradiction in saying that imperialism has ceased to bring appreciable benefits to the advanced countries (without ceasing to be ruinous for the undeveloped) and agreeing that, in theory at least, Hobson's nightmare was real. Only that nightmare was hardly capable of realisation without a much more thoroughgoing change in the existing social and economic system than he, or Lenin, or anyone else, realised. . . .

Many people—from conservatives to communists—sincerely believe that "if we lose the empire we shall be ruined". They ignore the fact that we have "lost" nearly nine-tenths of the empire already, with, as we have seen, no observable effect on the rate at which we exchange our products with those of the rest of the world. They suffer under the illusion that it is possible, by means of governmental authority, based in the last resort on armed force, to turn our terms of trade as a whole substantially in our favour. Certainly this was done in particular instances in the past, and it is still being done, to some extent, in the case of that, after all, relatively minor part of our trade which we do with the remaining colonies. But the main, decisive part of our overseas trade is already conducted, as we have seen, with nations, both members and non-members of the Commonwealth, which are completely self-governing and against which we could not possibly use force, even if we would. Whether or not we exploit their primary producers, as we certainly did in the 'thirties (but almost as much to our own detriment as to theirs) has not, as we have seen, much to do with imperialism (in the strict sense of the rule of one people by another) but is governed by the much broader question of what the terms of trade between primary producers and manufacturers in general are likely to be. When we are no longer able to use force to exploit anyone, we may indeed suffer some economic loss but it will be of the order of 1% or so of the national income and even that is without taking into account the possibly greater expense of attempting to continue our rule in areas which are determined that they will no longer remain our colonies.

The specifically Marxist contention that any improvement which, it is sometimes reluctantly admitted, may have taken place in the standard of life of the wage-earners in the advanced capitalisms, is simply due to intensified imperialist exploitation has at length been adequately answered. That contention was noted and briefly denied. . . . But comprehensive comment upon it had to be postponed to the part of the study dealing specifically with imperialism. We are now in a position to see that if we use the term imperialism in its habitual, and surely proper, sense of the rule (open or concealed) of one country over another, there is to-day little substance in the communist assertion. If on the other hand we extend the term, as contemporary communist writers habitually, if tacitly do to mean any bargaining advantage which the developed countries can exert against the undeveloped, then indeed it is entirely true that this is one of the factors which tend to keep the poor countries poor and the rich countries rich. But if we extend the term imperialism as widely as this it ceases to have any very clear meaning.

What is then really at issue is the far broader question of the tendency of highly developed countries continually to widen the gap in wealth between themselves and the undeveloped world. And we shall note that this tendency, whether it is to be called imperialism or not, is not confined to the capitalist part of the world. It seems therefore better to use the word imperialism to mean some degree at least of political, and in the last resort physical, power of one country over another. But if we do adopt this narrower usage we must not for one moment seem to deny that the wider issue—call it what you will—of the economic relationship, between the developed and the undeveloped world, is of crucial importance. The best way, perhaps, to express that issue is to write that we shall find that the liquidation of the specifically imperial, or colonial, relationship which is going on so fast to-day, will prove to be not enough. In order to make a viable world it will not be enough for imperial or ex-imperial states such as Britain to cease from ruling and exploiting their colonies: it will prove indispensable for them actively to help those ex-colonies—and the undeveloped world as a whole for that matter—to develop. That will be the subject of a later stage in this study. Here we are concerned to overcome the fear of national ruin which obstructs the indispensable preliminary process of freeing the colonies, as this becomes feasible, from external rule.

We have seen that the fear that without her empire Britain will not be able to obtain her food and raw materials, or will have to obtain them at ruinously high prices, will not stand up to an examination of the figures. There are however more than figures to prove the point. There is striking evidence to be derived from the fortunes of two neighbours of Britain's.

We have already noted the tragic circumstances of contemporary France. There can be few observers still left to deny that the largest single cause of her misfortunes is the passion with which she clings to the remainder of her empire. True, France emerged from the second World War far more severely injured, both materially and morally than Britain; for she had had the searing experience of occupation. None the less, her innate powers of recovery are second to none, and, sure enough, the industry and good sense of her people have been steadily rebuilding her in these last fourteen years. To-day, in 1959, she would be far along the road to complete recovery, were it not for the fact that since 1945 she has not known a single year of peace. She has been engaged in colonial warfare, often on the largest scale, from the very moment of her liberation until the present, and, if her imperial policies continue, there seems little prospect of relief. We have already mentioned the havoc that the struggle in Indo-China wrought in the military, financial and moral strength of France. But no sooner was she quit of that, than the struggle in North Africa became intense. Though, I repeat, it is far less sanguinary, it is perhaps equally costly. France is in 1959 said to be maintaining the almost incredible number of five hundred thousand troops, permanently under arms, in North Africa. No wonder that she has been reduced to almost total military impotence in Europe, unable any longer even to make her promised contribution to the N.A.T.O. forces guarding Europe's eastern frontiers. And at home she was up till 1958 unable to check the increasingly grave inflationary disorder of her finances. (One has only to think of what Britain's plight would be if we tried to maintain five hundred thousand men abroad, continuously under arms, in order to seek for no further explanations of France's difficulties.)

And what is it all for? The loss of Indo-China when it came turned out to have no observable evil effects upon the French economy. Algeria is a far less rich possession. The fact is that a settlement with the Algerians upon the basis of their independence, far from reducing France to "a Portugal", as is suggested, would immediately restore her to her natural position as a leading European nation. For then she would have troops and money and energy to spare. No concern for the future of the French settlers in Algeria, natural as such concern is, should really weigh with a patriotic Frenchman on this issue. For the brutal fact is that her imperial policy is ruining France. Still less should any hopes of immense profits from Saharan oil be allowed seriously to weigh in the balance. No doubt certain French companies may make high profits out of the oil: but France will not if she has to sink the wells, run the oil trains and guard the pipe-lines in the midst of a chronic civil war. Actually the only hope of the really profitable operation of the Saharan wells is an Algerian settlement. And such a settlement must involve at the very least half of the profits going to the Algerians, just as it has in Arabia. In any case, the profits which can possibly be got from such oil will form a far smaller fraction of the French national income than is usually imagined. France is ruining herself for a reminiscence of glory and a mirage of oil profits.

If the French warning were not conclusive, the Western German example would be. Lack of imperialism on the part of Western German capitalism is, perhaps, involuntary. Nevertheless the fact remains that West Germany, besides all the other consequences which she suffered as a result of the most catastrophic defeat of recent history, was stripped of every acre of her imperial possessions. And what is the result? She is universally held up as an example of the most prosperous, the strongest, the most stable economy of Europe. As a matter of fact some of the praise is exaggerated. Nevertheless present-day Western Germany incontestably demonstrates that it is possible to maintain a stable, prosperous and progressive economy without imperial possessions. Of course there are many other facts to account for the so-called "West German miracle". There is the influx of skilled refugees from East Germany combined with German power of organisation and German industry; there is the apparently undestroyable asset of mature industrial know-how; there is American help. Nevertheless the fact that Germany has not had to devote any of her resources to trying to maintain threatened imperial possessions has been one of her most useful assets. The position of influence and general importance which West Germany has already achieved in the world, only fourteen years after her utter prostration, proves conclusively that imperial possessions are not, to say the least of it, indispensable for material strength. It suggests strongly that, on the contrary, they are likely to prove "running sores" which destroy both the economic and the moral vigour of a nation's life. Exactly contrary to popular prejudice, a nation is likely to-day to be strong or weak in inverse ratio to her imperial possessions.

K. M. Panikkar
THE END OF COLONIALISM

The Effects of the Russian Revolution upon Asia

Though the effects of the October Revolution on the peoples of Asia are outside the scope of this study, a brief analysis of the forces generated by that historic event is necessary for a proper appreciation of the relations between Europe and Asia in the vital period between 1918 and 1948. This period marked the end of Western authority on the Asian continent and as the national movements in the countries of Asia which finally won their freedom were influenced, and in some cases inspired, by the existence of the Soviet State and the growth of Soviet power, it is necessary to understand in what way this influence worked. The question

From *Asia and Western Dominance* by K. M. Panikkar, pp. 189–193, 197–202. Reprinted by permission of the publisher, George Allen & Unwin Ltd.

K. M. Panikkar (1895–   ) is a writer on Asiatic history and the former Indian Ambassador to China (1948–1952).

is therefore discussed here only to the extent of trying to discover what influence the October Revolution and the ideas it generated had on the relations of Asia with Europe. . . .

It should be remembered that the Revolution had a well-defined national policy which had an irresistible appeal to the struggling dependencies, colonies and semi-colonial countries in Asia. The Declaration of the Rights of the Peoples of Russia, over the joint signatures of Lenin and Stalin, proclaimed the equality and sovereignty of the peoples of Russia, and the right of the peoples of Russia to freedom of development of national minorities. This was indeed an explosive statement and all the nations of Asia, struggling for freedom, heard it with a new hope. This emphasis on national self-determination and ethnic separateness of minorities had an immense effect in shaping opinion in Asia during the next quarter of a century.

From the first the Soviets also announced their support for the struggle for independence in India, China, Indonesia and Indo-China, not only as a Revolutionary slogan, but on the ground that imperialism is in itself the summation of capitalism and its destruction by bourgeois nationalist movements is a progressive stage in evolution. It therefore deserved support. There is no doubt that the nationalist movements in all Asian countries gained moral strength by the mere existence of a Revolutionary Russia. In countries where the nationalist movements had already been in existence for a considerable time, like India, the Communist theory gained but little support; but in Indonesia and Indo-China, where the movements for independence became effective in the period after the Russian Revolution, the Communists became a major factor in the forces working for liberation. In each one of these countries Communist parties came into existence in the period between 1920–23. In Indonesia they were able to gain considerable influence by 1926, when their hand was suspected in the widespread disturbances directed against the Dutch, which broke out in Java in that year. In Indo-China also it spread quickly among the nationalist groups.

In China the Communist Party was founded in Shanghai in 1921. But the small groups which established the party were no index of the wide influence of the Revolution on the progressive national leaders of the time. This could be judged from the fact that Sun Yat-sen, the Father of the Revolution and the spokesman of Chinese nationalism, stated publicly after he became fully aware of the attitude of the Western Powers and of America towards a strong and rehabilitated China: 'We no longer look to the West. Our faces are turned towards Russia.' The Soviet leaders also began to realize that the main stream of national awakening in China was represented then by Sun Yat-sen and his party, and following a report by H. Maring, who visited China to study the problem on the spot, the Soviet Government sent Adolphe Joffe to establish contact with Sun Yat-sen. The discussions between the two leaders, conducted in the safety of the international settlement at Shanghai, led to a joint statement regarding Sino-Soviet co-operation. In this famous document the Soviet representative gave expression to the view that 'China's paramount and most pressing problem is to achieve national unification and full national independence'. The support of Asian nationalism by Revolutionary Russia was thus publicly proclaimed.

Even more important than the added strength that the nationalist movements received was the change in the character of nationalism itself which is to be attributed mainly to the doctrines of the Revolution. Before the October Revolution, the nationalist movements in India and China were liberal and exclusively political. The issue was solely one of freedom from foreign domination. Such political content as the nationalist movements had was based on parliamentary liberalism, and on representative government. The movements had neither a defined social nor an economic objective, and were in that sense vague and Utopian. The Russian Revolution altered all this. The San Min Chu I, the Three People's Principles, confused though they may appear, formulated an economic doctrine, the central point of which was Land to the Tiller. The Indian Congress Party put in the forefront of its programme the abolition of untouchability—itself a revolutionary measure of immense significance. Also national movements thought in terms of 'planning'. The achievements of the successive five-year plans gave an impetus to all Asian countries to organize their economy for production in order to take them out of colonial systems which had made them weak, disorganized and dependent. The attack on the West came where it touched Europe most—in the sphere of economic life. The Asian countries were no longer content to be markets for Europe's industries; and the way a 'backward' country like Russia had in a few years of planned production emerged as a leading industrial country gave to the peoples of Asia the hope of industrial regeneration and economic independence.

That the Russian Revolution quickened the pulse of the peoples of Asia no one would deny. That it also helped to awaken the masses, to create doubts in the minds of thinking people about the validity of many things which they had accepted without question from the West, could not also be doubted. Equally it would be accepted that its general effect was to weaken the hold of the West on the peoples of Asia. But beyond all this there is one significant point: and that is, it affected different people differently. In countries like India, where social reorganization had to some extent taken place and the old tradition broken down as a result of a hundred years of reform, the message of the Russian Revolution did not have the same force as in China and Indo-China where, owing to the historical factors previously analysed, the West had only helped to undermine the old society without helping to build anything to take its place. In the social and ethical anarchy thus created, the doctrines of the Russian Revolution had a dominant influence which they failed to secure in India. In countries like Iran and Afghanistan, where the social structure, however reactionary, had held together and was not subjected to the same pressures as in China and in India, its direct influence has been even less. Thus we have the significant phenomenon of Communism moving in to fill a vacuum in China and in Annam, while in India, where the vacuum had been previously filled by a partial readjustment of society and a reform of religion, Communist thought has been mainly an intellectual development, helping to oust the hold of the West. And, finally, in independent countries like Iran, Afghanistan and Siam, where there has been but little social or religious aggression, Communist thought has on the whole failed to have any appeal.

The case of Japan stands in an entirely different category. The October Revolution instead of raising any hopes in Japan caused it the greatest alarm. Japan had joined the ranks of 'aggressors' and her interest naturally was that any revolution in Asia against the West should be solely for national independence and not for radical changes in society. Therefore the Russian Revolution with its appeal to the proletariat and with active encouragement of 'the exploited classes' was a threat as much to her as to the Western nations. She was among the most vociferous advocates of intervention in Russia, and unsuccessfully tried to separate Eastern Siberia from Soviet territory. While the other Asian countries, even the most conservative of them, were inclined to see in the new Russia a possible ally in their struggle against the West, Japan saw in her the most dangerous enemy to her national greatness. It is this feeling, together with the sense of suffering injustice at the hands of Britain and America, that forced her to join Germany and Italy in the anti-Comintern Pact. . . .

The Effects of World War I upon Asia

The Great War of 1914–8 was from the Asian point of view a civil war within the European community of nations. The direct participation of Asian countries, during some stages of this conflict, was at the invitation and by the encouragement of one of the parties, the *entente* Powers, and was greatly resented by the Germans. It is necessary to emphasize this internal character of the European conflict to realize its full significance on the development of events in Asia.

We have already noticed that at the beginning of the twentieth century the European nations, in the enjoyment of unprecedented economic prosperity and political prestige, remained unshakably convinced that they had inherited the earth, and that their supremacy in Asia was permanent and was something in the nature of a predetermined Divine Order. It was the age of Kipling and the white man's burden, and it seemed the manifest destiny of the white race to hold the East in fee. But though the edifice seemed impregnable two cracks had already appeared. The first was, as we noticed, the ambition of the new German Empire under Wilhelm II for a place in the Asian sun. Contradictions and rivalries of a kind which never existed before, when Britain's authority in the East was unchallenged, developed within the ranks of colonial Powers. The partition of China, at least into spheres of influence, was the great objective and seemed to be on the point of realization when the rivalries of territorial and non-territorial imperialists clashed, and China got a welcome and, as it happened, a decisive respite. America, which at that time disclaimed all territorial interests and was concerned with the policy of deriving maximum benefits from privileges granted to others, constituted a non-territorial imperialism whose claims could not be reconciled with a territorial partition of China. The old system, therefore, felt the strain of a double attack by the newcomers among the imperialists, Germany and Japan, who desired to gain control over territories and by America who desired that all parts of China should be equally open to her.

The second crack in the European hegemony was the growth of Japan as a Great Power in the Far East. From 1895, Japan had declared that she would line up with the European Powers, that in effect she would follow the same policies and expected to be treated in the same manner as the European Powers. Though in form Japan had therefore joined the forces arrayed against China, it was clear from the beginning that she was only utilizing the machinery of collective European action against China for the purpose of aggrandizing herself with the object of excluding European influence wherever possible in the Far East.

The immediate result of the European war was to effect an irreparable breach in Western solidarity in Asia. The major scene of action in this matter was, of course, China. Though at the very beginning, on August 3, 1914, China asked that her neutrality should be respected and no hostilities should take place in Chinese territories leased to foreigners, the Powers wantonly disregarded it and refused to respect her territorial integrity. A Japanese force, assisted by a British contingent, landed on Chinese territory, attacked and reduced Tsingtao and took over the Kiaochow Peninsula. The extraordinary course that the Japanese authorities followed and the Twenty-one Demands made on China will be discussed elsewhere, but the point necessary to emphasize here is that by this act one major European Power in Asia was for the first time driven out by an Asian Power and excluded from further influence in Asian affairs, and this was done with the active assistance of Britain, whose general, it will be remembered, fought under a Japanese commander-in-chief, General Kamio.

Secondly, as time went on and the war situation became more and more critical, Britain and France, in a frenzy of anti-Germanism, instigated a reluctant Chinese Government on one pretext or another to take over German properties and to eradicate all German influence in China. Britain especially was anxious to get control of German ships interned in Chinese ports. Under French pressure, German industries in China, banking and commercial houses and other enterprises, were closed. The concessions were taken over and, of course, extra-territorial rights denounced. A precedent of great future value to China was thus established. Finally, China was encouraged to declare war on the Central Powers.

In 1914, when the German invaders had reached the Marne, divisions of the Indian Army under British officers had been rushed to France and had helped at the critical moment to stem the German tide. Later, they were extensively used in the defence of the Suez Canal and the Middle East and in campaigns elsewhere in Africa. In 1917, Siam declared war on Germany. An Indo-Chinese labour force had been re-cruited and was working in France. On August 14, 1917, China also joined the Allies. Thus all the nations of Asia were brought into the European civil war. However, opinion in India, China and even in Japan was at the time more pro-German than pro-Ally. In India, except among the ruling princes, there was no pro-British feeling, and public opinion rejoiced at every report of German victory and felt depressed when the Allies were winning. China declared war only with the greatest reluc-tance and for the express purpose of checking Japanese plans of aggres-sion. In Japan itself, after the Shantung campaign, feeling against the Allies was most marked, and a Press campaign of great virulence was conducted against Britain at the end of 1916. Actually, though the Asian countries fought on the side of the Allies, public opinion in the East looked upon the conflict as a civil war in which neither party had a claim to the friendship of the peoples of Asia, and if any party could appeal to the sympathy of Asians it was the Germanic alliance which had no tradi-tion of Asian conquest and was allied with the chief Muslim Power, Turkey.

But the participation of Asian people in the war had far-reaching consequences.

The Indian soldier who fought on the Marne came back to India with other ideas of the *Sahib* than those he was taught to believe by decades of official propaganda. Indo-Chinese Labour Corps in the South of France returned to Annam with notions of democracy and republicanism which they had not entertained before. Among the Chinese who went to France at the time was a young man named Chou En-lai, who stayed on to become a Communist and had to be expelled for activities among the members of the Chinese Labour Corps.

More important than these influences was the fact that the French and British administrations in Asia had to appeal to their subjects for moral support. To ask Indians and Indo-Chinese to subscribe to war loans for the defence of democracy and to prevent the world being overwhelmed by German *Kultur,* would have sounded as strange and callous irony unless accompanied by promises of democracy for themselves and freedom for their own cultures. When, besides subscriptions for war loans, Indians and Indo-Chinese were pressed to join up and fight to save democracy, the contradictions of the position became too obvious even for the colonial administrators. In India the demand was made openly by the nationalist leaders that prior agreement on political problems was necessary before support of the war could be considered a national programme.

Politically, a further weakening of the colonial and imperialist position came about as a result of President Wilson's declaration of fourteen points. In 1917, the doctrine of the 'self-determination of peoples' had the ring of a new revelation. Whatever its effect was on the suppressed nationalities of Europe, in Asia it was acclaimed as a doctrine of liberation. As every Allied Power hastened to declare its faith in the new formula of Wilson (and it was soon raised to the position of an accepted 'war aim' in the propaganda campaign against the Germans), the colonial Powers found it difficult to oppose openly or resist publicly the claims of Asian nations based on this formula. It became difficult to proclaim self-determination of peoples as a great ideal for the establishment of which Asian peoples should co-operate with Europeans and fight and lose their lives in distant battlefields, but which, however excellent, could not be applied to themselves. Self-government for colonial countries had thus to be accepted, and the claim to it could no longer be brushed aside as premature or stigmatized as sedition.

In China, naturally, self-determination had a wide and ready-made field for immediate application. Apart from disabilities resulting from unequal treaties, there were areas where foreigners were exercising jurisdiction. The retention of Kiaochow by Japan would be a clear violation of the doctrine of self-determination. The limitations on Chinese customs, the numerous concession areas at ports, the maintenance of foreign troops on Chinese soil, all these seemed to militate against the self-determination of the Chinese.

Apart from these political considerations economic forces generated by the war were also helping to undermine the supremacy of the West. Japan utilized the four years of war for a planned expansion of her trade in the East. German competition had been eliminated. Britain and France, engaged in a mortal struggle when their entire resources of production had to be directed towards victory, had also left the field fairly open. India gained her first major start on the industrial road and, with the strain on British economy, Indian national capital was placed in a position of some advantage. In fact the full results of the weakening of European capitalism become evident only after the war when the preeminence of London was challenged by America, and British capital, though still powerful, began to be on the defensive in India. The growth of capitalist enterprise in India, and the development of industries and participation by Indian capital in spheres so far monopolistically held by Britain, like jute, resulted directly from the weakening of the economic position of Britain.

Two other results of a general character may be indicated. The first, the growth of a powerful left-wing movement in the countries of Western Europe had a direct effect on shaping events in the Eastern Empire. The Labour Party in England during the days of its growth had been closely associated with the nationalist movement in India. In fact, Ramsay MacDonald, the leader of the Socialist Party after the war, had been one of its champions from the earliest days. Similarly, Annamite nationalism had worked hand in hand with left-wing parties in France. In the period that immediately followed the war these parties had come to possess considerable influence in national affairs and, as we shall see, were instrumental in giving effect to policies which loosened the old bonds of political domination.

The second factor was, of course, the influence of the Russian Revolution which has been dealt with separately. Here it is sufficient to say that the October Revolution, as one of the results of the Great War, gave to the principles which all the Allies had accepted as their objectives a new content. Imperialism meant something totally different after Lenin's definition of it as the last phase of capitalism and his insistence that the liberation of subject peoples from colonial domination was a part of the struggle against capitalism.

Finally, the war had accelerated the pace of movements everywhere. For example, in India, the movement for independence which was confined to the intelligentsia in 1914 became a mass movement of immense proportions in 1919. Everywhere the case was similar. The *tempo* of events had acquired a momentum which few had foreseen and none had forecast in 1918. The war was a great world revolution which divided by a deep gulf the days before August 1914 and after November 1918.

One fact which stands out clear and illustrates this chasm in thought is the lack of faith in imperialist ideals in the period that followed the war. With the solitary exception of Churchill, there was not one major figure in any of the British parties who confessed to a faith in the white man's mission to rule. Successive Viceroys of India, Liberal, Conservative and non-party, professed publicly their adherence to the cause of Indian freedom. Secretaries of State from Edwin Montagu (1917–22) to Pethick Lawrence, including such stalwarts of Conservatism as Sir Samuel Hoare (Lord Templewood), claimed that they were working for the freedom of the Indian people and not for the maintenance of British rule. The French were no doubt more brave in their words, but the faith had gone out of them also.

Nowhere did this come out more clearly than in the treatment of China. Incidents which previously would have been dealt with sternly and for which territories and indemnities would have been exacted, were now only the subjects of a mild protest. Chiang Kai-shek's armies occupied the concessions at Hankow, and for months Hong Kong was subjected to an intensive trade boycott; these events would earlier have immediately led to a display of overwhelming naval strength. Britain in 1926 was prepared patiently to negotiate. Even the 'old China hands', who had watched with regret the sudden eclipse of European prestige, though they acted the Blimps in their clubs, never seriously felt that Western authority could be re-established over China by the use of gunboats. There was no conviction left of the European's superiority or sense of vision.

Lau Shaw
ASIA NEEDS WESTERNIZATION

Grandma Takes Charge

You couldn't blame old Mrs. Wang for wanting a grandson, for what was the use of getting a daughter-in-law if it was not to pave the way for a grandson? And you couldn't blame the daughter-in-law, either.

Reprinted by permission of the translator, Chi-Chen Wang.
Lau Shaw (1899–   ) is a Chinese novelist and Vice Chairman of the Union of Chinese Writers, as of 1965.

It is not that she hadn't tried, but what could one do if the baby didn't live after it was born, or was born without any life at all? Take the first birth, for instance. As soon as the mother became pregnant, old Mrs. Wang forbade her to do anything whatsoever, forbade her even to turn over in bed. You can't say that's not being careful. But after five months, she had a miscarriage, probably because she blinked her eyes once or twice too often. And it was a boy, too!

During her second pregnancy, she did not even dare to blink her eyes without due deliberation or indulge in a yawn without two maids on either side to make sure that nothing went wrong. Indeed, carefulness pays and the mother gave birth to a big, plump boy. But for some reason or other, the child had lived barely five days when it took eternal leave of this world without so much as a cheep or without even a ghost knowing. That happened in mid-winter. There were four open stoves in the nursery, without so much as a single pinhole in any of the windows. Not only was it impossible for any wind to get in, it would have been pretty difficult for the God of Wind himself to have found his way in. Moreover, the baby had piled on it four quilts and five woolen blankets. You can't say that he wasn't warmly covered, ca\ you? But the baby died just the same. It was simply fate and no one coul1 do anything about it.

Now young Mrs. Wang was aga.in blessed. The size of her belly was astonishing, like stone rollers that road gangs use. Was old Mrs. Wang tickled! It was as if her heart had grown two little hands that kept on tickling her and making her laugh. Judging by the mother's size, it would be a wonder if it did not turn out to be twins! The Goddess of Children had answered her prayers and was going to reward her with a pair of them. She was ready to do more than offer prayers and burn incense; she could hardly have refused her daughter-in-law if she had wanted human brains for dinner. For midnight supper she gave her stewed fresh bacon, chicken noodles, and similar rich delicacies.

The daughter-in-law was very obliging on her part. The more she lay motionless, the hungrier she became. She would eat a couple of pounds of moon cakes for a between-meal snack, so that oil fairly oozed out of her onto the pillow, and you could have swept out mincemeat and crumbs from under her covers by the bowlful. How could a pregnant woman give birth to a plump baby if she did not eat as much as she could? Both mother-in-law and daughter-in-law were agreed on that. And of course the maternal grandma was not to be outdone. She came every few days to "hasten the birth," and every time she came, she brought at least eight trays of food. It has been discovered long since by philosophers that in-laws are implacable foes. And so the more things maternal grandma brought, the more convinced the other grandma became that the former was just trying to show off and shame her; and the more paternal grandma tried to press food upon her daughter-in-law, the more convinced maternal grandma became that her daughter did not get enough to eat. The result of this wholesome competition was a boon to the young woman, who ate and ate until her mouth was worn thin.

The midwife had been on hand for seven days and seven nights, but to no purpose. They had tried all sorts of weird prescriptions and quantities of pills and powders and incense ash from the temple of the Goddess of Children, but nothing worked. On the eighth day, the young woman couldn't even be tempted with chicken broth. She just rolled and groaned with pain. Old Mrs. Wang burned incense to the Goddess of Children and maternal grandma summoned a holy woman to read the charm for hastening birth; still it was no use. Thus they struggled on toward midnight, when the top of the reluctant child's head finally came into view. The midwife tried all her tricks but accomplished nothing more than to maul and bruise the young mother. The child just would not come out. The minutes, each as long as a year dragged on until it was almost an hour, but still only the top of the child's head could be seen.

Someone suggested the hospital, but old Mrs. Wang would not hear of such a thing, for that would mean that the mother would have to be disemboweled and the child "gouged" out by force. Foreign devils and foreign devils once removed could do that if they wanted to, but not the Wangs. The Wangs wanted their grandchild to be born naturally, not gouged out by force. Maternal grandma didn't like the idea, either. You couldn't exactly hasten the birth of a child. Even a hen has to take her time about laying an egg. Moreover, the holy woman hadn't yet finished incanting her charm and to slight her was to be disrespectful to the gods. What was the hurry?

Another hour went by. The child was as stubborn as ever. The mother's eyes became glassy. With tears in her eyes, old Mrs. Wang made up her mind to save the child and forget the mother. You could always get another daughter-in-law; the child was more important. It was time to be resolute and pull the child out by brute force if necessary. A wet nurse would do just as well in case the mother died. She told the midwife to pull hard. Maternal grandma, however, had a different reaction. To her a daughter was a daughter, much closer than a grandson. It was better to get her to the hospital, without waiting for the holy woman to finish. Who knows what she was mumbling, anyway? What if it wasn't the birth-hastening charm, after all? Wouldn't that be wasting valuable time? The holy woman was dismissed, but paternal grandma was obdurate against gouging. There was little that maternal grandma could do. A married daughter is like water that has been thrown out of the pail. As long as her daughter lived, she was a member of the Wang family and when she died, she would still be a Wang ghost. The in-laws glared at each other, each ready to bite off a hunk of the other's flesh.

Another half hour went by, and the child was as unhurried and reluctant to come out as before. The midwife decided it was hopeless and sneaked off at the first opportunity. Her departure weakened old Mrs. Wang's position and gave more weight to maternal grandma's plea: "Even the midwife has sneaked off. What are we waiting for? Do you want the child to die in the womb?"

The juxtaposition of "death" and "child" made a deep impression on old Mrs. Wang, but still, gouging would hardly do under any circumstances.

"Lots of people go to the hospital nowadays; they don't always resort to gouging," maternal grandma vehemently argued, though she was not so sure of it herself. As for old Mrs. Wang, she naturally did not believe it at all; to her, going to the hospital meant only one thing and that was gouging.

Fortunately, maternal grandpa arrived on the scene, immediately improving the position and morale of maternal grandma. He, too, was for going to the hospital. There was little else to do after that. After all, he was a man and in a matter of life and death a man's word carries weight, though childbearing is strictly a woman's business.

And so the in-laws, the young mother, and the grandson, who had only his hair showing, all went to the hospital in a motorcar. The in-laws shed tears at the cruel fate of the grandson who had to be carted about in a motorcar when he had just barely showed his hair.

Old Mrs. Wang exploded almost as soon as they got to the hospital. What? they had to register? What did they mean by registering? It was a case of childbirth, not as if they had come for their quota of rice at government prices, or to get a bowl of free gruel. Old Mrs. Wang was outraged and declared that she would sooner give up the idea of a grandson than to submit to such a humiliation. But when she found that if she refused to register, they would refuse to let them in, she decided to swallow her pride, hard as it was for her to do, for the sake of her emerging grandson. If only her husband were still alive—it would have been a wonder indeed if he did not tear down the hospital then and there. A widow couldn't do that; she had to put up with things even though she had money. It was no time to ruminate over her grievances; the most pressing thing was to coax her grandson out. So she registered and was told that she had to pay fifty dollars in advance. That gave her her opportunity. "Fifty dollars? Even five hundred is nothing to me. Why didn't you come to the point? Why this nonsense about registration? Do you think my grandson is a letter?"

The physician came and again old Mrs. Wang exploded. It was a man—a man was to act as midwife. She wouldn't have a man attend to her daughter-in-law. Before she had a chance to recover from this shock, two more men came out and proceeded to lift up her daughter-in-law and put her on a stretcher. She was so outraged that even her ears quivered. Why, it was worse that revolution and rebellion! What did they mean by letting a crowd of men handle a young pregnant woman? "Put her down! Isn't there anyone here who knows what human decency means? If so, you'd better ask a few women to come out. Otherwise, we leave."

It happened that she had to deal with a very good natured physician. "All right," he said. "Put her down and let them go!"

Old Mrs. Wang swallowed hard and what she had to swallow burned her heart. If it were not for the sake of her grandson, she would give him a few resounding slaps at least. But "an official in authority is not as important as a flunky in charge," and what could she do, since her grandson had decided to be difficult? All right, take her and waste no more words. As soon as the two men put the daughter-in-law on the stretcher, the physician began to press her abdomen with his hands. Old Mrs. Wang closed her eyes to the horror of it and cursed maternal grandma in her heart: "It's your daughter and you let a man press her belly without uttering a word of protest! Oh, the indecency of it!" She was about to say something aloud when her thought again turned to her grandson. For more than ten months, he had never suffered any indignity or discomfort. Would he, with his tender skin and bone, be able to stand the physician's rough handling? She opened her eyes and was about to warn the physician when the latter anticipated her by asking, "What have you been feeding the mother? Look at her! I don't know what to do with people like you. You keep feeding the mother everything you can think of until the child is so large. You would not come for checkups. Then you come to us when everything else fails." Then, without waiting for old Mrs. Wang to say anything, he said to the two men, "Carry her in!"

Old Mrs. Wang had never suffered such a humiliation in all her life. It was as if the Goddess of Wisdom herself were being taught how to be wise! That was not the worst of it if there had been a grain of sense to what the man said. If a pregnant woman did not eat nourishing food, how was she to bear a child, how was the child to grow? Did the physician thrive on northwest wind when he was in his mother's womb? But Western-style physicians are all foreign devils once removed and you couldn't reason with them. She would take it out on maternal grandma, wherewith she glared at her. The latter was too busy thinking about her daughter to mind. She tried to follow the carriers. Old Mrs. Wang followed suit, but the physician turned around and said to them, "Wait here!"

Both women's eyes turned red with indignation. What, they would not let them in to watch? How were they to know where they were going to take her, and what they were going to do to her? After the physician left them, old Mrs. Wang unloosed the acrid smoke of her rage on maternal grandma. "You said they would not have to gouge him out, but see now, they would not even let you go in and see what's going on! Why, they may even have her quartered twice over. It would serve you right to have your daughter cut up like that. But if anything should happen to my grandson, I shall not live. I'll match my life against yours!"

Maternal grandma was frightened. What if they really did cut up her daughter? It was not beyond these foreign devils once removed. Didn't they exhibit a human leg and a torso in glass jars the last time the medical school was opened to the public? "Now you are blaming me! Who was it that kept on stuffing my daughter from morning till night? Didn't you hear what the doctor said? It was you who insisted on stuffing her. Now see what you have done. I have seen a lot of people in my time, but I have never seen a mother-in-law like you!"

"Yes, I have fed her well, but that's because I wasn't sure that she ever got enough to eat before she was married into our house," sneered in-law Wang.

"And I suppose it's because we never gave her enough to eat in our own house that I had to bring eight food trays every time I visited my daughter at your house!"

"Now you have admitted it yourself. Yes, eight trays. Yes, I have stuffed her and you haven't!"

Thus the in-laws battled on, neither willing to weaken. Their jibes and retorts were highly original and effectively delivered.

The physician came back, and said, as paternal grandma had anticipated, that an operation was necessary. The term operation had an unfamiliar ring, but there was no question as to the implication: it meant that they were going to cut her up. If they operated, the physician said, they might save both mother and child; if not, both would probably die. The child was hours overdue and was definitely too big to come out without an operation. But a member of the family must sign before they could operate.

Old Mrs. Wang did not hear a word of what the physician had said. She was saying to herself that she would not stand gouging.

"What are you going to do?" the physician said impatiently. "You must decide right away!"

"Gouging won't do!"

"Are you going to sign? Hurry up and make up your mind!" the physician again urged.

"My grandson must be born the natural way!"

Maternal grandma became anxious. "Would it be all right if I signed?"

Old Mrs. Wang flared up at maternal grandma's presumptuousness. "She is my daughter-in-law! Who are you?"

The physician became more and more impatient. He shouted into old Mrs. Wang's ear, "This is a matter of two lives!"

"Gouging won't do!"

"Then you don't care about a grandson?" The physician adopted a new line of attack.

For a while she was silent. Many ancestral ghosts presented themselves before her, and all of them seemed to say to her: "We want someone to keep on burning incense to us. We are willing to compromise on the issue of gouging."

She surrendered. Of course the ancestors must have an heir; let them resort to gouging, if necessary. "But just one thing—it must be alive!" She had hearkened to the ancestors' wishes and given her permission to the physician to cut open her daughter-in-law and gouge the child out, but she must make it clear that she wanted a live baby. What good would a dead one be? As for the mother, it didn't matter so long as the grandson lived.

Maternal grandma, however, was not so indifferent to the patient's fate. "Are you sure that both mother and child will live?"

"Hush!" said paternal grandma.

"I believe that there will be no danger," the physician said, wiping his forehead. "But the birth has been very much delayed and we can guarantee nothing. Otherwise, why should you be asked to sign?"

"You wouldn't guarantee anything? Then let us not go through all this for nothing!" Paternal grandma was very responsible in her attitude toward the ancestors; it wouldn't do anyone any good if only a dead child came out of all this horror.

"All right, then," said the physician, suffocating with exasperation. "Take her back and do what you like. But remember, two lives!"

"What if it were three lives, since you would not guarantee anything?"

Old Mrs. Wang suddenly decided that perhaps she had better let them try. She would not have thought of this if the physician had not started to walk away. "Doctor, doctor, come back! Supposing you try what you can." The physician was so exasperated that he hardly knew whether to laugh or to cry. He read the release to her and she signed it with a cross.

The grandmas waited and waited for they did not know how long. It was not until almost dawn that they succeeded in gouging the child out. What a big baby it was, fully thirteen pounds! Old Mrs. Wang was overwhelmed with happiness. She took maternal grandma's hands, laughing with tears streaming down her cheeks. The latter was no longer her enemy but her "dear elder sister." The physician was no longer a foreign devil once removed but a benefactor of the Wang family. She wished she could reward him with a hundred dollars at once. If he had not resorted to gouging, her nice, fat grandson might have suffocated. How would she then face her ancestors? She wished she could kneel down then and there and do some good old kowtowing, but they did not have any shrine for the Goddess of Children in the hospital.

The baby was now washed and put in the nursery. The grandmas wanted to go in and take a look. Not only to take a look but to pat and fondle the child with their wrinkled hands that had not been washed all night. The nurse would not let them go in; they were only allowed to look through the glass partition. There was their own grandson inside, their very own grandson, and yet they were not even allowed to touch it! Paternal grandma took out a red envelope—which she had planned to give to the midwife—and handed it to the nurse. She would surely let them in after that! But nothing seemed to go right; the nurse actually refused to accept the gift! Old Mrs. Wang rubbed her eyes and contemplated the nurse for a long while. "She does not appear to be a foreign-devil girl," she said to herself. "Then why is it that she would not accept a gift? Perhaps she is shy and feels embarrassed." She had it! She would strike up a conversation with her. Everything would be all right after she had broken down her shyness. She pointed to the row of baskets in the nursery and asked, "I suppose they were all gouged out?"

"No, only yours. All the others were born naturally."

"Nonsense," old Mrs. Wang said to herself. "All those who come to hospitals must be gouging cases."

"Only when you feed rich and fattening food to the mother is it necessary to operate," the nurse said.

"But would the child be so big if the mother didn't have enough to eat?" said maternal grandma, standing on a united front with old Mrs. Wang on the issue.

"A big, fat baby is better than a skinny monkey, though one may be gouged out and the other born naturally," old Mrs. Wang said, beginning to feel that none but gouging cases had any business to come to the hospital. "And who ever heard of natural cases coming to the hospital? That would be as unnecessary as letting down the pants in order to break wind!"

But they remained on the outside of the nursery, for all the talking they did.

Old Mrs. Wang had another idea. "Maid," she said to the nurse, addressing her as if she were a servant girl, "give the baby to us and let us take him home. We have a lot to do to get ready for the Third Day bathing ceremony."

"I am not a maid and I cannot give you the baby," said the nurse, none too politely.

"He is my grandson! You dare to refuse me? We can't invite guests to the hospital and do things properly."

"The mother can't nurse the child right away when we have to operate; we have to feed the child."

"And so can we! I am getting on toward sixty and I have borne sons and given birth to daughters. I should know more about such things than you do. Have you ever borne any children?" Old Mrs. Wang wasn't sure whether the nurse was married or not. Who could tell what these white-helmeted women were, anyway?

"We can't give you the child without the doctor's permission, no matter what you say."

"Then go and get the doctor and let me talk to him. I don't want to waste words with you!"

"The doctor has not yet finished; he has to sew up the incision."

This reminded maternal grandma of daughter, though old Mrs. Wang was still too full of her grandson to give any thought to her daughter-in-law. Before the birth of the grandson, her daughter-in-law always came to her mind when she thought of her grandson, but now that her grandson was born, it was no longer necessary to think of her daughter-in-law. Maternal grandma, however, wanted to see her daughter. Who knew what a big hole they made in her belly? They would not let anyone into the operating room and there was nothing for maternal grandma to do except to gaze at the child with old Mrs. Wang from the distance.

Finally the physician came out and old Mrs. Wang went up to parley with him.

"In operating cases, it is best for mother and child to stay in the hospital for a month," the physician said.

"Then what are we going to do about the Third Day and the Full Month?" old Mrs. Wang asked.

"Which is more important, their lives or the feasts? How can the mother stand the strain of entertaining before her incision heals?" the physician asked.

Old Mrs. Wang undoubtedly believed that the Third Day celebration was more important than her daughter-in-law's life, but she could not very well say so with maternal grandma listening. As to how her daughter-in-law was to receive the guests, that was easily managed: she would let her receive them lying in bed.

The physician still refused. Old Mrs. Wang got another idea. "I suppose it is money that you are after? All right, then, we'll pay you, but let us take mother and child home."

"You go and take a look at her yourselves, and see if she is in a condition to be moved," the physician said.

Both grandmas hesitated. What if she still had a gaping hole in her, as big as a washbasin? Wouldn't that be horrible? Love of her daughter finally enabled maternal grandma to summon up enough courage to go in and there was nothing for paternal grandma to do but to follow.

In the sickroom daughter-in-law lay on the bed, propped up on a reclining rest, her face like a sheet of white paper. Her mother cried out, not sure whether her daughter was dead or alive. Old Mrs. Wang had more fortitude and shed only a tear or two, which were immediately followed by an indignant protest: "Why won't you let her lie down flat and proper? What kind of foreign torture are you subjecting her to?"

"It would put a strain on the stitches to have her lie flat, understand?" the physician said.

"Can't you bind her up with plaster tape?" Old Mrs. Wang could not get over her distrust of the physician's foreign ideas.

The physician would not even let maternal grandma talk to her daughter, which made both grandmas suspect that the physician must have done something or other to the patient that he was anxious to hide. It was fairly evident that she could not be moved out of the hospital for a while. In that case they could at least take the grandson away so that they could plan on the Third Day festivities.

Again the physician refused. Old Mrs. Wang became desperate. "Do you observe the Third Day bathing ceremony in the hospital? If you do, I shall invite all our friends and relatives here. If you don't, then let me take him away. He is my first grandson. I can't live and face people if I do not celebrate his Third Day appropriately."

"Who is going to nurse the child?" the physician asked.

"We'll hire a wet nurse!" old Mrs. Wang said triumphantly.

The baby was brought out and surrendered to her. She began to sneeze as soon as she got into the car and sneezed all the way home, each sneeze being well aimed at her grandson's face. A man was sent out immediately to find a wet nurse. Grandma kept the baby so that she could sneeze into him. Yes, she knew that she had caught a cold, but she would not relinquish her grandson. By noon, the infant had received at least two hundred sneezes and was beginning to develop a temperature. That made old Mrs. Wang even more reluctant to give it up. By three o'clock in the afternoon, the child burned like fire. By night, they had hired two wet nurses, but the grandson died without having had one swallow of milk.

Old Mrs. Wang cried a long while. As soon as she finished crying her old eyes popped wide open with passion. "It is because they had to gouge him out! Of course he couldn't live! I'll sue the hospital. Such a big, heavy child living only one day—who ever heard of such a thing! It's all the hospital's fault, the foreign devils once removed!"

She got maternal grandma to go to the hospital with her and make life miserable for them down there. The latter wanted to get her daughter out of the hospital too. You never could depend on hospitals!

The daughter-in-law was duly taken away from the hospital; you couldn't sue them before that was done. Her incision broke open not long afterward. The "spring restoring plasters" for use after childbirth, that they bound her up with did not do any good and she died without much ado.

Now old Mrs. Wang was able to sue the hospital on both counts. Life now held nothing for her except to avenge her grandson and her daughter-in-law.

F. S. C. Northrop
THE MEETING OF EAST AND WEST

This aesthetic component or any part of it has one other characteristic. It must be immediately experienced to be known. Unlike that factor in the nature of things which is designated by theory, the aesthetic component cannot be conveyed syntactically and deductively by the postulational, formalized technique of a Newton or a St. Thomas Aquinas. This is the reason why no amount of verbal description will enable one to convey the sensed color blue to a person born blind. This is also why neither mathematical calculation nor logical deduction can ever take one from the theoretically known number of the wave length for

Reprinted with permission of The Macmillan Company from *The Meeting of East and West*, pp. 304, 458–465, 473–478, by F. S. C. Northrop. Copyright 1946 by The Macmillan Company.

F. S. C. Northrop (1893–   ) is Emeritus Professor of Philosophy and Law at Yale University.

blue in electromagnetic theory to the sensed blue of the differentiated aesthetic continuum. For this reason both components must be regarded as elementary, irreducible the one to the other—and hence ultimate. . . .

An interesting contrast appears between the rule for reforming a culture based on the aesthetic component and the rule for improving one grounded in the theoretic component. In the former case, the more the contemporary institutions and practices conform to the original aesthetic intuition of the ancient and primitive past the better; in the latter case, the more they conform to the most technical scientific conceptions of the present the better. The reasons for this contrast are clear: Since the aesthetic component is immediately apprehended, and since mature reflection and the attendant social habits tend to obscure the original pure intuition, a society grounded in this component is likely to be more correct to the extent that it returns, as the Buddha, Confucius, and Lao Tzu counseled, to the original experience of its ancient past. Because the theoretic component is known only by hypothesis, and one's hypothesis becomes more and more trustworthy to the extent that it is reconstructed to bring under its domain more and more facts, which accumulate with passage of time, a society resting on this component comes nearer the ideal to the extent that it conceives of it in terms of the latest and technically formulated experimentally verified scientific theory.

But our philosophical principle prescribes that both the aesthetic and theoretic components are required. Thus the ideal society must return to the primitive intuition of the past with respect to its aesthetically grounded portion and advance to the sophisticated science of the present with respect to its theoretically based part. This has one very radical consequence for Westerners. It means that the traditional Western tendency to regard the primitive as inferior or evil must be rejected with respect to the aesthetic component in culture. A people leaves the primitive aesthetic intuitions of its past at its peril. It must move forward to the scientific theory of the future, taking along the primitive aesthetic intuition of the past. But rare is the individual who can master both components. Thus every society needs those who cultivate intuition and contemplation with respect to things in their naïve aesthetic immediacy as well as those who pursue science to the philosophical articulation of the theoretically known factor in things. It is precisely at this point that the native Indians of the entire American continent and the Negroes in the United States can take their place immediately in the good society, with something of their own to offer, leading and teaching with respect to the things of intuition and feeling, just as the white people can lead and teach them with respect to those things which must be known by inference and by theoretically constructed, and scientifically verified, doctrine.

The rule that the part of culture grounded in the theoretic component must reform its idea of the good by identifying it with the latest scientific conceptions, moving away from ancient doctrines, is important for the theistic religions such as Shintoism, Mohammedanism, Judaism and Christianity. Because they affirm the determinate personality to be immortal when the immediately apprehended determinate self is seen to die, and because they affirm the divine to be determinate and immortal when all immediately apprehended determinate factors are mortal, these religions rest on the inferred, unseen theoretically designated component in ourselves and nature. Consequently, unless these theistic religious concepts are identified with the technical theoretical content of present scientifically verified knowledge, they degenerate, on the one hand, into mere verbiage, as is the case with much of contemporary Protestantism, or, on the other hand, into an arbitrary, provincial, intolerant, dictatorial and inquisitorial absolutism and obscurantism above all evidence and all criticism, as is the case with contemporary Japanese Shintoism.

More specifically, this means that *determinate* moral and religious commandments or theses arrived at by nomadic tribes in the Mediterranean region in the time of Moses or the time of Christ simply cannot be taken as perfect and sufficient determinate theses for the definition of the good life in the twentieth century, even in the West, to say nothing of the Orient. Remarkable and adequate as they were for the times in which they were uttered, and permanently valid as a rough approximation as certain of their insights remain, they simply do not represent, nor do they adequately designate what the present stage of human knowledge indicates the theoretic component in man and nature to be. Only if this is first recognized and then actually realized by the construction of a theistic theology in which all its concepts are identified with the content of present scientific knowledge of the theoretic component in things, after the manner of St. Thomas with respect to the scientific knowledge of the thirteenth century, can the theistic religions of the world slough off their tribal provincialisms and their obscurantism and take on the more universal character and the more universal validity which is their birthright, thereby eliminating the still persisting religious prejudice between Christian and Jew, Protestant and Catholic, Jew and Arab, and Mohammedan and Christian which are such obviously outmoded evils in our contemporary world.

But of equal importance with this reform in the theistic religions and in all other parts of culture which are grounded in the theoretic component, is the addition of the religious and cultural values of the Orient which are rooted in the aesthetic component. The analysis of the culture of the Orient in which this immediately apprehended part of oneself and all things is pursued for its own sake, has led to description of this aesthetic component in its totality as the differentiated aesthetic continuum. This complex aesthetic continuum is made up of two factors: one the determinate sensed or introspected differentiations which are transitory; the other, the undifferentiated aesthetic continuum, within which the determinate differentiations come and go. Since time has to do with the transitory differentiations, the Oriental affirms the undifferentiated aesthetic continuum to be outside time and hence not transitory.

It has previously been established that the two-termed relation of epistemic correlation has the consequence of making the aesthetic component an ultimate real and essential part of the self and all things. Consequently, human beings, all natural objects other than human beings, and the medium joining them must be regarded as in part constituted of the aesthetic differentiations which are transitory and the otherwise indeterminate all-embracing aesthetic continuum which is not transitory. In terms of concrete appreciation, what does this mean?

The Self in Its Aesthetic Nature

The aesthetic self is a continuum which is as much, and with precisely the same immediacy, in the aesthetic sky, the aesthetic other person, the aesthetic table, the aesthetic flower, the aesthetic molecule, the aesthetic electron, and the aesthetic ionization, as it is in the aesthetic self. This explains how it is possible for one to apprehend in his own self-consciousness the blueness of the sky and the color of the rose and the moving beauty of the sunset with precisely the same immediacy with which the pain of one's own local toothache is apprehended. It is only with respect to the differentiations in this all-embracing aesthetic continuum that the aesthetic self is different from the aesthetic sky, the aesthetic flower, or any other human or non-human natural object. Thus, it is quite erroneous to conceive of a person, after the manner of the Lockean mental substance and traditional modern Anglo-American culture, as a completely local, independent thing having nothing in common with all other persons and things. There is an all-embracing indeterminate continuum of feeling common to all creatures in their aesthetic immediacy.

It must be remembered also that all these aesthetic materials, including the all-embracing aesthetic continuum, are the kind of thing which can be known only by being immediately experienced. No syntactically formulated, mathematically or logically abstract, indirectly and experimentally verified theory can ever designate them. They are, by virtue of this very character, ineffable. They are also emotionally moving. In short, the aesthetic continuum within the essential nature of all things is, to use the language of Shakespeare, "Such stuff as dreams are made on." But there are other differentiations in this ineffable, all-embracing aesthetic component than the introspected images which constitute dreams. There are also the equally immediately inspected images which constitute the colors, fragrances, and flavors of the sky, the earth, the flowers, the sea, and other natural objects. The aesthetic component is therefore also the stuff that these are made of.

Now it is precisely this ineffable, emotional, moving quale that constitutes what is meant by spirit and the spiritual. Thus in order to do justice to the spiritual nature of human beings and of all things it is not necessary to have recourse to idle speculations, by means of which one tries to pierce through the glass beyond which we now see darkly, to supposedly unaesthetic material substances behind, or into some unreachable and unknowable realm where mental substances are supposed to be. On the contrary, the spiritual, the ineffable, the emotionally moving, the aesthetically vivid—the stuff that dreams and sunsets and the fragrance of flowers are made of—is the immediate, purely factual portion of human nature and the nature of all things. This is the portion of human knowledge that can be known without recourse to inference and speculative hypotheses and deductive logic, and epistemic correlations, and rigorously controlled experiments. This we have and are in ourselves and in all things, prior to all theory, before all speculation, with immediacy and hence with absolute certainty. One is able to say with the Spaniards, the Mexicans and the Tantric Hindus that in part at least the essence of the soul is passion.

Consequently, the relating of the aesthetic or sensed, to the theoretical in scientific knowledge, by the two-termed relation of epistemic correlation makes the recourse to Locke's and Descartes's troublesome mental substances quite unnecessary in order to account for the spiritual, aesthetic, and emotional religious character of man, and of all other natural objects. Here, in this conception of the spiritual and in this conception of religion, are the intuitive and contemplative, indeterminate, aesthetic and emotional religion of the Orient, the negative theology of the West, the mysticism of San Juan de la Cruz, and the cult of the Virgin at Chartres and Guadalupe; rather than the theoretical, doctrinal, orthodox religion of the male Moses, Christ, or Mohammed and their determinate unseen Yahweh or God the Father. We have also the basis for understanding the individualistic philosophy of the Spaniard Unamuno, and the *existence* philosophy of Kierkegaard and Heidigger. But this is precisely what any adequate philosophy must have if it is to do justice to certain unique insights and cultural achievements of the Orient, Spain and Latin America, and merge them with the equally unmatched but different values of the traditional orthodox West, without bloodshed, devastation, and tragedy. Also, it explains why, throughout the history of Catholicism, as Henry Adams notes in Chartres Cathedral and as can be seen even today in Mexico, surreptitiously or explicitly, men have instinctively insisted upon taking the aesthetic emotional Virgin Mary and the Virgin of Guadalupe as Divine in Her own right, and not simply because she is the earthly Mother of Christ and merely through Him a sensuous symbol of the theoretically and doctrinally known, but unseen, God the Father.

The theory also restores to natural objects their aesthetically rich luminous quality. The earth, as any farmer boy who has followed the plow in the springtime knows, is a warm and fragrant earth. It is, as the Orientals and all peoples close to the soil have clearly seen, the mother of us all. From her come the creation and the nourishment of all living things both plants and animals. Thus it is that she has been appropriately and properly named "Mother Earth," or "the Good Earth." So strong is the feeling of this inseparable bond between man and nature that the experienced explorer of China's soil and geography G. B. Cressey, and the informed student of Chinese culture Lucius C. Porter, have affirmed that "Perhaps the finest summary of Chinese philosophy is the desire to be 'in tune with nature.'"

As Tagore and the Taoist painters and the Americans Emerson and Thoreau have seen, nature fairly presses her beauty upon us always on all occasions. And as the Taoist painters have noted in their quiet contemplation, the all-embracing aesthetic continuum which is nature is the same emotionally moving aesthetic continuum which is man in the aesthetic ineffable spiritual component of his being. In the language of Hinduism, Brahman (the cosmic principle in the universe) and Atman (the psychic principle in man) are one.

It is for these reasons that there will be no religion nor culture which adequately meets the spiritual as well as the intellectual needs of men until the traditional Western theism, after being reformed to bring it abreast of contemporary knowledge of the theoretic component in things upon which it rests, is also supplemented with the primitive traditional Oriental religion of intuition and contemplation with its cultivation of the aesthetic component. And before this is possible there must be an art in the West, like that of the Orient, but our own, in which the female aesthetic intuitive principle in things speaks in its purity, conveying itself for its own sake. Only if such an art is created can the West break itself of the habit of regarding feelings and emotions and the immediately given portion of man's nature and the nature of all things as mere superficial appearance, or mere symbol of the theoretic component beyond. Only then can we grasp the positive experience that the ineffable spiritual immediately felt part of oneself and all things is something ultimate, elementary, and good. Such is the importance of the painting of Georgia O'Keeffe.

The Self in Its Theoretic Nature

Having accounted for the emotional, aesthetic, ineffably spiritual nature of man and the universe, with the aesthetic component or end-term in the two-termed relation of epistemic correlation, it is no longer necessary in the conception of the other end-term, the theoretic component, to include within it an inferred or postulated mental substance. Instead, the theoretic component of human knowledge can be restricted to precisely what the expert natural scientists with their scientific methods of hypothesis, deduction, and experimental confirmation indicate it to be. This means, in the case of man, that in the theoretic component of his nature he is precisely what experimental physicists, chemists, biologists, and psychologists find him to be. Thus the theoretic component of man is man conceived as a physical-chemical system, an electrodynamic field, with the particular structure which exhibits itself in man's body and especially in his nervous system and its cortex.

Man in this sense we do not immediately apprehend. The reader has but to inspect himself with all the immediacy of which he is capable, to realize that he does not immediately apprehend himself either in the data of sense or in the images of the imagination as a being with a cortex or a complicated nervous system involving electromagnetic and chemical relations with the electromagnetic field of the rest of nature. Man in this sense is known by postulated theory which is checked through its deductive consequences against the aesthetic component of oneself which is immediately apprehended, by recourse to the two-termed epistemic correlations. Thus one knows himself to be a creature with a physical-chemical-electromagnetic-biological body by indirectly verified theory, rather than by immediate inspection or observation alone. But this factor in man's nature is nonetheless real, and it is no less an essential part of his nature, because it is known in this logically inferred, scientifically and experimentally verified manner.

At this point, the theory provides the valid part of Russian communism. For the basic, unique factor in Russian communistic theory is precisely the thesis indicated just above that the physically, chemically, biologically, thermodynamically, physiologically, and anatomically known man is the essential man, and hence the economic and political person. This unique valid element in the philosophy of Karl Marx and in Russian communism, it will be recalled, came from Hobbes and Feuerbach. It is provided in the theory of epistemic correlation by what is termed the theoretic component of man's nature, since the theoretic component of anything is that thing precisely as it is known by the natural scientists' postulationally designated, indirectly and experimentally confirmed theory. . . .

Since it has been shown that the culture of the traditional Orient is grounded in the aesthetic component, and since the Feuerbachian unique, basic element in Marxian communism is provided by the theoretic component, the two-termed relation of epistemic correlation joining these two components specifies the manner in which the traditional Oriental culture and the valid Feuerbachian element in Russian communism can be related without conflict. . . .

Western science has shown that the pains and pleasures and colors and flavors in one's aesthetic nature, besides being determinate and in part relative, are also in part determined by fixed laws which indirect experimental verification has shown to govern the comings and goings of their epistemic correlates in the theoretic component. For example, the sharp pain which one immediately apprehends may be the epistemic correlate of the scientifically inferred acidity of one's physico-chemical digestive processes. Similarly, the dark round patch in the aesthetic continuum may be an epistemic correlate of the astronomical body termed the moon, when, as governed by the indirectly verified laws of celestial mechanics, this moon moves into a certain relation with the sun and the earth, which we call an eclipse of the sun. Thus an adequate comprehension of human nature must consider not merely the differentiated aesthetic component, but also the relation of its sensed qualities to the scientifically inferred theoretic component in all things. This theoretic component has one very important characteristic. Since it is not immediately apprehensible as a local particular, and since any part of it, such as a person, can be defined only relationally and syntactically by the postulates of systematic deductively formulated scientific theory, it is of necessity relational and systematic in character. Thus, by no stretching of the imagination can one's legal, political, economic or religious concept of a person in the theoretic component of its definition and essential nature be conceived, after the manner of Locke's mental substance and the traditional modern laissez-faire economic and political theory, as a self-sufficient, completely independent, purely local thing, free of all essential and internal relations to other persons and things. Instead, man in the theoretically inferred and scientifically verified part of his nature is a determinate relationally defined, and hence a social being. Again, Aristotelian, Elizabethan, and medieval truths and values are reconciled with those of contemporary modern science.

Moreover, the theoretic component in man as designated by contemporary biological and psychological science is defined systematically and relationally by the same laws which define the theoretic component in all other natural objects. Thus the social nature of man, as constituted by the theoretic component of his nature, is, like the indeterminate, all-embracing, undifferentiated continuum in the aesthetic component of his nature, a communal nature which, in a basic and systematic and fundamental sense, makes him one not merely with all human beings, as Christ taught, but also with all other natural objects—plants, animals, the good earth, and the most distant stars—as Buddha, Lao Tzu and Confucius taught. Again, traditional Christian and contemporary Western scientific values are reconciled with and supplemented to include Oriental values.

Furthermore, without the earth and the energy of the sun and the creative photosynthesis of the plants, man as we know him scientifically in the theoretic component of his nature would not be. This being the communal social nature of man in both the aesthetic and the theoretic components of his nature, clearly the old Lockean theory of the person as an absolutely free and independent mental substance, having no governmental need of his fellow men, except to preserve his private property, is a figment of the imagination as erroneous and untenable in theory as it has turned out to be inadequate and outmoded in practice before the inescapable social and international problems of the contemporary world. Consequently, to be a person, in a much more far-reaching sense than even Aristotle conceived, is to be, in one's very nature in the all-embracing aesthetic component and in the systematically defined, equally all-embracing theoretic component of one's being, a social natural object, a political animal. Hence, to have a good government is to have one which gives expression not merely to man's social nature as a human being and a living animal but also to man's social nature as part of the system of all natural objects. In this respect also justice is done to the social and systematic character of man and nature which was the merit of the Hegelian and Anglo-American idealistic social philosophy and the Marxian dialectic materialism.

But this does not occur to such an extreme degree that freedom is denied and the social becomes identical with the absolutely determined and the regimented. For it is only the theoretic component in things which is both determinate and socially systematic in character, and even knowledge of this is by hypothesis and hence, tentative and subject to change with further information. Consequently, in practice there is freedom here and open-mindedness, tempered always with the recognition that though the inferred part of human nature and things is determinate, social and systematic in character, any human being's knowledge of precisely what specific content it has, is at best approximate and probable rather than absolutely certain. With respect to the aesthetic component, not merely knowledge of it, but it in itself is in part indeterminate. This is unqualifiedly true with respect to that portion of it—namely the undifferentiated aesthetic continuum—which is the common all-embracing immediately experienced factor in all things. Thus, justice is done to the independence, integrity and freedom of the individual, which it is to the everlasting credit of Descartes, Locke, Hume, Bentham and Mill and traditional modern Protestantism and democracy to have fostered.

But this integrity and freedom of the individual is carried far beyond the traditional modern conception of it. Man in the theoretic component of his nature is not a blank tablet but has specific character as designated by the investigations of the most recent science. According to this science men vary tremendously because of determinate differences in their genes, their glandular secretions, and the structure of their nervous systems. Thus, men have individual integrity not because of a blank uniformity or because they are all mental substances but because each has in the theoretically known, scientifically verified component of his nature a unique, specific character. A free society, therefore, must do more than allow each person to vote, it must also as far as is possible allow the unique determinate traits of each person to come to fulfillment. Thus, to Anglo-American political freedom to vote and to Marxist economic freedom from want there must be added individual physiological freedom to be oneself.

The most important ground of freedom, however, as has been noted, is in the aesthetic component of man's nature. This is not merely in part irreducibly indeterminate, thereby introducing potentiality into the essence of man's nature; it is also emotional, ineffable and luminous in character. With respect to this type of freedom of the sentiments and the emotions the traditional modern Anglo-American cultures have been weak; as Grant Wood's portraits show, and as the spiritually mature British author Rebecca West indicates, when she writes of "the grey ice that forms on an Englishman's face" and of "the mean and puny element in the Gentile nature, at its worst among the English, which cannot stand up to anything abundant and generous." Even Thomas Jefferson wrote of the United States: "This country, which has given to the world the example of physical liberty, owes to it that of moral [and it should be added, emotional] emancipation also, for as yet it is but nominal with us. The inquisition of public opinion overwhelms, in practice, the freedom asserted by the laws in theory." One could expect little else from a people brought up in a philosophy and religion which removed the emotional and aesthetic factor in oneself and things from the essential natures of both the self and the natural object to turn it into mere appearance and the principle of evil. To regard the aesthetic component as possessing reality and irreducibility on an equal footing with the theoretic component, as the substitution of the two-termed relation of epistemic correlation for the traditional modern three-termed relation of appearance requires, is to change all this. Then, to be one's true self is to give expression to the ineffable emotional spontaneity and indeterminacy of the aesthetic component of one's essential nature, as well as to bring the more determinate theoretically known constitution of oneself to expression. Thus, to political, economic and physiological freedom there is also added psychological freedom of the emotions and the sentiments. In this manner justice is done to the Latin, Mexican, Spanish, Freudian, Middle Eastern and Oriental concept of freedom as well as to the more purely political freedom of the French, and English-speaking, modern West.

It is at this point also that previous emphasis upon leaving, or reconstructing, the traditional precepts which may have been reasonable in ancient times, or even in the eighteenth century, in the light of contemporary scientific and philosophical knowledge becomes important. Because of failure to bring the traditional moral doctrines referring to the theoretic component into accord with the advance in scientific knowledge, not only do outmoded provincial beliefs and practices persist in the name of morality, religion, economic science and politics but men are actually held morally responsible for items in their conduct which a scientific study of the biological, psychological, and psychiatric character of man indicates to be factors over which the individual has no control. If moralists are to insist that freedom is the precondition for a meaningful moral life, then they must also accept the corollary of this thesis, and not pass moral judgments upon human beings with respect to matters in their conduct over which the specific beings in question have in fact no control.

This must also be a guiding principle in the passage of laws in the nation and throughout the world. The community has a right to prescribe for everybody in it only laws referring to those factors which a correct, intuited and theoretically designated knowledge of the nature of man and his universe indicates to hold for everybody. There is plenty of scope for the operation of universal, unqualified laws, and for the pressing of our good works upon other people, in this realm of the nature of things alone. With respect to those matters in ourselves and the universe which a positivistic and scientific study of the aesthetic and theoretic components in the nature of things shows to be different from person to person, time to time, circumstance to circumstance, and nation to nation, both the layman and the governmental official must keep hands off in passing moral judgments upon other people and nations.

And by the same token a person or a government guided by a correct conception of man and nature has the right to affirm certain principles which hold for everybody. Otherwise, even the local individual would not be true to himself, since he would not be free to express the communal factors in his own nature; nor would the public agreement of at least a majority, necessary to prevent political freedom from destroying itself, be present. For man is not merely his own local, differentiated, aesthetic self, and his own local, differentiated, scientifically verified, theoretically known self. He is also (1) the indeterminate, otherwise undifferentiated aesthetic continuum common to all other persons and things in the aesthetic component of their nature and (2) the systematic, essentially social relatedness of the entire theoretic component of all things, apart from which his own more local theoretically known nature cannot be defined or conceived. Hence, these two factors insure positivistic and scientifically verifiable philosophical foundations for a limited application of the federal principle in international as well as national affairs.

Philosophical Foundations for World Sovereignty

Just as the relative local differentiations, both aesthetic and theoretic, which distinguish individuals and peoples from each other, provide for the limited absolute independence and freedom of the individual and for the limited sovereignties of local self-government, so the indeterminate aesthetic continuum and the determinate, theoretically designated systematic relatedness which are common to all men, guarantee the limited sovereignty of a world self-government. It is to be noted that a world government or a federal government is as much a self-government as is a village government or a government of an individual by himself alone, since the factors which are the same in all men are as much a part of the self as are the factors which distinguish that self from other persons and things. Thus, a philosophy of the state seems to be at hand with the specific criterion of private, local and world sovereignties that is required if the full freedom and integrity of the individual, which is one source of every great creative advance in civilization, is to be preserved, and if at the same time the sanctions for "one world" are to be guaranteed, which are so obviously required to solve by sympathetic, intelligent, lawful and peaceful means the inescapable national and international problems of these times.

It appears, therefore, when the paradoxically confusing and tragic conflicts of the world are analyzed one by one and then traced to the basic philosophical problem underlying them, and when this problem of the relation between immediately apprehended and theoretically inferred factors in things is then solved by replacing the traditional three-termed relation of appearance by the two-termed relation of epistemic correlation, that a realistically grounded, scientifically verifiable idea of the good for man and his world is provided in which the unique achievements of both the East and the West are united and the traditional incompatible and conflicting partial values of the different parts of the West are first reconstructed and then reconciled, so that *each* is seen to have something unique to contribute and *all* are reformed so as to supplement and reinforce instead of combat and destroy each other.

Edward Conze
ANXIETY—EAST AND WEST

The repudiation of everything which constitutes or attracts the empirical self, has earned for Buddhism the reputation of being a 'pessimistic' faith. It is true that this world, i.e. everything conditioned and impermanent, is emphatically regarded as wholly ill, as wholly pervaded with suffering, as something to be rejected totally, abandoned totally, for the one goal of Nirvana. I am not quite sure, however, that 'radical pessimism' is really a good word for this attitude to the world. Observers of such Buddhist countries as Burma and Tibet record that their inhabitants are spontaneously cheerful, and even gay—laymen and monks alike. It is rather puzzling that the pessimistic gloom which one reads into the Buddhist doctrine of universal suffering should reflect itself in a cheerful countenance. This world may be a vale of tears, but there is joy in shedding its burden. It must be renounced. But if there is a kingdom of God to win by renouncing it, the gain infinitely outweighs the loss. In any case, the best thing we can do with such a word as 'pessimism' is to discard it and look the problem straight in the face.

The negative attitude of Buddhist thinkers to this world is obviously bound up with the question of the meaning of life, and the problem of the destiny of man. However difficult this problem may be, however unscientific it may be to concern ourselves with it, we must come to a decision on it, because the entire happiness and fruitfulness of our lives depends on the answer. The views on the nature and destiny of man, or the meaning of human existence, fall roughly into two classes. According to some, man is a product of the earth. The earth is his home.

From *Buddhism* by Edward Conze, pp. 21–23. Reprinted by permission of Harper & Row, Publishers, Inc.
Edward Conze (1904–   ) is a British authority on Buddhism.

His task is to make himself at home on the earth. Self-preservation is the highest law, and even duty, of man. Others, however, believe that man is a spirit ill at ease, a soul fallen from heaven, a stranger on this earth. His task is to regain the state of perfection which was his before he fell into this world. Self-denial is the highest law and duty of man.

Our modern civilisation favours the first view-point, Buddhism the second. It would, of course, be futile to contend that such issues can be decided by argument alone. In all decisions on values one must be careful not to exalt one's own personal tastes, temperament, and preferences to the dignity of an objective and natural law. One should only define one's position, and not coerce others into it. The Buddhist point of view will appeal only to those people who are completely disillusioned with the world as it is, and with themselves, who are extremely sensitive to pain, suffering, and any kind of turmoil, who have an extreme desire for happiness, and a considerable capacity for renunciation. No Buddhist would assume that all men are either able or willing to understand his doctrine.

The Buddhist seeks for a total happiness beyond this world. Why should he be so ambitious? Why not be content with getting as much happiness out of this world as we can, however little it may be? The answer is that in actual practice we are seen not to be content. If increase in physical comfort and earthly satisfactions would make us content, then the inhabitants of the suburbs of London should be immeasurably more radiant and contented than Chinese coolies or Spanish peasants. The exact opposite is the case. Our human nature, according to the Buddhist contention, is so constituted that we are content with nothing but complete permanence, complete ease, complete security. And none of that can we ever find in this shifting world.

The discoveries which philosophers and psychologists have made in recent years about the central importance of anxiety at the very core of our being, have quite a Buddhist ring about them. According to the views elaborated by Scheler, Freud, Heidegger and Jaspers, there is in the core of our being a basic anxiety, a little empty hole from which all other forms of anxiety and unease draw their strength. In its pure form, this anxiety is experienced only by people with an introspective and philosophical turn of mind, and even then only rarely. If one has never felt it oneself, no amount of explanation will convince. If one has felt it, one will never forget, however much one may try. It may come upon you when you have been asleep, withdrawn from the world; you wake up in the middle of the night and feel a kind of astonishment at being there, which then gives way to a fear and horror at the mere fact of being there. It is then that you catch yourself by yourself, just for a moment, against the background of a kind of nothingness all around you, and with a gnawing sense of your powerlessness, your utter helplessness in the face of this astonishing fact that you are there at all. Usually, we avoid this experience as much as we possibly can, because it is so shattering and painful. Usually, I am very careful not to have myself by myself, but the I plus all sorts of other experiences. People who are busy all the time, who must always think of something, who must always be doing something, are incessantly running away from this experience of the *basic* or *original* anxiety. What we usually do is to lean and to rely on something else than this empty centre of ourselves. The Buddhist contention is that we will never be at ease before we have overcome this basic anxiety, and that we can do that only by relying on nothing at all.

6
Reevaluation in Religion

The world of the past few centuries has long been regarded as one of increasing secularism, in which the state has grown at the expense of the church. The crises of the twentieth century plus the dominant role played by science and technology have painfully accelerated this process of secularization, and the forces at variance with religion now seem to have the upper hand.

Among these forces, aside from the technological transformation of the world, modern scholarship and psychology are particularly important. The application of the methods of scientific research to religious literature, as in the work of Johannes Weiss, can be as fatal to conservative Christianity as evolution has been; and the psychologist has largely replaced the priest (with no Reformation in sight). Sigmund Freud explains (or explains away) religion in psychological terms, but Seward Hiltner argues that psychology is a "significant ally" of Christian morality. The relationship between religion and psychology, whatever its nature, has become one of stylish interest, and many people now include in their vocabulary such words as *angst,* or anxiety.

Paradoxically, perhaps, the intellectual approach to religion, if it cannot revive faith, can at least make it more respectable. Nietzsche has come into his own as a religious thinker and prophet of the twentieth century: his pronouncement, "God is dead," could hardly be more timely. And even the most agnostic intellectual can feel the attraction of the "neo-orthodoxy" of Reinhold Niebuhr, where a wealth of learning and a deep social consciousness accompany the religious message. Despite its famous atheistic proponents, existentialism, according to David Roberts, is very much an element of the Christian heritage, though an element to be used with care since it is both a stimulus and a threat to the religious life.

Unlike God, religion may be very much alive, but as Pope John XXIII suggested, religion needs to be brought up-to-date (*aggiornamento*).

Friedrich Nietzsche
THE DEATH OF GOD

Have you not heard of that madman who lit a lantern in the bright morning hours, ran to the market place, and cried incessantly, "I seek God! I seek God!" As many of those who do not believe in God were standing around just then, he provoked much laughter. Why, did he get lost? said one. Did he lose his way like a child? said another. Or is he hiding? Is he afraid of us? Has he gone on a voyage? or emigrated? Thus they yelled and laughed. The madman jumped into their midst and pierced them with his glances.

"Whither is God?" he cried. "I shall tell you. *We have killed him—* you and I. All of us are his murderers. But how have we done this? How were we able to drink up the sea? Who gave us the sponge to wipe away the entire horizon? What did we do when we unchained this earth from its sun? Whither is it moving now? Whither are we moving now? Away from all suns? Are we not plunging continually? Backward, sideward, forward, in all directions? Is there any up or down left? Are we not straying as through an infinite nothing? Do we not feel the breath of empty space? Has it not become colder? Is not night and more night coming on all the

From *The Portable Nietzsche*, translated and edited by Walter Kaufmann. Copyright 1954 by The Viking Press, Inc. Reprinted by permission of The Viking Press, Inc.

Friedrich Nietzsche (1844–1900) was one of the most influential German philosophers and an outspoken critic of Christianity.

while? Must not lanterns be lit in the morning? Do we not hear anything yet of the noise of the grave-diggers who are burying God? Do we not smell anything yet of God's decomposition? Gods too decompose. God is dead. God remains dead. And we have killed him. How shall we, the murderers of all murderers, comfort ourselves? What was holiest and most powerful of all that the world has yet owned has bled to death under our knives. Who will wipe this blood off us? What water is there for us to clean ourselves? What festivals of atonement, what sacred games shall we have to invent? Is not the greatness of this deed too great for us? Must not we ourselves become gods simply to seem worthy of it? There has never been a greater deed; and whoever will be born after us—for the sake of this deed he will be part of a higher history than all history hitherto."

Here the madman fell silent and looked again at his listeners; and they too were silent and stared at him in astonishment. At last he threw his lantern on the ground, and it broke and went out. "I come too early," he said then; "my time has not come yet. This tremendous event is still on its way, still wandering—it has not yet reached the ears of man. Lightning and thunder require time, the light of the stars requires time, deeds require time even after they are done, before they can be seen and heard. This deed is still more distant from them than the most distant stars—*and yet they have done it themselves.*"

It has been related further that on that same day the madman entered divers churches and there sang his *requiem aeternam deo.* Let out and called to account, he is said to have replied each time, "What are these churches now if they are not the tombs and sepulchers of God?"

Johannes Weiss
A CRITICAL APPROACH TO SCRIPTURE

Generally speaking, the popular view is dominated by the accounts of 'Luke' and 'John,' according to which the disciples, accompanied by a larger group of followers and in obedience to an express command of Jesus (Luke 24:49; Acts 1:4), remained as a body in Jerusalem (Acts 1:14), and prayerfully awaited the promised Spirit of God

From *Earliest Christianity* by Johannes Weiss, pp. 15–18, 27–31. Copyright 1937 by Wilson-Erickson, Inc. Reprinted by permission of Harper & Row, Publishers, Inc.

Johannes Weiss (1863–1914) was a German New Testament scholar.

until his coming on Pentecost (Acts 2). It was at this moment that the oldest Christian community was founded, and grew at one step from 120 to 3000 souls. The direct line of development, thus outlined, only faintly suggests that Jesus' followers were greatly upset by his death. Only a few light strokes—the depression of the disciples *en route* to Emmaus (Luke 24:17), their disappointment (24:21), the weeping of Mary Magdalene (John 20:11), the disciples gathered behind closed doors for fear of the Jews (20:19), the grave doubt of Thomas (20:25), the laments of the disciples and their weak faith (Mark 16:10, 14)—only such mild and touching details are used, to convey the discouragement and sorrow of the disciples, but they indicate nothing like a mood of despair. For had they not been prepared, by many a word of Jesus, to anticipate his resurrection (Luke 24:6f)? Hence there is absent from this harmonizing account, that swift transition from the utter darkness of the valley of shadow to the streaming brilliance of Easter morning, which we should otherwise have expected. The historical critic, however, suspects that at this point a deep gulf has been overbridged, a dark patch painted over with brighter colors.

Further grounds for this suspicion are to be found in the representations of Mark and Matthew. In sharpest contrast with Luke and John, the Risen Lord orders his disciples, through the women, to proceed to Galilee (Mark 16:7; Matt. 28:10), where they are to see him. The narrative of Mark breaks off at this point, but Matthew goes on to relate that the Eleven actually went to Galilee and there received from Christ their mission to the peoples of the earth (Matt. 28:16–20). These narratives are simply incompatible with those of Luke. It is no use trying to insert this Galilean journey between the dates of the Ascension and Pentecost (i.e. between Acts 1 and 2); for Luke states explicitly that the disciples did not leave Jerusalem until after the outpouring of the Spirit (Acts 1:4; Luke 24:49). It is equally impossible to slip in the story of Pentecost before the journey to Galilee (e.g. before Matt. 28:16). As it so often appears, both traditions arose independently, had no contacts one with another, took no account of each other, and are accordingly simply incompatible.

Present-day criticism is inclined to prefer the Marcan-Matthean account to that of Luke and John. It assumes that after the death of Jesus the disciples returned to Galilee and resumed their normal occupations. Further evidence of this is found in the appended chapter of the Gospel of John (ch. 21) and in the apocryphal Gospel of Peter, the surviving fragment of which concludes: 'But we, the twelve disciples of the Lord, mourned and were filled with grief; and each one, dismayed by what had taken place, returned to his own home. But I, Simon Peter, and my brother Andrew, took our nets and went down to the sea; and with us went Levi, the son of Alphaeus, to whom the Lord . . .' Of course one must not base the assumption upon such precarious foundations as this apocryphal tradition or the appendix to John—which is itself apocryphal enough. The testimony has weight only to the extent that it points back to earlier information regarding an appearance of Jesus which one of the disciples experienced in Galilee. Even the account in Mark commands credence, not because the evangelist narrates it—in truth long after the event—but because Mark offers us a fragment of the primitive tradition, which, as ordinarily understood, seems to provide incontrovertible historical evidence of the dispersion of the disciples in Galilee. It is found in a prediction of Jesus (Mark 14:27f): 'All ye shall be offended: for it is written, I will smite the shepherd, and the sheep shall be scattered abroad. Howbeit, after I am raised up, I will go before you into Galilee.' In these words we see reflected a not altogether happy reminiscence of those days, a hard fact which the old tradition could not altogether make away with—though Luke and John have suppressed it—namely, that the disciples 'wandered' and 'fell away.' A kind of justification, or at least mitigation, of this dark fact was discovered when it could be shown from the word of the prophet Zechariah (13:7) that the event was divinely foreseen. But the less the 'scattering' of the disciples could thereby be excused, the more certain it appears that such a dispersal actually took place. And this is what many scholars[1] now describe as 'the flight to Galilee.'

But this interpretation is by no means so certain as is often assumed. Matthew at any rate did not so understand the narrative of Mark; for he adds, 'this night' (26:31), i.e. he refers the words, 'Ye shall be offended in me,' and the 'scattering' of the disciples, to the flight of the disciples in Gethsemane when Jesus was arrested. And Mark himself must so have understood the saying, for he assumes that Peter and the others were still in Jerusalem on Easter morning (16:7), and that at the command of Jesus—not at all in precipitate flight—they returned to Galilee. Apparently, he already understood the words, 'I go before you into Galilee,' in the sense that the Risen Master was now on the way there, in order to meet his followers at the appointed place. But this interpretation of the words is even in Mark a complete misunderstanding, repeated now by modern critics.

For what reason will Jesus not manifest himself to his followers in Jerusalem, but only in Galilee? And why does he 'go before' them, in the meantime? Must he, as one risen from the dead, necessarily appear in Galilee? Can he not show himself anywhere, whenever he will? Cannot he manifest himself to his own, when he stands suddenly in their midst? Is he not exalted above the limitations of distance and place?

[1] [E.g. the late Professor B. W. Bacon: *The Beginnings of Gospel Story* (1909), *The Gospel of Mark* (1925), *Jesus the Son of God* (1930), etc.] Cf. Weizsäcker, *Apostolic Age*, pp. 1–4. [The more recent debate on this question between K. Lake and F. C. Burkitt is summarized in BC, v. 7ff.]

'I will go before you'—that scarcely means, 'I will precede you by a brief interval,' but rather, 'I will place myself at your head and lead you to Galilee.' Hence the passage in Mark (14:28) lacks the continuation, 'there shall ye see me'; for the presupposition was originally, 'After I have rejoined you here in Jerusalem, following my resurrection, I will lead you back home; there will come the fulfillment of our hopes—the Kingdom of God.' This saying, so understood, must rate as a very old and historical datum, for the very reason that it voices an expectation never realized. Whether or not it is an authentic word of Jesus, it reflects an expectation of the disciples, and one that was disappointed: the Lord did not lead them back to Galilee. Accordingly, some later authors, like Luke and John, simply ignored it, while others gave it a different meaning—Mark, for example, whose false interpretation (16:7) is the common one to this day. Thus we can readily see how 'the Galilean tradition' arose. From the words given in 14:27f, Mark himself inferred that the disciples were to see Jesus first in Galilee; it satisfies him simply to have this direction conveyed to them by the angel. Matthew carries the line further: the Eleven actually go to Galilee, to the mountain where Jesus had commanded them. The apocryphal narratives in John 21 and Pseudo-Peter further develop the scene of the appearance to Peter, in a colorful, novelistic direction, combining it with the story of the Draught of Fishes (Luke 5:1ff). Hence, contrary to the popular view, 'the Galilean tradition' must be looked upon as a product of fantasy. In opposition to it, Mark 14:27f clearly proves that at the very earliest period the disciples expected that the Risen Lord would lead them from Judea to Galilee. In other words, they were still in Jerusalem. Whether or not, as Luke relates, they were observing a command of Jesus in doing so, may be passed over. And certainly there is not the fragment of an indication that the disciples wandered back to Jerusalem again after fleeing to Galilee. . . .

A peculiar, and to us an unaccustomed, conception of the death of Jesus lies at the basis of these narratives, one that is reflected in the early sources but has been forced more or less into the background—the conception namely that Jesus returned to God at the very moment of his death. As Lazarus was transported at once by the angels into Abraham's bosom, without mention of his burial or resurrection (Luke 16:22), so Jesus says to the penitent thief, 'Today shalt thou be with me in Paradise' (Luke 23:43), as if he expected to enter immediately into the presence of God. The same meaning is reflected three verses later in Luke: 'Father, into thy hands I commend my spirit'; similarly in the Fourth Gospel[2] Jesus always says that he goes 'to the Father,' without any mention of burial and resurrection. Even before the high priest he expresses the same

[2] [E.g. 14:12; cf. Wellhausen, *Das Evangelium Johannis* (Gospel of John, 1908), *passim*.]

conviction, that 'from now on the Son of Man will sit at the right hand of Power' (Luke 22:69). In naïvely popular manner, the question is not raised whether only the soul of Jesus, or his spirit, and not his body as well, will thus be carried away;[3] the question, 'whether in the body or out of the body,' remains as much without an answer as in Paul's experience of rapture (II Cor. 12:2). Wherever this conception prevails, we also find the idea that the death of Jesus carried with it his immediate exaltation. It was in this state of heavenly glory that he manifested himself to his disciples. Had this conception become the dominant and exclusive one, there would have been no need, so to speak, for any doctrine of the Resurrection of Jesus. The idea which it suggested, the conviction namely that Jesus, far from succumbing to a divine judgment, had been exalted to the divine presence, was sufficiently established for all those concerned by the appearances of the glorified Christ.

Let us now inquire, How are we to judge these appearances from the present-day scientific viewpoint? The traditional conception, that what took place was purely miraculous, and that the exalted Christ in his body of light came within the disciples' range of vision, still satisfies many Christians—at least they believe themselves able to accept it; and many give the matter no further thought. For those, on the other hand, who take account of the modern scientific doctrine of the unbroken sequence of causation, there is scarcely any alternative to the view that these experiences of the disciples were simply 'visions.' The scientific meaning of this term is that an apparent act of vision takes place for which there is no corresponding external object. The optic nerve has not been stimulated by any outward waves of light or vibrations of the ether, but has been excited by a purely inner physiological cause. At the same time the sense-impression of sight is accepted by the one who experiences the vision as completely as if it were wholly 'objective'; he fully believes the object of his vision to be actually before him.

Is it permissible now to apply this scientifically evolved definition of vision to the experiences of the earliest disciples? Certainly the word 'visions' meant something different from this, as Paul used the term (see p. 26). He is convinced that the glorified Lord actually appeared before his eyes. The modern conception of 'vision' was totally unknown to him; and had he known it he would certainly have repudiated it. When the Book of Acts records that Peter beheld a vision in a moment of ecstasy, preceding the conversion of Cornelius (Acts 10:10–17), this is a far remove from any description of a merely subjective experience. The appearance makes so strongly objective an impression upon Peter that his

---

[3] [How then was he to 'lead' the disciples back to Galilee? Evidently this reflects the expectation of the disciples, rather than of Jesus himself.]

whole later course of life is decisively altered thereby. Similarly, the bold proclamation of the message of the resurrection, by the first disciples, would be simply inexplicable had they felt the slightest doubt of the objective reality of the Lord's appearances. All the more impossible must it then seem for us to explain these appearances as merely subjective events. However, the disciples are scarcely to be thought impartial witnesses, on this question, since it is characteristic of the vision-experience that the one who has had it is convinced of the complete physical objectivity of what he has seen.[4]

But is it not a depressing thought, that these fundamental facts of the Christian religion were no more than delusions, fancies, hallucinations? On such a view does not whole fabric of the faith crash irrevocably into ruin? Can we discover anything in the belief of these men that is fundamentally veracious or exemplary?

It is easy to see how disturbing this point of view must be for those to whom it is unaccustomed. On the contrary, anyone who believes in the divine guidance of history, and who in particular recognizes the hand of God in the beginnings of Christianity, will also have sufficient faith to leave with God the choice of the means whereby he called into existence the thing he willed to create. We must admit this much, viz. that under the circumstances, if the disciples were to carry forward the cause of their Master, it was essential and indispensable that they should be fully convinced of his survival and exaltation. And if this was the divine purpose, does it not still remain a question, which none of us is in a position to answer, what means God must choose in order to arouse in them this conviction? Who will maintain that the only method worthy of the divine will was the miracle of an actual manifestation of the Glorified Christ? And for what reason should God not make use of the means which again and again in the religious history of the ancient world, from Isaiah to John the Seer, provided the determinative, driving power, namely the vision? Conceived as visions, the events of the first Easter may lose something of their apologetic value *for us;* but then they scarcely took place for our benefit, but rather in the interest of those immediately concerned. For them, the vision sufficed, and produced a certainty of conviction which made them inspired missionaries and martyrs.

There is no doubt that the hypothesis of vision makes the events

---

[4] [On the other hand, the visions in the Book of Revelation are doubtless 'subjective', not to say more or less merely literary. On the subject of the literary and the psychological elements in Apocalyptic, see R. H. Charles, *Eschatology, Hebrew, Jewish, and Christian* (2d ed., 1913), pp. 174ff; *Commentary on the Revelation of St. John* (1920), vol. i. Int., ch. xi.]

more intelligible to us, and brings them closer home, than the older conception of miracle succeeds in doing. If the disciples were convinced by an external miracle, their conviction or—as in the case of Paul—their conversion turns out to be an act of violence, wholly unorganic, i.e. unconnected with any inner preparation for the change. Peter and the others might have been far more deeply plunged in despair than was in all probability their case; James might have lost faith completely, in fact might even have been opposed to his Brother—but the miracle of his awaking was simply incontrovertible. But on such terms their faith—as we should view it—would not possess very much in the way of moral or religious value. Little real faith or courage would be required in advocacy of what was so positively and undeniably a fact. Their conviction takes on the quality of genuine confidence, and carries with it a personal significance, only when the appearance of the glorified Lord comes as the final confirmation and reward of a faith already victorious over despair, one which has faced doubt and won through in spite of all that stood opposed to it. Under such conditions, their faith in the miracle was really rooted in their love and loyalty to Jesus, and its deepest, most genuine source was not their experience of a supernatural event, but was in fact everything they had lived through with their Master and had observed in him. Indeed, their later loyalty and courage can be explained only if their faith was more firmly anchored, ethically and religiously, than in those experiences of Eastertide. Precisely because after his death they could not get away from him, and in spite of his apparent defeat, were still convinced in their very souls that he had been divinely ordained to rule, the Easter-experience had a determinative influence upon their whole future. If one can accept this view, it is an easy step to affirm that the appearances were not external phenomena but were merely the goals of an inner struggle in which faith won the victory over doubt. They are the sign of a deep disturbance, but they show clearly what ideas and hopes were uppermost in their souls. To this extent the appearances were not the basis of their faith, though so it seemed to them, so much as its product and result. Our interpretation is no devaluing, but on the contrary a fresh vitalizing of the Easter-experiences. Instead of a faith rendered compulsory by miracle, we have to do with a profound inner conviction which through an overwhelming final experience emerges at last into certainty and reality. Accordingly, what began then was not something wholly new, but carried on—in another register and key—the old disciple-relationship, tempered now as by fire, made more inward through suffering and ardent longing, transfigured through relationship to the Lord and Master who was now exalted above everything earthly.

Reinhold Niebuhr
CHRISTIANITY AND CULTURE

Protestant Christianity in America is, unfortunately, unduly dependent upon the very culture of modernity, the disintegration of which
would offer a more independent religion a unique opportunity. Confused
and tormented by cataclysmic events in contemporary history, the "modern mind" faces the disintegration of its civilization in alternate moods of
fear and hope, of faith and despair. The culture of modernity was the
artifact of modern civilization, product of its unique and characteristic
conditions, and it is therefore not surprising that its minarets of the spirit
should fall when the material foundations of its civilization begin to
crumble. Its optimism had no more solid foundation than the expansive
mood of the era of triumphant capitalism and naturally gives way to
confusion and despair when the material conditions of life are seriously
altered. Therefore the lights in its towers are extinguished at the very
moment when light is needed to survey the havoc wrought in the city and
the plan of rebuilding.

At such a time a faith which claims to have a light, "the same
yesterday, today, and forever," might conceivably become a source of
illumination to its age, so sadly in need of clues to the meaning of life and
the logic of contemporary history. The Christian churches are, unfortunately, not able to offer the needed guidance and insight. The orthodox
churches have long since compounded the truth of the Christian religion
with dogmatisms of another day, and have thereby petrified what would
otherwise have long since fallen prey to the beneficent dissolutions of the
processes of nature and history. The liberal churches, on the other hand,
have hid their light under the bushel of the culture of modernity with all
its short-lived prejudices and presumptuous certainties.

To be more specific: Orthodox Christianity, with insights and
perspectives, in many ways superior to those of liberalism, cannot come
to the aid of modern man, partly because its religious truths are still
imbedded in an outmoded science and partly because its morality is

From *An Interpretation of Christian Ethics* by Reinhold Niebuhr, pp. 13–15,
17–20. Copyright 1935 by Harper & Brothers. Reprinted with the permission of
Harper & Row, Publishers, Inc., New York.

Reinhold Niebuhr (1892–   ) is the most famous Protestant theologian
in recent America and a leading writer and teacher. He became dean of Union
Theological Seminary in New York City in 1950.

expressed in dogmatic and authoritarian moral codes. It tries vainly to meet the social perplexities of a complex civilization with irrelevant precepts, deriving their authority from their—sometimes quite fortuitous —inclusion in a sacred canon. It concerns itself with the violation of Sabbatarian prohibitions or puritanical precepts, and insists, figuratively, on tithing "mint, anise, and cummin," preserving the minutiae of social and moral standards which may once have had legitimate or accidental sanctity, but which have, whether legitimate or accidental, now lost both religious and moral meaning.

The religion and ethics of the liberal church is dominated by the desire to prove to its generation that it does not share the anachronistic ethics or believe the incredible myths of orthodox religion. Its energy for some decades has been devoted to the task of proving religion and science compatible, a purpose which it has sought to fulfill by disavowing the more incredible portion of its religious heritage and clothing the remainder in terms acceptable to the "modern mind." It has discovered rather belatedly that this same modern mind, which only yesterday seemed to be the final arbiter of truth, beauty, and goodness, is in a sad state of confusion today, amidst the debris of the shattered temple of its dreams and hopes. In adjusting itself to the characteristic credos and prejudices of modernity, the liberal church has been in constant danger of obscuring what is distinctive in the Christian message and creative in Christian morality. Sometimes it fell to the level of merely clothing the naturalistic philosophy and the utilitarian ethics of modernity with pious phrases. . . .

High religions are . . . distinguished by the extent of the unity and coherence of life which they seek to encompass and the sense of a transcendent source of meaning by which alone confidence in the meaningfulness of life and existence can be maintained. The dimension of depth in religion is not created simply by the effort to solve the problem of unity in the total breadth of life. The dimension of depth is really prior to any experience of breadth; for the assumption that life is meaningful and that its meaning transcends the observable facts of existence is involved in all achievements of knowledge by which life in its richness and contradictoriness is apprehended. Yet the effort to establish coherence and meaning in terms of breadth increases the sense of depth. Thus the God of a primitive tribe is conceived as the transcendent source of its life; and faith in such a God expresses the sense of the unity and value of tribal solidarity. But when experience forces an awakening culture to fit the life of other peoples into its world, it conceives of a God who transcends the life of one people so completely as no longer to be bound to it. Thus a prophet Amos arises to declare, "Are ye not as the children of the Ethiopians unto me sayeth the Lord." What is divided, incompatible, and conflicting, on the plane of concrete history is felt to be united, harmonious, and akin in its common source ("God hath made of one blood all the nations of men") and its common destiny ("In Christ there is neither Jew nor Greek, neither bond nor free").

The dimension of depth in the consciousness of religion creates the tension between what is and what ought to be. It bends the bow from which every arrow of moral action flies. Every truly moral act seeks to establish what ought to be, because the agent feels obligated to the ideal, though historically unrealized, as being the order of life in its more essential reality. Thus the Christian believes that the ideal of love is real in the will and nature of God, even though he knows of no place in history where the ideal has been realized in its pure form. And it is because it has this reality that he feels the pull of obligation. The sense of obligation in morals from which Kant tried to derive the whole structure of religion is really derived from the religion itself. The "pull" or "drive" of moral life is a part of the religious tension of life. Man seeks to realize in history what he conceives to be already the truest reality—that is, its final essence.

The ethical fruitfulness of various types of religion is determined by the quality of their tension between the historical and the transcendent. This quality is measured by two considerations: The degree to which the transcendent truly transcends every value and achievement of history, so that no relative value of historical achievement may become the basis of moral complacency; and the degree to which the transcendent remains in organic contact with the historical, so that no degree of tension may rob the historical of its significance.

The weakness of orthodox Christianity lies in its premature identification of the transcendent will of God with canonical moral codes, many of which are merely primitive social standards, and for development of its myths into bad science. The perennial tendency of religion to identify God with the symbols of God in history, symbols which were once filled with a sanctity, of which the stream of new events and conditions has robbed them, is a perpetual source of immorality in religion. The failure of liberal Christianity is derived from its inclination to invest the relative moral standards of a commercial age with ultimate sanctity by falsely casting the aura of the absolute and transcendent ethic of Jesus upon them. A religion which capitulates to the prejudices of a contemporary age is not very superior to a religion which remains enslaved to the partial and relative insights of an age already dead. In each case religion fails because it prematurely resolves moral tension by discovering, or claiming to have realized, the *summum bonum* in some immediate and relative value of history. The whole of modern secular liberal culture, to which liberal Christianity is unduly bound, is really a devitalized and secularized religion in which the presuppositions of a Christian tradition have been rationalized and read into the processes of history and nature, supposedly discovered by objective science. The original tension of Christian morality is thereby destroyed; for the transcendent ideals of Christian morality have become immanent possibilities in the historic process. Democracy, mutual coöperation, the League of Nations, international trade reciprocity, and other similar conceptions are regarded as the ultimate ideals of the human spirit. None of them are without some degree of absolute validity, but modern culture never discovered to what degree they had emerged out of the peculiar conditions and necessities of a commercial civilization and were intimately related to the interests of the classes which have profited most by the expansion of commerce and industry in recent decades. The transcendent impossibilities of the Christian ethic of love became, in modern culture, the immanent and imminent possibilities of an historical process; and the moral complacence of a generation is thereby supported rather than challenged. This is the invariable consequence of any culture in which no "windows are left open to heaven" and the experience of depth in life is completely dissipated by a confident striving along the horizontal line of the immediate stream of history.

Pope John XXIII

AGGIORNAMENTO (BRINGING UP-TO-DATE)

Insufficiency of Modern States to Insure the Universal Common Good

The unity of the human family has always existed because its members are human beings all equal by virtue of their natural dignity. Hence there will always exist the objective need to promote in sufficient measure the universal common good, that is, the common good of the entire human family.

In times past, one could be justified in feeling that the public authorities of the different political communities might be in a position to provide for the universal common good, either through normal diplomatic channels or top-level meetings, or by making use of juridical instru-

From *Pacem in Terris—Peace on Earth* by Pope John XXIII, pp. 41–42, 44, 49–51. Reprinted by permission of America Press, Inc., New York 10019.
Pope John XXIII (1881–1963) reigned from 1958 to 1963 and won popular acclaim through many public appearances.

ments such as conventions and treaties and other means suggested by the natural law, or by the law of nations or by international law.

As a result of the far-reaching changes which have taken place in the relations of the human family, on the one hand the universal common good gives rise to problems which are complex, very grave and extremely urgent, especially as regards security and world peace. On the other hand, the public authorities of the individual political communities—placed as they are on a footing of equality one with the other—no matter how much they multiply their meetings or sharpen their wits in efforts to draw up new juridical instruments, are no longer able to face the task of finding an adequate solution to the problems mentioned above. And this is not due to a lack of good will or of a spirit of enterprise, but because of a structural defect which hinders them.

It can be said, therefore, that at this historical moment the present system of organization and the way its principle of authority operates on a world basis no longer correspond to the objective requirements of the universal common good.

Connection Between the Common Good and Political Authority

There exists an intrinsic connection between the common good on the one hand and the structure and function of public authority on the other. The moral order, which needs public authority in order to promote the common good in human society, requires also that the authority be effective in attaining that end. This demands that the organs through which the authority is institutionalized, becomes operative and pursues its ends, must be constituted and act in such a manner as to be capable of bringing to realization the new meaning which the common good is taking on in the historical evolution of the human family.

Today the universal common good poses problems of world-wide dimensions which cannot be adequately tackled or solved except by the efforts of public authorities endowed with a breadth of powers, structure and means of the same proportions: that is, of public authorities which are in a position to act in an effective manner on a world-wide basis. The moral order itself, therefore, demands that such a form of public authority be established. . . .

Principle of Subsidiarity

Just as within each political community the relations between individuals, families, intermediate associations and public authority are governed by the principle of subsidiarity, so too the relations between the public authority of each political community and the public authority of the world community must be regulated by the same principle. This means that the public authority of the world community must tackle and solve problems of an economic, social, political or cultural character which are posed by the universal common good. For, because of the vastness, complexity and urgency of those problems, the public authorities of the individual states are not in a position to tackle them with any hope of a positive solution.

The public authority of the world community is not intended to limit the sphere of action of the public authority of the individual political community, much less to take its place. On the contrary, its purpose is to create, on a world basis, an environment in which the public authorities of each political community, its citizens and intermediate associations, can carry out their tasks, fulfill their duties and exercise their rights with greater security. . . .

Relations Between Catholics and Non-Catholics in Social and Economic Affairs

The doctrinal principles outlined in this document derive from or are suggested by the requirements of human nature itself, and are, for the most part, dictates of the natural law. They provide Catholics, therefore, with a vast field in which they can meet and come to an understanding both with Christians separated from this Apostolic See, and also with human beings who are not enlightened by faith in Jesus Christ, but who are endowed with the light of reason and with a natural and operative honesty.

In such relations let the faithful be careful to be always consistent in their actions, so that they may never come to any compromise in matters of religion and morals. At the same time, however, let them be, and show themselves to be, animated by a spirit of understanding and detachment, and disposed to work loyally in the pursuit of objectives which are of their nature good, or conducive to good.[1]

However, one must never confuse error and the person who errs, not even when there is question of error, or inadequate knowledge of truth, in the moral or religious field.

The person who errs is always and above all a human being, and in every case he retains his dignity as a human person. He must always be regarded and treated in accordance with that lofty dignity. Besides, in every human being there is a need that is congenital to his nature and never becomes extinguished, one that compels him to break through the web of error and open his mind to the knowledge of truth. And God will

[1] Cf. Encycl. *Mater et Magistra. Acta Apostolicae Sedis* LIII (1961), 456.

never fail to act on his interior being, with the result that a person, who at a given moment of his life lacks the clarity of faith or even shall have adhered to erroneous doctrines, can at a future date be enlightened and believe the truth.

Meetings and agreements, in the various sectors of daily life, between believers and those who either do not believe or believe insufficiently because they adhere to error, can be occasions for discovering truth and paying homage to it.

It must be borne in mind, furthermore, that neither can false philosophical teachings regarding the nature, origin and destiny of the universe and of man be identified with historical movements that have economic, social, cultural or political ends, not even when these movements have originated from those teachings and have drawn and still draw inspiration therefrom.

This is so because the teachings, once they are drawn up and defined, remain always the same, while the movements, working in constantly evolving historical situations, cannot but be influenced by these latter and cannot avoid, therefore, being subject to changes, even of a profound nature. Besides, who can deny that those movements, insofar as they conform to the dictates of right reason and are interpreters of the lawful aspirations of the human person, contain elements that are positive and deserving of approval?

It can happen, then, that meetings for the attainment of some practical end, which formerly were deemed inopportune or unproductive, might now or in the future be considered opportune and useful.

But to decide whether this moment has arrived, and also to lay down the ways and degrees in which work in common might be possible for the achievement of economic, social, cultural and political ends which are honorable and useful, are problems which can be solved only with the virtue of prudence, which is the guiding light of the virtues that regulate the moral life, both individual and social.

Therefore, as far as Catholics are concerned, this decision rests primarily with those who live and work in the specific sectors of human society in which those problems arise, always, however, in accordance with the principles of the natural law, with the social doctrine of the Church, and with the directives of ecclesiastical authority. For it must not be forgotten that the Church has the right and the duty not only to safeguard the principles of ethics and religion, but also to intervene authoritatively with her children in the temporal sphere when there is a question of judging the application of those principles to concrete cases.

Sigmund Freud
RELIGION AS ILLUSION

I had sent him [a friend] my small book that treats religion as an illusion, and he answered that he entirely agreed with my judgement upon religion, but that he was sorry I had not properly appreciated the true source of religious sentiments. This, he says, consists in a peculiar feeling, which he himself is never without, which he finds confirmed by many others, and which he may suppose is present in millions of people. It is a feeling which he would like to a call a sensation of 'eternity', a feeling as of something limitless, unbounded—as it were, 'oceanic'. This feeling, he adds, is a purely subjective fact, not an article of faith; it brings with it no assurance of personal immortality, but it is the source of the religious energy which is seized upon by the various Churches and religious systems, directed by them into particular channels, and doubtless also exhausted by them. One may, he thinks, rightly call oneself religious on the ground of this oceanic feeling alone, even if one rejects every belief and every illusion. . . .

To me the claim does not seem compelling. After all, a feeling can only be a source of energy if it is itself the expression of a strong need. The derivation of religious needs from the infant's helplessness and the longing for the father aroused by it seems to me incontrovertible, especially since the feeling is not simply prolonged from childhood days, but is permanently sustained by fear of the superior power of Fate. I cannot think of any need in childhood as strong as the need for a father's protection. Thus the part played by the oceanic feeling, which might seek something like the restoration of limitless narcissism, is ousted from a place in the foreground. The origin of the religious attitude can be traced back in clear outlines as far as the feeling of infantile helplessness. There may be something further behind that, but for the present it is wrapped in obscurity.

I can imagine that the oceanic feeling became connected with religion later on. The 'oneness with the universe' which constitutes its ideational content sounds like a first attempt at a religious consolation, as

Reprinted from *Civilization and Its Discontents* by Sigmund Freud. Translated from the German and edited by James Strachey (pp. 11, 19, 28, 31–32). By permission of W. W. Norton & Company, Inc. Copyright © 1961 by James Strachey.
    Sigmund Freud (1856–1939), an Austrian physician, was the founder of psychoanalysis.

though it were another way of disclaiming the danger which the ego recognizes as threatening it from the external world. . . .

[The] attempt to procure a certainty of happiness and a protection against suffering through a delusional remoulding of reality is made by a considerable number of people in common. The religions of mankind must be classed among the mass-delusions of this kind. No one, needless to say, who shares a delusion ever recognizes it as such. . . .

Religion . . . imposes equally on everyone its own path to the acquisition of happiness and protection from suffering. Its technique consists in depressing the value of life and distorting the picture of the real world in a delusional manner—which presupposes an intimidation of the intelligence. At this price, by forcibly fixing them in a state of psychical infantilism and by drawing them into a mass-delusion, religion succeeds in sparing many people an individual neurosis. But hardly anything more. There are, as we have said, many paths which *may* lead to such happiness as is attainable by men, but there is none which does so for certain. Even religion cannot keep its promise. If the believer finally sees himself obliged to speak of God's 'inscrutable decrees', he is admitting that all that is left to him as a last possible consolation and source of pleasure in his suffering is an unconditional submission. And if he is prepared for that, he could probably have spared himself the *détour* he has made.

Seward Hiltner
PSYCHOLOGY IN SUPPORT OF RELIGION

Though I emphatically do not share it, there is a widespread conviction among intelligent people that modern dynamic psychologies like that of Freud are, however unwittingly or unintentionally, helping to undermine some aspects of traditional morality. This suspicion is quite different from the popular misinterpretations of Freud, for instance, as an advocate of sexual license. Thoughtful persons who know quite well that Freud was a highly moral man, and that popular attacks on his alleged immorality or citations from him that appear to support liber-

Reprinted, with permission, from *University: A Princeton Quarterly,* Fall 1964. Copyright 1964 by Princeton University.

Seward Hiltner (1909–   ) is a professor of theology and personality at Princeton Theological Seminary.

tinism are equally mistaken, are nevertheless, with some justice, concerned at the way in which such psychologies seem to "expose" traditional moralities.

Freud and others have certainly shown that there are often great discrepancies between the stated motives for morality and the underlying motives. The sexually continent young man may be hugging the dregs of his Oedipus complex; the older man may be avoiding a test that would expose his impotence. The person who is vociferous and diligent on behalf of minority groups may be impelled by unsolved authority problems; while the reactive member of a persecuted minority group may have found an approved channel for his aggression. Conformists to moral patterns may have regressed to a Peter Pan kind of stage, solving the problem of adolescence by acting as if it had never appeared. Clingingly dependent persons, who take the juice out of those they meet, may in fact be motivated by strong desires to dominate even though they may represent themselves as supporters of "love." The list of such exposures could be almost endless. Some behavior that conforms to moral norms is indeed motivated by immature, neurotic, childish, or concealed patterns. Of the fact there can be no question.

The suspicion of psychology's bad effect on moral patterns grows when the focus is shifted to the general psychological elucidation of conscience. The Freudian Super-ego, for instance, reveals the part of the conscience that is most primitive, that developed first, that is most inaccessible to education, and that has astonishing pertinacity in even sophisticated and wise people. The original German "Uber-Ich" conveys the meaning better than the Latinized English version. It is something that "hangs over me." If taught in early life that motion pictures were bad or sinful, an adult may still have strange symptoms before his television set even if later on he, his parents, and his community of origin changed their views on this matter. The Super-ego may be a ruthless task-master. The man apparently so devoted to his business that he cannot take a vacation, the advocate of cold showers on arising, or the woman whose house is perpetually spotless, may all read a kind of moral significance into their patterns, when actually, according to many psychologies, they may simply be slaves of the Super-ego.

Since no reputable psychology has declared the Super-ego, or its equivalent, to be the whole phenomenon of conscience, comfort was taken, for a time, in the illusion that parents who were open, honest, alert, sensitive, firm, and loving to their children could prevent the development of nasty Super-egos. But clinical evidence now stands against them. The Super-egos of the children tend to be like the partly-concealed Super-egos of the parents, not like what the conscious behavior and concern of the parents is. So the Super-ego seems more like fate, and less like a habit that can be altered by education, or reward, or relaxation, or insight. It seems to tie some aspects of morality with virtually atavistic dimensions of personality.

In the West morality has always been associated with decision, and decision with freedom. Freud has shown convincingly that the usual subjective feeling of freedom—ability to make this choice or that regardless of what has gone before—is an illusion. To be sure, this fact is misinterpreted if alleged to mean a denial of all human freedom. Freud himself felt that a major aim of psychoanalysis was to increase genuine psychic freedom. But if no human behavior is without meaning and antecedents, then the notion that one can decide whatever he wants at any time is exposed as evasion of the real situation. When the conditions are met, freedom may be real. But the foremost of those conditions is the acknowledgment of the nature and strength of the forces that have molded one. Thus, the illusion about making decisions arbitrarily cuts off at the root any chance of meeting the conditions for real freedom. Thus any morality that professes to be the result of free decisions is under suspicion of being in invincible ignorance about what, in fact, is cooking.

In his penetrating analysis of adolescents in large-city high schools, Edgar Z. Friedenberg attempts to show why there is an increase in delinquency, and in conformist behavior, at the same time. When the dominant pattern becomes a kind of "organization man" imitation of adults, then the majority group becomes not only diligent, apparently moral and good, but also seemingly responsible in a way the adult culture approves. This may be, says Friedenberg, at the price of not really experiencing adolescence as a period of leaving primary loyalties and finding new ones. But when the majority pattern becomes strongly conformist, then the rebels will be punished or ostracized even for light deviations; and it is only a step to the reasoning: If I will get clobbered anyhow, why stop with something small?

There is indeed, as history should have shown us, an underlying psychic kinship between conformity and rebellion. We see this in Friedenberg's high schools. It was evident in the emergence of monasticism in the midst of Hellenistic libertinism. The American wild west gave place to the most dogmatic of moralisms. Thus dynamic psychologies suggest that traditional moralities themselves probably also have a kind of secret pact with their detractors, and are thus not quite what they profess themselves to be. If everyone lived up to them, it could only be for part of the time—and there would have to be Jubilees, license days, or Seven-Year-Itch celebrations to take up the slack.

Modern dynamic psychologies have shown, then, that there is a psychopathology of morality. Allegedly good things may be done for the wrong reasons. Evil deeds may be avoided through shameful but hidden motives. Both a general moral aura and the conformist bent of traditional morality may contain hidden pathological elements. Is the price of morality to include some forms of regression, concealment, ignorance, and illusion?

But dynamic psychologies are no respecters of persons. As dissecters and elucidators, they turn the searchlight on immorality as well as on morality. Although their findings on immorality are less well known to the public, they are no less important.

Don Juan is not a sexual virtuoso but has gnawing inner doubts about his manliness which he has not the gumption to confront on the proper terms. The allegedly "good prostitute," currently having such a vogue on the stage, may be trying to get back at her father, or compensating for her extreme self-depreciation, or taking out her hostility toward men through a sexual smoke screen. The business or professional man who skirts the edge of the law may be trying to compensate, through prestige or possessions, for his Willy Loman-like emptiness. The gambler may be neurotic right down to his last quarter. The appeal of Fanny Hill may be rather less of an aphrodisiacal kind, and rather more a secret but weak-kneed confession that women ought to quit being what they really are and instead should act like *Playboy's* no-problem females, soft tonight and off your hands tomorrow.

A great deal of immorality, by any definition, involves acts of aggression, both against other people and the self. The self-directed aggression in both alcoholism and heavy drinking has long been noted. There is the "cold aggression" of no sympathy for persons beyond our borders, or for those of another skin color, or those who do not share our religious or economic views. There is the "hot aggression" of parents who maim or even kill their children, or the sweetheart murders. What psychology exposes is the inability of such persons to deal symbolically and relationally with their aggression; and thus, whether cold or hot, failing to integrate it into the whole personality so that it is not top dog. It is not aggression or aggressiveness, as a presence in the human being, that is immoral, but the symbolizing failure that produces immorality.

Generally speaking, American society is still permissive about expressions of aggression. The ubiquity of firearms, of westerns, and perhaps most ominously of the current association of sex and violence, are all indications of our culture's fear that aggression can not really be dealt with symbolically but must be allowed some allegedly "harmless outlets." Many, however, are far from harmless. It is a dubious morality that lets the villain be got rid of by any means at hand, and a clear anti-morality when sex is portrayed as more interesting when associated with violence. If I had to choose between Mike Hammer's masochism and Fanny Hill's illusions, I think I should prefer Fanny.

Dynamic psychologies suggest that the core of immoralities lies in the relative absence of "fellow feeling" or empathy for others that can appear in persons who have at least some basic self-respect. The essence of real love in the grown-up sense is the capacity to feel for another person's interests as strongly as we feel for our own. Developmentally, this capacity seems not to emerge (and then backhandedly) until the pre-adolescent period. Before that, children are astonishingly legalistic about "rights." Thereafter, in normal development, the positive-relational factor should transcend the law although not destroy it. When this process is arrested at any significant point, the result is the absence of the fellow-feeling that is the sole durable foundation of morality and even the sole context in which law can finally operate.

Thus psychology is equally capable of exposing the psychopathology within morality, and within immorality. It is no accident that Freud declared human beings to be, at the same time, both more moral and more immoral than they realize.

As a theologian, I am profoundly impressed with the insights into morality and immorality that are coming from psychiatry and clinical psychology, the two principal branches of dynamic psychology that are involved in direct help to people. My discussion thus far has illustrated the negative aspects, the exposure of the falsities, hypocrisies, and distortions. We may also take a look at the positive and constructive contributions.

One of the most misunderstood of the positive contributions is about guilt. The traditional moral understanding was: guilt is a fact, stemming from man's accountability for his acts; guilt feelings acknowledge this accountability; such feelings, while painful, are nevertheless necessary; thus the response to guilt means amendment of life, restitution, or at least repentance.

Psychiatry put in a word of caution: not all guilt feelings reflect real guilt, nor are all such feelings related to their actual source. The first effect of this finding is to show that some guilt feelings need to be got rid of, not acted on. But further work shows, even more significantly, that real guilt may masquerade under many names and apparent feelings, of which the modern favorite is anxiety. It demonstrates also that such guilt, when confronted and responded to properly, is an empowerment to constructive or restitutive action, and not a continuing negative feeling. Thus psychiatry has helped to clarify real guilt, by separating it from distorted guilt feelings. This is an important contribution to morality.

Closely related to the constructive contribution to understanding real guilt is insight into the meaning of human responsibility. In their early work, all modern clinical psychologies were impressed with how suffering people had been deprived and put upon, especially in their early lives. There was, therefore, a temptation to say, "Poor fellow, his neurosis or immoral habits were forced on him by society through his parents," with the correct suggestion that he was not primarily accountable for the condition that had developed. But actual therapeutic work was found ineffective when the sufferer said, in effect, "Poor me, since society produced my condition through my parents, no one can blame me if I remain as I am." Patiently, the clinical people, even before they had theorized about it, were helping such persons to realize that the past need not determine the future, because something had been added; and that the person who knew he had been put upon was not the same person as he who was put upon.

Out of these insights has emerged a conception of responsibility that is related to, but distinguishable from, past concepts of accountability. It is now believed that the essence of responsibility is prospective rather than retrospective in character. In therapeutic work, the turning point often comes when the patient soberly assumes responsibility for what his life is to be, even though, before therapy, he may have been so driven that his accountability was very small. The exercise of prospective responsibility cannot be defined abstractly out of context. A person who finds himself committing a violent but non-criminal act may be highly responsible if, in reflection on his lack of control, he yields himself temporarily to the guidance of others. If that yielding lands him temporarily in a mental hospital, so that the law regards him as, for the time being, "not responsible," the legal side of the matter ought not to obscure what is really taking place. This clarification of responsibility is of great significance for morality.

A third constructive contribution to morality by the clinical psychologies is about the relatedness of basic self-respect and concern for others. In coining the term "narcissism," Freud returned to Greek culture and the man dazzled by his reflection in the water. Narcissism is not, precisely, selfishness. It is preoccupied bondage that cannot get beyond its immediate interests, *because it has no respect for itself.* It is more affliction than indulgence. Furthermore love, or concern for others, is not "altruism" in the nineteenth-century sense, but the natural human reaction in the absence of narcissistic preoccupation. Thus concern for others comes from a certain kind of strength of selfhood, the energies of which are free for investment beyond its own boundaries.

When is self-respect too self-satisfied? When is concern for others either too foreshortened or too undiscriminating? Those are important questions which certainly cannot be answered in entirety by the clinical disciplines. But the right clue is given to morality by separating some kind of self-respect (as strength) from narcissism (as bondage), and genuine investment in other people from compulsive reaction against any positive valuation of one's own interests.

Finally, what is the contribution of psychiatry to the respective place, in morality, of faith and of works? Although this question is of special importance to religiously-based morality, it has general significance as well.

The person who has no faith or trust at all cannot even enter upon the "therapeutic contract." If he insists on complete and detailed guarantees in advance, no sign can be given him. So something of the general nature of faith is needed even to begin. As therapy proceeds, he discovers more and more unpleasant things about himself, and knows they have been true all along but that he lacked the courage to confront them. Now he can do so because the therapeutic relationship makes it possible. When he comes upon a basic and releasing insight, he is tempted to give up therapy. He see-saws between believing something was given him, and that he got better by his work. It is the complex interrelationship between these two beliefs that does, in fact, make for improvement. Thus, flat declarations that morality is simply work and rules, or that it is nothing but trust and surrender, both seem to violate the concrete reality. But, as religious ethics has alleged, faith does come first, in some very basic sense.

When we re-examine our understanding of basic Christian moral principles in the light of both kinds of psychological findings—the exposés and the positives—these principles come off pretty well.

The proper motive power for morality is personal initiative, and not behavior considered in itself. Such a capacity is an achievement and a gift, and does not first appear in pure form. The rules and discipline for the child are intended, however, not to perpetuate his reliance upon rules and outside guidance, but to evoke within him the latent capacities for exercising initiative in his valuation of and relationship to other people, and even to himself. Moral education is, therefore, education in the direction of both self-discipline and social fulfillment. It is not no's without yes's. But how, in actual fact, can such valuations and prospective responsibilities develop? Only through relationships in which the reality of basic trust makes possible the no-saying that is culturally necessary. The capacity for morality in the sense of responsible initiative does not appear, therefore, through an analogue to Pavlov's salivating dogs, but rather through acceptance that makes tolerable the setting of limits.

The proper mode of moral decision is not blind and conformist obedience, even to the right rule, but responsible decision on the basis of principles viewed in concrete context. Young people often ask whether there is anything wrong in sleeping together with no intention of getting married, provided that the man and woman love each other, are not hurting any one else, take steps to prevent pregnancies and syphilis, and are prepared to assume responsibility for consequences. If in reality everything were true that they allege, and in the proper context, what would be the difference (except legally) between their union and a marriage? The main answer is, of course, that their commitment is severely foreshortened, and that thus all their other claims· are partly false. According to the biblical view, which is rather more earthy than modern romanticism, they would already be married by their sexual union.

They might argue, in legitimate interpretation of the biblical view, that some unions may be defective. But if they have that much sophistication, they are exercising some reasonable facsimile of Christian principles in relation to concrete situations—regardless of whether or not they elect to act on such principles. What neither Christian thought nor clinical psychology can let them assume is that a sexual union may be non-serious in its meaning or effects. But the process of working through such decisions, in the light of principles, is of the essence of morality. Conformity is not enough.

The proper criterion of moral decision, from the Christian point of view, is to exercise as much *agape* (love in the sense that is heedless of benefits) as one is capable of, concentrating instead upon the need and value of the other person. No degree of this is possible if there is narcissistic preoccupation. But if one is freed at all, then he may use his uniquely human capacity to feel himself into the place of another; and, whether out of love for his wife, or from concern for a member of a persecuted minority group, joyfully assume some proper responsibility for meeting the other's needs. Since we usually rationalize most about our own interests, moralists are not wrong when they direct our attention to others' needs. But they are wrong psychologically if they try to make us feel guilty for having any acknowledged needs of our own.

From the Christian point of view, morality is not a social club held over each individual's head, nor a device for attaining social security by discouraging all risk and creative novelty. It is never, even in the family, the blessing for all time of even the best *status quo*. As some one has said, "Every family exists to be broken up." The entire process of rearing children is to enable each of them to achieve maturity, necessarily breaking his ties to the parental home in order to create his own home. Every marriage service has some such phrase as "forsaking all others." While this vow may take care of old girl friends, it is aimed far more at mama.

The intent of morality from the Christian point of view, then, is not goodness in the debased sense of doing no wrong because nothing at all is done. The essence of morality is responsible and productive *personal* contributions to society: including risks, temporary rebellions and regressions—all of which one conceives as inherent to his own fulfillment, in himself and in his relationships with others. Both the exposé side of modern psychology, and its positive contributions, help to this end. Real guilt is separated from distorted and inaccessible feelings of guilt. Responsibility is set in its properly future-oriented context. Self-respect and mature manhood are shown in proper relationship with concern for others. And the dialectic between faith and works, delegalizing morality without throwing away law, is reinforced.

There is a final and, in some respects, most important point of all about morality from the Christian point of view. This is that no one is ever wholly moral, and that God in his love has made forgiveness available. Many moderns reject such a notion as they understand it. If you can always be forgiven, then it doesn't matter what you do. O. Hobart Mowrer, University of Illinois psychologist, believes forgiveness may be too "cheap."

Modern psychology and psychiatry, despite Dr. Mowrer's view on this point, offers some useful suggestions about the relevance of forgiveness. It is precisely the most sensitive and imaginative person who, on realizing that his sins were as scarlet and not, as he had previously thought, just tinged with pink, turns back in revulsion, is liable to feel paralyzed and overwhelmed, and may be tempted to hopelessness about a new start. Actually, as the Christian tradition is clear, such acknowledgement or "conviction" of sin in itself shows that one has already made a new start. Only the redeemed man can know the enormity of his sin. True acceptance of forgiveness is always an acknowledgement of something that, in some degree, has already taken place. It is not cheap. It does not let us off the hook about the consequences. It testifies that, even in so basic a realm as morality, no one is or can be perfect, new starts are a part of creative living, and the one unpardonable sin is rejecting the strength that enables us to make them.

The psychology I know will certainly give little aid and comfort to any traditional morality that is rooted in legalism, conformity, mere external behavior, or hortatory injunctions to altruism. But if it is the mode and spirit of Christian morality, at least in my understanding of it, then I view psychology as a significant ally.

David E. Roberts
EXISTENTIALISM IN RELIGION

What is existentialism, and why should Christians pay any attention to it? There is no simple answer to this question because each of the writers whom we shall discuss gives his own account of what he is trying to do, and not all of these accounts are mutually compatible. Therefore

From *Existentialism and Religious Belief* by David E. Roberts, pp. 3–11. Copyright © 1957 by Oxford University Press, Inc. Reprinted by permission.

David E. Roberts (1911–1955) was professor of philosophy of religion at Union Theological Seminary.

we shall have to listen to what these thinkers actually have to say before we can even put forward an adequate definition of existentialism.

And one word of warning must be issued immediately. In recent years the word 'existentialism' has gained popular currency mainly through the works of Jean-Paul Sartre. People in Europe and America have seen his plays and read his novels and essays, and the idea has gotten abroad that existentialism means his particular brand of nihilism. Existentialism began, however, as a frankly Christian mode of thinking, and I shall hope to show that what is valid and illuminating in it can be held in perspective within the Christian faith. Yet I believe that these same emphases, when sundered from such faith, become particularly vivid expressions of the spiritual disintegration of our age.

Thus a study of existential philosophy brings into sharp focus the basic struggle between contemporary Christianity and so-called 'secularism.' The movement includes figures who represent both extremes, and many positions intermediate between them. Gabriel Marcel, the French Roman Catholic; Nicolai Berdyaev, the Russian Orthodox lay theologian; Martin Buber, the Jewish philosopher; and many Protestant thinkers have found in this sort of reflection a powerful impetus driving them toward the affirmation and expression of religious faith. At the other extreme stand Martin Heidegger, the influential German philosopher who was unfortunately associated with the Nazis, and Sartre, who played a role in the French underground resistance. Both of these men are avowed atheists, and they are close together philosophically even though they stood at opposite poles politically during the war. Karl Jaspers provides a very interesting example of an intermediate position. He is not an atheist —on the contrary he is a deeply religious person; yet he holds aloof from his Protestant heritage and determinedly attacks the very center of Christian belief.

In all its forms, however, existentialism should be of compelling interest to the Christian thinker today. For it protests against those intellectual and social forces which are destroying freedom. It calls men away from stifling abstractions and automatic conformity. It drives us back to the most basic, inner problems: what it means to be a self, how we ought to use our freedom, how we can find and keep the courage to face death. And even more important, it bids each individual thinker wrestle with these problems until he has grown into personal authenticity, instead of simply taking his answers from someone else.

Yet in my opinion existentialism cannot serve as a self-sufficient philosophy. Its chief value is that of a corrective. By clearing away philosophical underbrush it brings us face to face with the urgency of ultimate questions. But it does not answer them. It may lead a man to the point where he sees the momentousness of a decision for or against faith in

God. But the over-all value of existentialism depends upon the outcome. Where it leads to Christian faith, it offers a promising basis for a concordat between philosophy and theology. Indeed, anyone who takes Biblical revelation seriously must approach philosophical problems in a fashion which incorporates certain existential elements whether he uses this term or not. Yet even where existentialism leads to atheistic conclusions, it is of great importance that we understand it, for it offers a particularly poignant exposition of the predicament of modern man. Here we see individuals facing tragedy without any hope of salvation. We see them standing in utter loneliness and staring at bleak emptiness. And as Christians we need to understand these atheists because, unlike more complacent modern thinkers, they are honest enough to voice that sense of despair which is so widespread in our world. They speak, in fact, for millions of our contemporaries for whom God is dead. They tear away the masks of optimism, self-confidence, and indifference. They help us to understand how the will-to-power issues from hopelessness, how dictators can compel men to renounce their freedom for the sake of specious security, how emptiness lurks behind our amusements and our vices, and how men become enraged at a civilization which makes them cogs in a well-oiled economic and political machine.

Still, existentialism is difficult to define, even provisionally, because most of the writers I have mentioned are deliberately unsystematic. They are not in the slightest degree interested in purveying a set of findings like the answers to arithmetic problems which can be found at the back of the book. Rather are they interested in arousing the reader to a spiritual struggle. Hence the result of this kind of philosophy is what it does to you, not some answer which can be appropriated without going through the agony of figuring things out for yourself.

This is why these men so often produce plays, novels, journals, fugitive essays or meditations. For them, entering into the truth involves a profound kind of self-examination. The most significant thing, they feel, is a change in the man—his motives, feelings, and hopes—instead of an increase in his fund of knowledge. Such a method constitutes an explicit protest against traditional philosophizing by insisting that the personal commitments of a thinker be incorporated into his definition of truth. In fact, it accuses all objective philosophies of divorcing reason from life by trying to evade such human polarities as freedom-and-destiny, anxiety-and-courage, isolation-and-community, guilt-and-forgiveness, instead of recognizing that these polarities must remain perpetually at the center of vital thinking.

Ordinarily the student of philosophy assumes that his task is to master certain concepts and to get them straightened out rationally so that they will be free from inconsistency. He hopes thereby to arrive eventually at an explanation of nature, man, and God. But existentialism passionately protests that the truly great questions of life cannot really be answered by means of scientific information plus clear thinking. For example, I may learn and accept certain theories about immortality without moving one step toward fitness for eternal life. Or I may learn and accept arguments for the existence of God without making one step toward trusting Him in such a way as to incorporate His love in my own life.

The task which lies before us may seem, therefore, to be a contradictory one. We propose to survey and scrutinize existentialism, whereas a real grasp of it demands being on the inside rather than looking curiously at it from the outside. If the ghost of Kierkegaard were present, he would doubtless say that this book is a professor's project. Only the academic mind, he might say, could possibly be so stupid. And yet I cannot believe that this problem is totally insoluble. Is our danger very different from that of a teacher of literature? He can of course turn the study of Shakespeare or Dante into deadly pedantry, but need not. Admittedly, the problem of how to combine intense personal commitment with a critical detachment becomes most acute at the level of religious belief. But surely it is altogether possible to listen to another man's confession of faith (or unfaith) sympathetically, without feeling compelled to swallow it wholesale. And I, for one, can see no real contradiction in studying the general characteristics of existentialism, so long as it is remembered that acquiring information about it is very different from entering personally into the spiritual engagement which it exhibits. Therefore I shall make bold to suggest, in a preliminary way, a few of these general characteristics of existentialism.

First, it is a protest against all forms of rationalism which find it easy to assume that reality can be grasped primarily or exclusively by intellectual means. It is an emphatic denial of the assumption that construction of a logical system is the most adequate way to reach the truth.

In the second place, existentialism is a protest against all views which tend to regard man as if he were a thing, that is, only an assortment of functions and reactions. This means that in the sphere of philosophical theory existentialism stands against mechanism and naturalism; and in the sphere of social theory it stands against all patterns of human organization in which the mass mentality stifles the spontaneity and uniqueness of the individual person. Incidentally, this refusal to accept the dictates of mass-mindedness applies quite as much to the automatic conformities of a democratic, capitalistic society as it does to the obvious regimentation of a totalitarian ordering of life.

Thirdly, existentialism makes a drastic distinction between subjective and objective truth, and it gives priority to the former as against the latter. This word 'subjective' may be easily misunderstood. In ordinary speech when we say that someone has given a highly subjective interpretation, we imply that it is biased, prejudiced, and unreliable. When, however, existentialists speak of 'subjectivity' they have in mind something very different from this. They are not denying that through science, common sense, and logic men are able to arrive at genuinely objective truth. But they insist that in connection with ultimate matters it is impossible to lay aside the impassioned concerns of the human individual. They are calling our attention to the fact that in the search for ultimate truth the whole man, and not only his intellect or reason, is caught up and involved. His emotions and his will must be aroused and engaged so that he can live the truth he sees. The fundamental difference, then, is that between *knowing about* the truth in some theoretical, detached way and *being grasped* by the truth in a decisively personal manner. While the objective standpoint gets as far as it possibly can from the feelings, hopes, or fears of the individual human being, the subjective point of view puts the individual with his commitments and passions in the very center of the picture. And only by the latter approach, say the existentialists, can a man be so grasped and changed inwardly as to deepen and clarify his relationship to reality, even as a thinker.

In the fourth place, existentialism regards man as fundamentally ambiguous. This is very closely linked to its predominant stress on freedom. It sees the human situation as filled with contradictions and tensions which cannot be resolved by means of exact or consistent thinking. These contradictions are not due simply to the present limitations of our knowledge, and they will not be overcome merely by obtaining further scientific information or philosophical explanation because they reflect the stubborn fact that man is split down the middle—at war with himself. He is free, yes; he is conscious of responsibility, of remorse, of guilt for what he has done. Yet his whole life is enmeshed within a natural and social order which profoundly and inevitably determines him, making him what in fact he is. He is finite; but he is capable of rising above the limits of any particular situation through his action or his imagination. His life is bounded in time and is moving forward toward death; yet he has a strange kinship with eternity because he can rise above the present and see its relation to the past and the future. From top to bottom, as it were, man is a contradictory creature. Viewed from the outside, he is but an episode in the vast process of nature. Viewed from the inside, each man is a universe in himself.

Hence there can be no simple answers to what man should do with his freedom. In one sense, he must himself create the answer by using his freedom to find out just what he wants to become. He will not avoid this dilemma by returning to the level of the animal who does not ask metaphysical and religious questions. Nor can he avoid it by accepting some ethical or religious system which purports to give him infallible guidance as to what he should do. For man himself has a hand in producing these systems, and does so for reasons which the systems cannot altogether conceal. All of us try to run away from this predicament. Everything would be simple if we could become either like animals or like God. As an animal, or as God, man would be liberated from the agonizing torments of moral conflict and inner strife. But so long as we remain human we must enter into the mystery of what it means to be a finite self possessing freedom.

It is quite obvious that some at least of these characteristics of existentialism are as old as human thought. For example, the Bible constantly tells us that only through a conversion of the whole man can we enter into the truth. One might then inquire why existentialists should be permitted to claim a monopoly on something which has been affirmed by virtually every Christian thinker. Yet writers like Pascal or Kierkegaard would gladly agree that there is no such thing as existentialism taken by itself. They would say that they were not trying to start something new, but were seeking to call men back to an inner realization of what Biblical revelation always has meant and always will mean. The crucial issue is not whether a philosophical outlook takes account of subjectivity, freedom, and inner conflict; every such outlook pays some attention to what these words stand for. The crucial issue is whether one regards these as central or peripheral. Many philosophers work them into a context which denatures them. They are woven into a fabric of thought where all contradiction is finally smoothed out into intelligibility and harmony. The genuinely existential thinker, on the contrary, regards contradiction as not merely the Alpha but the Omega; thought must not only begin here but must return to the given ambiguity of the human situation, and do so continually. In the end, moreover, thought cannot get beyond it.

One further word of clarification is necessary before taking up our study of individual existentialists. All stirring firsthand experience may be termed 'existential' in a fairly broad sense; for example, falling in love, being seized by some group loyalty such as patriotism, or possessing any type of moral earnestness. But this usage is so vague that the word becomes almost completely meaningless. In this regard it is helpful to focus upon the fact that man alone can ask ultimate questions, let alone answer them. Also, of course, we can ask pertinent questions about the weight or worth of a particular experience like serving our country or making a certain decision. Yet beyond such particular meanings and values we may ask why there is a world at all, why man exists at all, and whether our lives are at bottom meaningful or meaningless. These questions can be raised in a speculative and detached way, but whenever we come to face them with passionate earnestness, fully aware of the solemn risks and tremendous opportunities involved in them, we are entering into an 'existential attitude' in the narrower and stricter sense.

Now such an attitude has its potential weaknesses as well as its strengths. One may carry the contrast between subjective and objective to such a point that value or science or logic is unwisely deprecated. In theology, the contrast can be drawn so sharply that faith and reason are driven unwholesomely asunder. Let us be clear that wherever existentialism undercuts the elements of rational structure which are indispensable to both metaphysics and Christian theology, it must be rejected. Properly employed, however, this mode of thinking rightly opens the way to a reformulation of philosophy and Christian doctrine which can render them vital and dramatic instead of rigid and sterile.

Another potential weakness can be detected at that point where the isolated individual becomes so preoccupied with *his* freedom, *his* struggle, *his* inner conflicts, that he is shut off from fruitful contacts with nature, society, and God. Here again existentialism is primarily valuable as an antidote, but poisonous as an exclusive diet. As an antidote, it issues a not unimpressive protest against those tyrannical and legalistic elements which may be found in every society and every institution. But unless it is able to carry the human being in the direction of a restored and purified conception of community, it becomes a destructive and not a truly prophetic voice. So far as Christianity is concerned, this means that the acid test of an existentialist is his attitude toward the Church; and on this score some but not all of them betray a grave weakness.

Finally, stress upon freedom can lead toward either faith in God or downright atheism. That is why the movement which we are to study is divided roughly into two camps. One group is trying to make an atheistic acceptance of freedom and despair serve as the only possible answer. The other group is finding that the implications of human responsibility lead inescapably to a revival of religious faith. A deepened sense of human need and failure can lead toward readiness for faith in God. A keen recognition of our inability to heal ourselves through strenuous moral effort or through sustained theoretical knowledge can awaken us to the meaning of divine forgiveness. But on the other hand, the awareness of freedom may lead to the conviction that man must make himself self-sufficient, self-authenticating. It may prompt us to feel that dependence on God is no more than a form of slavery. It may cause us to take our last stand on a Stoic courage which is able to stare at emptiness, tragedy, and death unafraid. Thus existentialism has produced both the most penetrating forms of Christian faith and the most nihilistic types of human self-assertion.

Time Magazine
THE AGE OF ANGST

The automatic elevator stops with a jolt. The doors slide open, but instead of the accustomed exit, the passenger faces only a blank wall. His fingers stab at buttons: nothing happens. Finally, he presses the alarm signal, and a starter's gruff voice inquires from below: "What's the matter?" The passenger explains that he wants to get off on the 25th floor. "There is no 25th floor in this building," comes the voice over the loudspeaker. The passenger explains that, nonsense, he has worked here for years. He gives his name. "Never heard of you," says the loudspeaker. "Easy," the passenger tells himself. "They are just trying to frighten me."

But time passes and nothing changes. In that endless moment, the variously pleading and angry exchanges over the loudspeaker are the passenger's only communication with the outside world. Finally, even that ceases; the man below says that he cannot waste any more time. "Wait! Please!" cries the passenger in panic—"Keep on talking to me!" But the loudspeaker clicks into silence. Hours, days or ages go by. The passenger cowers in a corner of his steel box, staring at the shining metal grille through which the voice once spoke. The grille must be worshiped; perhaps the voice will be heard again.

This is not a story by Franz Kafka or by one of his contemporary imitators. It is a recent dream remembered in precise detail by a successful New Yorker (one wife, three children, fair income, no analyst) who works with every outward appearance of contentment in one of Manhattan's new, midtown office buildings. Whatever Freudian or other analysis might make of it, the dream could serve as a perfect allegory for an era that is almost universally regarded as the Age of Anxiety. It speaks of big city towers in which life is lived in compartments and cubicles. It speaks of the century's increasingly complex machines that no one man can control. It speaks of the swift ascents and descents not only in a competitive business existence but in an ever-fluid society. It speaks of man's dreaded loss of identity, of a desperate need to make contact with his fellow man, with the world and with whatever may be beyond the world. Above all, it speaks of God grown silent.

From "The Anxiety of Angst," *Time* (March 31, 1961), pp. 44–46, 51. Reprinted by permission of *Time*, The Weekly Newsmagazine; Copyright Time Inc., 1961.

STAGE WHINES   Anxiety seems to be the dominant fact—and is threatening to become the dominant cliché—of modern life. It shouts in the headlines, laughs nervously at cocktail parties, nags from advertisements, speaks suavely in the board room, whines from the stage, clatters from the Wall Street ticker, jokes with fake youthfulness on the golf course and whispers in privacy each day before the shaving mirror and the dressing table. Not merely the black statistics of murder, suicide, alcoholism and divorce betray anxiety (or that special form of anxiety which is guilt), but almost any innocent, everyday act: the limp or over-hearty handshake, the second pack of cigarettes or the third martini, the forgotten appointment, the stammer in mid-sentence, the wasted hour before the TV set, the spanked child, the new car unpaid for.

Although he died in 1855, the great Danish existentialist Sören Kierkegaard described the effects of anxiety in terms that are strikingly apt today. He spoke of his "cowardly age," in which "one does everything possible by way of diversions and the Janizary music of loud-voiced enterprises to keep lonely thoughts away." Yet all the noise is in vain: "No Grand Inquisitor has in readiness such terrible tortures as has anxiety, and no spy knows how to attack more artfully the man he suspects, choosing the instant when he is weakest, nor knows how to lay traps where he will be caught and ensnared, and no sharp-witted judge knows how to interrogate, to examine the accused, as anxiety does, which never lets him escape, neither by diversion nor by noise, neither at work nor at play, neither by day nor by night."

WAR OR PEACE   When a fact is as universal as love, death or anxiety, it becomes difficult to measure and classify. Man would not be human were he not anxious. Is his anxiety today really greater than ever before—different from Job's? Or is modern man simply a victim of distorted historical vision that always sees the present as bigger and worse than the past?

There is general agreement among psychiatrists, theologians, sociologists and even poets that in this era, anxiety is indeed different both in quantity and quality.

Other eras were turbulent, insecure and complex—the great migrations after the fall of the Roman Empire; the age of discovery; Copernicus' and Galileo's tinkering with the universe, removing the earth and man from its center; the industrial revolution. But in a sense, the 20th century U.S. is the culmination of all these upheavals—itself the product of a gigantic migration, itself both champion and victim of the industrial revolution, itself faced with the necessity not only of accepting a new universe but of exploring it.

The American today is told without pause that the world is up to him—war or peace, prosperity or famine, the welfare or literacy of the last, remotest Congolese, Tibetan or Laotian. And he is facing his demanding destiny in a state of psychological and religious confusion.

For centuries of Christian civilization (and not Christian alone), man assumed that anxiety and guilt were part of his nature and that as a finite and fallen being, he had plenty to be guilty about. The only remedies were grace and faith. When the age of reason repealed the Fall, man was thrust back onto himself and, for a time, reason seemed to be an adequate substitute for the certainties of faith. Spinoza could write confidently: "Fear arises from a weakness of mind and therefore does not appertain to the use of reason." But it was soon clear that reason alone could not answer all man's questions, could not provide what he desperately needs: order and purpose in the universe. And so man invented substitute deities—History, the State, Environment. But in the end all these only led back to the nearly unbearable message that man is alone in a meaningless cosmos, subject only to the blind forces of evolution and responsible only to himself. As Kirilov puts it in Dostoevskys' *The Possessed:* "If there is no God, then I am god."

The discovery of the unconscious depths of man's mind by Schopenhauer, Freud and others seemed to offer an escape; here was a dark, mysterious realm, irrational as man knew himself to be irrational, to which he might shift responsibility for his acts. But this worked only partly; ultimately even the cult of the unconscious (psychoanalysis) directed man back to himself and his own resources. Many rejoice that man has been freed from the fear of demons, not realizing that it may be worse to have to fear himself. Many similarly rejoice that, to some extent, he has been freed from the fear of hell-fire, not realizing that he has instead been condemned to the fear of nothingness—what Paul Tillich calls the fear of "nonbeing."

Widespread awareness of all this has itself contributed to the change. Psychologists report that 30 years ago the U.S. was in an "age of covert anxiety." It is now in an age of "overt anxiety." People tend to believe that it is wrong and "sick" to feel anxious or guilty; they are beset by guilt about guilt, by anxiety about anxiety.

BOUND AND FREE Psychiatrists and theologians know, of course, that a certain amount of guilt and anxiety is inevitable and necessary in man. They are like pain: "bad" because they are discomforting, but in normal quantities necessary for survival because they warn of danger and because they make a human being responsible to others. The rare individual who feels neither guilt nor anxiety is a monster—a psychopath with no conscience. What psychologists call *Urangst*, or original anxiety, the anxiety that is inevitably part of any human being, is well described by theologian Reinhold Niebuhr, who believes that it springs from man's dual character: on the one hand, man is involved in the contingencies of nature, like the animals; on the other, he has freedom and understanding of his position. "In short, man, being both bound and free, both limited and limitless, is anxious."

This basic, or existential, anxiety (which Niebuhr sees as the precondition of sin) is no more disturbing, in normal quantities, than is rational fear of danger. In contrast, neurotic anxiety is irrational fear, a response to a danger that is unknown, internal, intangible or unreal. Anxiety is fear in search of a cause. Authorities differ on the relationship of guilt to anxiety, but Dr. John Donnelly of Hartford's Institute of Living offers what is for laymen the most sense-making distinction: guilt is apprehension over some transgression in the past, whether actually committed or merely contemplated, whereas anxiety involves only the possible and the future. Because the German equivalent, *die Angst*, carries a stronger connotation of dread, many psychiatrists prefer this term to the English word. Of itself, anxiety is not a neurosis, but it is an essential ingredient in almost all neuroses, most major mental and psychosomatic illnesses. Its victims fall into three broad categories:

1. The whole men and women, who have such minor emotional disturbances as fear about thunder or a compulsion to twist and untwist paper clips (symbolically twisting the boss's neck). Their aggressiveness, perfectionism or shyness are not exaggerated.

2. The walking wounded, who can usually control their anxiety and its symptoms well enough to function as breadwinners or housewives, but periodically break down and wind up, in a severe anxiety state, in a psychiatrist's office or, briefly, in a mental hospital.

3. The ambulance cases, who spend months or years or drag out their lives in mental hospitals, or (in some cases still not recognized often enough) land in the emergency rooms of general hospitals with psychosomatic illnesses often mistaken for heart attacks, asthma or pregnancy complications.

All the neurotic symptoms, major or minor, originate in the same way: they are defenses against anxiety. The most common are the phobias in which—to cover up anxiety and guilt too painful to be acknowledged—people develop an irrational aversion to some act or object seemingly unconnected with their anxiety. Phobias seem to occur in dazzling profusion: Blakiston's *New Gould Medical Dictionary* lists 217 of them. More prevalent but less generally recognized as cover-ups for anxiety are compulsive forms of behavior and addictions to alcohol and narcotics. . . .

ORDER OUT OF CHAOS Beyond curing the obviously sick, psychologists and psychiatrists evidently must make an effort to teach people not so much to eliminate guilt and anxiety as to understand them and live with them constructively. That is the point made by Hans Hofmann, associate professor of theology at Harvard Divinity School, in a new book called *Religion and Mental Health* (Harper). Writes Hofmann:

> Our time is one of ferment and potential rebirth. This is so precisely because it is a time full of chaos . . . It was only natural that Sigmund Freud should at the beginning of his career have thought of the irrational aspects of the human personality as chaotic and potentially dangerous powers . . . It did not occur to him that chaos in itself may represent a very positive and fertile current of life. For the people of the Old Testament, especially in the creation story, the question was not: 'Why is there chaos?' but rather: 'Why is there order?' For them, order was the outgrowth of daily living . . . The unique function of man, in their view, is to live in close, creative touch with chaos, and thereby experience the birth of order . . . Surprisingly enough, modern psychotherapists share this ancient knowledge.

7
New Forms of
Aesthetic Expression

Who would venture into the labyrinth of modern art, elucidating novel, theater, music, painting, and film, if indeed these genres still have meaning in an era of anti-art, anti-novel, even anti-history? Eschewing any pretense at total coverage, but still taking the traditional categories at face value, this chapter offers readings on painting, music, and the theater, in the hope of presenting the main issues involved in twentieth century art.

Probably the arts get as much attention as any other aspect of contemporary life. Along with the war boom, we have a "cultural boom." Along with hawks and doves, we have "culture vultures." The "moderns," though difficult and perplexing, are very "in," and only reactionaries criticize them.

But by what critical canon do we accept or reject the art forms of our age? American art critic Harold Rosenberg emphasizes the irrelevance of art criticism in an era of action painting, when what goes on the canvas "is not a picture, but an event." Picasso himself finds the lack of "rigid standards" a "limitation" and bemoans the loss of "tradition." Marcel Duchamp sees the artistic value of today's art as measured only in shock value—*succès de scandale.*

If the painter is beyond aesthetic good and evil, what of the musician? Constant Lambert dismisses the artistic revolution in music as pre–World War I and devoid of meaning since that time. Calvin Tompkins points out that composer John Cage's basic creed contends that music is "purposeless play" and should have no direction. But if meaning is banished and if, as Cage feels, "everything we do is music," is there even meaning to the word "music," to say nothing of critical standards by which music should be judged?

And what of the theater? Is the theater of the absurd really absurd? In large measure it is, declares Mordecai Gorelik, research professor in theater. "The absence of true dramatic action and the dismal idea [portrayal] of the human condition . . . form the background of non-drama." But Martin Esslin, an authority on modern drama, feels that "the theater of the absurd isn't absurd at all." Modern plays confront their audiences with the great questions facing man today, says he. "If we want to master the despair arising from such basic elements of the human condition, we can only do so by facing up to them and steeling our minds to accept them."

Art today, according to Jacques Barzun, Dean of Faculties and Provost of Columbia University, is symptomatic of a crisis in intellect. The arts are replacing verbal communication and thus are weakening intellect. In their "love of confusion," says Barzun, artists are seeking "a release from responsibility."

Françoise Gilot
GETTING PAINTING BACK ON THE RAILS

Before I met Picasso and for some months after, my painting was figurative in an experimental way. Early in 1944 I decided that what people were referring to in the jargon as "the anecdote" was useless and I began to work in a completely nonfigurative manner. My grandmother used to come upstairs to my studio every evening to see what I had done during the day. Several months earlier I had done figurative portraits and

From *Life with Picasso* by Françoise Gilot and Carlton Lake, pp. 71–76, 77. Copyright © 1964 by McGraw-Hill, Inc. Used by permission of the publisher, McGraw-Hill Book Company.

Françoise Gilot (1921–   ) is a painter who was Picasso's mistress for a number of years. She later wrote a book about these years called *Life with Picasso*.

still lifes, rather tortured in their forms, and they had shocked her. But when I began to do nonfigurative painting, she liked it immediately.

"I didn't understand what you were doing before," she said, "and although I don't understand this either, I find it pleasing. I see the harmony of color and design, and since you don't twist and torture nature, I like it better." I told her I didn't have the impression that it was any more pleasing than what I had been doing before. On the contrary, in my own mind the compositions I was doing now had rather dramatic intentions and they were not pleasing for *me*. I asked her if she found them dramatic. She said, "Not at all. I can look at those by the hour and find them restful."

I told Pablo about that one afternoon before he settled down to painting. He laughed. "Naturally," he said. "Nonfigurative painting is never subversive. It's always a kind of bag into which the viewer can throw anything he wants to get rid of. You can't impose your thought on people if there's no relation between your painting and their visual habits. I'm not speaking of the connoisseur of painting. I mean the average person, whose visual habits are pretty conventional. He sees a tree in a certain fashion, in accordance with habits he formed in childhood. Someone who has a very cultivated vision may see a landscape of Aix as a Cézanne, a landscape of Arles as a van Gogh. But in general, people see nature in conventional fashion and they don't want anybody tampering with it. They are willing to be shown things that resemble nothing because those things correspond to a kind of invertebrate, unformulated interior dream. But if you take a commonplace way of seeing and try to change the slightest detail in it, everyone shouts, 'Oh, no, it's not possible. That's not the portrait of my grandmother.'

"When I paint, I always try to give an image people are not expecting and, beyond that, one they reject. That's what interests me. It's in this sense that I mean I always try to be subversive. That is, I give a man an image of himself whose elements are collected from among the usual way of seeing things in traditional painting and then reassembled in a fashion that is unexpected and disturbing enough to make it impossible for him to escape the questions it raises."

I told Pablo I thought nobody could have done completely nonfigurative painting better than he. "I suppose so," he said. "In those polyhedric Cubist portraits I did in tones of white and gray and ocher, beginning around 1909, there were references to natural forms, but in the early stages there were practically none. I painted them in afterwards. I call them 'attributes.' At that period I was doing painting for its own sake. It was really pure painting, and the composition was done as a composition. It was only toward the end of a portrait that I brought in the attributes. At a certain moment I simply put in three or four black touches and what was around those touches became a vest.

"I suppose I use that word 'attribute' in the way a writer might use it rather than a painter; that is, as one speaks of a sentence with a subject, verb, and attribute. The attribute is an adjective. It serves to qualify the subject. But the verb and the subject are the whole painting, really. The attributes were the few points of reference designed to bring one back to visual reality, recognizable to anyone. And they were put in, also, to hide the pure painting behind them. I've never believed in doing painting for 'the happy few.' I've always felt that painting must awaken something even in the man who doesn't ordinarily look at pictures, just as in Molière there is always something to make the very intelligent person laugh and also the person who understands nothing. In Shakespeare, too. And in my work, just as in Shakespeare, there are often burlesque things and relatively vulgar things. In that way I reach everybody. It's not that I want to prostrate myself in front of the public, but I want to provide something for every level of thinking.

"But to get back to the matter of attributes: You know my Cubist portrait of Kahnweiler?" I told him I did—in reproduction, at least. "All right," he said. "In its original form it looked to me as though it were about to go up in smoke. But when I paint smoke, I want you to be able to drive a nail into it. So I added the attributes—a suggestion of eyes, the wave in the hair, an ear lobe, the clasped hands—and now you can. You see, at that time and in those portraits I felt that what I had to say was fairly hard to understand. It's like Hegel. Hegel is a very interesting man but there aren't many people who want to take the trouble to read him. He's up there where he is for the few people who do want to give themselves that trouble and will go in search of whatever nourishment is there. If you want to give nourishment like that in painting, which is not easy to absorb for most people, who don't have the organs to assimilate it, you need some kind of subterfuge. It's like giving a long and difficult explanation to a child: you add certain details that he understands immediately in order to sustain his interest and buoy him up for the difficult parts. The great majority of people have no spirit of creation or invention. As Hegel says, they can know only what they already know. So how do you go about teaching them something new? By mixing what they know with what they don't know. Then, when they see vaguely in their fog something they recognize, they think, 'Ah, I know that.' And then it's just one more step to, 'Ah, I know the whole thing.' And their mind thrusts forward into the unknown and they begin to recognize what they didn't know before and they increase their powers of understanding."

That sounded very reasonable to me, I told him. "Of course it's reasonable," he said. "It's purest Hegel."

I told him these applications of Hegel were very impressive. How much of him had he read?

"None," he said. "I told you there weren't many people who

wanted to take the trouble to go that far. And I don't either. I picked up my information on the subject from Kahnweiler. But I keep getting away from my attributes. What you have to understand is that if the attributes—or, in a more general sense, the objects—were the main point of my painting, I would choose them with great care. For example, in a painting by Matisse the object plays a major role. It isn't any old object that is chosen to receive the honor of becoming an object in a painting by Matisse. They're all things that are most unusual in themselves. The objects that go into my paintings are not that at all. They're common objects from anywhere: a pitcher, a mug of beer, a pipe, a package of tobacco, a bowl, a kitchen chair with a cane seat, a plain common table— the object at its most ordinary. I don't go out of my way to find a rare object that nobody ever heard of, like one of Matisse's Venetian chairs in the form of an oyster, and then transform it. That wouldn't make sense. I want to tell something by means of the most common object: for example, a casserole, any old casserole, the one everybody knows. For me it is a vessel in the metaphorical sense, just like Christ's use of parables. He had an idea; he formulated it in parables so that it would be acceptable to the greatest number. That's the way I use objects. I will never paint a Louis XV chair, for example. It's a reserved object, an object for certain people but not for everybody. I make reference to objects that belong to everybody; at least they belong to them in theory. In any case, they're what I wrap up my thought in. They're my parables."

I told Pablo he was making progress in the order of sanctity: first Hegel, then Christ. Who next? He thought about that for a moment. "I'm not sure," he said. "Perhaps Aristotle. Someone, at least, who might be able to get painting back on the rails again." Where had it gone off, I asked him.

"That's a long story," he said, "but you're a good listener, so I'll tell you. You have to go all the way back to the Greeks and the Egyptians. Today we are in the unfortunate position of having no order or canon whereby all artistic production is submitted to rules. They—the Greeks, the Romans, the Egyptians—did. Their canon was inescapable because beauty, so-called, was, by definition, contained in those rules. But as soon as art had lost all link with tradition, and the kind of liberation that came in with Impressionism permitted every painter to do what he wanted to do, painting was finished. When they decided it was the painter's sensations and emotions that mattered, and every man could recreate painting as he understood it from any basis whatever, then there was no more painting; there were only individuals. Sculpture died the same death.

"Beginning with van Gogh, however great we may be, we are all, in a measure, autodidacts—you might almost say primitive painters.

Painters no longer live within a tradition and so each one of us must recreate an entire language. Every painter of our times is fully authorized to recreate that language from A to Z. No criterion can be applied to him *a priori*, since we don't believe in rigid standards any longer. In a certain sense, that's a liberation but at the same time it's an enormous limitation, because when the individuality of the artist begins to express itself, what the artist gains in the way of liberty he loses in the way of order, and when you're no longer able to attach yourself to an order, basically that's very bad."

I brought up the question of Cubism. Wasn't that a kind of order, I asked him. He shrugged. "It was really the manifestation of a vague desire on the part of those of us who participated in it to get back to some kind of order, yes. We were trying to move in a direction opposite to Impressionism. That was the reason we abandoned color, emotion, sensation, and everything that had been introduced into painting by the Impressionists, to search again for an architectonic basis in the composition, trying to make an order of it. People didn't understand very well at the time why very often we didn't sign our canvases. Most of those that are signed we signed years later. It was because we felt the temptation, the hope, of an anonymous art, not in its expression but in its point of departure. We were trying to set up a new order and it had to express itself through different individuals. Nobody needed to know that it was so-and-so who had done this or that painting. But individualism was already too strong and that resulted in a failure, because after a few years all Cubists who were any good at all were no longer Cubists. Those who remained Cubists were those who weren't really true painters. Braque was saying the other day, 'Cubism is a word invented by the critics, but we were never Cubists.' That isn't exactly so. We *were*, at one time, Cubists, but as we drew away from that period we found that, more than just Cubists, we were individuals dedicated to ourselves. As soon as we saw that the collective adventure was a lost cause, each one of us had to find an individual adventure. And the individual adventure always goes back to the one which is the archetype of our times: that is, van Gogh's— an essentially solitary and tragic adventure. That's why I said a few minutes ago that we were all autodidacts. That's literally true, I think, but I realized even when Cubism was breaking up that we were saved from complete isolation as individuals by the fact that however different we might have the appearance of being, we were all Modern-Style artists. There were so many wild, delirious curves in those subway entrances and in all the other Modern-Style manifestations, that I, even though I limited myself almost exclusively to straight lines, was participating in my fashion in the Modern-Style movement. Because even if you are against a movement, you're still part of it. The pro and the con are, after all, two aspects of the same movement. In that way those of us who attempted to escape from Modern-Style became more Modern-Style than anybody else. You can't escape your own period. Whether you take sides for or against, you're always inside it." . . .

I asked him how a painter could work like nature. "Well," he said, "aside from rhythm, one of the things that strikes us most strongly in nature is the difference of textures: the texture of space, the texture of an object in that space—a tobacco wrapper, a porcelain vase—and beyond that the relation of form, color, and volume to the question of texture. The purpose of the *papier collé* was to give the idea that different textures can enter into composition to become the reality in the painting that competes with the reality in nature. We tried to get rid of *trompe-l'oeil* to find a *trompe-l'esprit*. We didn't any longer want to fool the eye; we wanted to fool the mind. The sheet of newspaper was never used in order to make a newspaper. It was used to become a bottle or something like that. It was never used literally but always as an element displaced from its habitual meaning into another meaning to produce a shock between the usual definition at the point of departure and its new definition at the point of arrival. If a piece of newspaper can become a bottle, that gives us something to think about in connection with both newspapers and bottles, too. This displaced object has entered a universe for which it was not made and where it retains, in a measure, its strangeness. And this strangeness was what we wanted to make people think about because we were quite aware that our world was becoming very strange and not exactly reassuring."

Marcel Duchamp
and
William Seitz
KEEPING ART OFF THE RAILS

Editor's note: Undoubtedly the most scandalous, important, and exciting art exhibition ever held in this country took place February 17, 1913, when derisive New Yorkers saw their first full view of Picasso,

"What's Happened to Art?" by William Seitz from *Vogue Magazine*, pp. 110, 112–113, 129–130, 131. Reprinted by permission of the author.

Marcel Duchamp (1887–   ) is a French painter whose cubistic painting "Nude Descending a Staircase" caused quite a stir when it was exhibited at the New York Armory Show in 1913. Duchamp has been called the *enfant terrible* of modern art.

Matisse, Rouault, Seurat, Van Gogh, and many others, including the star of the affair, Marcel Duchamp's canvas, "The Nude Descending a Staircase." . . . To discuss that first Armory Show and its effect on Americans, Vogue asked the scholarly William Seitz to do a taped interview with Mr. Duchamp.

WILLIAM SEITZ: You said a few moments ago that the reception of your paintings in New York was not success in the accepted sense, but rather a *succès de scandale.*

MARCEL DUCHAMP: A *succès de scandale,* yes.

W.S.:   Yet coupled with the sale of the pictures this must have made you extremely happy.

M.D.:   It did.

W.S.:   And you were not resentful of the way it was received?

M.D.:   Oh! No. No. Of course not. I was delighted to be a *succès de scandale* because for me it was a form of revolutionary action. You see if I were accepted with open arms that would be the opposite of what I wanted.

W.S.:   Would you have been disappointed if it had been received as a beautiful and great painting?

M.D.:   Probably. Yes. At least it wouldn't have fulfilled my intentions or hopes. After all, the idea of the Cubists at that time was to be entirely revolutionary and disturb completely every conception of art as it was accepted at that time. Upset the standards.

W.S.:   While painting "The Nude" did you think of it as a picture which might be profoundly shocking to a lay audience?

M.D.:   Oh! Of course. From Courbet on, that had always been the idea of modern art, and every ten or fifteen years a new school would come up and start again on another slope.

W.S.:   You said once, when we were talking about this, that you wanted to shock yourself.

M.D.:   Yes. That's the point; it's very difficult to shock oneself, you see. And that's why I say it must have shocked me when I decided that descending was more important than ascending. That was a sort of refining of the idea of shocking. Not only the public but myself. I've been all my life in that attitude. I never do anything to please myself. None of the few things I have done in my life ever were finished with a feeling of satisfaction.

W.S.:   Does this have any connection with your decision, some ten years later, not to paint anymore?

M.D.:   Well, probably it had to . . . no, the decision is more general than that, and it was not a decision in the first place. It never was a decision; I can paint tomorrow if I wish. I don't find painting or the idea of painting or the painter or the artist today as suiting my attitude toward life. In other words, painting for me was a means to an end but not an end in itself. To be a painter for the sake of being a painter was never the ultimate aim of my life, you see. That's why I tried to go into different forms of activity—purely optical things and kineticism—which has nothing to do with painting.

w.s: You were interested in revolutionary acts or in upsetting the canons, not in painting as such. Painting was a tool.

m.d.:   Exactly. Painting was only a tool. A bridge to take me somewhere else. Where, I don't know. I wouldn't know because it would be so revolutionary in essence that it couldn't be formulated.

w.s.:   Your kind of revolutionary activity apparently was never political. What adjective would you use to describe it? "Aesthetic?" "Philosophical?"

m.d.:   No. No. "Metaphysical," if any. And even that is a dubious term. Anything is dubious. It's pushing the idea of doubt of Descartes, you see, to a much further point than they ever did in the School of Cartesianism: doubt in myself, doubt in everything. In the first place never believing in truth. In the end it comes to doubt "to be." Not doubt to say "to be or not to be"—that has nothing to do with it. There won't be any difference between when I'm dead and now, because I won't know it. You see the famous "to be" is consciousness, and when you sleep you "are" no more. That's what I mean—a state of sleepingness; because consciousness is a formulation, a very gratuitous formulation of something, but nothing else. And I go farther by saying that words such as truth, art, veracity, or anything are stupid in themselves. Of course it's difficult to formulate, so I insist *every word I am telling you now is stupid and wrong.*

w.s.:   Could it be otherwise? Can you conceive of finding words which would be appropriate?

m.d.:   No. Because words are the tools of "to be"—of expression. They are completely built on the fact that you "are," and in order to express it you have built a little alphabet and you make your words from it. So it's a vicious circle. I mean it's completely idiotic. I mean the language is a great enemy, in the first place. The language and thinking in words are the great enemies of man, if man exists. And even if he doesn't exist. . . .

w.s.:   Now to go back to the Armory Show: it was a tremendous success for the "revolutionary" artists in the United States. Suppose this group had been totally accepted. Or suppose, in France, the Cubists had been totally accepted: what effect would that have had on their *esprit de corps,* on their newness, on their commitment?

m.d.:   It would have been very bad, I think. It would have been terribly bad because there's nothing more demoralizing than success.

When you are trying to shock and you're not shocking anyone, it's a shock. You see you have to keep on shocking. In other words, you little by little get your own little group of people who are with you fighting the big mass against you. Art is a second-fiddle social expression. After all you don't have to have art to eat, to live, to be comfortable, to make wars, anything. It's a decorative element in society, so you don't see why the layman should take it in.

w.s.:   We keep applying the adjective "revolutionary" to painting and sculpture, or the term "avant-garde"—which after all is a military term. Do you think the idea of the "revolutionary artist" is valid?

m.d.:   No, I don't. I think it's an easy way of expressing oneself but it doesn't mean a thing. In other words there is no revolutionary spirit; actually there is a difference in time flowing. In other words, after 1952 comes 1953 and you can not expect '53 to be like '52.

w.s.:   But you, too, looked at yourself at one time as a revolutionary.

m.d.:   Yes, I spoke the word, I used it because everybody used it, but I'm against the word in itself. I mean, it doesn't mean a thing. It's a false use.

w.s.:   How would you compare the "revolutionary" artists of 1963 with those of your youth—let us say of 1910–1913?

m.d.:   Well, for one thing, at that time—1910—Kandinsky and Kupka produced abstract or "nonfigurative" works; then came the Cubist period, and then a second wind of nonfigurativeness appeared between the two wars. A man a thousand years from now—even two hundred years from now—will see it as much more compact. As one piece. It will be Kandinsky *and* Pollock. Together.

w.s.:   In 1960 we had what some called Dada. Was this, in your opinion, the same thing as . . .

m.d.:   No, it was not Dada. Just as Abstract Expressionism is not like Kandinsky at all. Pollock is not like Kandinsky at all, but time will unite them under the label: nonfigurativeness.

w.s.:   Would you agree that, after the Armory Show, the most important art-historical event in New York was the period just after the Second War? It was the first time when the movements from Europe began to be . . .

m.d.:   Terminated, yes. But all this comes to a very simple conclusion, you know: there is no art; there are only artists. In other words, the school has absolutely no importance. It's only a few names, a few men who are so powerful in themselves that they impose their work.

Whether it's figurative, nonfigurative, Cubistic, or anything else has absolutely no importance. "Pop Art" is the same thing. If you're "Pop" you're somebody today. But that doesn't mean you're the great artist of tomorrow. In other words it's just like newspaper appearing every day with the news.

w.s.:　Are you saying that the true history of art is the history of individual men? Of individual artists?

m.d.:　Yes, *uniquement;* that's the only thing that counts.

w.s.:　Their relationship to the society in which they worked—the fact that they happen to have been regarded as ultraconservatives, ultraradicals, or middle-of-the-roaders—is, in your opinion, totally irrelevant.

m.d.:　Yes, absolutely. The fortunate thing is that we in 1963 and people in the year 2000 will name the five or six top men. Those who have most chance of keeping on top are the ones who have worked in a very solid material that will defy time.

w.s.:　It's interesting that so many artists now work in very perishable materials, such as refuse and old newspapers.

m.d.:　Yes that's very interesting. It's the most revolutionary—if I want to use the word this time—attitude possible because they know they're killing themselves. It's a form of suicide, as artists go; they kill themselves by using perishable materials. They know it will last five years, ten years, and will necessarily be destroyed, destroy itself.

But today the integration of art into society forces the artist to submit to its demands. In 1913 the zero—the economic level at which an artist could subsist—was so low that bohemian life was possible. You didn't have to think every week of having to pay your rent or anything. You didn't pay your rent. Now the zero is too high. You can not afford to be a young man who doesn't do a thing. Who doesn't work? You can't live without working, which is a terrible thing. I remember a book called *The Right To Be Lazy:* that right doesn't exist now. You have to work to justify your breathing.

w.s.:　The integration of art: isn't this precisely what modern artists, teachers, dealers, collectors, and museum people have been seeking?

m.d.:　Oh, yes. It's a marvellous thing from a certain angle. But it has the opposite effect, too, if the mediocritization of the rest results. In other words, there are so many buyers and so many artists that the aesthetic part will become completely nonexistent because it will be completely levelled, from the bottom up.

w.s.:　The hostility levelled against the Postimpressionist art in the Armory Show was in reality a very important form of recognition.

m.d.:　Yes, yes. It's very simple: there was no integration then and they were pariahs, all of them. The era of pariahs. We were delighted to be pariahs. We didn't want to be integrated. After the two wars—especially after the second—there was complete integration. A man who would want to be a revolutionary today couldn't be known. He will have to be unknown. If he is integrated he is lost; if he succeeds, he fails, because the stamp of this society is derogatory and destructive.

w.s.:   Can you conceive of yourself now as being twenty-six, with the aspirations you had then?

M.D.:   I don't know what I'd do except that I know there was no money consideration at that time. I didn't expect to make a living. In other words the money question was not included. It didn't exist when I took that painting off the wall in the Independents show.

The idea was to give up any collaboration with the Cubists. I was a member of the Cubists and I just pulled out of it, rather than integrate myself into Cubism. So that's one form of revolution, or revolt, at least! Today I don't know whether I would have the same considerations. Of course, I would have to hate the mixture of art and money as water in your wine. It's a very good comparison because it dilutes into mediocrity. Water in wine. The bouquet disappears.

w.s.:   Less of one commodity and more and more of another until—I think I'd be interpreting you correctly—you feel that the more art becomes integrated into modern commerce the more it ceases to be art.

M.D.:   Exactly. But art doesn't interest me. Artists interest me.

w.s.:   In other words, you think that Leonardo or Rembrandt are more important than the "Mona Lisa" or "Aristotle Contemplating the Bust of Homer." . . .

M.D.:   Oh, yes. Of course. I saw many Rembrandts last summer in Amsterdam and they are remarkable compared to that thing here. Even Rembrandt didn't paint a masterpiece every time he went to his easel.

w.s.:   Such objects now seem to have more monetary than aesthetic value.

M.D.:   Yes. We have so many standards: the gold standard, the platinum standard, and now the burlap standard. It's surprising that a piece of cloth, a piece of burlap on a stretcher with a few nails, can bring such prices.

w.s.:   In a sense it was the pressure of alienation—of hostility from without—that enabled you to identify yourselves as revolutionary artists.

M.D.:   Yes. There was no danger of being sucked in by success, none whatsoever. It took twenty years for Picasso to become a great financial success. I remember going to the Sagot Gallery on the rue Laffitte in 1908 or '09 where Picasso's drawings were five francs—one dollar—framed in those blue mats.

So, it was really the pariah status of the artist at that epoch that made it possible for movements like Cubism and Fauvism to be "pure," as we say. At least not to be adulterated by money.

w.s.: Just since 1950—since the success of the "New York School"—one could cite many instances of works worth five hundred or a thousand dollars that today are worth thirty times that amount. In 1945 none of the avant-garde artists in New York—Arshile Gorky is one example—dreamed their works would ever sell at $10,000 and more.

M.D.: Exactly. It's a postwar phenomenon, decidedly. Between 1946 and now the thing has become a crazy machine of money.

w.s.: In the early thinking about modern art one finds a constant objection to "materialism." Artists spoke in terms of spiritual against material values. Are they fighting against them any longer?

M.D.: No. They accept them—because there is nothing else to do, probably. It's much too strong a *courant d'air*—a draft that you can not go against or you lose all your vitality.

w.s.: Do you feel there is now a capitulation on the part of the artist to materialism?

M.D.: Yes, it is a capitulation. It seems today that the artist couldn't survive if he didn't swear allegiance to the good old mighty dollar. That shows how far the integration has gone.

w.s.: But even you were greatly helped by a sympathetic and enlightened collector, Walter Arensberg, when you came to this country.

M.D.: Oh, yes, but that's a different thing, if you consider that there are thirty-five pieces in the Philadelphia Museum, and that those thirty-five pieces were bought over a period of thirty-five years. So it's not so much a year. I couldn't even live on it, because I remember giving French lessons in New York in '16, '17, and '18. I was very happy to give a few French lessons. It was a form of freedom.

In the case of Arensberg and myself it was a question of $200, $300 each time and no more. I don't think Arensberg ever gave me a check for $1,000. I remember he paid the rent for my studio a year or two when I was on Sixty-seventh Street—that was in exchange for "The Large Glass," which I was then working on.

w.s.: In the present situation, with the widespread acceptance of radical art by wealthy collectors, big business, and museums, can it continue to develop in the same way?

M.D.: No. I don't think so. It has the effect of dilution of quality.

w.s.: Each year we have a new avant-garde. Whether it's a . . .

M.D.: We know that every day we see the name of a new artist in our mail; a young artist. They can't continue multiplying like rabbits. . . .

w.s.: To return, perhaps as one of the last things we'll discuss, to the assimilation of "revolutionary" modern art into bourgeois culture:

is dilution an inevitable outcome of dissemination to a larger and larger audience, or is it related more to the fact that art has become a commercial thing?

M.D.:   It's both. One has brought the other. You see commercialism has brought in a number of collectors, semi-collectors, half collectors, and even laymen who are motivated by a sort of matter-of-fact impulse.

W.S.:   You mean the way they would have a swimming pool or two cars or belong to a country club?

M.D.:   Yes that goes with it. As long as it is connected with money and it can be an investment. The investment idea has brought in a great deal of that public, and that public, in turn, has completely accepted the idea of the avant-garde. They don't even call it avant-garde anymore: "You can't be avant-garde anymore. We accept it before you do it. There is nothing shocking to us. You can't shock us." Shocking is impossible today.

W.S.:   We still have a few journalists and critics who become incensed over modern art. Should we welcome these voices, which sometimes come from high positions, as manifestations that someone still exists who can be shocked? Perhaps we should be grateful for them.

M.D.:   One could put an ad in the papers saying, "We want somebody who will be shocked." It becomes a joke. The shock as it was originally—in the Armory Show, for example—was a genuine shock. The word "shock" did not exist as such. It came afterward. The phenomenon had taken place and it was called a shock.

W.S.:   Just as the avant-garde was labelled after it existed.

M.D.:   Exactly. When today it is the opposite: the shock is put before the cart.

Harold Rosenberg
NOT A PICTURE BUT AN EVENT

What makes any definition of a movement in art dubious is that it never fits the deepest artists in the movement—certainly not as well as, if successful, it does the others. Yet without the definition something essential in those best is bound to be missed. The attempt to define is like

Reprinted by permission of the publisher, Horizon Press, from *The Tradition of the New* by Harold Rosenberg. Copyright 1959, 1960.
Harold Rosenberg (1906–   ) is an American art critic.

a game in which you cannot possibly reach the goal from the starting point but can only close in on it by picking up each time from where the last play landed.

Modern Art? Or an Art of the Modern?

Since the War every twentieth-century style in painting has been brought to profusion in the United States: thousands of "abstract" painters—crowded teaching courses in Modern Art—a scattering of new heroes—ambitions stimulated by new galleries, mass exhibitions, reproductions in popular magazines, festivals, appropriations.

Is this the usual catching up of America with European art forms? Or is something new being created? For the question of novelty, a definition would seem indispensable.

Some people deny that there is anything original in the recent American painting. Whatever is being done here now, they claim, was done thirty years ago in Paris. You can trace this painter's boxes of symbols to Kandinsky, that one's moony shapes to Miró or even back to Cézanne.

Quantitatively, it is true that most of the symphonies in blue and red rectangles, the wandering pelvises and bird-bills, the line constructions and plane suspensions, the virginal dissections of flat areas that crowd the art shows are accretions to the "School of Paris" brought into being by the fact that the mode of production of modern masterpieces has now been all too clearly rationalized. There are styles in the present displays which the painter could have acquired by putting a square inch of a Soutine or a Bonnard under a microscope. . . . All this is training based on a new conception of what art is, rather than original work demonstrating what art is about to become.

At the center of this wide practicing of the immediate past, however, the work of some painters has separated itself from the rest by a consciousness of a function for painting different from that of the earlier "abstractionists," both the Europeans themselves and the Americans who joined them in the years of the Great Vanguard.

This new painting does not constitute a School. To form a School in modern times not only is a new painting consciousness needed but a consciousness of that consciousness—and even an insistence on certain formulas. A School is the result of the linkage of practice with terminology—different paintings are affected by the same words. In the American vanguard the words, as we shall see, belong not to the art but to the individual artists. What they think in common is represented only by what they do separately.

Getting Inside the Canvas

At a certain moment the canvas began to appear to one American painter after another as an arena in which to act—rather than as a space in which to reproduce, re-design, analyze or "express" an object, actual or imagined. What was to go on the canvas was not a picture but an event.

The painter no longer approached his easel with an image in his mind; he went up to it with material in his hand to do something to that other piece of material in front of him. The image would be the result of this encounter.

It is pointless to argue that Rembrandt or Michelangelo worked in the same way. You don't get Lucrece with a dagger out of staining a piece of cloth or spontaneously putting forms into motion upon it. She had to exist some place else before she got on the canvas, and paint was Rembrandt's means for bringing her there, though, of course, a means that would change her by the time she arrived. Now, everything must have been in the tubes, in the painter's muscles and in the cream-colored sea into which he dives. If Lucrece should come out she will be among us for the first time—a surprise. To the painter, she *must* be a surprise. In this mood there is no point to an act if you already know what it contains.

"B—is not modern," one of the leaders of this mode said to me. "He works from sketches. That makes him Renaissance."

Here the principle, and the difference from the old painting, is made into a formula. A sketch is the preliminary form of an image the *mind* is trying to grasp. To work from sketches arouses the suspicion that the artist still regards the canvas as a place where the mind records its contents—rather than itself the "mind" through which the painter thinks by changing a surface with paint.

If a painting is an action the sketch is one action, the painting that follows it another. The second cannot be "better" or more complete than the first. There is just as much in what one lacks as in what the other has.

Of course, the painter who spoke had no right to assume that his friend had the old mental conception of a sketch. There is no reason why an act cannot be prolonged from a piece of paper to a canvas. Or re-peated on another scale and with more control. A sketch can have the function of a skirmish.

Call this painting "abstract" or "Expressionist" or "Abstract-Ex-pressionist," what counts is its special motive for extinguishing the object, which is not the same as in other abstract or Expressionist phases of modern art.

The new American painting is not "pure" art, since the exclusion of the object was not for the sake of the esthetic. The apples weren't brushed off the table in order to make room for perfect relations of space and color. They had to go so that nothing would get in the way of the act of painting. In this gesturing with materials the esthetic, too, has been subordinated. Form, color, composition, drawing, are auxiliaries, any one of which—or practically all, as has been attempted logically, with unpainted canvases—can be dispensed with. What matters always is the revelation contained in the act. It is to be taken for granted that in the final effect, the image, whatever be or be not in it, will be a *tension*.

Dramas of As If

A painting that is an act is inseparable from the biography of the artist. The painting itself is a "moment" in the adulterated mixture of his life—whether "moment" means the actual minutes taken up with spotting the canvas or the entire duration of a lucid drama conducted in sign language. The act-painting is of the same metaphysical substance as the artist's existence. The new painting has broken down every distinction between art and life.

It follows that anything is relevant to it. Anything that has to do with action—psychology, philosophy, history, mythology, hero worship. Anything but art criticism. The painter gets away from art through his act of painting; the critic can't get away from it. The critic who goes on judging in terms of schools, styles, form—as if the painter were still concerned with producing a certain kind of object (the work of art), instead of living on the canvas—is bound to seem a stranger.

Some painters take advantage of this stranger. Having insisted that their painting is an act, they then claim admiration for the act as art. This turns the act back toward the esthetic in a petty circle. If the picture is an act, it cannot be justified *as an act of genius* in a field whose whole measuring apparatus has been sent to the devil. Its value must be found apart from art. Otherwise the "act" gets to be "making a painting" at sufficient speed to meet an exhibition date.

Art—relation of the painting to the works of the past, rightness of color, texture, balance, etc.—comes back into painting by way of psychology. As Stevens says of poetry, "it is a process of the personality of the poet." But the psychology is the psychology of creation. Not that of the so-called psychological criticism that wants to "read" a painting for clues to the artist's sexual preferences or debilities. The work, the act, translates the psychologically given into the intentional, into a "world"— and thus transcends it.

With traditional esthetic references discarded as irrelevant, what gives the canvas its meaning is not psychological data but *rôle*, the way the artist organizes his emotional and intellectual energy as if he were in a living situation. The interest lies in the kind of act taking place in the four-sided arena, a dramatic interest.

Criticism must begin by recognizing in the painting the assumptions inherent in its mode of creation. Since the painter has become an actor, the spectator has to think in a vocabulary of action: its inception, duration, direction—psychic state, concentration and relaxation of the will, passivity, alert waiting. He must become a connoisseur of the gradations between the automatic, the spontaneous, the evoked.

"It's Not That, It's Not That, It's Not That"

With a few important exceptions, most of the artists of this vanguard found their way to their present work by being cut in two. Their type is not a young painter but a re-born one. The man may be over forty, the painter around seven. The diagonal of a grand crisis separates him from his personal and artistic past.

Many of the painters were "Marxists" (WPA unions, artists' congresses); they had been trying to paint Society. Others had been trying to paint Art (Cubism, Post-Impressionism)—it amounts to the same thing.

The big moment came when it was decided to paint . . . just TO PAINT. The gesture on the canvas was a gesture of liberation, from Value—political, esthetic, moral.

If the war and the decline of radicalism in America had anything to do with this sudden impatience, there is no evidence of it. About the effects of large issues upon their emotions, Americans tend to be either reticent or unconscious. The French artist thinks of himself as a battleground of history; here one hears only of private Dark Nights. Yet it is strange how many segregated individuals came to a dead stop within the past ten years and abandoned, even physically destroyed, the work they had been doing. A far-off watcher unable to realize that these events were taking place in silence might have assumed they were being directed by a single voice.

At its center the movement was away from, rather than toward. The Great Works of the Past and the Good Life of the Future became equally nil.

The refusal of values did not take the form of condemnation or defiance of society, as it did after World War I. It was diffident. The lone artist did not want the world to be different, he wanted his canvas to be a world. Liberation from the object meant liberation from the "nature", society and art already there. It was a movement to leave behind the self that wished to choose his future and to nullify its promissory notes to the past.

With the American, heir of the pioneer and the immigrant, the foundering of Art and Society was not experienced as a loss. On the contrary, the end of Art marked the beginning of an optimism regarding himself as an artist.

The American vanguard painter took to the white expanse of the canvas as Melville's Ishmael took to the sea.

On the one hand, a desperate recognition of moral and intellectual exhaustion; on the other, the exhilaration of an adventure over depths in which he might find reflected the true image of his identity.

Painting could now be reduced to that equipment which the artist needed for an activity that would be an alternative to both utility and idleness. Guided by visual and somatic memories of paintings he had seen or made—memories which he did his best to keep from intruding into his consciousness—he gesticulated upon the canvas and watched for what each novelty would declare him and his art to be.

Based on the phenomenon of conversion the new movement is, with the majority of the painters, essentially a religious movement. In almost every case, however, the conversion has been experienced in secular terms. The result has been the creation of private myths.

The tension of the private myth is the content of every painting of this vanguard. The act on the canvas springs from an attempt to resurrect the saving moment in his "story" when the painter first felt himself released from Value—myth of past self-recognition. Or it attempts to initiate a new moment in which the painter will realize his total personality—myth of future self-recognition.

Some formulate their myth verbally and connect individual works with its episodes. With others, usually deeper, the painting itself is the exclusive formulation, a Sign.

The revolution against the given, in the self and in the world which since Hegel has provided European vanguard art with theories of a New Reality, has re-entered America in the form of personal revolts. Art as action rests on the enormous assumption that the artist accepts as real only that which he is in the process of creating. "Except the soul has divested itself of the love of created things . . ." The artist works in a condition of open possibility, risking, to follow Kierkegaard, the anguish of the esthetic, which accompanies possibility lacking in reality. To maintain the force to refrain from settling anything, he must exercise in himself a constant No.

Constant Lambert
MUSIC IN DECLINE

Revolutionaries themselves are the last people to realize when, through force of time and circumstance, they have gradually become conservatives. It is scarcely to be wondered at if the public is very nearly as slow in the uptake. To the public a red flag remains a red rag even when so battered by wind and weather that it could almost be used as a pink coat. Nothing is so common as to see a political upheaval pass practically unnoticed merely because the names of the leaders and their parties remain the same. Similarly in the world of music, the fact that some of the key-names in modern music, such as Stravinsky and Schön-berg, are the same as before the war has blinded us to the real nature of the present-day musical revolution. We go on using the words 'revolutionary composer' just as we go on using the words 'Liberal' and 'Bolshevik'; but between the modern music of pre-war days and that of to-day lies as much difference as that between the jolly old Gilbertian 'Liberal or Conservative' situation and the present mingled state of the parties, or that between the clear anarchical issues of the October revolution and the present situation in Russian politics with Stalin at the head of a frustrated Five Year Plan and Trotsky fuming in exile.

To the seeker after the new, or the sensational, to those who expect a sinister *frisson* from modern music, it is my melancholy duty to point out that all the bomb throwing and guillotining has already taken place. If by the word 'advanced' we mean art that departs as far as possible from the classical and conventional norm, then we must admit that pre-war music was considerably more advanced (if that is any recommendation) than the music of our own days. Schönberg's *Erwartung*, for example, still the most sensational essay in modern music from the point of view of pure strangeness of sound, was actually finished in 1909. If your ear can assimilate and tolerate the music written in 1913 and earlier, then there is nothing in post-war music that can conceivably give you an aural shock, though the illogicality of some of the present-day pastiches may give you 'a rare turn' comparable to the sudden stopping of a lift in transit. . . .

From *Music Ho! A Study of Music in Decline* by Constant Lambert, pp. 11–12, 14–15, 194–198, 200–201. Reprinted by permission of Faber & Faber Ltd.
Constant Lambert (1905–1951) was a British composer, conductor, and critic.

Experiments may take many forms, but only one general direction, whereas the spirit of pastiche has no guiding impulse. Once invoked it becomes like the magic broom of the sorcerer's apprentice, to whom indeed the average modern composer, with his fluent technique, but lack of co-ordinative sense, may well be compared. It is the element of deliberate pastiche in modern music that chiefly distinguishes it from the experimental period of before the war. The landmarks of pre-war music, such as *Le Sacre du Printemps, Pierrot Lunaire* and Debussy's *Iberia,* are all definitely antitraditional; but they are curiously linked to tradition by the continuous curve of their break-away, comparable to the parabola traced in the air by a shell. But this shell has reached no objective, like a rocket in mid air it has exploded into a thousand multicoloured stars, scattering in as many different directions, and sharing only a common brilliance and evanescence.

It may be said in defence of the present age that the elements of decay are already to be found in the period that immediately preceded it, that the experiments of the pre-war period were of a type to lead inevitably to the present cul-de-sac. . . . Apart from the one or two isolated and exceptional figures who constitute all that ultimately counts in contemporary music there are few composers who are not attached, either officially or unwittingly, to some one or other revolutionary 'movement'. Just as the various coloured-shirt political parties that have sprung up in Europe having nothing in common save their faith in the shirt as a symbol, so these various musical parties have nothing in common save their faith in the label 'revolutionary' or '*avant-garde*'.

The unsophisticated listener may well be puzzled as to what constitutes revolution in music when he is successfully asked to regard atonality, polytonality, highbrow jazz and neo-classicism as the dernier cri. He may, though, on closer acquaintance, detect two common threads which, however twisted and coloured, run through all contemporary musical movements. One is revolution, the other classicism; and their confused proximity is sufficient indication of their shallow spiritual foundation. The post-war composer is lacking in the genuine spirit of revolt that we find in a composer like Mussorgsky, or the genuine spirit of conservatism that we find in a composer like Cherubini; for to him revolution has become merely a mechanical reaction and classicism merely a receptacle, a roll-top desk into which he can thrust incongruous scraps of paper.

The label 'modern' is already become a stale joke, as one can see by the dreary comedy that is being played in advanced musical circles in Central Europe. Whereas before the war we had the familiar spectacle of old conservatives chiding youth for its earsplitting cacophony and bad manners, we now have the delicious spectacle of old revolutionaries chiding youth for its consonance and its good manners.

A particularly happy instance of this new development was provided by the reception accorded Walton's latest work at that officially revolutionary meeting the Festival of the International Society for Contemporary Music. Some ten years ago an immature quartet of Walton's, written in the then fashionable revolutionary manner of Central Europe, earned for him the title of 'International Pioneer'. In 1933 his mature but regrettably consonant *Belshazzar's Feast* was dismissed, particularly by the older critics, as 'routinier', conventional, and unworthy of its place in so selectly revolutionary a festival. The rest of the works were still in the style that Walton himself had used ten years before, but it so happened that Walton's development had led him away from official revolt to personal revolt. It would be a tenable hypothesis that Walton himself was the real revolutionary and the others the conservatives. In fact, if A accuses B of being reactionary, B can always reply 'On the contrary, I am merely reacting against your reaction against reaction'. Whatever else we may blame the post-war composer for, we can only be grateful to him for having deprived of any conceivable meaning the epithet 'revolutionary'.

In the present age the word classicism has become not so much deprived of meaning as degraded in meaning. The classic spirit should be something as positive as the revolutionary spirit, it should represent not a rejection, or even curbing, of the imagination, but the direction of it through interlinked channels—neither a flood nor a dam but an aqueduct. The neo-classicism of to-day . . . is a bare framework, a stereotyped scaffolding designed to give to the inconsequent and devitalized ideas of the post-war composers a superficial air of logic and construction. It is a conscious revival of formulas that were the unconscious inessentials of the age that originally produced them—as who should confuse archaic spelling or the use of the long 's' with the content of the writers in whom these devices are to be found.

The moment we realize that the revolutionary spirit and the classical spirit, which would appear to form such odd bedfellows in the work of the average post-war composer, are in fact not revolution and classicism at all but reaction and formalism, then we see that there is no real conflict between the two, that they are both expressions of the same underlying weakness—lack of faith, or, if that phrase be considered too sentimental, soft and yellow for this tough, red-blooded, poker-faced, heman age, shall we say, no sense of direction. The feverish fashionable reactions of post-war Paris, the mathematical revolutionary formulas of post-war Vienna, indicate that the average post-war composer has either nothing to say or does not know how to say it—possibly both. That so many works written to-day depend to such an unparalleled extent on the modern adaptation of academic device is a sign not of formal strength but of emotional weakness. We have almost no composer who has sufficient faith in himself to get to grips with his medium directly, in the fashion of Mussorgsky or Debussy, and create a personal yet intelligible idiom. We bolster up our lack of faith with party cries, and pour our bootleg gin into cracked leather bottles with olde-worlde labels.

The spiritual background of the eighteenth-century classics and the nineteenth-century romantics has gone, and it now seems that even the spiritual background of the pre-war revolutionaries has gone also. The composer finds himself in a spiritual waste land with only the cold and uncertain glimmer of intellectual theorizing to guide and console him. It is, of course, in his spiritual and social background that we must seek the reasons of his decline, of which technical mannerisms are only the outward expression. There is, I imagine, no critic who still thinks that the contemporary composer adapts any particular style through sheer lack of ability or through a desire to leg-pull. Technical craftsmanship is at as high a level as ever, and indeed is apt to intrude itself too much—not too little.

'The spirit of the age' is a vulgar and easily misapplied phrase, like 'the will of the people', but after all some peoples show a common will and some ages a common spirit. To say that the spirit of the romantic age found fuller and more successful expression in music than in painting may be a crude generalization, but it is undoubtedly a true one. Similarly we may say that the spirit of the present age finds its best expression not so much in music as in abstract painting and satire, whether literary or cinematic.

Abstraction and satire are not so opposed in impulse as might at first appear. The one is an escape from reality, the other an attack on it.

There is very little Whitmanesque acceptance of life about the artist of to-day. He is not a 'yea-sayer'. Faced with life, he either turns away from it or debunks it. Joyce's *Work in Progress,* abstract films, and Disney's *Silly Symphonies,* represent the escape attitude; Lewis's *Apes of God* and the James Cagney, Lee Tracy type of tough Hollywood film represent the debunking attitude. Both attitudes, though perhaps negative in impulse, have in certain media produced results that are positive in their excellence. But neither abstraction nor satire is suited to the medium of music, and consequently the typical composition of to-day is either a swan song echoing from another period or else a present-day echo from another art.

This state of affairs may only be a temporary lull due to present-day social conditions, or . . . it may be that the various arts are going to merge into the all-embracing medium of the surrealist film. In any case it can hardly be denied that the composer of today is out of joint with both his medium and his period. . . . Unable to progress any further in the way of modernity he has not a sufficiently sympathetic or stimulating background to enable him to start afresh or to consolidate his experiments. The stupider composers . . . escape from the situation either by an empty and wilful pastiche of an older tradition or by an equally fruitless concentration on the purely mechanical and objective sides of their arts. The more intelligent composer is forced in on himself and made to overconcentrate on his own musical personality, a process which is inclined to be dangerous and sterilizing.

The premature senility of so many modern composers can mainly be ascribed to this concentration on purely personal mannerisms. Most of the great figures of the past have been content to leave their personal imprint on the *materia musica* of the day without remodelling it entirely. It is only the minor figure whose every bar is recognizable, just as it is only the minor painter, like Marie Laurencin, whose handiwork can be detected at a hundred yards. The number of musical devices, turns of phrase and tricks of rhythm that a composer can appropriate to himself alone, is surprisingly few, and a refusal to lose caste by vulgarly moving outside these self-imposed barriers results in a similarly narrow and restricted content.

Calvin Tompkins
JOHN CAGE: MUSIC IN SILENCE

It must be conceded that the attitude of most subscription audiences—and of most concert musicians, for that matter—toward works by avant-garde composers is almost invariably hostile these days. Although recordings and FM-radio broadcasts, together with a few concerts put on by small groups in New York and elsewhere, are beginning to acquaint a predominantly youthful audience with the musical works of the last twenty-five years, it is still accurate to say that a very large section of the American music public—unlike the public for the visual arts—has been insulated from the developments in musical composition that have sprung from the two great revolutions in twentieth-century music: Schoenberg's abandonment of conventional tonality, and the more recent development of magnetic tape, which, after the war, ushered in the era of electronic music. In this atmosphere, it is hardly surprising that

From "Figure in an Imaginary Landscape" by Calvin Tompkins, *The New Yorker* (November 28, 1964). Reprinted by permission; © 1964 The New Yorker Magazine, Inc.

Calvin Tompkins (1926–   ) is an American writer on the contemporary arts.

the general public shows particular hostility to Cage's music, for it is certainly less familiar—less recognizable, that is, by nineteenth-century standards—than any other music now being written. Yet although the current crop of avant-garde leaders in Europe and the United States now tend to say that they have not been influenced by Cage—some of them spend a great deal of time explaining just how their music differs from his—it can hardly be denied that Cage's work and ideas continue to exert an extraordinary influence, for good or bad, on the work of contemporary composers throughout the world. When he was in his twenties (he is now fifty-two), his invention of the "prepared piano"—a technique of muting the strings that transformed an ordinary grand piano into a kind of percussion orchestra—won him awards from the Guggenheim Foundation and from the National Academy of Arts and Letters, which cited him for "having thus extended the boundaries of musical art." In his thirties, he started to employ techniques of composition by chance methods, thus anticipating, and directly influencing the European and American composers of what is now called "aleatory," or chance, music, which Igor Stravinsky has described (in some dismay) as the music of the nineteen-sixties. Cage was experimenting with electronic sounds ten years before the advent of magnetic tape, and his "Imaginary Landscape No. 5," a collage of recorded sounds, is the earliest piece of tape music to be produced in this country. In recent years, his work with contact microphones, phonograph-needle cartridges, and electronic circuits has kept him several jumps ahead of even his most devoted followers, and in his latest compositions he has moved out of the field of musical time altogether. When performing his "Variations IV," he simply obtains a map or plan of the performance area and then, by chance calculations, determines *where* the sounds will come from; any sounds will do—radios, conventional instruments, even the sound of a door slamming—for Cage is now convinced that "everything we do is music." And he continues to convince others. Looking back over his career in 1963, the music critic Peter Yates concluded that "John Cage would appear to be the most influential living composer today—whatever opinion you or I may hold about his music."

Cage would be very happy if his work were received more sympathetically, or at least more objectively, by audiences, critics, and musicians; as he puts it, he prefers to live "in a climate of agreement." Yet he himself is objective enough not to expect any general acceptance of his music or his ideas in the foreseeable future, for what he is proposing is, essentially, the complete overthrow of the most basic assumptions of Western art since the Renaissance. The power of art to communicate ideas and emotions, to organize life into meaningful patterns, and to realize universal truths through the self-expressed individuality of the artist are only three of the assumptions that Cage challenges. In place of a self-expressive art created by the imagination, tastes, and desires of the artist, Cage proposes an art born of chance and indeterminacy, in which every effort is made to extinguish the artist's own personality; instead of the accumulation of masterpieces, he urges a perpetual process of artistic discovery in our daily lives. Again and again in "Silence," the published collection of his lectures and writings up to 1961, Cage asks himself what the purpose is of writing music (or engaging in any other artistic activity), and answers with a restatement of his basic creed. The purpose, he wrote in 1957, is "purposeless play," and he added, "This play, however, is an affirmation of life—not an attempt to bring order out of chaos nor to suggest improvements in creation, but simply a way of waking up to the very life we're living, which is so excellent once one gets one's mind and one's desires out of its way and lets it act of its own accord."

Cage is by no means alone in pursuing an art that goes beyond individual self-expression. A number of painters, writers, and composers in various countries have been moving in roughly the same direction in recent years, and many of them have used chance methods as a means to that end. The young French composer Pierre Boulez said last year that "if it were necessary to find a profound motive for the work I have tried to describe [his own], it would be the search for *anonymity*." Painters like the late Jackson Pollock, in America, and Georges Mathieu, in France, whose goal was and is certainly not anonymity, have nevertheless sought in the accidents of thrown or dripping paint a key to creation beyond the reach of the artist's conscious mind and will. The "absurd" theatre of Ionesco and Beckett, the so-called "new novel" of French authors like Alain Robbe-Grillet, and a good deal of the choreography done by young modern–dance groups in New York and elsewhere can also be seen as part of a general revolt against self-expressive, meaningful art in the Renaissance tradition. Summing up these trends in an article in the *Hudson Review* entitled "The End of the Renaissance?," Professor Leonard B. Meyer, of the University of Chicago, gave the movement the scholarly title of "radical empiricism." The basis for the new aesthetic, he wrote, is "a conception of man and the universe that is almost the opposite of the view that has dominated Western thought since its beginnings," for it proceeds from the conviction that "man is no longer . . . the center of the universe." Radical-empiricist art reflects a loss of belief in man's ability to control nature or his own destiny, and finds support for its position in the contemporary scientific revolution, which has shown that nature's processes are inherently indeterminate, unpredictable, and, ultimately, unknowable. Also—and especially in Cage's case—it draws much of its philosophical underpinning from Oriental thought, notably

Zen Buddhism, which sees nature as an interrelated field or continuum, no part of which can be separated from the rest or valued above the rest. Nature is thus interpreted as being an unending process with no inherent design and no predictable goals. As Cage states it, "The highest purpose is to have no purpose at all. This puts one in accord with nature in her manner of operation."

The main difference between Cage and other radical empiricists is that he is willing to go a great deal farther than they are. Composers like Pierre Boulez and Karlheinz Stockhausen have used methods of chance and indeterminacy in their writings, but generally without giving up control of their use. Cage, on the other hand, favors abandoning all vestiges of control and turning the entire composition over to chance. All his efforts are directed toward the difficult end of getting rid of his own taste, imagination, memory, and ideas, so that he will then be able to "let sounds be themselves." To many of his old friends, this is pure heresy. "John is just spitting in people's faces now," says Robert Motherwell, the painter. "It's a kind of compulsion, this pushing an absurd premise to its logical conclusion. He's just not in the real world anymore." The sculptor Richard Lippold, who has known Cage for many years, says that he now finds it difficult to talk with him at all. "John has the most brilliant intellect of any man I've ever met," Lippold declared last summer, "and for years he's been trying to do away with it." Even the composer Earle Brown, who has worked in close association with Cage for twelve years, has parted company with him aesthetically over the issue of eliminating control. "There's no real freedom in John's approach," Brown says. "I think that a really indeterminate situation is one where the self can enter in, too. I feel you should be able to toss coins and then decide to use a beautiful F sharp if you want to—be willing to chuck the system, in other words. John won't do that."

To all these complaints and criticisms Cage's answer is basically the same. He believes that the world is changing more rapidly and more drastically than most people realize. A great many of the traditional attitudes of Western thought are becoming obsolete, he feels, and a great many of the older traditions of Oriental thought are becoming increasingly relevant to life in the West. Cage insists that the true function of art in our time is to open up men's minds and hearts to the immensity of these changes, in order that they may be able to "wake up to the very life" they are living in the modern world. But—and this is crucial to Cage's argument—only by getting completely out of the imprisoning circle of his own wishes and desires can the artist be free to enter the miraculous new field of human awareness, and thereby help others to enter it as well. Thus, even in Cage's view, art turns out to have a purpose after all, and a very important purpose at that. The "purposeless play" of the artist, which is really an imitation of Nature in her newly perceived manner of operation (indeterminate, chancy, without design), should serve, ideally, to lead his audience into the promised land of a totally new form of experience, where, as Cage picturesquely describes it, "everyone is in the best seat." For Cage, art and life are not separate entities, as they have been in the past, but very nearly identical, and Cage's whole career can, in fact, be seen as a long campaign to break down all lines of demarcation between the two. . . .

Through a friend, he met one of the pioneers of abstract film-making, Oskar Fischinger, and was commissioned to do the music for one of Fischinger's films. Fischinger had the idea that every inanimate object possessed its own indwelling spirit, which was released when the object made a sound. This slightly whimsical notion suddenly opened up for Cage a whole new world of musical possibilities—a world that did not depend on harmony for its structure, and thus pointed the way out of the impasse to which his studies with Schoenberg were leading. There had been a flurry of interest in percussion music during the nineteen-twenties, stimulated in part by Luigi Russolo's 1916 Italian Futurist manifesto, which called for an "art of noises." Then, in the early thirties, Edgard Varèse had, as Cage puts it, "Fathered forth noise into twentieth-century music"—Varèse's famous score "Ionization," with parts for forty-one percussion instruments and two sirens, was written in 1931—and some of Henry Cowell's work had come close to pure noise. "I believe that the use of noise to make music will continue and increase until we reach a music produced through the aid of electrical instruments that will make available for musical purposes any and all sounds that can be heard," Cage said in a 1937 lecture. "Whereas in the past the point of disagreement has been between dissonance and consonance, it will be, in the immediate future, between noise and so-called musical sounds." And he had an answer to the charge that noise itself could not be music: "A single sound by itself is neither musical nor not musical. It is simply a sound. And no matter what kind of a sound it is, it can become musical by taking its place in a piece of music." His own contribution to this development was his use of silence—not simply as a gap in the continuity or as a pause to lend emphasis to sounds but as an element of composition in itself, in much the same way that contemporary sculptors were using open space, or "negative volume," in their sculpture. The music he wrote in this period is full of silences—some of them rather long—woven into the context of delicate, generally quiet noises, which Cowell once described as "a shower of meteors of sound." Cage organized his own orchestra to play his new music, and its members—as was proper for this breaking of new ground—were not musicians at all. Actually, they were bookbinders; Cage and his wife were friends of a well-known Los Angeles bookbinder named Hazel Dreis, who had a large house that was usually filled with apprentices, and Cage set them to work on a variety of novel percussion instruments, salvaged for the most part from local junk-yards—automobile brake drums, hubcaps, and so on. Cage invited Schoenberg to come to a concert, but Schoenberg said he was busy that night. He was busy every other night, too.

Fortunately for Cage, there was a branch of the music world that welcomed all such experiments. For some time, the modern dance had been the real patron of twentieth-century music. The followers of Martha Graham not only took an interest in the innovations and experiments of young composers but commissioned new works and used them as scores for their own performances. "My percussion music would have been fine, but there was no room in the dance theatre for all those instruments," he recalls. His solution was to invent a totally new instrument, the prepared piano, and this marked a turning point in his career. "I was still writing twelve-tone music for piano then, but I knew that wouldn't do for 'Bacchanale,' which was rather primitive—almost barbaric," he says. "I worked and worked without getting anywhere. The performance was only three days off. Then suddenly I decided that what was wrong was not me—it was the piano. I remembered that Henry Cowell had used his hands *inside* the piano, and had even slid a darning egg along the strings, so I began trying things inside the piano, too—magazines, newspapers, ashtrays, pie plates. These seemed to change the sound in the right direction, making it percussive, but they bounced around too much. I tried using a nail, but it slipped around, too. Then I realized that a bolt or a large wood screw inserted between two strings was the answer. This changed every aspect of the sound. I soon had a whole new gamut of sounds, which was just what I needed. The piano had become, in effect, a percussion orchestra under the control of a single player." In its subsequent refinements, which included the use of rubber, wood, glass, and other materials between the strings, the prepared piano became the most widely known of all Cage's innovations. . . . "Schoenberg had always stressed the structural function of harmony as a means of relating the parts to the whole," Cage said recently. "But traditional harmonic structure had been in a process of disintegration ever since Beethoven—a process that shows up very clearly in the music of Wagner and of Schoenberg himself. I realized, moreover, that harmony relates only to pitch, but pitch does not really apply to percussion music—to noise—and certainly does not apply to silence, which I had come to regard as an essential complement of sound. Now, when you analyze the physical nature of sound, you find that it has three characteristics besides pitch—timbre, loudness, and duration. The only one of these four characteristics that *does* relate to both sound and silence is, quite obviously, duration. And so I came to realize that any structure for percussion music—for a situation in which harmony does not exist—must be based on duration, or *time.*" . . .

Then, just as he was beginning to feel ready to stop what he called "window-shopping" among the world's philosophies and religions, he discovered Zen Buddhism. Dr. Daisetz T. Suzuki, the first important spokesman for Zen in the West, had recently come to America and was giving weekly lectures at Columbia University that were attended by psychoanalysts, scientists, painters, sculptors, and philosophy students. They were also attended by Cage. He went regularly for two years, and he feels that for him they took the place of psychoanalysis. "I had the impression that I was changing—you might say growing up," he says. "I realized that my previous understanding was that of a child." He saw that Zen, like psychoanalysis, was an attempt to open up the psyche from within to a more intense awareness (enlightenment, or *satori*) of everyday life. Therefore, he felt, it could be said that music should try to do externally what Zen and psychoanalysis attempted internally; it should not be concerned primarily with entertainment or communication or the symbolic expression of the artist's ideas and tastes but, rather, should perform the specifically useful function of helping men and women attain a more intense awareness of their own lives, not only in the concert hall but during every waking moment. By a rare coincidence, Cage found this Oriental idea perfectly summed up in the words of the seventeenth-century English music commentator Thomas Mace, who once wrote that the function of music was "to sober and quiet the mind, thus rendering it susceptible to divine influences." How could music do this? Cage found his answer in the statement by Coomaraswamy that all art should "imitate Nature *in her manner of operation*"—that is to say, rather than in her outward appearances—and this is precisely what he has tried to make his music do ever since. "I would like to think that the sounds people hear in a concert could make them more aware of the sounds they hear in the street, or out in the country, or anywhere they may be," he has said. . . .

In the spring of 1950, while Cage was working on a dance score for Merce Cunningham, he drew up a series of large charts to facilitate the plotting of his rhythmic structures. In working with these charts, he caught his first glimpse of a whole new approach to musical composition—an approach that led very quickly to the use of chance. "Somehow, I reached the conclusion that I could compose according to moves on these charts instead of according to my own taste," he has said. "Until that time, my music had been based on the traditional idea that you had to say something. The charts gave me my first indication of the possibility of saying nothing." The move into chance operations, which he began to investigate seriously soon afterward, represents a dividing line in Cage's career. Up to that point, he had won praise and serious consideration from some of the leading musicians of the day; from that point on, he was to experience little but rejection and hostility. It is characteristic of Cage that he pursued his new and highly unpopular course without hesitation and in the very best of spirits. Many years before, he had accepted Gertrude Stein's dictum that all vigorous art was irritating at first, and that when it ceased to be irritating and became pleasing it was no longer useful. Cage denies the charge that his whole purpose now is to be irritating merely for the sake of being irritating. "But whenever I've found that what I'm doing has become pleasing, even to one person, I have redoubled my efforts to find the next step," he says. In 1950, the next step seemed clearly indicated: to discover, through chance operations, a kind of music that would more truly imitate Nature in her manner of operation. . . .

The use of chance in music was not altogether without precedent. Charles Ives, the turn-of-the-century American composer, had written pieces in which performers were free to make certain choices, and Mozart himself is said to have composed a set of contredanses in which dice were thrown to determine which of certain measures were to be performed. But such instances were few. In the visual arts, which are usually a generation or two ahead of music in applying new techniques, chance effects of a far more advanced nature had, of course, been in vogue for many years, and Cage, who had known Max Ernst, Marcel Duchamp, and other leading members of the Surrealist group (he had written the music for the Duchamp sequence in Hans Richter's Surrealist film "Dreams That Money Can Buy"), and who had stayed close to the world of painting ever since he came to New York, began to find himself turning more and more to painters for friendship. When Robert Motherwell and a group of his fellow-artists started a series of weekly lecture-and-discussion meetings in a loft on Eighth Street—a series that led to the formation of the Artists' Club, which played such an important role in the evolution of Abstract Expressionism—Cage became an active participant. (His "Lecture on Nothing"—written, as most of his lectures were and are, in the manner of his musical compositions, with silences of up to several minutes in length—was a great sensation; so was his subsequent "Lecture on Something," the "something" in this case being the music of Feldman.) Generally speaking, his painter friends saw chance as a means of getting past their conscious control, so that their subconscious might express itself more directly on canvas. This had never been Cage's idea; he was as anxious to rule out the subconscious, with all *its* desires and tastes, as to rule out the conscious mind. And yet, as Virgil Thomson observed in his review of "Music of Changes," there was a good deal more to Cage's music than mere hazard. "The sounds of it, many of them quite complex, are carefully chosen, invented by him," Thomson wrote. "And their composition in time is no less carefully worked out." The point comes up again and again in discussions of Cage's music. If Cage selects the materials he uses, and makes all the decisions necessary to set up the mechanism of chance, is the result really controlled by chance at all? "What happens is that a human being has to decide what goes into the chances," Henry Cowell said recently. "And since he's human, his expression enters into it." . . .

Cage was persuaded that the theatre offered more opportunity than music did to imitate Nature in her manner of operation. He defined "theatre" as everything going on at the same time, including music, and in his view it came close to being synonymous with life. "Theatre takes place all the time wherever one is," he wrote soon afterward, "and art simply facilitates persuading one this is the case." The clearest possible expression of this idea may very well be the famous "silent" piece in three movements that Cage composed at Black Mountain that summer and called "4'33"." (The title refers to the number of minutes and seconds the piece takes to perform, but Cage liked the thought that it could also refer to feet and inches—a sort of personal space-time continuum.) Cage had come to realize that there is really no such thing as silence. This was brought home to him with great force when he was taken into a sound-proof room, called an anechoic chamber, in the physics laboratory at Harvard; instead of the total silence he had expected, he heard two sounds, one high and one low, and was told that the high sound was his nervous system in operation and the low one was his blood circulating. If true silence did not exist in nature, then the silences in a piece of music, Cage decided, could be defined simply as "sounds not intended," and he made up his mind to compose a piece consisting entirely of just such sounds, much in the manner of Rauschenberg's all-white paintings, on which the only images to be seen are the shadows and reflections of the painting's environment. Cage's "4'33"" received its first performance in August, 1952, at the Maverick Concert Hall in Woodstock, New York. David Tudor, who performed it, solved the problem of the piece's division into three parts by closing the cover of the piano keyboard at the start of each movement and opening it at the end of the specified time; aside from that, he did nothing but sit on his bench, immobile but intent. The Woodstock audience considered the piece either a joke or an affront, and this has been the general reaction of most people who have heard it, or not heard it, ever since. From Cage's point of view, however, the performance was highly successful. In the hall, which was wide open to the woods at the back, attentive listeners could hear the sound of the wind in the trees during the first movement, the patter of raindrops on the roof during the second, and, during the third, the audience's own perplexed mutterings. Whether this was a case of art imitating Nature in her manner of operation or Nature imitating art is perhaps an open question. . . .

His situation today is essentially what it has been for the last

fifteen years. In spite of the influence of his ideas on the younger generation of painters, musicians, and intellectuals, he has no status in the music
Establishment. One day recently, sitting on the floor of the glass-walled
living room of a monkish two-room house near Stony Point that is his
home between lecture and dance tours, Cage told a friend that he sometimes feels as though he had come to the point reached many years ago
by Marcel Duchamp when he stopped painting pictures. "I understand
Duchamp's not doing things," Cage said. "And it seems to me that I am
somewhat in Duchamp's situation now, except that instead of not doing
things I will keep on doing whatever there is to do. One does what there
is to do, that's all. I remember during the rehearsals for the Philharmonic
concerts the contact microphones seemed to be causing all kinds of
trouble, and Morty Feldman tried to persuade me not to use them. 'Think
how shimmeringly beautiful it would sound with just the instruments
playing that star music, with no electronics!' he said. 'Yes,' I said, 'but
think how magnificently ugly it will sound with the microphones on!'
That's how I feel now. I am going toward violence rather than tender-
ness, Hell rather than Heaven, ugly rather than beautiful, impure rather
than pure, because if one does these things they become transformed,
and we all become transformed."

Richard D. Freed
AN AVANT-GARDE FESTIVAL HAPPENS

The third annual Avant-Garde Festival ground to its dreary end
at Judson Hall Saturday night. The place was packed, as it had been for
most of the preceding dozen events in the series.

In addition to the faithful hangers-on, one noticed a greater
proportion of the curious and, perhaps, the hopeful. The program, a non-
musical one, comprised only two works, Al Hansen's "Time-Space
Drama" and John Cage's "Theater Piece."

The Cage had already been given on the three preceding eve-
nings, although not, of course, in quite the same form.

On this occasion it included a man hanging upside-down and wrapped in a black plastic cocoon; a watermelon sliced in the sling that had held the upside-down man; a film of Charlotte Moorman playing one of Mr. Cage's other works on the cello as the composer placed a cigar in her mouth and removed it now and then (Miss Moorman, the festival's producer, was actually on stage with her cello at the time); a tiny Japanese waving silken banners on a huge bamboo pole; an oil drum rolled down the stairs outside the auditorium, and the usual assortment of balloons, buzzers and electronic sound effects.

Nam June Paik, whose "action music" began the festival on Aug. 25, put his back into the Cage work, literally, when he stripped to the waist and knelt before Miss Moorman, who bowed and fingered his back. Earlier, he sat in the center of the floor with a fishing rod, his line dangling to the floor, but no bites.

Even this tired procession of sight gags and sound effects came almost as a restorative after the inanities of the "Time-Space Drama." Not that there is anything wrong with inanity per se, but what was dished up simply didn't entertain.

Young women in bathing suits sauntered on and off the floor (in the center of the audience area, not the stage) carrying flowers, toy guns and each other. Another, in a bright red union suit, flapped her trap door provocatively at a young man who responded predictably.

From time to time Steve Balkin, Mr. Hansen's associate, gave instructions over a public address system. He and other members of the troupe took turns climbing a ladder and blowing a note or two on a trumpet, and from time to time either a pianist, a phonograph or both played snippets of Beethoven, Verdi, Schumann, Wagner, Tchaikovsky and several national anthems. And so on, ad infinitum, ad tedium.

By contrast, the Cage piece, by an old hand at this sort of thing, at least showed how fast-moving, relatively well organized and at times even funny, such an undertaking could be.

In general, though, depressing is the word for the evening, and for most of the 13-part series. Miss Moorman and her colleagues showed that their collective heart belongs to Dada and, as in most cases involving the heart, this meant that enthusiasm obscured good sense, balance and judgment.

Nearly all the exceptions were confined to the evening of Aug. 26, devoted to the music of Erik Satie. It was fitting that Satie be so honored, since he was, after all, the personification of the avant-garde in his time.

But Satie was a musician. His works were music when they were new and remain so now. This could not be said of the bloop-bleeps, furniture-building, piano-smashing, strip-teases and measured silences that dominated the other programs.

Mordecai Gorelik
THE ABSURDITY OF THE THEATER

If the theater of the absurd leaves me less than wildly enthusiastic, that may not prove, necessarily, that I am a relic of the *ancien regime*. I am the American translator (as well as the director, both at California State College, L.A., and at Southern Illinois University) of Max Frisch's "The Firebugs," a play certified as absurdist by no less an authority on the subject than Martin Esslin himself.

Nor is "The Firebugs" the only absurdist play that I have found entertaining. I recall the clownish innocence of "Waiting for Godot," the evil glitter of "The Blacks," the sick humor of "The Connection." "Rhinoceros" is obviously a sardonic parable of conformism; "The Caretaker" depicts a squalid world of social irresponsibility; "Oh Dad, Poor Dad, etc." is a lampoon of momism and the "international set," one of the funniest vaudeville skits in years. The plays of the absurd are undoubtedly an expression of our times and have a devoted following among the younger American stage people. Some of the absurdist dramas are inventive in a way that adds to the resources of grotesque irony onstage. They even provide a mild psychotherapy for certain audiences. And they are part of a significant rebellion against the mildewed family dramas and stale domestic comedies that are the standard brand of canned goods on Broadway.

Enough, Enough

But when I am presented with callow, pseudo-philosophic plays like "Tiny Alice" and hear them praised for their "awesome depths," or am told that they are "a shaft driven deep down into the core of being," or when I am informed, oracularly, that Goldberg and McCann, the two mysterious gents in "The Birthday Party," are an embodiment of the Judaeo-Christian tradition, I begin to feel that enough is enough. The importance of these sophomoric charades has been tremendously overrated.

"The Absurd Absurdists" by Mordecai Gorelik from *The New York Times* (August 8, 1965). © 1965 by The New York Times Company. Reprinted by permission.

Mordecai Gorelik is research professor in theater at Southern Illinois University in Carbondale, Illinois.

Theater is a special, remarkable form of social communication, one that, when it is healthy, celebrates the highest aspiration and deepest wisdom of its communicants. Therefore the apologists of absurdism are correct when they say that the absurdist dramas (or non-dramas) describe non-communication. Not only do these plays describe it, but they also form part of it themselves. The more lucid absurdist products, such as those named in my first paragraph, reflect, with typical ambiguity, the conflicts that rage in the outer world of today. The others depict only the inner life of their authors, with a symbolism that is always obscure and eccentric, and often flagrantly repulsive. Nor will you get anywhere by calling an absurdist play irrational, for its author disdains rationality and has nothing but scorn for the "squares" who look for a minimum of sense in a dramatic story. He thinks he is being communicative enough if the story can be interpreted by his psychoanalyst.

A Diagnosis

At least one such analyst, Dr. Donald M. Kaplan, of New York, has taken note of certain aspects of homosexual ideology that bear a striking resemblance to the absurdist phenomenon onstage: ". . . the homosexual's ideologic style does not champion humanity but merely himself . . . behavior without responsibility—a program ultimately without action. . . . Intelligence, discrimination and reason . . . have little status in the homosexual ideological style . . .

"The audience is splintered into a mere collection of individuals, each now troubled by a return to his own obscene secrets."[1] I have no moralistic purpose in quoting Dr. Kaplan, nor am I ready to follow him in all of his conclusions: I rather think that there are all kinds of homosexuals, with all kinds of ideologies. But the diagnosis is too telling to be dismissed offhand; the irrationality, the inner preoccupations, the need to astonish an audience, the absence of a true dramatic action, the dismal idea of the human condition—all form the background of non-drama and metatheatre.

Absurdism's feeling of nausea when confronted with the realities of life can be traced through its current spokesmen, Eugene Ionesco and Jean Genet, through the stage theorist Antonin Artaud, with his lunatic cult of the "theater of cruelty," back to Sören Kierkegaard, who called reason and science an illness, and Martin Heidegger, who views life as a state of permanent anxiety, depression and guilt. According to Ionesco, the world is "a desert of dying shadows" in which learned men, tyrants and revolutionists alike have arisen and died without accomplishing any-

[1] "Homosexuality and the American Theater." Tulane Drama Review. Spring, 1965.

thing. In an exchange of polemics with the English drama critic, Kenneth Tynan, he advised, sarcastically, "Don't try to better man's lot if you wish him well." For the metadramatist, existence is at one and the same time utterly depressing and totally unknowable: Beckett, who has somehow "retained a terrible memory of life in his mother's womb," when asked by Alan Schneider to explain Godot, could only reply, "If I knew I would have said so in my play."

Not only are the absurdists baffled by their own compositions, but nothing could be further from their thought than a call to remedial action. It cannot be surprising that Beckett puts his characters inside rubbish cans or vases, or buries them up to the chin in a sandpile. The two tramps in "Waiting for Godot" stand around stupidly waiting, and Krapp, in "Krapp's Last Tape," is a decayed old man who keeps mumbling to himself or munches toothlessly on a banana. Senile or moronic types abound in these anti-dramas—alleged human beings made of mud, with arms and legs as inoperative as their minds. The argument is, of course, that the Estragons and Vladimirs and Krapps are not people but tokens of the human race in general. But it may still be questioned whether these cardboard figures involved in no valid dilemma and with no hope of any resolution except idiotic despair, are a true picture of humanity.

The dramatic, or rather, anti-dramatic, action of the absurdist figurines resembles the spasms of a dead laboratory frog or mouse under an electric charge. That sort of action is far removed from anything like the developing struggle of protagonists who have the breath of life, who fight with all their energy on one side or another of vital issues. (And among these protagonists I include even the troubled Hamlet, Prince of Denmark.)

Action may seem useless to those "intellectuals" who feel impotent in the face of today's problems. The rest of the human race believes in action, as anyone can tell who reads the daily papers. And we might wish that some of the monsters of history had felt as powerless as the philosophers of absurdism: a certain Corporal Adolf Hitler, for instance, who took action to turn the world into a permanent hell, and who might have done it, too, if some other people, unaware of the uselessness of action, had not stopped him in his tracks.

It may suit Ionesco to tell us that life is nothing more substantial than a nightmare, but he himself keeps turning out new works and collecting royalties. And Beckett, in spite of a leaden *weltschmerz*, took time off to be a member of the French Resistance, according to Esslin. We have not had to wait for metatheatre to tell us that life is neither simple nor easy: Hamlet's "To be or not to be" speech describes it better than anything in Ionesco, Beckett, Arrabal, Genet or Pinter. Besides, it is a complete nonsequitur that if life is brutal one must let oneself be trampled on. To quote Friedrich Dürrenmatt, who is no cheerful optimist: "The world (hence the stage which represents this world) is for me something monstrous, a riddle of misfortunes which must be accepted but before which one must not capitulate."

If absurdism is an "expression of our times," that does not automatically ennoble it or give it stature. (Vandalism, juvenile delinquency and race hatred are also an expression of our times.) It is true that many of us do destructive things that make no sense. Indeed, the whole modern world is in an absurd state, unbalanced by gigantic conflicts. Two frightful world wars have solved nothing basic, and now the culminating imbecility of the Cold War threatens the existence of everyone on this planet—at the very time when atomic energy has opened the way to an undreamt-of richness and splendor. One might imagine that, in the face of the great issues before us, dramatic writing would reach heights never known before. Instead we have the jejune diversions and cheap obscurities of the absurdists.

And suddenly the immensely difficult craft of playwriting has turned almost childishly simple. Esslin complains, "Everybody who writes a crazy script now sends it to me." As a scene designer I am reminded of the good old days when any beginning designer could establish a reputation if he slanted walls, windows and doors. This device made it possible to be imaginative without really trying—so much so that expressionist scene design has persisted in the university theaters for almost forty years. We may expect a like popularity for absurdist writing. Especially when the younger dramatists have an example like "Who's Afraid of Virginia Woolf?" to encourage them. To be sure, "Who's Afraid" was no mere piece of automatic scribbling; but what it did was to create a formula that paid off handsomely at the box office and even reached for the Pulitzer Prize.

I don't believe for a moment that Albee thought up, deliberately, this combination of soap opera and absurdist cynicism souped up with "true-to-life," four-letter-word dialogue. Albee is both talented and sincere, and instead of making further use of his golden invention he earned two box-office failures by reverting to the more uncompromising principles of absurdism in "The Ballad of the Sad Cafe" and "Tiny Alice." But his formula will serve others, if not himself: the weird hipster lingo, the juvenile gutter words, will be sprinkled over the latest helping of schmalz. We may also look for some second-hand Pinters—for Pinter, too, has hit upon a successful formula. Endowed with an excellent stage sense, he has turned out Grand Guignol melodramas such as "The Birthday Party" in which the basic motivations are simply omitted, thus inviting critical acclaim in terms of the cosmos and the infinite.

It may have been natural for absurdism to take root in a conquered and war-exhausted France. But who has conquered the United States? This country is a mighty nation at the height of its power; and even if it does not always know what is good for it, that is no reason to describe it in terms of misery. The vigor of America is discounted by the American playwright, who, under stress of the Cold War, has abandoned the responsibility of the mind and has entered on a path known to the Germans, at the time of Hitler, as the "inner migration." But theater itself is not so easily betrayed. If its audiences are not wiped out by the holocaust that is now in preparation, it will arrive, one day, at a maturity worthy of the atomic age.

Martin Esslin
THE THEATER OF THE ABSURD ISN'T ABSURD AT ALL

I sympathize with Professor Mordecai Gorelik's impassioned outcry against absurdist drama, but I must say that I feel he has misunderstood a good many things, both about the theater of the absurd and the present situation in the world.

First, it is logically indefensible to attack a whole convention of an art form wholesale. There are great plays in the absurdist convention and there are others that are execrable. To single out some that are bad and use them as arguments to condemn the entire convention is as illogical as it is unfair. It is a mistake that is often made: In the 18th century, the whole of Elizabethan drama, including Shakespeare, was condemned by the ruling school of criticism as coarse and irregular. And today there are still those who reject nonfigurative art or twelve-tone composition on similar grounds.

Second, Professor Gorelik attacks the absurdists, not so much on artistic as on moralistic or ideological grounds. This presupposes that they represent a moral or ideological position. And this is certainly not the case. In present-day Poland, for example, there are decidedly left-

"The Theater of the Absurd Isn't Absurd At All" by Martin Esslin from *The New York Times* (August 29, 1965). © 1965 by The New York Times Company. Reprinted by permission.
Martin Esslin (1918–   ) is an authority on modern drama.

wing absurdists, while in France a writer like Ionesco is under fire from the Communists for holding a right-wing position. Genet's latest play "The Screens" uses absurdist techniques to attack colonial oppression in Algeria. Hence Professor Gorelik's line of argument that the absurdists merely lament the state of the world without indicating lines of social action is factually wrong.

After all, most of Ionesco's work is a satire on the fossilized and dehumanized lives of an affluent bourgeoisie. Satire may be negative in form, but it always represents a call for positive action. Similarly, Professor Gorelik has misunderstood what "Waiting for Godot" is about. But, of course, there are two other characters as well in that play, Pozzo and Lucky, who spend their time wildly careening about the countryside. One of the questions that the play poses to the audience concerns the relative merits of the contemplative and the wildly active life.

Far from being an expression of "idiotic despair" this particular play, by increasing the audience's awareness of some basic truths about the human situation, will make them able to face reality more calmly and as more integrated human beings, which is the only good basis for rational social behavior and action. Indeed, if Professor Gorelik says that "the rest of the human race believes in action," he ought to have examined the subject matter of some of the absurdists' despair, before demanding that they should always recommend some remedial action. If Beckett or Ionesco express a sense of the inevitability of death, for example, what action would Professor Gorelik recommend to remedy that state of affairs? And, indeed, what action does Shakespeare recommend in plays that deal with similar subject matter, for example, "King Lear?"

Must all drama be political? Even the most socially committed dramatist of our time, Brecht, dealt with these subjects repeatedly without suggesting any remedy. Indeed, the fact of dealing with the subject is itself the remedy. If we want to master the despair arising from such basic elements of the human condition, we can only do so by facing up to them and steeling our minds to accept them. That is the subject matter and aim of all tragedy and of most of man's religions.

If some human beings in a scientific age find it impossible to accept supernatural consolations like the promise of eternal life, they can still find comfort in the nobility of facing the void with gay defiance and in such values as beauty and total sincerity. These are the values which the best absurdist plays embody, the values that also inspire much other great tragic drama, from Sophocles to Shakespeare and Ibsen. The artistic expression of the stark facts of the human condition is itself its sublimation and the conquest of despair.

Third, Professor Gorelik complains that absurdist drama is formless, meaningless and easily imitated. This, I am afraid, is another argument on the level of: "Fancy Picasso getting thousands of dollars for this drawing, my little girl of five can do better!" It is simply not true that any child could draw better than Picasso. It is also simply not true that absurdist drama is formless and meaningless. On the contrary, the best absurdist plays are masterpieces of controlled form. In fact, the freer and more associative the subject matter of a work of art, the more rigidly structured must it be. Hence the plays of Beckett, Pinter, or the best of Ionesco are as rigidly constructed as the most formal poetry.

Total Pattern

Each word, even each pause, is inevitable and forms an irremovable part of the total pattern. As regards the apparent ease with which this kind of drama can be imitated: it is true that I have somewhere said that, having written my book on the theater of the absurd, I have become the recipient of many a crazy play. But, on the other hand, in my work as head of radio drama for the British Broadcasting Corporation I get a far greater number of plays that are childishly untalented imitations of Ibsen, Sardou, Brecht or Noel Coward. Ultimately, bad imitations are made of every successful formula and the fact that many people make bad imitations of absurdist plays is merely due to their phenomenal success in the last ten years.

Moreover, a bad absurdist play is more easily detected than a bad imitation of many other conventions precisely because the naive idea that to write such a play you need merely to write down whatever comes into your mind is totally wrong. The need for sense is manifestly greatest in a form that uses the element of nonsense as an artistic device, just as design and pictorial sense are most needed in abstract painting where ugly forms cannot be excused as being reproductions of ugly models. The premium on originality and genuine invention is highest in the sphere where the crutches of mere reportage of real life have been removed.

Not So Easy

Nothing could be further from the truth than Professor Gorelik's statement that, with the coming of the absurdists, "the immensely difficult craft of playwriting has turned almost childishly simple." This will appear so only to very childish people, who may also think that ballet dancing is very easy because Nureyev and Fonteyn seem to do it without effort.

Fourth, Professor Gorelik wonders why absurdism, which could naturally take root in a conquered and war-exhausted France, should also have become so popular among intellectuals in the United States. Here

Professor Gorelik has misunderstood both our times and the function of this kind of art. It was not the physical conquest of France that gave rise to absurdist writing 20 years ago, it was the ideological malaise caused by the evident failure of some of the cherished ideals of the 19th century—religious, political and social.

In the United States these ideals may not have crumbled as obviously and as decisively as in continental Europe, but they are certainly also being questioned in a world living under the shadow of the atomic bomb and escalating wars. This is the reason why a searching examination of some of the ultimate and inescapable facts of the human condition, a questioning of fossilized beliefs of the past, certainly is at least justifiable, even in the United States, which today, prosperous as the nation may be, has to bear the burden of all the world's ills, simply by being the most powerful country on earth. It would be an unhealthy and alarmingly callous nation whose intellectuals at such a moment did not put searching questions and steel themselves to face even the grimmest answer.

Questions

I may be wrong, but my impression is that Professor Gorelik is particularly angry with Edward Albee and especially so with "Tiny Alice."

I must say I personally found "Tiny Alice" neither particularly obscure, nor particularly pretentious. It is a play, which, as I understood it, examined Man's inability ever to hold or ever to attain to the ideal, which he nevertheless is bound to pursue. This may not be a particularly novel conclusion, nor does it recommend remedial social action. But then, Ibsen's "Master Builder" deals with a similar subject in very similar symbolical terms. What remedial action does that play recommend? And is it any worse for not recommending any?

The theater, after all, is not a collection of recipes for social improvement, but a place where human beings can purge their emotions and attain spiritual insight through contact with the emotional world of its artists. "Romeo and Juliet" is no worse a play for not providing a recipe for the avoidance of unhappy love. Why should "Tiny Alice" be faulted for not solving one of Man's basic problems if it has been able to communicate a strong and exhilarating emotional experience?

But even if Professor Gorelik were right in maintaining that "Tiny Alice" is a bad play, and a bad absurdist play at that (which I personally doubt), this would prove nothing about other plays in an absurdist convention, some of which are very bad, while others are enduring masterpieces.

Jacques Barzun
ART AGAINST INTELLECT

. . . Artists are today the most persistent denouncers of Western civilization; and their lay following zealously presses the indictment. Beside theirs, the political animus against society seems tame. This is something new, in form as well as spirit. For the artistic outcry tends to be vague, abstract, and often absurd. It affects to despise materialism and the world of trade, but the ground of attack is that trade gives artists too little material reward. Being intellectually feeble, these complaints cannot lead to action; they merely poison the air and the lives of those that breathe it.

This autointoxication, which contributes to the modern intellectual's sense of martyrdom, is linked with another social change that has stolen upon us unregarded—the recent education of the artist to the ways of Intellect. In itself, art can exist without learning and, in a sense, without reason. Painters, sculptors, musicians, actors, dancers, even poets and playwrights, resemble engineers and physical scientists in that they can follow modes of thought quite other than those of discursive intellect; some scarcely need literacy, as history proves; and they certainly have no obligation to traffic in established ideas. Some of the greatest have in fact been virtually inarticulate—to cite examples at random: Schubert, Daumier, George Stephenson, Ghiberti.

During the last century, the current has been reversed; artists of every kind have become men of words and ideas, bent on joining the Great Conversation. In youth, they no longer resist a liberal arts training; later, they accept academic posts, they set up as critics and social philosophers, they are caught—sometimes ridden—by political and other systems. This was notable in the Marxist decade and it still is so in the so-called religious revival of today. And now the artists have been joined by an increasing group of natural scientists, late-awakened by the noise of an explosion. In both groups, talent, education, and a fresh appetite for ideas produce an effervescence which has the coloring, though not always the substance, of Intellect.

Nor has the rapprochement been from one side only. The artist turning toward ideas has been met halfway by a public turning aside

From *The House of Intellect* by Jacques Barzun, pp. 15–19. Copyright ©
1959 by Jacques Barzun. Reprinted by permission of Harper & Row, Publishers.

Jacques Barzun (1907–   ) is Professor of History at Columbia University.

from words and greedy for speechless art. The new pastimes of the educated amateur are the arts of nonarticulate expression: music and painting. While fiction languishes and the theater is in the doldrums, ballet has risen to popularity, Sunday painting is fashionable, and chamber music thrives. Everywhere picture and sound crowd out text. The Word is in disfavor, not to say in disrepute—which is indeed one way of abolishing the problem of communication.

Nor should we be surprised: This shift in taste has been gathering momentum for three generations. From the Symbolist period on, Western art has been based on the repudiation of what is common— common speech, common life, common knowledge—and its replacement by the singular and indefinable. Excellent reasons can be shown for the choice, and the right of artists to do as they see fit is not here in question. But neither is the effect in doubt, for art has never been so quick and potent in its influence: the revulsion from words, syntax, and coherence accounts for the widespread anarchy in the handling of the mother tongue, as well as the now normal preference for the abnormal in our conceptions of the real. Whereas the 'experimental' in art used to take a generation to be recognized, now we encounter the latest modernisms overnight in the work of the commercial artist and the writer of advertising copy. The public approves and encourages, having learned to swallow and even to enjoy what shocks feeling and defies reason.[1]

Subtler, but equally strong, has been the result of what we pedantically call 'aesthetic experience.' For many people art, displacing religion, has become the justification of life, whether as the saving grace of an ugly civilization or as the pattern of the only noble career. In sustaining this role, art has put a premium on qualities of perception which are indeed of the mind, but which ultimately war against Intellect. The cant words of modern criticism suggest what these qualities are: *ambiguity, sensibility, insight, imagination, sensitive, creative, irony.* All these, in art, declare the undesirability, perhaps the impossibility, of articulate precision and thus defy, counteract, or degrade the chief virtue of Intellect.

The bearing of this observation must itself be understood precisely: there is a difference between the artist and the refugees from life who hide their nakedness in artistic toggery; there is a parallel difference between criticism which is the gateway of understanding and that which is a substitute for artistic work. I do not depart here from my lifelong

---

[1] A trade magazine advises professional writers to make use of: 1. *Clever wackiness;* 2. *Exotic, quaint, or off-beat characters;* and 3. *Fresh and unusual props for showing characters.* Follows an example showing the hero's just resentment of his fiancée's mother by the 'symbolic' act of drowning a monkey. *The Writer,* 71:7, 1958, 14.

conviction that art is miraculously precise and communicative in its own domain of fused spirit and sensation. It awakens knowledge of a kind no other means can reach. But that kind is not the only kind, and the means that art uses are always less than explicit. This is the root of the distinction between poetry and prose, between painting and illustration; between narrative or dialogue that 'shows' and the kind that merely 'tells'; in short between Meaning and Information. And the point here is that explicitness in the mode of prose is also desirable: thanks to it, Intellect can steadily pursue one of its great tasks, which is to refine and enlarge the common language for ideas.

Now a devotion to art does not preclude being articulate in this mode, but an *exclusive* devotion, except in a professional, is almost surely hostile to Intellect. For cultivating art out of fear or spite means preferring always what is ambiguous, what touches only the sensibility, what titillates through irony, what plunges the imagination into a sea of symbols, echoes, and myths, from which insights may be brought up to the surface but no arguable views. And this preference is at bottom love of confusion—confusion sought as a release from responsibility. The purest emotions of the aesthetic quest, it is said, are private; one partakes only after illumination, as formerly after mystical conversion. And it is true that the unique messages of poetry, music, painting, and serious fiction refuse to be decanted into common prose. When this is said in contempt of all other uses of the mind, it amounts to a denial of Intellect's declarative powers and social obligations.

That contempt and denial modern artists have not troubled to conceal. 'Every day,' said Proust in the opening sentence of his manifesto *Contre Sainte-Beuve*, 'I set less store by the intellect.' Today, after eighty years or more of this open war, most educated men and women have been persuaded that all the works of man's mind except art are vulgar frauds: law, the state, machinery, the edifice of trade, are worthless. More, men and women feel that they themselves are worthless, they despise their own existence, because it fails in loveliness when compared with the meanest *objet d'art*. The abandonment of Intellect in favor of communion through quartet playing and amateur ceramics has bred a race of masochist-idolaters, broken up into many sects, but at one in their worship of the torturing indefinite. ·

I dwell at this length on the influence of art upon the intellectual life of today because it is all-pervasive. A member of the educated class nowadays need not have any direct or vivid contact with art to fall under the sway of the aesthetical creed and its emotions. He feels about life, business, society, the Western world, what the art-inspired critics of the last eighty years have felt, and he speaks the phrases appropriate to his borrowed disgust. He may be a minor foundation official living rather comfortably on the earnings of some dead tycoon, but he talks like Baudelaire. Indeed, the attitudes I describe are no longer confined to those engaged in intellectual or semi-intellectual occupations. They have touched the wider public whose exposure to ideas is through the press, where readers find reflected not only the worship of art but also its attendant contempt of the world, both alike taken for granted as the natural response of any intelligent and 'sensitive' modern. A deep unconscious anti-intellectualism thus comes to be the natural adjunct of any degree of literacy and culture; and this at the very time when new social groups, fresh from the educational mills and thoroughly aestheticized, think of themselves as intellectuals and mean to live as artists.

8
Mass Culture

While many problems of the twentieth century present clear analogies to past history, in one respect there can be no question of our century's uniqueness. The twentieth century is the age of that widely discussed phenomenon "mass society." So much is explained by invoking this condition (or theory), which accounts for violence and alienation, that it is fitting that this new type of society should have its own form of artistic expression. It is also inevitable that this new art should have a new name, "mass culture," and a new interpretation.

Perhaps "mass culture" is not art at all, or possibly we need a new theory of aesthetics. In any case, along with the "serious" art discussed in the foregoing chapter, we are just beginning to recognize this vast realm. Irving Howe, American literary critic, offers a tentative definition of the "mass society" which presupposes new aesthetic values. American writer Dwight Macdonald explores the mysteries of masscult and pretentious *Kitsch*—a new art "bad in a new way." "Up to the eighteenth century," says Macdonald, "bad art was of the same nature as good art, produced for the same audience, accepting the same standards. The difference was simply one of individual talent. But masscult is something else. It is not just unsuccessful art. It is non-art." German novelist Thomas Mann had already sensed these phenomena in that remarkable anticipation of later twentieth century life, first published in 1924, *The Magic Mountain.* Observing the early cinema, Mann saw an empty parade of actors performing for a passive audience, with no real involvement on either side.

In short, critics have been overwhelmingly critical of what they have labeled as "mass culture." But critic Harold Rosenberg approaches the problem in a somewhat different fashion by asking what the new public is. He claims that "the public is not a single entity of high or low intelligence, but a sum of shifting groupings, each with its own mental focus. . . . Incomprehensibility in the arts is inseparable from the fragmentation of the public." Only Marshall McLuhan defends the new media. Much-discussed author of two recent books, *Understanding Media* and *The Medium Is the Massage,* Professor McLuhan points out that electric technology "is forcing us to reconsider and reevaluate every thought, every action, and every institution formerly taken for granted." Instant communication has changed the world into "a global village."

Irving Howe
DEFINING MASS SOCIETY

In the last two decades there has occurred a series of changes in American life, the extent, durability and significance of which no one has yet measured. No one can. We speak of the growth of a "mass society," a term I shall try to define in a moment; but at best this is merely a useful hypothesis, not an accredited description. It is a notion that lacks common consent, for it does not yet merit common consent. Still, one can say with some assurance that the more sensitive among the younger writers, those who feel that at whatever peril to their work and careers they must grapple with something new in contemporary experience, even if, like everyone else, they find it extremely hard to say what that "newness" consists of—such writers recognize that the once familiar social categories and place-marks have now become as uncertain and elusive as

From *Partisan Review* (Summer 1959), pp. 426–428. © 1959 by Partisan Review. Reprinted by permission of the publisher.
Irving Howe (1920–   ) is an American literary critic.

the moral imperatives of the nineteenth century seemed to novelists of fifty years ago. And the something new which they notice or stumble against is, I would suggest, the mass society.

By the mass society we mean a relatively comfortable, half welfare and half garrison society in which the population grows passive, indifferent and atomized; in which traditional loyalties, ties and associations become lax or dissolve entirely; in which coherent publics based on definite interests and opinions gradually fall apart; and in which man becomes a consumer, himself mass-produced like the products, diversions and values that he absorbs.

No social scientist has yet come up with a theory of mass society that is entirely satisfying; no novelist has quite captured its still amorphous symptoms—a peculiar blend of frenzy and sluggishness, amiability and meanness. I would venture the guess that a novelist unaware of the changes in our experience to which the theory of mass society points, is a novelist unable to deal successfully with recent American life; while one who focussed only upon those changes would be unable to give his work an adequate sense of historical depth.

This bare description of the mass society can be extended by noting a few traits or symptoms:

1. Social classes continue to exist, and the society cannot be understood without reference to them; yet the visible tokens of class are less obvious than in earlier decades and the correlations between class status and personal condition, assumed both by the older sociologists and the older novelists, become elusive and problematic—which is not, however, to say that such correlations no longer exist.

2. Traditional centers of authority, like the family, tend to lose some of their binding-power upon human beings; vast numbers of people now float through life with a burden of freedom they can neither sustain nor legitimately abandon to social or religious groups.

3. Traditional ceremonies that have previously marked moments of crisis and transition in human life, thereby helping men to accept such moments, are now either neglected or debased into mere occasions for public display.

4. Passivity becomes a widespread social attitude: the feeling that life is a drift over which one has little control and that even when men do have shared autonomous opinions they cannot act them out in common.

5. As perhaps never before, opinion is manufactured systematically and "scientifically."

6. Opinion tends to flow unilaterally, from the top down, in measured quantities: it becomes a market commodity.

7. Disagreement, controversy, polemic are felt to be in bad taste; issues are "ironed out" or "smoothed away"; reflection upon the nature of society is replaced by observation of its mechanics.

8. The era of "causes," good or bad, comes to an end; strong beliefs

seem anachronistic; and as a result, agnostics have even been known
to feel a certain nostalgia for the rigors of belief.

9. Direct and first-hand experience seems to evade human beings,
though the quantity of busy-ness keeps increasing and the number of
events multiplies with bewildering speed.

10. The pressure of material need visibly decreases, yet there
follows neither a sense of social release nor a feeling of personal joy;
instead, people become increasingly aware of their social dependence
and powerlessness.

Now this is a social cartoon and not a description of American
society; but it is a cartoon that isolates an aspect of our experience with a
suggestiveness that no other mode of analysis is likely to match. Nor does
it matter that no actual society may ever reach the extreme condition of a
"pure" mass society; the value of the theory lies in bringing to our attention a major historical drift.

Dwight Macdonald
MASSCULT, MIDCULT, CULTURE

For about two centuries Western culture has in fact been two
cultures: the traditional kind—let us call it High Culture—that is chron-
icled in the textbooks, and a novel kind that is manufactured for the
market. This latter may be called Mass Culture, or better Masscult, since
it really isn't culture at all. Masscult is a parody of High Culture. In the
older forms, its artisans have long been at work. In the novel, the line
stretches from the eighteenth-century "servant-girl romances" to Edna
Ferber, Fannie Hurst and such current ephemera as Burdick, Drury,
Michener, Ruark and Uris; in music, from Hearts and Flowers to Rock 'n
Roll; in art, from the chromo to Norman Rockwell; in architecture, from
Victorian Gothic to ranch-house moderne; in thought, from Martin
Tupper's *Proverbial Philosophy* ("Marry not without means, for so
shouldst thou tempt Providence;/But wait not for more than enough, for
marriage is the DUTY of most men.") to Norman Vincent Peale. (Think-
ers like H. G. Wells, Stuart Chase, and Max Lerner come under the head

Condensed from *Against the American Grain*, by Dwight Macdonald, pp.
3–75. © Copyright 1960 by Dwight Macdonald. Reprinted by permission of Random
House, Inc.
     Dwight Macdonald (1906–   ) is an American journalist and writer.

of Midcult rather than Masscult.) And the enormous output of such new media as the radio, television and the movies is almost entirely Masscult.

This is something new in history. It is not that so much bad art is being produced. Most High Culture has been undistinguished, since talent is always rare—one has only to walk through any great art museum or try to read some of the forgotten books from past centuries. Since only the best works still have currency, one thinks of the past in their terms, but they were really just a few plums in a pudding of mediocrity.

Masscult is bad in a new way: it doesn't even have the theoretical possibility of being good. Up to the eighteenth century, bad art was of the same nature as good art, produced for the same audience, accepting the same standards. The difference was simply one of individual talent. But Masscult is something else. It is not just unsuccessful art. It is non-art. It is even anti-art.

> There is a novel of the masses but no Stendhal of the masses; a music for the masses but no Bach or Beethoven, whatever people say. . . . It is odd that no word . . . designates the common character of what we call, separately, bad painting, bad architecture, bad music, etc. The word "painting" only designates a domain in which art is possible. . . . Perhaps we have only one word because bad painting has not existed for very long. There is no bad Gothic painting. Not that all Gothic painting is good. But the difference that separates Giotto from the most mediocre of his imitators is not of the same kind as that which separates Renoir from the caricaturists of *La Vie Parisienne*. . . . Giotto and the Gaddi are separated by talent, Degas and Bonnat by a schism, Renoir and "suggestive" painting by what? By the fact that this last, totally subjected to the spectator, is a form of advertising which aims at selling itself. If there exists only one word . . . it is because there was a time when the distinction between them had no point. Instruments played real music then, for there was no other.[1]

But now we have pianos playing Rock 'n Roll and *les sanglots longs des violons* accompanying torch singers.

Masscult offers its customers neither an emotional catharsis nor an aesthetic experience, for these demand effort. The production line grinds out a uniform product whose humble aim is not even entertainment, for this too implies life and hence effort, but merely distraction. It may be stimulating or narcotic, but it must be easy to assimilate. It asks nothing of its audience, for it is "totally subjected to the spectator." And it gives nothing.[2]

[1] André Malraux in "Art, Popular Art and the Illusion of the Folk"—(*Partisan Review*, September–October, 1951).

[2] "Distraction is bound to the present mode of production, to the rationalized and mechanized process of labor to which . . . the masses are subject. . . . People want to have fun. A fully concentrated and conscious experience of art is pos-

Some of its producers are able enough. Norman Rockwell is technically skilled, as was Meissonier—though Degas was right when he summed up the cavalry charge in *Friedland, 1806:* "Everything is steel except the breastplates." O. Henry could tell a story better than many contributors to our Little Magazines. But a work of High Culture, however inept, is an expression of feelings, ideas, tastes, visions that are idiosyncratic and the audience similarly responds to them as individuals. Furthermore, both creator and audience accept certain standards. These may be more or less traditional; sometimes they are so much less so as to be revolutionary, though Picasso, Joyce and Stravinsky knew and respected past achievements more than did their academic contemporaries; their works may be seen as a heroic breakthrough to earlier, sounder foundations that had been obscured by the fashionable gimcrackery of the academies. But Masscult is indifferent to standards. Nor is there any communication between individuals. Those who consume Masscult might as well be eating ice-cream sodas, while those who fabricate it are no more expressing themselves than are the "stylists" who design the latest atrocity from Detroit.

The difference appears if we compare two famous writers of detective stories, Mr. Erle Stanley Gardner and Mr. Edgar Allan Poe. It is impossible to find any personal note in Mr. Gardner's enormous output— he has just celebrated his centenary, the hundredth novel under his own name (he also has knocked off several dozen under pseudonyms). His prose style varies between the incompetent and the nonexistent; for the most part, there is just no style, either good or bad. His books seem to have been manufactured rather than composed; they are assembled with the minimum expenditure of effort from identical parts that are shifted about just enough to allow the title to be changed from *The Case of the Curious Bride* to *The Case of the Fugitive Nurse.* Mr. Gardner obviously has the production problem licked—he has rated his "native abilities" as Very Good as a lawyer, Good as a business analyst, and Zero as a writer, the last realistic estimate being the clue to his production-line fertility— and his popularity indicates he has the problem of distribution well in hand. He is marketing a standard product, like Kleenex, that precisely because it is not related to any individual needs on the part of either the producer or the consumer appeals to the widest possible audience. The obsession of our fact-minded culture with the processes of the law is probably the lowest common denominator that has made Mr. Gardner's unromantic romances such dependable commodities.

Like Mr. Gardner, Mr. Poe was a money-writer. (That he didn't

sible only to those whose lives do not put such a strain on them that in their spare time they want relief from both boredom and effort simultaneously. The whole sphere of cheap commercial entertainment reflects this dual desire."—T. W. Adorno: *On Popular Music.*

make any is irrelevant.) The difference, aside from the fact that he was a good writer, is that, even when he was turning out hack work, he had an extraordinary ability to use the journalistic forms of his day to express his own peculiar personality, and indeed, as Marie Bonaparte has shown in her fascinating study, to relieve his neurotic anxieties. (It is simply impossible to imagine Mr. Gardner afflicted with anything as individual as a neurosis.) The book review, the macabre-romantic tale, the magazine poem, all served his purposes, and he even invented a new one, the detective story, which satisfied the two chief and oddly disparate drives in his psychology—fascination with horror (*The Murders in the Rue Morgue*) and obsession with logical reasoning or, as he called it, "ratiocination" (*The Purloined Letter*). So that while his works are sometimes absurd, they are rarely dull.

It is important to understand that the difference between Mr. Poe and Mr. Gardner, or between High Culture and Masscult, is not mere popularity. From *Tom Jones* to the films of Chaplin, some very good things have been popular; *The Education of Henry Adams* was the top nonfiction best seller of 1919. Nor is it that Poe's detective stories are harder to read than Gardner's, though I suppose they are for most people. The difference lies in the qualities of Masscult already noted: its impersonality and its lack of standards, and "total subjection to the spectator." The same writer, indeed the same book or even the same chapter, may contain elements of both Masscult and High Culture. In Balzac, for instance, the most acute psychological analysis and social observation is bewilderingly interlarded with the cheapest, flimsiest kind of melodrama. In Dickens, superb comedy alternates with bathetic sentimentality, great descriptive prose with the most vulgar kind of theatricality. All these elements were bound between the same covers, sold to the same mass audience, and, it may well be, considered equally good by their authors—at least I know of no evidence that either Dickens or Balzac was aware of when he was writing down and when he was writing up. Masscult is a subtler problem than is sometimes recognized.

"What is a poet?" asked Wordsworth. "He is a man speaking to men . . . a man pleased with his own passions and volitions, and one who rejoices more than other men in the spirit of life that is in him." It is this human dialogue that Masscult interrupts, this spirit of life that it exterminates. Evelyn Waugh commented on Hollywood, after a brief experience there: "Each book purchased for motion pictures has some individual quality, good or bad, that has made it remarkable. It is the work of a great array of highly paid and incompatible writers to distinguish this quality, separate it and obliterate it." This process is called "licking the book"—i.e., licking it into shape, as mother bears were once thought to lick their amorphous cubs into real bears; though here the process is reversed and the book is licked not into but out of shape. The other meaning of "licked" also applies; before a proper Hollywood film can be made, the work of art has to be defeated.

The question of Masscult is part of the larger question of the masses. The tendency of modern industrial society, whether in the USA or the USSR, is to transform the individual into the mass man. For the masses are in historical time what a crowd is in space: a large quantity of people unable to express their human qualities because they are related to each other neither as individuals nor as members of a community. In fact, they are not related *to each other* at all but only to some impersonal, abstract, crystallizing factor. In the case of crowds, this can be a football game, a bargain sale, a lynching; in the case of the masses, it can be a political party, a television program, a system of industrial production. The mass man is a solitary atom, uniform with the millions of other atoms that go to make up "the lonely crowd," as David Riesman well calls our society. A community, on the contrary, is a group of individuals linked to each other by concrete interests. Something like a family, each of whose members has his or her special place and function while at the same time sharing the group's economic aims (family budget), traditions (family history), sentiments (family quarrels, family jokes), and values ("That's the way we do it in *this* family!"). The scale must be small enough so that it "makes a difference" what each person does—this is the first condition for human, as against mass, existence. Paradoxically, the individual in a community is both more closely integrated into the group than is the mass man and at the same time is freer to develop his own special personality. Indeed, an individual can only be defined in relation to a community. A single person in nature is not an individual but an animal; Robinson Crusoe was saved by Friday. The totalitarian regimes, which have consciously tried to create the mass man, have systematically broken every communal link—family, church, trade union, local and regional loyalties, even down to ski and chess clubs—and have reforged them so as to bind each atomized individual directly to the center of power.

The past cultures I admire—Periclean Greece, the city-states of the Italian Renaissance, Elizabethan England, are examples—have mostly been produced by communities, and remarkably small ones at that. Also remarkably heterogeneous ones, riven by faction, stormy with passionate antagonisms. But this diversity, fatal to that achievement of power over other countries that is the great aim of modern statecraft, seems to have been stimulating to talent. (What could be more deadly than the usual post-Marx vision of socialism as equality and agreement? Fourier was far more perceptive when he based his Utopia on cabals, rivalry, and every kind of difference including what he called "innocent mania.") A mass society, like a crowd, is inchoate and uncreative. Its atoms cohere not according to individual liking or traditions or even interests but in a purely mechanical way, as iron filings of different shapes and sizes are pulled toward a magnet working on the one quality they have in common. Its morality sinks to the level of the most primitive members—a crowd will commit atrocities that very few of its members would commit as individuals—and its taste to that of the least sensitive and the most ignorant.

Yet this collective monstrosity, "the masses," "the public," is taken as a human norm by the technicians of Masscult. They at once degrade the public by treating it as an object, to be handled with the lack of ceremony of medical students dissecting a corpse, and at the same time flatter it and pander to its taste and ideas by taking them as the criterion of reality (in the case of the questionnaire-sociologists) or of art (in the case of the Lords of Masscult). When one hears a questionnaire-sociologist talk about "setting up" an investigation, one realizes that he regards people as mere congeries of conditioned reflexes, his concern being which reflex will be stimulated by which question. At the same time, of necessity, he sees the statistical majority as the great Reality, the secret of life he is trying to unriddle. Like a Lord of Masscult, he is—professionally—without values, willing to take seriously any idiocy if it is held by many people (though, of course, *personally* . . .). The aristocrat's approach to the masses is less degrading to them, as it is less degrading to a man to be shouted at than to be treated as nonexistent. But the *plebs* have their dialectical revenge: indifference to their human quality means prostration before their statistical quantity, so that a movie magnate who cynically "gives the public what it wants"—i.e., assumes it wants trash—sweats with anxiety if the box-office returns drop 5 per cent.

Whenever a Lord of Masscult is reproached for the low quality of his products, he automatically ripostes, "But that's what the public wants, what can I do?" A simple and conclusive defense, at first glance. But a second look reveals that (1) to the extent the public "wants" it, the public has been conditioned to some extent by his products, and (2) his efforts have taken this direction because (a) he himself also "wants" it—never underestimate the ignorance and vulgarity of publishers, movie producers, network executives and other architects of Masscult—and (b) the technology of producing mass "entertainment" (again, the quotes are advised) imposes a simplistic, repetitive pattern so that it is easier to say the public wants this than to say the truth which is that the public gets this and so wants it. The March Hare explained to Alice that "I like what I get" is not the same thing as "I get what I like," but March Hares have never been welcome on Madison Avenue.

For some reason, objections to the giving-to-the-public-what-it-wants line are often attacked as undemocratic and snobbish. Yet it is precisely because I do believe in the potentialities of ordinary people that I criticize Masscult. For the masses are not people, they are not The Man in the Street or The Average Man, they are not even that figment of liberal condescension, The Common Man. The masses are, rather, man as non-man, that is man in a special relationship to other men that makes it impossible for him to function as man (one of the human functions being the creation and enjoyment of works of art). "Mass man," as I use the term, is a theoretical construction, an extreme toward which we are being pushed but which we shall never reach. For to become wholly a mass man would mean to have no private life, no personal desires, hobbies, aspirations, or aversions that are not shared by everybody else. One's behavior would be entirely predictable, like a piece of coal, and the sociologists could at last make up their tables confidently. It is still some time to 1984 but it looks unlikely that Orwell's anti-Utopia will have materialized by then, or that it will ever materialize. Nazism and Soviet Communism, however, show us how far things can go in politics, as Masscult does in art. And let us not be too smug in this American temperate zone, unravaged by war and ideology. "It seems to me that nearly the whole Anglo-Saxon race, especially of course in America, have lost the power to be individuals. They have become social insects like bees and ants." So Roger Fry wrote years ago, and who will say that we have become less apian?

Like the early capitalism Marx and Engels described in *The Communist Manifesto,* Masscult is a dynamic, revolutionary force, breaking down the old barriers of class, tradition, and taste, dissolving all cultural distinctions. It mixes, scrambles everything together, producing what might be called homogenized culture, after another American achievement, the homogenization process that distributes the globules of cream evenly throughout the milk instead of allowing them to float separately on top. The interesting difference is that whereas the cream is still in the homogenized milk, somehow it disappears from homogenized culture. For the process destroys all values, since value-judgments require discrimination, an ugly word in liberal-democratic America. Masscult is very, very democratic; it refuses to discriminate against or between anything or anybody. All is grist to its mill and all comes out finely ground indeed.

Life is a typical homogenized magazine, appearing on the mahogany library tables of the rich, the glass cocktail tables of the middle class, and the oilcloth kitchen tables of the poor. Its contents are as thoroughly homogenized as its circulation. The same issue will present a serious exposition of atomic energy followed by a disquisition on Rita Hayworth's love life; photos of starving children picking garbage in Calcutta and of sleek models wearing adhesive brassières; an editorial hailing

Bertrand Russell's eightieth birthday ("A Great Mind Is Still Annoying and Adorning Our Age") across from a full-page photo of a matron arguing with a baseball umpire ("Mom Gets Thumb"); nine color pages of Renoir paintings followed by a picture of a roller-skating horse; a cover announcing in the same size type two features: "A New Foreign Policy, by John Foster Dulles" and "Kerima: Her Marathon Kiss Is a Movie Sensation."[3] Somehow these scramblings together seem to work all one way, degrading the serious rather than elevating the frivolous. Defenders of our Masscult society like Professor Edward Shils of the University of Chicago—he is, of course, a sociologist—see phenomena like *Life* as inspiriting attempts at popular education—just think, nine pages of Renoirs! But that roller-skating horse comes along, and the final impression is that both Renoir and the horse were talented. . . .

As a marketable commodity, Masscult has two great advantages over High Culture. One has already been considered: the post-1750 public, lacking the taste and knowledge of the old patron class, is not only satisfied with shoddy mass-produced goods but in general feels more at home with them (though on unpredictable occasions, they will respond to the real thing, as with Dickens' novels and the movies of Chaplin and Griffith). This is because such goods are standardized and so are easier to consume since one knows what's coming next—imagine a Western in which the hero loses the climactic gun fight or an office romance in which the mousy stenographer loses out to the predatory blonde. But standardization has a subtler aspect, which might be called The Built-In Reaction. As Clement Greenberg noted in "Avant-garde and *Kitsch*" many years ago in *Partisan Review*, the special aesthetic quality of *Kitsch*—a term which includes both Masscult and Midcult—is that it "predigests art for the spectator and spares him effort, provides him with a shortcut to the pleasures of art that detours what is necessarily difficult in the genuine art" because it includes the spectator's reactions in the work itself instead of forcing him to make his own responses. That standby of provincial weddings, "I Love You Truly," is far more "romantic" than the most beautiful of Schubert's songs because its wallowing, yearning tremolos and glissandos make it clear to the most unmusical listener that some-

---

[3] The advertisements provide even more scope for the editors' homogenizing talents, as when a full-page photo of a ragged Bolivian peon grinningly drunk on cocoa leaves (which Mr. Luce's conscientious reporters tell us he chews to narcotize his chronic hunger pains) appears opposite an ad of a pretty, smiling, well-dressed American mother with her two pretty, smiling, well-dressed children (a boy and a girl, of course—children are always homogenized in our ads) looking raptly at a clown on a TV set, the whole captioned in type big enough to announce the Second Coming: RCA Victor Brings You a New Kind of Television—Super Sets with "Picture Power." The peon would doubtless find the juxtaposition piquant if he could afford a copy of *Life*, which, luckily for the Good Neighbor Policy, he cannot.

thing very tender indeed is going on. It does his feeling for him; or, as T. W. Adorno has observed of popular music, "The composition hears for the listener." Thus Liberace is a much more "musical" pianist than Serkin, whose piano is not adorned with antique candelabra and whose stance at it is as businesslike as Liberace's is "artistic." So, too, our Collegiate Gothic, which may be seen in its most resolutely picturesque (and expensive) phase at Yale, is more relentlessly Gothic than Chartres, whose builders didn't even know they *were* Gothic and so missed many chances for quaint effects.[4] And so, too, Boca Raton, the millionaires' suburb that Addison Mizener designed in Palm Beach during the Great Bull Market of the 'twenties, is so aggressively Spanish Mission that a former American ambassador to Spain is said to have murmured in awe, "It's more Spanish than anything I ever saw in Madrid." The same Law of the Built-In Reaction also insures that a smoothly air-brushed pin-up girl by Petty is more "sexy" than a real naked woman, the emphasis of breasts and thighs corresponding to the pornographically exaggerated Gothic details of Harkness. More *sexy* but not more *sexual*, the relation between the terms being similar to that of *sentimentality* to *sentiment* or *modernistic* to *modern*, or *arty* to *art*. . . .

In these more advanced times, the danger to High Culture is not so much from Masscult as from a peculiar hybrid bred from the latter's unnatural intercourse with the former. A whole middle culture has come into existence and it threatens to absorb both its parents. This intermediate form—let us call it Midcult—has the essential qualities of Masscult— the formula, the build-in reaction, the lack of any standard except popularity—but it decently covers them with a cultural figleaf. In Masscult the trick is plain—to please the crowd by any means. But Midcult has it both ways: it pretends to respect the standards of High Culture while in fact it waters them down and vulgarizes them.[5]

The enemy outside the walls is easy to distinguish. It is its am-

---

[4] When I lived in Harkness Memorial Quadrangle some thirty years ago, I noticed a number of cracks in the tiny-paned windows of my room that had been patched with picturesquely wavy strips of lead. Since the place had just been built, I thought this peculiar. Later I found that after the windows had been installed, a special gang of artisans had visited them; one craftsman had delicately cracked every tenth or twentieth pane with a little hammer and another had then repaired the cracks. In a few days, the windows of Harkness had gone through an evolution that in backward places like Oxford had taken centuries. I wonder what they do in Harkness when a window is broken by accident.

[5] It's not done, of course, as consciously as this suggests. The editors of the *Saturday Review* or *Harper's* or the *Atlantic* would be honestly indignant at this description of their activities, as would John Steinbeck, J. P. Marquand, Pearl Buck, Irwin Shaw, Herman Wouk, John Hersey and others of that remarkably large group of Midcult novelists we have developed. One of the nice things about Zane Grey was that it seems never to have occurred to him that his books had anything to do with literature.

biguity that makes Midcult alarming. For it presents itself as part of High Culture. Not that coterie stuff, not those snobbish inbred so-called intellectuals who are only talking to themselves. Rather the great vital mainstream, wide and clear though perhaps not so deep. You, too, can wade in it for a mere $16.70; pay nothing now, just fill in the coupon and receive a full year six hard-cover lavishly illustrated issues of *Horizon: A Magazine of the Arts*, "probably the most beautiful magazine in the world . . . seeks to serve as guide to the long cultural advance of modern man, to explore the many mansions of the philosopher, the painter, the historian, the architect, the sculptor, the satirist, the poet . . . to build bridges between the world of scholars and the world of intelligent readers. It's a good buy. Use the coupon *now.*" *Horizon* has some 160,000 subscribers, which is more than the combined circulations, after many years of effort, of *Kenyon, Hudson, Sewanee, Partisan, Art News, Arts, American Scholar, Dissent, Commentary*, and half a dozen of our other leading cultural-critical magazines.

Midcult is not, as might appear at first, a raising of the level of Masscult. It is rather a corruption of High Culture which has the enormous advantage over Masscult that while also in fact "totally subjected to the spectator," in Malraux's phrase, it is able to pass itself off as the real thing. Midcult is the Revised Standard Version of the Bible, put out several years ago under the aegis of the Yale Divinity School, that destroys our greatest monument of English prose, the King James Version, in order to make the text "clear and meaningful to people today," which is like taking apart Westminster Abbey to make Disneyland out of the fragments. Midcult is the Museum of Modern Art's film department paying tribute to Samuel Goldwyn because his movies are alleged to be (slightly) better than those of other Hollywood producers—though why they are called "producers" when their function is to prevent the production of art (cf., the fate in Hollywood of Griffith, Chaplin, von Stroheim, Eisenstein and Orson Welles) is a semantic puzzle. Midcult is the venerable and once venerated *Atlantic*—which in the last century printed Emerson, Lowell, Howells, James, and Mark Twain—putting on the cover of a recent issue a huge photograph of Dore Schary, who has lately transferred his high-minded sentimentality from Hollywood to Broadway and who is represented in the issue by a homily, "To A Young Actor," which synthesizes Jefferson, Polonius and Dr. Norman Vincent Peale, concluding: "Behave as citizens not only of your profession but of the full world in which you live. Be indignant with injustice, be gracious with success, be courageous with failure, be patient with opportunity, and be resolute with faith and honor." Midcult is the Book-of-the-Month Club, which since 1926 has been supplying its members with reading matter of which the best that can be said is that it could be worse, i.e., they get

John Hersey instead of Gene Stratton Porter. Midcult is the transition from Rodgers and Hart to Rodgers and Hammerstein, from the gay tough lyrics of *Pal Joey*, a spontaneous expression of a real place called Broadway, to the folk-fakery of *Oklahoma!* and the orotund sentimentalities of *South Pacific*. Midcult is or was, "Omnibus," subsidized by a great foundation to raise the level of television, which began its labors by announcing it would "be aimed straight at the average American audience, neither highbrow nor lowbrow, the audience that made the *Reader's Digest*, *Life*, the *Ladies' Home Journal*, the audience which is the solid backbone of any business as it is of America itself" and which then proved its good faith by programming Gertrude Stein and Jack Benny, Chekhov and football strategy, Beethoven and champion ice skaters. "Omnibus" failed. The level of television, however, was not raised, for some reason. . . .

What is to be done? Conservatives like Ortega y Gasset and T. S. Eliot argue that since "the revolt of the masses" has led to the horrors of totalitarianism and of California roadside architecture, the only hope is to rebuild the old class walls and bring the masses once more under aristocratic control. They think of the popular as synonymous with the cheap and vulgar. Marxian radicals and liberal sociologists, on the other hand, see the masses as intrinsically healthy but as the dupes and victims of cultural exploitation—something like Rousseau's "noble savage." If only the masses were offered good stuff instead of *Kitsch*, how they would eat it up! How the level of Masscult would rise! Both these diagnoses seem to me fallacious because they assume that Masscult is (in the conservative view) or could be (in the liberal view) an expression of *people*, like Folk Art, whereas actually it is, as I tried to show earlier in this essay, an expression of *masses*, a very different thing.

The conservative proposal to save culture by restoring the old class lines has a more solid historical basis than the liberal-cum-Marxian hope for a new democratic, classless culture. Politically, however, it is without meaning in a world dominated by the two great mass nations, the USA and the USSR, and a world that is becoming more industrialized and mass-ified all the time. The only practical thing along those lines would be to revive the spirit of the old avant-garde, that is to re-create a cultural—as against a social, political or economic—elite as a counter-movement to both Masscult and Midcult. It may be possible, in a more modest and limited sense than in the past—I shall return to this point later—but it will be especially difficult in this country where the blurring of class lines, the lack of a continuous tradition and the greater facilities for the manufacturing and distribution of *Kitsch*, whether Masscult or Midcult, all work in the other direction. Unless this country goes either fascist or communist, there will continue to be islands above the flood for those determined enough to reach them and live on them; as Faulkner has shown, a writer can use Hollywood instead of being used by it, if his purpose be firm enough. But islands are not continents.

The alternative proposal is to raise the level of our culture in general. Those who advocate this start off from the assumption that there has already been a great advance in the diffusion of culture in the last two centuries—Edward Shils is sure of this, Daniel Bell thinks it is probably the case—and that the main problem is how to carry this even further; they tend to regard such critics of Masscult as Ernest van den Haag, Leo Lowenthal or myself as either disgruntled Left romantics or reactionary dreamers or both. Perhaps the most impressive—and certainly the longest—exposition of this point of view appears in Gilbert Seldes' *The Great Audience*. Mr. Seldes blames the present sad state of our Masscult on (1) the stupidity of the Lords of *Kitsch* (who underestimate the mental age of the public), (2) the arrogance of the intellectuals (who make the same mistake and so snobbishly refuse to try to raise the level of the mass media), and (3) the passivity of the public itself (which doesn't insist on better Masscult). This diagnosis seems to me superficial because it blames everything on subjective, moral factors: stupidity (the Lords of *Kitsch*), perversity (the intellectuals), or failure of will (the public). My own notion is that—as in the case of the "responsibility" of the German (or Russian) people for the horrors of Nazism (or of Soviet Communism)—it is unjust and unrealistic to blame large social groups for such catastrophes. Burke was right when he said you cannot indict a people. Individuals are caught up in the workings of a mechanism that forces them into its own pattern; only heroes can resist, and while one can hope that everybody will be a hero, one cannot demand it.

I see Masscult—and its recent offspring, Midcult—as a reciprocating engine, and who is to say, once it has been set in motion, whether the stroke or the counterstroke is responsible for its continued action? The Lords of *Kitsch* sell culture to the masses. It is a debased, trivial culture that avoids both the deep realities (sex, death, failure, tragedy) and also the simple, spontaneous pleasures, since the realities would be too real and the pleasures too lively to induce what Mr. Seldes calls "the mood of consent": a narcotized acceptance of Masscult-Midcult and of the commodities it sells as a substitute for the unsettling and unpredictable (hence unsalable) joy, tragedy, wit, change, originality and beauty of real life. The masses—and don't let's forget that this term includes the well-educated fans of *The Old Man and the Sea, Our Town, J.B.,* and *John Brown's Body*—who have been debauched by several generations of this sort of thing, in turn have come to demand such trivial and comfortable cultural products. Which came first, the chicken or the egg, the mass demand or its satisfaction (and further stimulation), is a question as academic as it is unanswerable. The engine is reciprocating and shows no signs of running down.

"Our fundamental want today in the United States," Walt Whitman wrote in 1871, "is of a class and the clear idea of a class, of native authors, literatures, far different, far higher in grade than any yet known, sacerdotal, modern, fit to cope with our occasions, lands, permeating the whole mass of American mentality, taste, belief, breathing into it a new life, giving it decision, affecting politics far more than the popular superficial suffrage. . . . For know you not, dear, earnest reader, that the people of our land may all read and write, and may all possess the right to vote—and yet the main things may be entirely lacking? . . . The priest departs, the divine literatus comes."

The divine literatus is behind schedule. Masscult and Midcult have so pervaded the land that Whitman's hope for a democratic culture shaped by a sacerdotal class at once so sublime and so popular that they can swing elections—that this noble vision now seems absurd. But a more modest aspiration is still open, one adumbrated by Whitman's idea of a new cultural class and his warning that "the main things may be entirely lacking" even though everybody knows how to read, write and vote. This is to recognize that two cultures have developed in this country and that it is to the national interest to keep them separate. The conservatives are right when they say there has never been a broadly democratic culture on a high level. This is not because the ruling class forcibly excluded the masses—this is Marxist melodrama—but quite simply because the great majority of people at any given time (including most of the ruling class for the matter) have never cared enough about such things to make them an important part of their lives. So let the masses have their Masscult, let the few who care about good writing, painting, music, architecture, philosophy, etc., have their High Culture, and don't fuzz up the distinction with Midcult.

Whitman would have rejected this proposal as undemocratic, which it is. But his own career is a case in point: he tried to be a popular bard but the masses were not interested, and his first recognition, excepting Emerson's lonely voice, came from the English pre-Raphaelites, a decadent and precious group if ever there was one. If we would create a literature "fit to cope with our occasions," the only public the writer or artist or composer or philosopher or critic or architect should consider must be that of his peers. The informed, interested minority—what Stendhal called "We Happy Few." Let the majority eavesdrop if they like, but their tastes should be firmly ignored.

There is a compromise between the conservative and liberal

proposals which I think is worth considering—neither an attempt to re-create the old avant-garde nor one to raise the general level of Masscult and Midcult. It is based on the recent discovery—since 1945—that there is not One Big Audience but rather a number of smaller, more specialized audiences that may still be commercially profitable. (I take it for granted that the less differentiated the audience, the less chance there is of something original and lively creeping in, since the principle of the lowest common denominator applies.) This discovery has in fact resulted in the sale of "quality" paperbacks and recordings and the growth of 'art' cinema houses, off-Broadway theatres, concert orchestras and art museums and galleries. The mass audience is divisible, we have discovered—and the more it is divided, the better. Even television, the most senseless and routinized expression of Masscult (except for the movie newsreels), might be improved by this approach. One possibility is pay-TV, whose modest concept is that only those who subscribe could get the program, like a magazine; but, also like a magazine, the editors would decide what goes in, not the advertisers; a small gain but a real one. The networks oppose this on philanthropic grounds—they don't see why the customer should pay for what he now gets free. But perhaps one would rather pay for bread than get stones for nothing.

As long as our society is "open" in Karl Popper's sense—that is unless or until it is closed by a mass revolution stimulated by the illusion of some "total solution" such as Russian-type Communism or Hitler-type Fascism, the name doesn't really matter—there will always be happy accidents because of the stubbornness of some isolated creator. But if we are to have more than this, it will be because our new public for High Culture becomes conscious of itself and begins to show some *esprit de corps,* insisting on higher standards and setting itself off—joyously, implacably—from most of its fellow citizens, not only from the Masscult depths but also from the agreeable ooze of the Midcult swamp.

In "The Present Age," Kierkegaard writes as follows:

> In order that everything should be reduced to the same level it is first of all necessary to procure a phantom, a monstrous abstraction, an all-embracing something which is nothing, a mirage—and that phantom is the public. . . .
> The public is a concept which could not have occurred in antiquity because the people *en masse in corpore* took part in any situation which arose . . . and moreover the individual was personally present and had to submit at once to applause or disapproval for his decision. Only when the sense of association in society is no longer strong enough to give life to concrete realities is the Press able to create that abstraction, "the public," consisting of unreal individuals who never are and never can be united in an actual situation or organization—and yet are held together as a whole.

The public is a host, more numerous than all the peoples together, but it is a body which can never be reviewed; it cannot even be represented because it is an abstraction. Nevertheless, when the age is reflective [i.e., the individual sees himself only as he is reflected in a collective body] and passionless and destroys everything concrete, the public becomes everything and is supposed to include everything. And . . . the individual is thrown back upon himself. . . .

A public is neither a nation nor a generation nor a community nor a society nor these particular men, for all these are only what they are through the concrete. No single person who belongs to the public makes a real commitment; for some hours of the day, perhaps, he belongs to a real public—at moments when he is nothing else, since when he really is what he is, he does not form part of the public. Made up of such individuals, of individuals at the moment when they are nothing, a public is a kind of gigantic something, an abstract and deserted void which is everything and nothing. But on this basis, any one can arrogate to himself a public, and just as the Roman Church chimerically extended its frontiers by appointing bishops *in partibus infidelium,* so a public is something which every one can claim, and even a drunken sailor exhibiting a peep-show has dialectically the same right to a public as the greatest man. He has just as logical a right to put all those noughts *in front of* his single number.

This is the essence of what I have tried to say.

Thomas Mann

THE CINEMA—ART FORM OF THE AGE

Life flitted across the screen before their smarting eyes: life chopped into small sections, fleeting, accelerated; a restless, jerky fluctuation of appearing and disappearing, performed to a thin accompaniment of music, which set its actual *tempo* to the phantasmagoria of the past, and with the narrowest of means at its command, yet managed to evoke a whole gamut of pomp and solemnity, passion, abandon, and gurgling sensuality. It was a thrilling drama of love and death they saw silently reeled off; the scenes, laid at the court of an oriental despot,

From *The Magic Mountain,* by Thomas Mann. Copyright 1927 and renewed 1955 by Alfred A. Knopf, Inc. Reprinted by permission.

Thomas Mann (1875–1955) was a well-known German novelist who won the Nobel Prize for literature in 1929.

galloped past, full of gorgeousness and naked bodies, thirst of power and raving religious self-abnegation; full of cruelty, appetite, and deathly lust, and slowing down to give a full view of the muscular development of the executioner's arms. Constructed, in short, to cater to the innermost desires of an onlooking international civilization. Settembrini, as critic, Hans Castorp thought, and whispered as much to his cousin, would doubtless have sharply characterized what they saw as repugnant to a humanistic sense, and have scarified with direct and classic irony the prostitution of technical skill to such a humanly contemptible performance. On the other hand, Frau Stöhr, who was sitting not far from our three friends, seemed utterly absorbed; her ignorant red face was twisted into an expression of the hugest enjoyment.

And so were the other faces about them. But when the last flicker of the last picture in a reel had faded away, when the lights in the auditorium went up, and the field of vision stood revealed as an empty sheet of canvas, there was not even applause. Nobody was there to be applauded, to be called before the curtain and thanked for the rendition. The actors who had assembled to present the scenes they had just enjoyed were scattered to the winds; only their shadows had been here, their activity had been split up into millions of pictures, each with the shortest possible period of focus, in order to give it back to the present and reel it off again at will. The silence of the crowd, as the illusion passed, had about it something nerveless and repellent. Their hands lay powerless in face of the nothing that confronted them. They rubbed their eyes, stared vacantly before them, blinking in the brilliant light and wishing themselves back in the darkness, looking at sights which had had their day and then, as it were, had been transplanted into fresh time, and bedizened up with music.

The despot died beneath the knife, with a soundless shriek. Then came scenes from all parts of the world: the President of the French Republic, in top-hat and cordon, sitting in a landau and replying to a speech of welcome; the Viceroy of India, at the wedding of a rajah; the German Crown Prince in the courtyard of a Potsdam garrison. There was a picture of life in a New Mécklenburg village; a cock-fight in Borneo, naked savages blowing on nose-horns, a wild elephant hunt, a ceremony at the court of the King of Siam, a courtesans' street in Japan, with geishas sitting behind wooden lattices; Samoyeds bundled in furs, driving sledges drawn by reindeer through the snowy wastes of Siberia; Russian pilgrims praying at Hebron; a Persian criminal under the knout. They were present at all these scenes; space was annihilated, the clock put back, the Then and There played on by music and transformed into a juggling, scurrying Now and Here. A young Moroccan woman, in a costume of striped silk, with trappings in the shape of chains, bracelets, and rings, her swelling breasts half bared, was suddenly brought so close to the camera as to be life-sized; one could see the dilated nostrils, the eyes full of animal life, the features in play as she showed her white teeth in a laugh, and held one of her hands, with its blanched nails, for a shade to her eyes, while with the other she waved to the audience, who stared, taken aback, into the face of the charming apparition. It seemed to see and saw not, it was not moved by the glances bent upon it, its smile and nod were not of the present but of the past, so that the impulse to respond was baffled, and lost in a feeling of impotence. Then the phantom vanished. The screen glared white and empty, with the one word *Finis* written across it. The entertainment was over, in silence the theatre was emptied, a new audience took the place of that going out, and before their eager eyes the cycle would presently unroll itslf again.

Harold Rosenberg
IS THERE A PUBLIC?

The image of the simple layman waiting on the doorstep of art is a morbid fancy of modern thought. In actuality there exists no such thing as an "uncultivated mass." If there is anyone in America who has managed to elude being educated by free compulsory schools and by the millions of pictures and written and spoken words poured into every crevice of this country hourly, he is so hard to catch he may as well be written off as prospective audience material. Today everybody is already a member of some intellectually worked-over group, that is, an audience. And in the sense that it is literate, selective and self-conscious in its taste, every audience is an audience of intellectuals. Science fiction, tabloid sports columns, rock 'n roll gab, the New Criticism, presuppose various levels of technical preparation and familiarity with terminology on the part of their readers (I am not saying which way is up). Even the daytime broadcast designed for the suburban housewife addresses itself to an expertise gained through womansday and digest journalism with its encyclopedic how-to-do-it training and inside stories on heroes and heroines. The member of the soap-show audience may differ from the

Reprinted by permission of the publisher, Horizon Press, from *The Tradition of the New* by Harold Rosenberg. Copyright 1959, 1960.
Harold Rosenberg (1906–   ) is an American art critic.

Museum of Modern Art first nighter in vocabulary and self-estimation, but not necessarily in intellectual background or capacity; each is where she is largely because of chance or social environment. Moreover, American audiences interlock and their components easily pass over from one to another.

The Public is not a single entity of high or low intelligence but a sum of shifting groupings, each with its own mental focus. Which intellectual category an individual belongs to is *not* decided by his appreciation of the fine arts—all modern geniuses are known to read detective stories and one doubts that Einstein's record collection included Schönberg or Varèse. The existence of a mass of generic art appreciators is a myth left over from European aristocratic and pseudo-aristocratic meditations on lost peasant cultures and noble savages. In America today this myth serves the purposes not of art nor of the public but of salesmanship or political propaganda—one who speaks on behalf of an art for The Public is trying to recruit a new public out of existing publics.

The novelty about the situation of the fine arts in the twentieth century is that for the first time in history no one is sure who the art audience is. Today, it is possible to ask: For Whom Do You Paint (or Write)? and for this question to be the beginning of a speculation, to say nothing of a fight. Proust's idea that the real audience of an original work is slowly shaped by the work itself merely confirms the presence of the enigma. To the tattoo artist on Melville's Pacific island who covered the village headman with an over-all design previously tried out on some bottom dog used as a sketch pad, the problem did not present itself. His audience was there in advance. The same for the painters and poets commissioned by the princes of church and court, and even for those whose acquaintance the educated bourgeoisie of the nineteenth century felt obliged to make. The radical twist in the art situation begins in earnest when the typical art audience is no longer recognizable by the insignia of its social function. The turnout at a current art show, which consists almost exclusively of artists and of practitioners of closely allied professions—art teachers, museum employees, decorators, architects, designers, photographers—is by comparison with the élites of other days a very odd group; not only does it fail to represent social authority, it does not even represent its own social function as a professional group, since other artists and members of the same professions as those present, with an education, income, prestige, equivalent to theirs, despise this art or regard it as irrelevant to their work; as a *New Yorker* novelist once said to me, "Kafka is interesting, but of course he's not in my field."

Lacking objective cohesion, the new audience is truer esthetically than former ones to the extent that it comes into being not through social status but through the magnetic attraction of the work of art upon random human particles.

On the other hand, the social amalgam that constitutes an audience today tends to be charged with currents of mood and opinion originating in the uncertain conditions of its existence and in the gratuitousness of its interest in any given work or style. These emotional and mental currents it diffuses upon the arts.

The study of the influences thus set into motion in art is the only appropriate ground for social criticism of contemporary work; while theories about what "Society" demands of the artist, or of what art might communicate with an audience of everybody, are as out-of-date and useless as the idea of shocking or defying this phantom.

Notes on the New Public

The intellectualistic character of all current audiences is an effect of the steady transformation of the whole populace into professionals and semi-professionals; sociologists who classify people by the colors of their collars find a spectacular trend toward white and blue.

The professional mass keeps expanding and as it expands it divides. Old professions break up and each fragment becomes the center of a new constellation—it is not only that all doctors have become specialists but that the practice of medicine, like that of warfare, involves scores of other professions. At the same time the trades keep propelling themselves upwards into the professions; as the dentist not so long ago suppressed his past as a barber and assumed the rank of surgeon, so the kitchen manager becomes a dietitian and stockbreeders and policemen set up academic qualifications and conduct "prestige" campaigns to convince society of the learned nature of their pursuits. Bricklayers, I am told, now lay exclusively on a fee-per basis, and their public relations representatives will soon, no doubt, have traced their craft back to Amenhotep's magicians and succeeded in ranking it with performance on the dulcimer—that is, assuming that there are still bricks. . . .

Traditionalists resent this inexorable liquidation of the proletariat into the intellectual caste. They might console themselves with the thought that the process renders obsolete Lenin's conception of a vanguard of professional revolutionists hustling a semi-literate mass up this incline, and that the change of collars occurring spontaneously is probably the fundamental reason for the failure of Bolshevism in technologically advanced nations.

A form of work establishes itself as a profession not only through the complication of its technique—many of the ancient crafts involved more complex recipes than their counterparts today—but through self-consciousness with regard to this technique. A cop stops being a mere armed watch when he is aware of general reasons for his particular way of lounging on street corners. Thus the essential mark of a profession is its evolution of a unique language or jargon into which it translates its subject matter and in which its methods, purposes and relations to other arts and sciences are formulated. The more incomprehensible this lingo is to outsiders,[1] the more thoroughly it identifies the profession as such and elevates it out of the reach of mere amateurs and craftsmen.

One of the effects of the "universal audience" illusion is that, while gnomic language is taken for granted in the sciences and in newer modes of study, its use in the arts is treated as if they were still in an age when craftsmen bent silently over their tools. It would not, for instance, occur to the humanists of the picture weeklies to object to the following exposition of method in cultural anthropology:

> When it is asserted that a certain behaviour is "typical" in a certain culture, it is not implied that there is no other culture in which it is, at the same or some other time, equally "typical." What has hitherto turned out to be rather unique is the syndrome of each culture (the ensemble of its regularities), but not each element of the syndrome.[2]

Yet anyone who thought as closely (no one goes *that* far) about the implications of his practices in painting would be treated as a genocide by audience builders, and perhaps also by Leites. In their turn, artists, responding to the surrounding professionalization, become convinced that the secret of art, as well as its honor as a calling, resides in the jargon of the studios.

In any case, incomprehensibility in the arts is inseparable from the fragmentation of the public through the expansion of professionalism. The segregation of occupations within the mazes of their technical systems increasingly demolishes the old mental cohesions of class and nation. Outside each profession there is no social body to talk to, and apart from the forms in which the thought of the profession is embodied there is nothing to say. One who calls for mass communication in the arts is like a sergeant who wants to go back to good old simple drill in what the Defense Department, following the trend, calls "our new *professional army*."

[1] The continued use of Latin by the medical profession appears as simple-minded compared to what newer professions have been able to accomplish in "English."

[2] *Psycho-Cultural Hypotheses About Political Acts,* Nathan Leites.

Marshall McLuhan
MEDIUM, MESSAGE, MASSAGE

The medium, or process, of our time—electric technology—is reshaping and restructuring patterns of social interdependence and every aspect of our personal life. It is forcing us to reconsider and reevaluate practically every thought, every action, and every institution formerly taken for granted. Everything is changing—you, your family, your neighborhood, your education, your job, your government, your relation to "the others." And they're changing dramatically.

Societies have always been shaped more by the nature of the media by which men communicate than by the content of the communication. The alphabet, for instance, is a technology that is absorbed by the very young child in a completely unconscious manner, by osmosis so to speak. Words and the meaning of words predispose the child to think and act automatically in certain ways. The alphabet and print technology fostered and encouraged a fragmenting process, a process of specialism and of detachment. Electric technology fosters and encourages unification and involvement. It is impossible to understand social and cultural changes without a knowledge of the workings of media.

The older training of observation has become quite irrelevant in this new time, because it is based on psychological responses and concepts conditioned by the former technology—mechanization.

Innumerable confusions and a profound feeling of despair invariably emerge in periods of great technological and cultural transitions. Our "Age of Anxiety" is, in great part, the result of trying to do today's job with yesterday's tools—with yesterday's concepts.

Youth instinctively understands the present environment—the electric drama. It lives mythically and in depth. This is the reason for the great alienation between generations. Wars, revolutions, civil uprisings are interfaces within the new environments created by electric informational media. . . .

Ours is a brand-new world of allatonceness. "Time" has ceased, "space" has vanished. We now live in a global village . . . a simulta-

From *The Medium Is the Massage* by Marshall McLuhan and Quentin Fiore, pp. 8–9, 63, 113–114, 122–131. Copyright © 1967 by Bantam Books, Inc. All rights reserved.

Marshall McLuhan (1911–   ) is a communications specialist and Director of the Center for Culture and Technology at the University of Toronto in Canada. At present, he is professor of humanities at Fordham University.

neous happening. We are back in acoustic space. We have begun again to structure the primordial feeling, the tribal emotions from which a few centuries of literacy divorced us.

We have had to shift our stress of attention from action to re-action. We must now know in advance the consequences of any policy or action, since the results are experienced without delay. Because of electric speed, we can no longer wait and see. George Washington once re-marked, "We haven't heard from Benj. Franklin in Paris this year. We should write him a letter."

At the high speeds of electric communication, purely visual means of apprehending the world are no longer possible; they are just too slow to be relevant or effective.

Unhappily, we confront this new situation with an enormous backlog of outdated mental and psychological responses. We have been left d-a-n-g-l-i-n-g. Our most impressive words and thoughts betray us— they refer us only to the past, not to the present.

Electric circuitry profoundly involves men with one another. In-formation pours upon us, instantaneously and continuously. As soon as information is acquired, it is very rapidly replaced by still newer infor-mation. Our electrically-configured world has forced us to move from the habit of data classification to the mode of pattern recognition. We can no longer build serially, block-by-block, step-by-step, because instant com-munication insures that all factors of the environment and of experience coexist in a state of active interplay. . . .

Homer's "Illiad" was the cultural encyclopedia of pre-literate Greece, the didactic vehicle that provided men with guidance for the management of their spiritual, ethical, and social lives. All the persuasive skills of the poetic and the dramatic idiom were marshaled to insure the faithful transmission of the tradition from generation to generation.

These Bardic songs were rhythmically organized with great formal mastery into metrical patterns which insured that everyone was psychologically attuned to memorization and to easy recall. There was no ear illiteracy in pre-literate Greece.

In the "Republic," Plato vigorously attacked the oral, poetized form as a vehicle for communicating knowledge. He pleaded for a more precise method of communication and classification ("The Ideas"), one which would favor the investigation of facts, principles of reality, human nature, and conduct. What the Greeks meant by "poetry" was radically different from what we mean by poetry. Their "poetic" expression was a product of a collective psyche and mind. The mimetic form, a technique that exploited rhythm, meter, and music, achieved the desired psycho-logical response in the listener. Listeners could memorize with greater ease what was sung than what was said. Plato attacked this method because it discouraged disputation and argument. It was in his opinion the chief obstacle to abstract, speculative reasoning—he called it "a poison, and an enemy of the people."

"Blind," all-hearing Homer inherited this metaphorical mode of speech, a speech which, like a prism, refracts much meaning to a single point.

"Precision" is sacrificed for a greater degree of suggestion. Myth is the mode of simultaneous awareness of a complex group of causes and effects.

Electric circuitry confers a mythic dimension on our ordinary individual and group actions. Our technology forces us to live mythically, but we continue to think fragmentarily, and on single, separate planes.

Myth means putting on the audience, putting on one's environment. The Beatles do this. They are a group of people who suddenly were able to put on their audience and the English language with musical effects—putting on a whole vesture, a whole time, a Zeit.

Young people are looking for a formula for putting on the universe—participation mystique. They do not look for detached patterns—for ways of relating themselves to the world, à la nineteenth century. . . .

"Authorship" in the sense we know it today, individual intellectual effort related to the book as an economic commodity—was practically unknown before the advent of print technology. Medieval scholars were indifferent to the precise identity of the "books" they studied. In turn, they rarely signed even what was clearly their own. They were a humble service organization. Procuring texts was often a very tedious and time-consuming task. Many small texts were transmitted into volumes of miscellaneous content, very much like "jottings" in a scrapbook, and, in this transmission, authorship was often lost.

The invention of printing did away with anonymity, fostering ideas of literary fame and the habit of considering intellectual effort as private property. Mechanical multiples of the same text created a public—a reading public. The rising consumer-oriented culture became concerned with labels of authenticity and protection against theft and piracy. The idea of copyright—"the exclusive right to reproduce, publish, and sell the matter and form of a literary or artistic work" was born.

Xerography—every man's brain-picker—heralds the times of instant publishing. Anybody can now become both author and publisher. Take any books on any subject and custom-make your own book by simply xeroxing a chapter from this one, a chapter from that one—instant steal!

As new technologies come into play, people are less and less convinced of the importance of self-expression. Teamwork succeeds private effort.

A ditto, ditto device.
„   „   „   „
A ditto, ditto device.
„   „   „   „
A ditto, ditto device.
„   „   „   „

Even so imaginative a writer as Jules Verne failed to envisage the speed with which electric technology would produce informational media. He rashly predicted that television would be invented in the XXIXth Century.

Science-fiction writing today presents situations that enable us to perceive the potential of new technologies. Formerly, the problem was to invent new forms of labor-saving. Today, the reverse is the problem. Now we have to adjust, not to invent. We have to find the environments in which it will be possible to live with our new inventions. Big Business has learned to tap the s-f writer.

Television completes the cycle of the human sensorium. With the omnipresent ear and the moving eye, we have abolished writing, the specialized acoustic-visual metaphor that established the dynamics of Western civilization.

In television there occurs an extension of the sense of active, exploratory touch which involves all the senses simultaneously, rather than that of sight alone. You have to be "with" it. But in all electric phenomena, the visual is only one component in a complex interplay. Since, in the age of information, most transactions are managed electrically, the electric technology has meant for Western man a considerable drop in the visual component, in his experience, and a corresponding increase in the activity of his other senses.

Television demands participation and involvement in depth of the whole being. It will not work as a background. It engages you. Perhaps this is why so many people feel that their identity has been threatened. This charge of the light brigade has heightened our general awareness of the shape and meaning of lives and events to a level of extreme sensitivity.

It was the funeral of President Kennedy that most strongly proved the power of television to invest an occasion with the character of corporate participation. It involves an entire population in a ritual process. (By comparison, press, movies, and radio are mere packaging devices for consumers.) In television, images are projected at you. You are the screen. The images wrap around you. You are the vanishing point. This creates a sort of inwardness, a sort of reverse perspective which has much in common with Oriental art.

The television generation is a grim bunch. It is much more serious than children of any other period—when they were frivolous, more whimsical. The television child is more earnest, more dedicated.

Most often the few seconds sandwiched between the hours of viewing—the "commercials"—reflect a truer understanding of the medium. There simply is no time for the narrative form, borrowed from earlier print technology. The story line must be abandoned. Up until very recently, television commercials were regarded as simply a bastard form, or vulgar folk art. They are influencing contemporary literature. Vide "In Cold Blood," for instance.

The main cause for disappointment in and for criticism of television is the failure on the part of its critics to view it as a totally new technology which demands different sensory responses. These critics insist on regarding television as merely a degraded form of print technology. Critics of television have failed to realize that the motion pictures they are lionizing—such as "The Knack," "Hard Day's Night," "What's New Pussycat?"—would prove unacceptable as mass audience films if the audience had not been preconditioned by television commercials to abrupt zooms, elliptical editing, no story lines, flash cuts.

Movies are better than ever!

Hollywood is often a fomenter of anti-colonialist revolutions.

Sukarno: "The motion picture industry has provided a window on the world, and the colonized nations have looked through that window and have seen the things of which they have been deprived. It is perhaps not generally realized that a refrigerator can be a revolutionary symbol—to a people who have no refrigerators. A motor car owned by a worker in one country can be a symbol of revolt to a people deprived of even the necessities of life . . . [Hollywood] helped to build up the sense of deprivation of man's birthright, and that sense of deprivation has played a large part in the national revolutions of postwar Asia."

9
The Welfare State

Of all the issues of the twentieth century, the welfare state seems to have been the most dominant in domestic politics. Like so many other contemporary experiences, it was given great support by the wars of the century, even though the Left, with which the welfare state is so often identified, has generally opposed war.

Writing early in the century (before the wars) British novelist, sociological writer, and historian H. G. Wells argued that socialism was the very expression of reason: "Just as science aims at a common organized body of knowledge to which all its servants contribute and in which they share, so socialism insists upon its ideal of an organized social order which every man serves and by which every man benefits." Still, the word "socialism" has been less honorific than the word "scientific," and a good many proponents of welfare legislation have explicitly rejected any association with socialism. Winston Churchill in his youth did "not want to pull down the structures of science and civilization," which presumably socialism would, and insisted that liberalism was not socialistic. John Maynard Keynes also professed to be rescuing, not destroying capitalism, and rescuing it through the scientific analysis of economics. He felt that

306

increased public spending would bring increased prosperity and that the way out of depression was greater investment.

Yet the very apostles of violence and irrationalism, the Nazis, seemed to have created an economic "miracle" through national socialism, employing Keynesian economics. Austrian economist Gustav Stolper dismisses this miracle: "an armament boom never creates prosperity." A. J. P. Taylor, by contrast, accepts as commonplace the German "miracle" and the Keynesian revelation that unemployment need not be "regarded as a law of nature."

John Kenneth Galbraith is concerned with affluence. Although a follower of Keynes, he urges us to grapple with a new set of problems in a new age. "The miserable consumption of the poor," says he, "is partly the result of the ostentatious demands of the rich. There isn't enough for both, and the latter get far more than they need. If possible, something should be done about inequality . . ." That something, according to Galbraith, should be increased taxation, for "poverty can only be corrected at increased public cost." Taxation is necessary to achieve social balance.

It is, to be sure, a new age built on debt and armament; the new mass society is "half welfare and half garrison." American writer John T. Flynn warns not of the road to communism, but of the road to fascism, and the old Winston Churchill of 1950 conjures up an ugly vision of the all-powerful socialist state, the very negation of freedom. But if author Michael Harrington is correct, the whole process of increasing government control, in whatever country, is simply a product of the capitalistic system itself. Capitalism is being destroyed by the practice of capitalism.

H. G. Wells
FUNDAMENTALS OF SOCIALISM

The fundamental idea upon which Socialism rests is the same fundamental idea as that upon which all real scientific work is carried on. It is the denial that chance impulse and individual will and happening

From *New Worlds for Old* by H. G. Wells, pp. 22–26, 73–74, 75–76, 92–94, 96–97. Reprinted by permission of The Executors of H. G. Wells.

H. G. Wells (1866–1946) was a British novelist and social critic. His works included such popular science fiction books as *The Invisible Man* and *War of the Worlds*.

constitute the only possible methods by which things may be done in the world. It is an assertion that things are in their nature orderly, that things may be computed, may be calculated upon and foreseen. In the spirit of this belief Science aims at a systematic knowledge of material things. "Knowledge is power," knowledge that is frankly and truly exchanged— that is the primary assumption of the *New Atlantis* which created the Royal Society and the organization of research. The Socialist has just that same faith in the order, the knowableness of things and the power of men in co-operation to overcome chance; but to him, dealing as he does with the social affairs of men, it takes the form not of schemes for collective research but for collective action and the creation of a comprehensive design for all the social activities of man. While Science gathers knowledge, Socialism in an entirely harmonious spirit criticizes and develops a general plan of social life. Each seeks to replace disorder by order.

Each of these systems of ideas has, of course, its limits; we know in matters of material science that no calculated quantity is ever exact, no outline without a fogging at the edge, no angle without a curve at the apex; and in social affairs also, there must needs always be individuality and the unexpected and incalculable. But these things do not vitiate the case for a general order, any more than the different sizes and widths and needs of the human beings who travel prevent our having our railway carriages and seats and doors of a generally convenient size, nor our sending everybody over the same gauge of rail.

Now Science has not only this in common with Socialism that it has grown out of men's courageous confidence in the superiority of order to muddle, but these two great processes of human thought are further in sympathy in the demand they make upon men to become less egotistical and isolated. The main difference of modern scientific research from that of the middle ages, the secret of its immense successes, lies in its collective character, in the fact that every fruitful experiment is published, every new discovery of relationships explained. In a sense scientific research is a triumph over natural instinct, over that mean instinct that makes men secretive, that makes a man keep knowledge to himself and use it slyly to his own advantage. The training of a scientific man is a training in what an illiterate lout would despise as a weakness; it is a training in blabbing, in blurting things out, in telling just as plainly as possible and as soon as possible what it is he has found. To "keep shut" and bright-eyed and to score advantages, that is the wisdom of the common stuff of humanity still. To science it is a crime. The noble practice of that noble profession medicine, for example, is to condemn as a quack and a rascal every man who uses secret remedies. And it is one of the most encouraging things for all who speculate upon human possibility to consider the multitude of men in the last three centuries who have been content to live laborious, unprofitable, and for the most part quite undistinguished lives in the service of knowledge that has transformed the world. Some names indeed stand out by virtue of gigantic or significant achievement, such names as Bacon, Newton, Volta, Darwin, Faraday, Joule; but these are but the culminating peaks of a nearly limitless Oberland of devoted toiling men, men one could list by the thousand. The rest have had the smallest meed of fame, small reward, much toil, much abandonment of pleasure for their lot. One thing ennobles them all in common—their conquest over the meanness of concealment, their systematic application of energy to other than personal ends!

And that, too, Socialism pre-eminently demands. It applies to social and economic relationships the same high rule of frankness and veracity, the same subordination of purely personal considerations to a common end that Science demands in the field of thought and knowledge. Just as Science aims at a common organized body of knowledge to which all its servants contribute and in which they share, so Socialism insists upon its ideal of an organized social order which every man serves and by which every man benefits. Their common enemy is the secret-thinking, self-seeking man. Secrecy, subterfuge and the private gain; these are the enemies of Socialism and the adversaries of Science. At times, I will admit, both Socialist and scientific man forget this essential sympathy. You will find specialized scientific investigators who do not realize they are, in effect, Socialists, and Socialists so dull to the quality of their own professions, that they gird against Science, and are secretive in policy. But such purblind servants of the light cannot alter the essential correlation of the two systems of ideas.

Now the Socialist, inspired by this conception of a possible frank and comprehensive social order to which mean and narrow ends must be sacrificed, attacks and criticizes the existing order of things at a great number of points and in a great variety of phraseology. At all points, however, you will find upon analysis that his criticism amounts to a declaration that there is wanting a sufficiency of *constructive design.* That in the last resort is what he always comes to.

He wants a complete organization for all those human affairs that are of collective importance. He says, to take instances almost haphazard, that our ways of manufacturing a great multitude of necessary things, of getting and distributing food, of conducting all sorts of business, of begetting and rearing children, of permitting diseases to engender and spread are chaotic and undisciplined, so badly done that here is enormous hardship, and there enormous waste, here excess and degeneration, and there privation and death. He declares that for these collective purposes, in the satisfaction of these universal needs, mankind presents the appearance and follows the methods of a mob when it ought to follow the method of an army. In place of disorderly individual effort, each man doing what he pleases, the Socialist wants organized effort and a plan. And while the scientific man seeks to make an orderly map of the half-explored wilderness of fact, the Socialist seeks to make an orderly plan for the half-conceived wilderness of human effort.

That and no other is the essential Socialist idea. . . .

With land, with all sorts of property and all sorts of businesses and public services, just as with the old isolated private family, the old separateness and independence is giving way to a new synthesis. The idea of Private Ownership, albeit still the ruling idea of our civilization, does not rule nearly so absolutely as it did. It weakens and falters before the inexorable demands of social necessity—manifestly under our eyes.

The Socialist would be able to appeal to a far greater number of laws in the nature of limitation of the owner of property than could be quoted to show the limitation of the old supremacy of the head of the family. In the first place he would be able to point to a constantly increasing interference with the right of the landowner to do what he liked with his own, building regulations, intervention to create allotments and so forth. Then there would be a vast mass of factory and industrial legislation, controlling, directing, prohibiting; fencing machinery, interfering on behalf of health, justice and public necessity with the owner's free bargain with his work-people. His business undertakings would be under limitations his grandfather never knew—even harmless adulterations that merely intensify profit, forbidden him!

And in the next place and still more significant is the manifest determination to keep in public hands many things that would once inevitably have become private property. For example, in the middle Victorian period a water supply, a gas supply, a railway or tramway was inevitably a private enterprise, the creation of a new property; now, this is the exception rather than the rule. While gas and water and trains were supplied by speculative owners for profit, electric light and power, new tramways and light railways are created in an increasing number of cases by public bodies who retain them for the public good. Nobody who travels to London as I do regularly in the dirty, over-crowded carriages of the infrequent and unpunctual trains of the South-Eastern Company, and who then transfers to the cleanly, speedy, frequent—in a word, "civilized" electric cars of the London County Council, can fail to estimate the value and significance of this supersession of the private owner by the common-weal.

All these things, the Socialists insist, are but a beginning. They point to a new phase in social development, to the appearance of a collective intelligence and a sense of public service taking over appliances, powers, enterprises, with a growing confidence that must end finally in the substitution of collective for private ownership and enterprise throughout the whole area of the common business of life. . . .

In relation to quite a number of large public services it can be shown that even under contemporary conditions Private Ownership does work with an enormous waste and inefficiency. Necessarily it seeks for profit; necessarily it seeks to do as little as possible for as much as possible. The prosperity of all Kent is crippled by a "combine" of two ill-managed and unenterprising railway companies, with no funds for new developments, grinding out an uncertain dividend by clipping expenditure.

I happen to see this organization pretty closely, and I can imagine no State enterprise west of Turkey or Persia presenting even to the passing eye so deplorable a spectacle of ruin and inefficiency. The South-Eastern Company's estate at Seabrook presents the dreariest spectacle of incompetent development conceivable; one can see its failure three miles away; it is a waste with an embryo slum in one corner protected by an extravagant sea-wall, already partly shattered, from the sea.

To-day (Nov. 4, 1907) the price of the ordinary South-Eastern stock is 65 and its deferred stock 31; of the London, Chatham and Dover ordinary stock 10½; an eloquent testimony to the disheartened state of the owners who now cling reluctantly to this disappointing monopoly. Spite of this impoverishment of the ordinary shareholder, this railway system has evidently paid too much profit in the past for efficiency; the rolling stock is old and ageing—much of it is by modern standards abominable—the trains are infrequent, and the shunting operations at local stations, with insufficient sidings and insufficient staffs, produce a chronic dislocation and unpunctuality in the traffic that is exaggerated by the defects of direction evident even in the very time-tables. The trains are not well planned, the connections with branch lines are often extremely ill managed. The service is bad to its details. It is the exception rather than the rule to find a ticket-office in the morning with change for a five-pound note; and, as a little indication of the spirit of the whole machine, I discovered the other day that the conductors upon the South-Eastern trams at Hythe start their morning with absolutely no change at all. Recently the roof of the station at Charing Cross fell in—through sheer decay. . . . A whole rich county now stagnates hopelessly under the grip of this sample of private enterprise, towns fail to grow, trade flows sluggishly from point to point. No population in the world would stand such a management as it endures at the hands of the South-Eastern Railway from any responsible public body. . . .

I want now to point out that Socialism seeks to ennoble the intimate personal life, by checking and discouraging passions that at present run rampant, and by giving wider scope for passions that are now thwarted and subdued. The Socialist declares that life is now needlessly dishonest, base and mean, because our present social organization, such as it is, makes an altogether too powerful appeal to some of the very meanest elements in our nature.

Not perhaps to the lowest. There can be no disputing that our present civilization does discourage much of the innate bestiality of man; that it helps people to a measure of continence, cleanliness and mutual toleration; that it does much to suppress brute violence, the spirit of lawlessness, cruelty and wanton destruction. But on the other hand it does also check and cripple generosity and frank truthfulness, any disinterested creative passion, the love of beauty, the passion for truth and research, and it stimulates avarice, parsimony, overreaching, usury, falsehood and secrecy, by making money-getting its criterion of intercourse.

Whether we like it or not, we who live in this world to-day find we must either devote a considerable amount of our attention to getting and keeping money, and shape our activities—or, if you will, distort them—with a constant reference to that process, or we must accept futility. Whatever powers men want to exercise, whatever service they wish to do, it is a preliminary condition for most of them that they must, by earning something or selling something, achieve opportunity. If they cannot turn their gift into some saleable thing or get some propertied man to "patronize" them, they cannot exercise these gifts. The gift for getting is the supreme gift—all others bow before it.

Now this is not a thing that comes naturally out of the quality of man; it is the result of a blind and complex social growth, of this set of ideas working against that, and of these influences modifying those. The idea of property has run wild and become a choking universal weed. It is not the natural master-passion of a wholesome man to want constantly to own. People talk of Socialism as being a proposal "against human nature," and they would have us believe that this life of anxiety, of parsimony and speculation, of mercenary considerations and forced toil we all lead, is the complete and final expression of the social possibilities of the human soul. But, indeed, it is only quite abnormal people, people of a narrow, limited, specialized intelligence, Rockefellers, Morgans and the like, people neither great nor beautiful, mere financial monomaniacs, who can keep themselves devoted to and concentrated upon gain. To the majority of capable good human stuff, buying and selling, saving and investing, insuring oneself and managing property, is a mass of uncongenial, irrational and tiresome procedure, conflicting with the general trend of instinct and the finer interests of life. The great mass of men and women, indeed, find the whole process so against nature, that in spite of all the miseries of poverty, all the slavery of the economic disadvantage, they cannot urge themselves to this irksome cunning game of besting the world, they remain poor. Most, in a sort of despair, make no effort; many resort to that floundering endeavour to get by accident, gambling; many achieve a precarious and unsatisfactory gathering of possessions, a few houses, a claim on a field, a few hundred pounds in some investment as incalculable as a kite in a gale; just a small minority have and get—for the most part either inheritors of riches or energetic people who, through a real dulness toward the better and nobler aspects of life, can give themselves almost entirely to grabbing and accumulation. To such as these, all common men who are not Socialists do in effect conspire to give the world. . . .

Now not only is it true that the subordination of our affairs to this spirit of gain places our world in the hands of a peculiar, acquisitive, uncreative, wary type of person, and that the mass of people hate serving the spirit of gain and are forced to do so through the obsession of the whole community by this idea of Private Ownership, but it is also true that even now the real driving force that gets the world along is not that spirit at all, but the spirit of service. Even to-day it would be impossible for the world to get along if the mass of its population was really specialized for gain. A world of Rockefellers, Morgans and Rothschilds would perish miserably after a vigorous campaign of mutual skinning; it is only because the common run of men is better than these profit-hunters that any real and human things are achieved.

Peter de Mendelssohn
THE NEW LIBERALISM

It was a fact that the Labour Party by now numbered more than half a million members, nine-tenths of whom came from the Trade Unions. It was a fact also that the Labour Party insisted that the poor and weak must henceforth look after their own interests since the Liberals, despite their professions, showed no more sign of doing so than the Conservatives. That was the reason why the Labour Party had de-

From *The Age of Churchill*, by Peter de Mendelssohn. © Copyright 1961 by Peter de Mendelssohn. Reprinted by permission of Alfred A. Knopf, Inc.

    Peter de Mendelssohn (1908–   ) is a German-born novelist and journalist.

cided that it must exist; and presumably Mr. Mawdsley, had he survived, would now be with them. As he reflected on this, a new scheme of things lit up in Churchill's mind. It was simple, clear-cut, and as fascinating as a military plan of operation.

There were two upheavals threatening—one from the right, the other from the left. There were two major weapons to hand to beat them back, or down, if necessary. Free Trade was the weapon against the threatening revolution from the right; Radicalism was the weapon against that from the left. It was a struggle on two fronts. Between these two fronts there stretched a pathway of organic continuity and reasonable evolutionary progress. Along this road Lloyd George was already marching at a great pace. Churchill made up his mind to catch up with him. He issued himself with marching orders, not sealed but open, and waved them as a flag for everyone to see, as he set out.

On 11 October 1906, Churchill made a speech at St. Andrew's Hall, Glasgow, which immediately revealed his new route. This speech, called "Liberalism and Socialism," is contained in his volume of collected addresses, *Liberalism and the Social Problem*, published when he was just thirty-five. The book, which has never been reprinted, is a source of the first importance; for it contains, on four hundred small pages, Churchill's entire Radical period, and a general exposition of Radical thought such as cannot easily be found in the writings or speeches of any of his Liberal contemporaries. It is a long time since it last received the attention it deserves. . . .

> We are often told that there can be no progress for democracy until the Liberal Party has been destroyed. Let us examine that. Labour in this country exercises a great influence upon the Government. That is not so everywhere. It is not so, for instance, in Germany, and yet in Germany there is no Liberal Party worth speaking of. Labour there is very highly organized, and the Liberal Party there has been destroyed. In Germany there exists exactly the condition of affairs, in a party sense, that Mr. Keir Hardie and his friends are so anxious to introduce here. A great social democratic party, on the one hand, are bluntly and squarely face to face with a capitalist and military confederation on the other. And what is the result? In spite of the great numbers of the Socialist Party in Germany, in spite of the high ability of its leaders, it has hardly any influence whatever upon the course of public affairs. That is rather a disquieting result to working men of having destroyed the Liberal Party.

In short, the Liberal Party was in a far better position to help the workers than any Socialist Party. Indeed, all the Labour movements would be able to do for the workers, managed as it was by visionaries, dreamers, and political adventurers, would be to hurl them into an abyss. "Any violent movement," Churchill proclaimed, "would infallibly encounter an overwhelming resistance" from "millions of persons who would certainly lose by anything like a general overturn." These millions of "haves," in whom resided "the essential stability of modern States," were "everywhere the strongest and best organized millions"; and they would put up an effective resistance which would bring any such movement "to sterility and to destruction." Such a conclusion was correct enough; but the premise was nevertheless a fallacy again. The Labour Party was not nearly as visionary or adventurous as Churchill made it out to be; and it was quite as horrified by the idea of a "general overturn" as was the prophet of doom himself.

But had the Liberals admitted this, it would largely have spoilt their case. This case rested on the assertion that Liberalism in contrast to Socialism proceeded "by courses of moderation," and that these were best suited to the interests of organized workers. "By gradual steps," Churchill said, "by steady effort from day to day, from year to year, Liberalism enlists hundreds of thousands upon the side of progress and popular democratic reform whom militant Socialism would drive into violent Tory reaction. That is why the Tory Party hate us. . . . The cause of the Liberal Party is the cause of the left-out millions; and because we believe that there is in all the world no other instrument of equal potency and efficacy available at the present time for the purposes of social amelioration, we are bound in duty and in honour to guard it from all attacks, whether they arise from violence or from reaction." It was self-evident that the workers had everything to gain from subscribing to Liberal "courses of moderation," and stood to lose all from opposing them with doctrines of militant Socialism.

Still, there was the question of doctrine. Churchill was well aware that it represented a barrier. He therefore proceeded to dismantle it, and remove it piece by piece from the working-man's mind; and this part of his Glasgow speech showed him as a very dexterous dialectician. There was no necessity, he declared, to "plunge into a discussion of the philosophical divergencies between Socialism and Liberalism." Come to think of it, there really was nothing much in them. "It is not possible to draw a hard-and-fast line between individualism and collectivism. You cannot draw it either in theory or in practice. That is where the Socialist makes a mistake. Let us not imitate that mistake. No man can be a collectivist alone or an individualist alone. He must be both an individualist and a collectivist. The nature of man is a dual nature. The character of the organization of human society is dual. For some purposes man must be a collectivist, for others he is, and he will for all time remain, an individualist. . . . Collectively we light our streets and supply ourselves with water. But we do not make love collectively, and the ladies do not marry us collectively. . . ." In short, "no view of society can possibly be complete which does not comprise within its scope both collective organization and individual incentive."

What conclusions must be drawn from this?

There was no denying, Churchill went on, that the whole tendency of civilization was towards the multiplication of the collective functions of society; and this being so there was a danger of all these new services, which by nature were monopolies, passing into private hands. There was anxiety about this, and he shared this anxiety. The only safe and salutary way of avoiding it was to place these collective functions under the control of the State; and there was no reason why the State should not show some creative initiative in this respect; indeed, there was every reason why it should. For once the State had entered this field, there were many excellent things it could do for the general benefit which private initiative could not achieve or perform efficiently. Churchill declared:

> I should like to see the State embark on various novel and adventurous experiments. I am of opinion that the State should increasingly assume the position of the reserve employer of labour. I am very sorry we have not got the railways of this country in our hands. We are all agreed that the State must increasingly and earnestly concern itself with the care of the sick and the aged, and, above all, of the children. I look forward to the universal establishment of minimum standards of life and labour, and their progressive elevation as the increasing energies of production may permit. . . . I do not want to see impaired the vigour of competition, but we can do much to mitigate the consequences of failure. We want to draw a line below which we will not allow persons to live and labour, yet above which they may compete with all the strength of their manhood. We want to have free competition upwards; we decline to allow free competition downwards. We do not want to pull down the structures of science and civilization, but to spread a net over the abyss . . . and I would recommend you not to be scared in discussing any of these proposals, just because some old woman comes along and tells you they are Socialistic.[1]

We must remind ourselves that this was said fifty years ago. Today it may seem to state the obvious. But in the England of 1906 it was an almost desperately bold conception. It went considerably beyond the programme of reform that Campbell-Bannerman and Asquith had in mind, and far beyond anything Asquith and Lloyd George were eventually able to achieve. Some of its features remained pious hopes for forty years. State-ownership of the railways and other public utilities was not achieved until 1947; and it was achieved by a Labour Government which remained unmoved by Churchill's reproach that it was following a course

[1] Speech at St. Andrew's Hall, Glasgow, 11 October 1906, reprinted in *Liberalism and the Social Problem*, pp. 67–84.

dictated by social prejudice and doctrinaire theory. "We have not been elected," said Mr. Attlee, "to patch up an old system but to make something new."[2] It was not as new as all that, as he and Churchill well knew.

In 1945, it was Socialism. In 1906, Churchill did his best to prove that it was not. But if it wasn't, what was it?

It was pure Lloyd Georgian Radicalism. Only coming from the lips of Winston Churchill, scion of the aristocracy, it was no rousing Welsh sermon, but had the measured tones of Disraeli. "An insular people," wrote Disraeli, "subject to fogs and possessing a powerful middle-class, requires grave statesmen." It was characteristic of Churchill to have perceived this.[3] The ideas of the Glasgow speech were hardly his own. They had been in the air for some time. The Webbs had been preaching them tirelessly for years; and there was growing literature about them. It was not difficult to sniff them up. But they belonged to a world which until very recently had been totally alien to Churchill; in which he had shown no interest; and where he was supported by no personal experience. Yet with him they fell on peculiarly fertile soil. His contemporaries in the Liberal Party recognized with much admiration and not a little envy that this novice formulated their concepts with greater polish, and argued their case more effectively than they had been able to do themselves. How was it done, and was it genuine? They wondered, and were never quite sure.

[2] C. R. Attlee: *As It Happened*, p. 163.
[3] Churchill quoted the phrase (which is from Disraeli's *Endymion*) in *Lord Randolph Churchill*, p. 497.

Gustav Stolper
THE ECONOMIC "MIRACLE"

The "economic miracle" is even less miraculous than the military achievement of the Nazis. In fact, compared with what the German Republic accomplished in the 1920's, the economic performance of the Nazis in the 1930's is hardly impressive.

From *This Age of Fable* by Gustav Stolper, pp. 319–320, 325–327. Copyright, 1942, by Gustav Stolper. Reprinted by permission of Harcourt, Brace & World, Inc.

Gustav Stolper (1888–1947) was an Austrian economist and writer.

Hitler abolished unemployment. So did Stalin. So did Mussolini. So did Winston Churchill and Franklin D. Roosevelt. So does every country that bends all its efforts to war economy irrespective of costs. There was no unemployment in Germany from 1914 to 1918. There was little unemployment during the inflation boom. There was hardly any real unemployment in the genuine boom of the Republican 1920's. But an armament boom never creates prosperity. It can be borne by every nation without impairment of its living-standard to the limits of its idle reserves in man power and resources. Beyond this point it is bound to lower the living-standard of the people, no matter how much money the average worker receives in his weekly envelope.

The German industries and the German genius for organization once more performed marvels, not because it was Nazi, but because it was German, the same genius that has performed similar miracles time and again, the same genius that made Germany in the last decades before the First World War the leading industrial Power of Europe, the same genius that brought back the industrial leadership to Germany in the 1920's. And like the reconstruction of the army, the reconstruction of industry was accomplished by the same old people brought up at educational institutions of the pre-Nazi era in which sciences blossomed and discovery and invention enjoyed every encouragement, freedom, and incentive—without which they cannot thrive or indeed survive. What so far has saved Germany industrially is the fact that the Nazi regime has lasted only eight years. Another decade of this regime, which has already ruined the German universities and intellectually and morally crippled the adolescent generation, would do away with the remnants of the past that may save Germany when the "Future" is over.

The German reality ["economic miracle"] freed from the confusion of emotional ignorance is simple enough. When the Hitler regime came to power, it embarked on a program of outright inflation, continuing on a large scale the technique of tax anticipation notes introduced under the Papen regime. A vast program of public works was launched—roads, railway equipment, housing, land reclamation, and so forth. It was initially financed by more or less direct resort to Central Bank credit, not by either loans or taxes. At the same time, the labor supply was diminished by the withdrawal of women from employment and subsidies for marriage conditional on the retirement of the bride from her job. Work was spread by reducing hours, many hundreds of thousands of boys were called into labor camps, other hundreds of thousands were sent to concentration camps. Thus in two years unemployment fell from 6,000,000 to 2,600,000. Inflationist effects were prevented from the very beginning by a well-co-ordinated system of restrictions rigidly enforced by police terror.

These restrictions were: First, the complete separation of the German world from the world outside. The foreign exchange value of the mark was what the Government said it was. There was no such thing as a market for German currency, because no German currency could be offered for sale without a license from the Reichsbank, and no one abroad would buy German marks unless he was assured in advance by the Reichsbank that he could use the mark for certain purchases in Germany.

Second, at the same time the Government enlarged its own resources of foreign exchange, both by open default on all foreign obligations and by outright confiscation of all foreign assets of German Jews and other politically persecuted groups, as far as the Government could get hold of them.

Third, German exports were forced onto world markets by lavish subsidies, incidentally greatly aided by the fortunate fact that world markets after 1932 were once more in the recovery phase.

Fourth, while exports into countries with free currencies were encouraged, imports were largely drawn from poorer Southeastern countries utterly dependent on the German market, which therefore involuntarily became the new creditors of Germany, for they never received the promised compensation in manufactured goods.

Fifth, while thus Germany's economic relations with the outside world were kept under control, inflationist effects at home were nipped in the bud. The Government simply decreed that wages should not be raised above the level of 1933. Therefore the income of the working class could only rise parallel with the output. The income of a worker's family could expand (and did expand), though only with the growing number of hours worked or with the growing number of family members working at the same rates.

Even these measures, however, would not suffice unless there was also direct control of the entire economic process. It was not enough to cut off German money completely from possible foreign interference, to establish a watertight foreign-trade monopoly equaled in effectiveness only by the Russians, and to fix wage rates. It was also necessary on a rapidly expanding scale to fix prices and even to direct production by prescribing not only what must, and must not, be produced but even the methods and techniques to be applied, and finally even the channels of distribution.

In the first two years of the Nazi regime the financial methods and the methods used in combating unemployment were rather primitive. Nevertheless, among the first steps taken by the regime was the suppression of any information about the national budget or the national debt. No one even before this war knew how much the Government spent, how large the deficit or the debt actually was. (The guesses differed by huge margins.) But the "real thing" came in 1935 with the military conscription, when the Government openly started the greatest armament drive of all time. Even so, full employment was not reached until the spring of 1938.

By that time, German economy was completely socialized in everything except the emptied title to property. By that time the financial problem of Germany had ceased to exist. A socialist economy has no financial problem. If both production and distribution are directed and controlled by the Government, money is no more than a vehicle for the movement of goods. It has lost its dynamic function, which it can exercise only in a system of more or less free markets. If money cannot buy anything because the goods desired are not offered for sale, then the money readily flows back to its source; whether it is pumped back by taxes or by forced loans does not matter. In a free country the citizen in possession of money is free to compete with his Government for the available goods. In the shadow of gallows and concentration camps such an idea would cross the mind of a German only in a nightmare.

A. J. P. Taylor
DIPLOMACY AND THE NEW ECONOMICS

In 1929 the system of security against Germany, devised in the treaty of Versailles, was still complete. Germany was disarmed; the Rhineland was demilitarised; the victors were ostensibly united; and the system was reinforced by the authority of the League of Nations. Seven years later all this had gone without a blow being struck. International stability was first shaken by the collapse of economic stability in the great Depression which began in October 1929. The Depression had little to do with the preceding war, though men did not think so at the time. It had nothing to do with the surviving provisions of the peace-treaty. The Depression was started by the collapse of a speculative boom in the United States; and the unemployment which followed was swelled by the failure of purchasing power to keep pace with the increased resources of production. Everyone understands this now; just as they know that the way out

From *The Origins of the Second World War* by A. J. P. Taylor. Copyright © 1961 by A. J. P. Taylor, Hamish Hamilton, London, and Atheneum Publishers, N.Y.

of a depression is to increase government spending. In 1929 hardly anyone knew it; and the few who did had no influence on policy. It was generally believed that deflation was the only cure. There must be sound money, balanced budgets, cuts in government expenditure, and reductions in wages. Then, presumably, prices would somehow become low enough for people to start buying again.

This policy caused hardship and discontent in every country where it was applied. There was no reason why it should cause international tension. In most countries the Depression led to a turning-away from international affairs. In Great Britain the lowest arms-estimates between the wars were introduced by Neville Chamberlain, chancellor of the exchequer in the National government, in 1932. The French became even less assertive than they had been before. American policy under F. D. Roosevelt became in 1933 markedly more isolationist than it had been under his Republican predecessor. Germany was a special case. The Germans had experienced the terrible evils of inflation in 1923, and now went equally far in the opposite direction. Most Germans regarded this as inevitable; but the results were highly unpopular. Everyone applauded the measures when applied to others, yet resented them when applied to himself. The Reichstag failed to provide a majority for a deflationist government, though such a government was what it wanted. As a result Brüning governed Germany for more than two years without a majority, imposing deflation by presidential decree. High-minded and sincere, he would not win popularity by mitigating the rigours of deflation; but his government sought popularity by success in foreign affairs. Curtius, his foreign minister, tried to carry economic union with Austria in 1931—a project which offered no economic advantage; and Treviranus, another member of his government, started an agitation against the Polish frontier. In 1932 Papen, Brüning's successor, demanded equality of armaments for Germany. All these things were irrelevant to the economic difficulties, but the ordinary German could not be expected to understand this. He had been told for years that all his troubles were due to the treaty of Versailles; and now that he was in trouble he believed what he had been told. Moreover the Depression removed the strongest argument for doing nothing: prosperity. Men who are well off forget their grievances; in adversity they have nothing else to think about.

The Western powers made two mistakes. They failed to allow for the fact that Hitler was a gambler who would play for high stakes with inadequate resources. They also failed to allow for the economic achievement of Schacht, who ensured that German resources were less inadequate than they would otherwise have been. Countries with the more or less free economy of the time operated to 75% of their efficiency. Schacht first worked the system of full employment and so used German economic power almost to capacity. This is all commonplace now. It seemed wizardry beyond imagination then.

The British government feared to offend economic principle even more than to offend Hitler. The secret of Pandora's box which Schacht had opened in Germany and which the American New Deal had also revealed, was still unknown to them. Wedded to stable prices and a stable pound, they regarded increased public spending as a great evil, excusable only in the event of actual war, and even then lamentable. They had no inkling that public spending on anything, even on armaments, brought with it increased prosperity. Like nearly all contemporary economists except of course J. M. Keynes, they still treated public finance as though it were the finance of a private individual. When an individual spends money on wasteful objects, he has less to spend elsewhere, and there is less "demand". When the state spends money, this creates an increased "demand", and therefore increased prosperity, throughout the community. This is obvious to us now. Few knew it then. Before we condemn Baldwin and Neville Chamberlain too contemptuously, we should reflect that even in 1959 an economist was elevated to the House of Lords for preaching the very doctrine of public miserliness which stultified British policy before 1939. Perhaps we are not more enlightened; merely more fearful of the popular explosion which would be caused if the economists got their way, and there was a return to mass unemployment. Before 1939 this unemployment was regarded as a law of nature; and the government could claim, in all sincerity, that there were no unused resources in the country when nearly two million men remained unemployed.

Here again, Hitler had a great advantage over the democratic countries. His principal achievement was the conquest of unemployment; and most Germans did not mind what heretical methods he used, so long as he did it. Moreover, even if German bankers objected, they had no effective means of saying so. When Schacht himself grew anxious, he could only resign; and few Germans cared. A dictatorship like Hitler's could escape the usual consequences of inflation. Since there were no trade unions, wages could be kept stable, and prices too; while a rigorous exchange control—backed by the weapons of terror and the secret police—prevented any depreciation of the mark. The British government still lived in the psychological atmosphere of 1931: more terrified of a flight from the pound than of defeat in war. Its measures of rearmament were therefore determined less by strategic need, even if that had been known, than by what the taxpayer would stand; and he, constantly assured that the government had already made Great Britain strong, would not stand much. Limitation of income-tax, and the confidence of the City of London, came first; armaments came second. Under such circumstances, it is not necessary to invoke the opposition of the Labour party in order to understand why British preparations for war before 1939 lagged behind those of Gemany. The wonder is rather that, when war came, Great Britain was as well prepared as she was—a triumph of scientific and technical ingenuity over the economists.

John Maynard Keynes
THE KEYNESIAN REVOLUTION

We have magneto trouble. How, then, can we start up again? Let us trace events backwards:—

1. Why are workers and plant unemployed? Because industrialists do not expect to be able to sell without loss what would be produced if they were employed.

2. Why cannot industrialists expect to sell without loss? Because prices have fallen more than costs have fallen—indeed, costs have fallen very little.

3. How can it be that prices have fallen more than costs? For costs are what a business man pays out for the production of his commodity, and prices determine what he gets back when he sells it. It is easy to understand how for an individual business or an individual commodity these can be unequal. But surely for the community as a whole the business men get back the same amount as they put out, since what the business men pay out in the course of production constitutes the incomes of the public which they pay back to the business men in exchange for the products of the latter? For this is what we understand by the normal circle of production, exchange, and consumption.

4. No! Unfortunately this is not so; and here is the root of the trouble. It is not true that what the business men pay out as costs of production necessarily comes back to them as the sale-proceeds of what they produce. It is the characteristic of a boom that their sale-proceeds exceed their costs; and it is the characteristic of a slump that their costs

From *Essays in Persuasion* by John Maynard Keynes, pp. 140–146, 150–154. Reprinted by permission of Harcourt, Brace & World, Inc.

John Maynard Keynes (1883–1946) was the most influential economist of the twentieth century. His book, *The General Theory of Employment, Interest, and Money*, written in 1936, revolutionized economic thinking.

exceed their sale-proceeds. Moreover, it is a delusion to suppose that they can necessarily restore equilibrium by reducing their total costs, whether it be by restricting their output or cutting rates of remuneration; for the reduction of their outgoings may, by reducing the purchasing power of the earners who are also their customers, diminish their sale-proceeds by a nearly equal amount.

5. How, then, can it be that the total costs of production for the world's business as a whole can be unequal to the total sale-proceeds? Upon what does the inequality depend? I think that I know the answer. But it is too complicated and unfamiliar for me to expound it here satisfactorily. (Elsewhere I have tried to expound it accurately.) So I must be somewhat perfunctory.

Let us take, first of all, the consumption-goods which come on to the market for sale. Upon what do the profits (or losses) of the producers of such goods depend? The total costs of production, which are the same thing as the community's total earnings looked at from another point of view, are divided in a certain proportion between the cost of consumption-goods and the cost of capital-goods. The incomes of the public, which are again the same thing as the community's total earnings, are also divided in a certain proportion between expenditure on the purchase of consumption-goods and savings. Now if the first proportion is larger than the second, producers of consumption-goods will *lose* money; for their sale proceeds, which are equal to the expenditure of the public on consumption-goods, will be less (as a little thought will show) than what these goods have cost them to produce. If, on the other hand, the second proportion is larger than the first, then the producers of consumption-goods will make exceptional *gains*. It follows that the profits of the producers of consumption-goods can only be restored, either by the public spending a larger proportion of their incomes on such goods (which means saving less), or by a larger proportion of production taking the form of capital-goods (since this means a smaller proportionate output of consumption-goods).

But capital-goods will not be produced on a larger scale unless the producers of such goods are making a profit. So we come to our second question—upon what do the profits of the producers of capital-goods depend? They depend on whether the public prefer to keep their savings liquid in the shape of money or its equivalent or to use them to buy capital-goods or the equivalent. If the public are reluctant to buy the latter, then the producers of capital-goods will make a loss; consequently less capital-goods will be produced; with the result that, for the reasons given above, producers of consumption-goods will also make a loss. In other words, *all* classes of producers will tend to make a loss; and general unemployment will ensue. By this time a vicious circle will be set up, and, as the result of a series of actions and reactions, matters will get worse and worse until something happens to turn the tide.

This is an unduly simplified picture of a complicated phenomenon. But I believe that it contains the essential truth. Many variations and fugal embroideries and orchestrations can be superimposed; but this is the tune.

If, then, I am right, the fundamental cause of the trouble is the lack of new enterprise due to an unsatisfactory market for capital investment. Since trade is international, an insufficient output of new capital-goods in the world as a whole affects the prices of commodities everywhere and hence the profits of producers in all countries alike.

Why is there an insufficient output of new capital-goods in the world as a whole? It is due, in my opinion, to a conjunction of several causes. In the first instance, it was due to the attitude of lenders—for new capital-goods are produced to a large extent with borrowed money. Now it is due to the attitude of borrowers, just as much as to that of lenders.

For several reasons lenders were, and are, asking higher terms for loans than new enterprise can afford. First, the fact, that enterprise could afford high rates for some time after the war whilst war wastage was being made good, accustomed lenders to expect much higher rates than before the war. Second, the existence of political borrowers to meet Treaty obligations, of banking borrowers to support newly restored gold standards, of speculative borrowers to take part in Stock Exchange booms, and, latterly, of distress borrowers to meet the losses which they have incurred through the fall of prices, all of whom were ready if necessary to pay almost any terms, have hitherto enabled lenders to secure from these various classes of borrowers higher rates than it is possible for genuine new enterprise to support. Third, the unsettled state of the world and national investment habits have restricted the countries in which many lenders are prepared to invest on any reasonable terms at all. A large proportion of the globe is, for one reason or another, distrusted by lenders, so that they exact a premium for risk so great as to strangle new enterprise altogether. For the last two years, two out of the three principal creditor nations of the world, namely, France and the United States, have largely withdrawn their resources from the international market for long-term loans.

Meanwhile, the reluctant attitude of lenders has become matched by a hardly less reluctant attitude on the part of borrowers. For the fall of prices has been disastrous to those who have borrowed, and any one who has postponed new enterprise has gained by his delay. Moreover, the risks that frighten lenders frighten borrowers too. Finally, in the United States, the vast scale on which new capital enterprise has been undertaken in the last five years has somewhat exhausted for the time being—at any rate so long as the atmosphere of business depression continues—the profitable opportunities for yet further enterprise. By the middle of 1929 new capital undertakings were already on an inadequate scale in the world as a whole, outside the United States. The culminating blow has been the collapse of new investment inside the United States, which to-day is probably 20 to 30 per cent less than it was in 1928. Thus in certain countries the opportunity for new profitable investment is more limited than it was; whilst in others it is more risky.

A wide gulf, therefore, is set between the ideas of lenders and the ideas of borrowers for the purpose of genuine new capital investment; with the result that the savings of the lenders are being used up in financing business losses and distress borrowers, instead of financing new capital works.

At this moment the slump is probably a little overdone for psychological reasons. A modest upward reaction, therefore, may be due at any time. But there cannot be a real recovery, in my judgement, until the ideas of lenders and the ideas of productive borrowers are brought together again; partly by lenders becoming ready to lend on easier terms and over a wider geographical field, partly by borrowers recovering their good spirits and so becoming readier to borrow.

It is beyond the scope of this essay to indicate lines of future policy. But no one can take the first step except the central banking authorities of the chief creditor countries; nor can any one Central Bank do enough acting in isolation. Resolute action by the Federal Reserve Banks of the United States, the Bank of France, and the Bank of England might do much more than most people, mistaking symptoms or aggravating circumstances for the disease itself, will readily believe. In every way the most effective remedy would be that the Central Banks of these three great creditor nations should join together in a bold scheme to restore confidence to the international long-term loan market; which would serve to revive enterprise and activity everywhere, and to restore prices and profits, so that in due course the wheels of the world's commerce would go round again.

The worst of it is that we have one excellent excuse for doing nothing. To a large extent the cure lies outside our own power. The problem is an international one, and for a country which depends on foreign trade as much as we do there are narrow limits to what we can achieve by ourselves. But this is not the only reason why we are inactive. Nor is it a sufficient reason. For something we can do by ourselves. The other principal reason, in my opinion, is a serious misunderstanding as to what kind of action is useful and what kind is not. There are to-day many well-wishers of their country who believe that the most useful thing which they and their neighbours can do to mend the situation is to *save* more than usual. If they refrain from spending a larger proportion of their incomes than usual they believe that they will have helped employment. If they are members of Town or County Councils they believe that their right course at such a time as this is to oppose expenditure on new amenities or new public works.

Now, in certain circumstances all this would be quite right, but in present circumstances, unluckily, it is quite wrong. It is utterly harmful and misguided—the very opposite of the truth. For the object of saving is to release labour for employment on producing capital-goods such as houses, factories, roads, machines, and the like. But if there is a large unemployed surplus already available for such purposes, then the effect of saving is merely to add to this surplus and therefore to increase the number of the unemployed. Moreover, when a man is thrown out of work in this or any other way, his diminished spending power causes further unemployment amongst those who would have produced what he can no longer afford to buy. And so the position gets worse and worse in a vicious circle.

The best guess I can make is that whenever you save five shillings, you put a man out of work for a day. Your saving that five shillings adds to unemployment to the extent of one man for one day—and so on in proportion. On the other hand, whenever you buy goods you increase employment—though they must be British, home-produced goods if you are to increase employment in this country. After all, this is only the plainest common sense. For if you buy goods, some one will have to make them. And if you do not buy goods, the shops will not clear their stocks, they will not give repeat orders, and some one will be thrown out of work.

For take the extreme case. Suppose we were to stop spending our incomes altogether, and were to save the lot. Why, every one would be out of work. And before long we should nave no incomes to spend. No one would be a penny the richer, and the end would be that we should all starve to death—which would surely serve us right for refusing to buy things from one another, for refusing to take in one another's washing, since that is how we all live. The same is true, and even more so, of the work of a local authority. Now is the time for municipalities to be busy and active with all kinds of sensible improvements.

The patient does not need rest. He needs exercise. You cannot set men to work by holding back, by refusing to place orders, by inactivity. On the contrary, activity of one kind or another is the only possible means of making the wheels of economic progress and of the production of wealth go round again.

Nationally, too, I should like to see schemes of greatness and magnificence designed and carried through. I read a few days ago of a proposal to drive a great new road, a broad boulevard, parallel to the Strand, on the south side of the Thames, as a new thoroughfare joining Westminster to the City. That is the right sort of notion. But I should like to see something bigger still. For example, why not pull down the whole of South London from Westminster to Greenwich, and make a good job of it—housing on that convenient area near to their work a much greater population than at present, in far better buildings with all the conveniences of modern life, yet at the same time providing hundreds of acres of squares and avenues, parks and public spaces, having, when it was finished, something magnificent to the eye, yet useful and convenient to human life as a monument to our age. Would that employ men? Why, of course it would! Is it better that the men should stand idle and miserable, drawing the dole? Of course it is not.

John Kenneth Galbraith
THE AFFLUENT SOCIETY

Up to twenty or twenty-five years ago—say the middle years of the thirties—the broad impact of economic ideas was clear. It could not but leave a man with a sense of the depth, pervasiveness, and burden of the economic problem and, on the whole, with the improbability of a happy outcome. "Depend on it," Dr. Johnson observed, "when a man knows he is going to be hanged in a fortnight, it concentrates his mind wonderfully."[1] For the same reasons men's minds were focused on the perils of economic life.

In particular, although it was no longer the lesson of the central economic tradition that men would starve, neither was it the lesson that they would do very well. Privation was still normal. Men might lift themselves by lifting their marginal product; with increasing efficiency and increasing supplies of capital, marginal productivity and hence wages might rise. But no one could suppose that the result could be more than barely adequate. Certainly no one could suggest that any opportunity for

From *The Affluent Society* by John Kenneth Galbraith, pp. 67–68, 109–112, 224–226, 244–246. Reprinted by permission of the publisher, Houghton Mifflin Company.

John Kenneth Galbraith (1908–   ) is professor of economics at Harvard University.

[1] The saying owes its modern fame to Winston Churchill, who noted that his mind had been so focused by the prospect of the invasion of Britain in 1940.

such improvement could be overlooked. On the contrary, to relax such effort in the slightest would be extreme social dereliction. The privation, already great, would be greater—and unnecessarily so. The man of conscience and compassion must see that efficiency is increased by all possible means. To do less was to be profoundly callous, even cruel.

Privation is also enhanced by the intransigent inequality of the income. The miserable consumption of the poor is partly the result of the ostentatious demands of the rich. There isn't enough for both, and the latter get far more than they need. If possible, something should be done about inequality, for no sensitive man could be indifferent to the social strains and conflicts that it was producing and seemed likely to produce as the proletariat became increasingly conscious of its inferior position. But could anything serious really be done about it?

Finally, there was the nerve-racking problem of insecurity. The competitive model made episodic unemployment for the worker, and occasional insolvency for the farmer or businessman, a part of the system. This insecurity was enhanced by the growing severity of depressions and now in the thirties by the most devastating depression of all. This latter was especially troublesome because the contemporary theory dismissed it as self-correcting. If self-correcting it was inevitable, and if inevitable it was intolerable.

Clearly there was much to bring productivity, inequality, and insecurity to the center of men's minds and to make them a preoccupying concern. And if there was any tendency in the central tradition of economics to conclude that all might in the end work out for the best, there were also voices from the wings to say it couldn't be so. From the right was the echo of the Social Darwinists saying struggle is not only inevitable but good. From the Marxist world, in tones of thunderous conviction, came the warning that the inequality and the insecurity would increase and increase until, in the end, their victims would destroy the whole edifice and, by implication, quite a few of its favored inhabitants.

These—productivity, inequality, and insecurity—were the ancient preoccupations of economics. They were never more its preoccupations than in the nineteen-thirties as the subject stood in a great valley facing, all unknowingly, a mountainous rise in well-being. We have now had that mountainous rise. In very large measure the older preoccupations remain. We should scarcely be surprised. This pre-eminently is an occasion when we would expect the conventional wisdom to lose touch with the reality. It has not disappointed us. . . .

We are curiously unreasonable in the distinctions we make between different kinds of goods and services. We view the production of some of the most frivolous goods with pride. We regard the production of some of the most significant and civilizing services with regret.

Economists in calculating the total output of the economy—in arriving at the now familiar Gross National Product—add together the value of all goods and all services of whatever sort and by whomsoever produced. No distinction is made between public and privately produced services. An increased supply of educational services has a standing in the total not different in kind from an increased output of television receivers. Nothing, however, could be more in conflict with popular attitudes, and indeed it is rather surprising that economists have not been reproached by the rather considerable number of individuals who, if they fully understood the nature of the calculation, would regard the inclusion of government spending as subversive.

In the general view it is privately produced production that is important, and that nearly alone. This adds to national well-being. Its increase measures the increase in national wealth. Public services, by comparison, are an incubus. They are necessary, and they may be necessary in considerable volume. But they are a burden which must, in effect, be carried by the private production. If that burden is too great, private production will stagger and fall.

At best public services are a necessary evil; at worst they are a malign tendency against which an alert community must exercise eternal vigilance. Even when they serve the most important ends, such services are sterile. "Government is powerless to create anything in the sense in which business produces wealth. . . ."[2]

Such attitudes lead to some interesting contradictions. Automobiles have an importance greater than the roads on which they are driven. We welcome expansion of telephone services as improving the general well-being but accept curtailment of postal services as signifying necessary economy. We set great store by the increase in private wealth but regret the added outlays for the police force by which it is protected. Vacuum cleaners to insure clean houses are praiseworthy and essential in our standard of living. Street cleaners to insure clean streets are an unfortunate expense. Partly as a result, our houses are generally clean and our streets generally filthy. In the more sophisticated of the conventional wisdom, this distinction between public and private services is much less sharp and, as I have observed, it does not figure in the calculation of Gross National Product. However, it never quite disappears. Even among economists and political philosophers, public services rarely lose their connotation of burden. Although they may be defended, their volume and quality are almost never a source of pride.

There are a number of reasons for these attitudes, but again tradition plays a dominant role. In the world into which economics was

2 Francis X. Sutton, Seymour E. Harris, Carl Kaysen, and James Tobin, *The American Business Creed* (Cambridge, Mass.: Harvard University Press, 1956), p. 195.

born the four most urgent requirements of man were food, clothing and shelter, and an orderly environment in which the first three might be provided. The first three lent themselves to private production for the market; given good order, this process has ordinarily gone forward with tolerable efficiency. But order which was the gift of government was nearly always supplied with notable unreliability. With rare exceptions it was also inordinately expensive. And the pretext of providing order not infrequently afforded the occasion for rapacious appropriation of the means of sustenance of the people.

Not surprisingly, modern economic ideas incorporated a strong suspicion of government. The goal of nineteenth-century economic liberalism was a state which did provide order reliably and inexpensively and which did as little as possible else. Even Marx intended that the state should wither away. These attitudes have persisted in the conventional wisdom. And again events have dealt them a series of merciless blows. Once a society has provided itself with food, clothing, and shelter, all of which so fortuitously lend themselves to private production, purchase, and sale, its members begin to desire other things. And a remarkable number of these things do not lend themselves to such production, purchase, and sale. They must be provided for everyone if they are to be provided for anyone, and they must be paid for collectively or they cannot be had at all. Such is the case with streets and police and the general advantages of mass literacy and sanitation, the control of epidemics, and the common defense. There is a bare possibility that the services which must be rendered collectively, although they enter the general scheme of wants after the immediate physical necessities, increase in urgency more than proportionately with increasing wealth. This is more likely if increasing wealth is matched by increasing population and increasing density of population. Nonetheless these services, although they reflect increasingly urgent desires, remain under the obloquy of the unreliability, incompetence, cost, and pretentious interference of princes. Alcohol, comic books and mouth wash all bask under the superior reputation of the market. Schools, judges, and municipal swimming pools lie under the evil reputation of bad kings.

Moreover, bad kings in a poorer world showed themselves to be quite capable, in their rapacity, of destroying or damaging the production of private goods by destroying the people and the capital that produced them. Economies are no longer so vulnerable. Governments are not so undiscriminating. In western countries in modern times economic growth and expanding public activity have, with rare exceptions, gone together. Each has served the other as indeed they must. Yet the conventional wisdom is far from surrendering on the point. Any growth in public services is a manifestation of an intrinsically evil trend. If the vigor of the race is not in danger, liberty is. And this may be threatened even by the activities of the local school board. The structure of the economy may also be at stake. In one branch of the conventional wisdom the American economy is never far removed from socialism, and the movement toward socialism may be measured by the rise in public spending. Thus even the most neutral of public services, for one part of the population, fall under the considerable handicap of being identified with social revolution.

Finally—also a closely related point—the payment for publicly produced services has long been linked to the problem of inequality. By having the rich pay more, the services were provided and at the same time the goal of greater equality was advanced. This community of objectives has never appealed to those being equalized. Not unnaturally, some part of their opposition has been directed to the public services themselves. By attacking these, they could attack the leveling tendencies of taxation. This has helped to keep alive the notion that the public services for which they pay are inherently inferior to privately produced goods.

While public services have been subject to these negative attitudes, private goods have had no such attention. On the contrary, their virtues have been extolled by the massed drums of modern advertising. They have been pictured as the ultimate wealth of the community. Clearly the competition between public and private services, apart from any question of the satisfactions they render, is an unequal one. The social consequences of this discrimination—this tendency to accord a superior prestige to private goods and an inferior role to public production—are considerable and even grave. . . .

The argument over the progressive income tax has long been concerned with its effect on efficiency. Some have argued that it impairs incentives to increased efficiency. Others have argued that it does not. But if efficiency is not decisive, then the debate must go forward on other grounds. These may well include the simple and uncouth question of who is to pay how much. However, it is with this question that many who now talk about efficiency are really concerned.

Moreover, if efficiency is no longer a prime criterion, tariff policy will have to be resolved on the basis of how far we should go in making trade the handmaiden of larger national policy or what part compassion should play in easing the problems of distressed industries or areas. But, in fact, trade policy is already partly subordinate to both international comity and local charity. Efficiency has already partly surrendered to these other and more urgent considerations.

If the modern corporation must manufacture not only goods but the desire for the goods it manufactures, the efficiency of the first part of this activity ceases to be decisive. One could indeed argue that human happiness would be as effectively advanced by inefficiency in want creation as efficiency in production. Under these circumstances, the relation of the modern corporation to the people who comprise it—their chance for dignity, individuality, and full development of personality—may be at least as important as its efficiency. These may be worth having even at higher cost of production. Evidently the unions, in seeking to make life tolerable on the job, were being governed by a sound instinct. Why should life be intolerable to make things of small urgency?

Attitudes toward the declining community may need to be revised. The happiness and contentment of the people of Lawrence and Lowell and their preference, remarkable as it may seem, for life in these ancient towns, now becomes a consideration to set against the efficiency with which they are employed. The rational and compassionate society may seek to avoid the heartbreaks of an industrial Diaspora. If the goods have ceased to be urgent, can we sternly command men to leave their homes to produce them with maximum efficiency?

Coal has numerous substitutes. The marginal urgency of its present employments is low. The workers who made their life more livable at the expense of the most efficient production of coal may well have had reason on their side. In any case the substitutes—oil, water power, and atomic energy—are cleaner and more pleasant to work with.

The Benthamite test of public policy was "what serves the greatest happiness of the greatest number," and happiness was more or less implicitly identified with productivity. This is still the official test. In modern times the test has not been very rigorously applied. We have sensed though we have not recognized the declining importance of goods. Yet even in its deteriorated form we cling to this criterion. It is so much simpler than to substitute the other tests—compassion, individual happiness and well-being, the minimization of community or other social tensions—which now become relevant. . . .

Even though the higher urgency of the services for social balance are conceded, there is still the problem of providing the revenue. And since it is income taxes that must be used, the question of social balance can easily be lost sight of in the reopened argument over equality. The truce will be broken and liberals and conservatives will join battle on this issue and forget about the poverty in the public services that awaits correction and, as we shall see presently, the poverty of people which can only be corrected at increased public cost. All this—schools, hospitals, even the scientific research on which increased production depends—must wait while we debate the ancient and unresolvable question of whether the rich are too rich.

The only hope—and in the nature of things it rests primarily with liberals—is to separate the issue of equality from that of social balance. The second is by far the more important question. The fact that a tacit truce exists on the issue of inequality is proof of its comparative lack of social urgency. In the past the liberal politician has countered the conservative proposal for reduction in top-bracket income taxes with the proposal that relief be confined to the lower brackets. And he has insisted that any necessary tax increase be carried more than proportionately by the higher-income brackets. The result has been to make him a co-conspirator with the conservative in reducing taxes, whatever the cost in social balance; and his insistence on making taxes an instrument of greater equality has made it difficult or impossible to increase them. Meanwhile, the individual with whom he sympathizes and whom he seeks to favor are no longer the tax-ridden poor of Bengal or the first Empire but people who, by all historical standards, are themselves comparatively opulent citizens. In any case, they would be among the first beneficiaries of the better education, health, housing, and other services which would be the fruits of improved social balance, and they would be the long-run beneficiaries of more nearly adequate investment in people.

The rational liberal, in the future, will resist tax reduction, even that which ostensibly favors the poor, if it is at the price of social balance. And, for the same reason, he will not hesitate to accept increases that are neutral as regards the distribution of income. His classical commitment to greater equality can far better be kept by attacking as a separate issue the more egregious of the loopholes in the present tax laws. These loopholes—preferential treatment of capital gains and the special depletion allowances for mineral, including in particular oil, recovery—are strongly in conflict with traditional liberal attitudes, for this is inequality sanctioned by the state. There is work enough here for any egalitarian crusader.

While there is much that the federal government must do by way of redressing balance, it is in state and local services that the imbalance is most striking. Here, however, the solution—although it involves another wrench in liberal attitudes—is most clear. It involves much expanded use of the sales tax.

So long as social balance is imperfect there should be no hesitation in urging high rates. Coverage should be general on consumer products and services. In the affluent society no useful distinction can be made between luxuries and necessaries. Food and clothing are as difficult as ever to do without. But they can be and frequently are among the most opulent of expenditures.

The relation of the sales tax to the problem of social balance is admirably direct. The community is affluent in privately produced goods. It is poor in public services. The obvious solution is to tax the former to provide the latter—by making private goods more expensive, public goods are made more abundant. Motion pictures, electronic entertainment, and cigarettes are made more costly so that schools can be more handsomely supported. We pay more for soap, detergents, and vacuum cleaners in order that we may have cleaner cities and less occasion to use them. We have more expensive cars and gasoline so that we may have highways and streets on which to drive them. Food being comparatively cheap and abundant, we tax it in order to have better medical services and better health in which to enjoy it. This forthright solution has the further advantage that sales taxation can be employed with fair efficiency by states and even by cities. It is in the services rendered by these governments that the problem of social balance is especially severe. The yield of the sales tax increases with increasing production. As wants are contrived for private goods more revenues are provided for public use. The general property tax, the principal alternative to the sales tax, is rigid and inflexible. Since its rates must ordinarily be raised for additional services, including those that are associated with increasing income and product, the burden of proving need is especially heavy. This tax is a poor servant of social balance.

During the present century the use of sales taxation by states and cities has been growing. Liberals have ordinarily resisted its use. At a minimum they have viewed it with grave misgiving. This has again made the liberal the effective enemy of social balance. The reasons for this opposition provide an interesting example of how ideas, as they remain stereotyped in face of change, can force those who hold them into roles inconsistent with their own professions. The American liberal has been, all things considered, the opponent of better schools, better communities, better urban communications, and indeed even of greater economic stability.

The effect of a sales tax varies greatly as between a poor and an affluent country, and the difference is one not of degree but of kind. Under the *ancien régime* in France the tax on salt achieved an enduring reputation for its oppressiveness which it retains in parts of modern India to this day. In the United States a tax on salt, even one that doubled or trebled its price, would work no perceptible hardship. It is not that salt is more dispensable now than in the day of the *gabelle*. But where it was then a major object of expenditure it is now an insignificant one. And where the price of salt once affected visibly and directly what remained for other use, it is now too small to have a noticeable effect.

As with salt so with other things. In a family which can buy only bread and cloth, a tax on bread and clothing means that children will be hungrier and less well clad. In a family which can buy many things the adjustment comes at the margin in spending for gasoline, installment payments, the races, or the quality of the ceremonial steak.

Thus does affluence alter the case against sales taxation. It will be argued that some people are still very poor. The sales tax, unlike the income tax, weighs heavily on the small consumption of such individuals. But if the income tax is unavailable or in service of other ends, the only alternative is to sacrifice social balance. A poor society rightly adjusts its policy to the poor. An affluent society may properly inquire whether, instead, it shouldn't remove the poverty. . . . Moreover, improved social balance is one of the first requisites for the elimination of poverty. The modern liberal rallies to protect the poor from the taxes which in the next generation, as the result of a higher investment in their children, would eliminate poverty.

Winston S. Churchill
THE THREAT OF SOCIALISM

Food, Work, and Homes

Socialism is based on the idea of an all-powerful State which owns everything, which plans everything, which distributes everything, and thus through its politicians and officials decides the daily life of the individual citizen. We have not of course got this—or anything like it—in Britain at the present time. The process of establishing the Socialist State has only begun. The practical question which we have to settle now is whether we shall take another deep plunge into State ownership and State control, or whether we shall restore a greater measure of freedom of choice and action to our people, and of productive fertility and variety to our industry and trade.

Before deciding upon this, it is well to look around. Except in Scandinavia, Socialism and Socialist parties are on the decline throughout Europe everywhere outside the Iron Curtain. Socialism has been found in all European countries, bond or free, to have been the weakest defence against Communism. In taking another lurch into Socialism at this juncture we should be moving contrary to the general trend and tide of reviving European society. Still more should we be out of harmony with the States and nations of the English-speaking world, the British Domin-

From *The War Speeches* by Sir Winston Churchill. Reprinted by permission of Houghton Mifflin Company and Cassell & Co., Ltd.

ions and the United States. Mr. Attlee at this moment is the head of the only Socialist government to be found anywhere in the whole English-speaking world, the birthplace and the home of parliamentary democracy—the only one.

New Zealand and Australia, which have given a prolonged trial to Socialist governments, though not of course to Socialism in its complete form, have recently shaken themselves free. A young nation, like Australia, dwelling in a continent growing ample food for itself and for export, may try experiments in Socialism without the risk of fatal injury, but the 50,000,000 gathered together in this small island are in a very different position. We are a highly artificial community, balanced precariously at a level of well-being which before the war was superior to anything in Europe, but whose means of existence have been seriously, though not yet irreparably, undermined by changes in the surrounding world, and also by the actions of our own Government during these last critical and difficult years.

No nation of equal size, no society of equal civilization, has ever been in time of peace in the economic peril in which we stand. We do not grow enough food at home to keep ourselves alive, nor have we many of the raw materials which we need to earn our living. I am sure that if we act wisely we can make our way through our dangers as we have done before. But if, through political thoughtlessness or wrong guidance, we make grave mistakes and consume our strength in domestic quarrels and class war, consequences may descend upon us the like of which we have never yet suffered or even imagined.

The main reason why we are not able to earn our living and make our way in the world is because we are not allowed to do so. The whole enterprise, contrivance and genius of the British nation is being increasingly paralysed by the wartime restrictions from which all other free nations have shaken themselves clear, but these are still imposed upon our people here in the name of a mistaken political philosophy and a largely obsolete mode of thought. Our Government is the only one glorying in controls for controls' sake. I am sure that a parliament resolved to set the nation free would soon enable it to earn its own living in the world. I am sure on the other hand that the Socialist policy of equalizing misery and organizing scarcity instead of allowing diligence, self-reliance and ingenuity to produce abundance, has only to be prolonged to be fatal to our British island home.

The scheme of society for which Conservatives and National Liberals stand is the establishment and maintenance of a basic standard of life and labour below which a man or a woman, however old or weak, shall not be allowed to fall. The food they receive, the prices they have to pay for basic necessities, the homes they live in, their employment, must be the first care of the State, and must have priority over all other peace-time needs. Once we have made that standard secure we propose to set the nation free as quickly as possible from the controls and restrictions which now beset our daily life. Above the basic standard there will be free opportunity to rise. Everyone will be allowed to make the best of himself, without jealousy or spite, by all the means that honour and the long respected laws of our country allow.

One of the main pillars of any modern society is a stable value for money. 'Honest money', as it is called, is the only means by which goods and services can be fairly interchanged for mutual benefit between fellow citizens. The Socialist Government has spent every penny which it could lay its hands on, or which it could beg or borrow. They have spent in their term of office over £17,000,000,000, including the enormous sums given or loaned to us from abroad. They have exacted from us the heaviest taxation in the world. We are now paying £500,000,000 more a year even than in the height of the war.

At the same time they have cut down the buying power of every pound we earn in wages, salaries or in trading with one another. The British pound has fallen since the war stopped by no less than 3s. 8d. This has struck a heavy blow at the social services, at pensions of every kind, at every form of national insurance and at all savings. Thus what is given with the one hand is taken away with the other, and Socialist claims about safeguarding or extending the social services are vitiated by the fraud of giving only 16s. 4d. and calling it a pound. This is one of the gravest evils which we have to face and, remember, we still have the consequences of devaluation coming upon us to make it worse. I hope, my friends, you will think carefully about this and what it means to all of us. As head of the wartime Government I proclaimed the Four-Years' Plan of social reform—Education, Family Allowances and the National Health Scheme. Although mauled and twisted a bit by ministerial inepti-tude, this programme has now largely been carried through. At that time I summed it up in three words: Food, Work and Homes.

Without food, work is impossible and homes a mockery. I am sorry indeed that Lord Woolton is not looking after our food as he did in the war. We should have a better diet now if he were and at about half the administrative cost. Cheap and abundant food is the foundation of our strength. It will be the foundation of our policy. But this can only come in the long run from the workings of a free market. There is, however, a larger aspect of the food problem. We must grow more food at home. We must set to work forthwith to raise our home-grown food supply. We must also make long-term arrangements inside the Empire for mutual trade, whereby our brothers in their spacious food lands will feel that they have an assured market in the Mother Country and can plan ahead to supply it.

Now I come to work. All parties are agreed that the prevention of unemployment ranks next to food in the duties of any government. The policy on unemployment which all parties will follow was set forth in the commanding scheme of the National Government to which the leading men of all parties bound themselves in 1944. The scheme has not had to be put into operation for two reasons. First, because all the world is still at work and engaged in repairing the damage of the war, and replacing all kinds of things that were not made while it was going on. And, secondly, there has been very little unemployment because the Americans and our own Dominions have lent or given us over £400,000,000 a year ever since the war stopped.

The Government calculate, and their leading members have declared, that but for the large subsidies which the United States have so generously supplied, but which the Socialists somewhat ungratefully do not even mention in their manifesto, there would have been between 1,500,000 and 2,000,000 unemployed in this island during these years. I am not prepared myself to challenge these calculations, though I think perhaps we could have done better than that. But that is what Mr. Morrison and Mr. Bevan say, and we must agree with our opponents on facts whenever we can.

Thus on the question of unemployment there is no real difference between the two political parties. Why then in this election should all kinds of wrongful charges and false claims of party achievements be bandied about, when we are all agreed that American aid has prevented the kind of unemployment which appeared after the last war and rose again to hideous heights under the Socialist Government of twenty years ago, and when we are also agreed on the kind of remedies we should use to cope with it should it occur? The Conservative and National Liberal Parties regard the prevention of mass unemployment as the most solemn duty of government. Great difficulties lie ahead when the consequences of devaluation come home to us and when American aid ends. If human brains and will-power can conquer these dangers, we shall, with God's blessing, succeed. It is not the first time we have been through a life and death struggle together.

Lastly our homes. It is the homes that I wish to end in tonight. Three years ago we were promised that by the time of this election there would be no housing shortage as far as the mass of the British people were concerned. But the council waiting-lists are longer than ever. Before the war under a Conservative Government we were building by the normal process of supply and demand 1,000 houses a day. With all this need, and the same labour force, we are building only half as many now, and every house costs three times as much. Surely something must have gone wrong—and very wrong.

What then will you do about all these problems? Will you simply go on melting down the treasures of the past, and shrug your shoulders at the perils of the future? If so, a terrible awakening lies not so far ahead. It will not only be worldly fame and power which will pass from Britain, but the long treasured theme of British history and British greatness will be broken. I am sure it is not too late for our nation to lift itself above its troubles and resume, amid world-wide thanksgiving, its share in guiding the upward march of man. But if we should sink into mere materialism, and petty calculations of immediate personal advantage and fleeting gain, it will not be our reputation only which will perish, but our power to keep ourselves independent and even alive.

Class quarrels, endless party strife, on a background of apathy, indifference and bewilderment, will lead us all to ruin. Only a new surge of impulse can win us back the glorious ascendancy which we gained in the struggle for right and freedom, and for which our forbears had nerved our hearts down the long aisles of time. Let us make a supreme effort to surmount our dangers. Let faith, not appetite, guide our steps. There still remain forces in our island that can bring back all our true glories and range our people once again in the vanguard of Christian civilization to revive and save the world. . . .

Down with Queues

I have no hesitation in saying that the new Socialist manifesto contains, under much smooth language, an effective design or plot—for that is a truer term—to obtain a power over their fellow-countrymen such as no British Government has ever sought before, and that this would be fatal alike to their freedom and prosperity. Here I must point out that there is no dispute between parties on this important point. 'The important fact,' says the *Tribune* weekly newspaper which is the voice of Mr. Aneurin Bevan, 'The important fact about the manifesto is that it will give a new Labour Government the mandate to go forward with the construction of a Socialist society in Britain.' This is indeed a clear case of 'You have been warned.' Before I leave the Socialist manifesto there is a point I noticed in the paragraph dealing with children's welfare. The admission is all the more revealing because it is unconscious. Here it is:

'The policy of putting the children at the head of the queue will be continued.'

We are all agreed that the children should come first in our thoughts and in our resources. But why should they be at the head of the queue? Why should queues become a permanent, continuous feature of our life? Here you see clearly what is in their minds. The Socialist dream is no longer *Utopia* but *Queuetopia*. And if they have the power this part of their dream will certainly come true. Our earnest hope is that it may be granted to us to proclaim not the continuance but the doom of the queues and restore the normal relations between the shopkeepers and the public. . . .

The Folly of Socialism

I always like to come to Wales. I was the friend and comrade of the most famous Welshman of our time, David Lloyd George. Most people are unconscious of how much their lives have been shaped by the laws for which Lloyd George was responsible. He it was who launched the Liberal forces of this country effectively into the broad stream of social betterment and social security along which all modern parties now steer. Nowadays this is called 'the Welfare State'. We did not christen it but it was our political child. I hope the Liberal Party whose aid we need so much will not forget all this now. When I first became his friend and active lieutenant nearly fifty years ago his deep love of the people, his profound knowledge of their lives and of the undue and needless pressures under which they lived made a deep impression on my mind. Nearly two generations have passed since those great days. I also served under his leadership in the First World War when he rendered lasting service to the British Empire and to the cause of freedom and brought world-wide honour upon the name of Wales. I must turn aside for a moment to make one observation. There can be no greater insult to his memory than to suggest that today Wales has a second Lloyd George. Oh, I think it much better not to mention names.

Mr. Lloyd George was a democrat if ever there was one, but he recoiled, like all those who are ready to fight for freedom must recoil, from the fallacy and folly of Socialism. This is what he said about it almost a quarter of a century ago. His words are vivid: they are also prophetic:

> You cannot trust the battle of freedom to Socialism. Socialism has no interest in liberty. Socialism is the very negation of liberty. Socialism means the community in bonds. If you establish a Socialist community it means the most comprehensive universal and pervasive tyranny that this country has ever seen. It is like the sand of the desert. It gets into your food, your clothes, your machinery, the very air you breathe. They are all gritty with regulations, orders, decrees, rules. That is what Socialism means.

These are the words of Lloyd George. See how they live and ring through the years. He might have said this yesterday. He knew what it would feel like long before it came upon us.

I hope you have all mastered the official Socialist jargon which our masters, as they call themselves, wish us to learn. You must not use the word 'poor'; they are described as the 'lower income group'. When it comes to a question of freezing a workman's wages the Chancellor of the Exchequer speaks of 'arresting increases in personal income'. The idea is that formerly income taxpayers used to be the well-to-do, and that therefore it will be popular and safe to hit at them. Sir Stafford Cripps does not like to mention the word 'wages', but that is what he means. There is a lovely one about houses and homes. They are in future to be called 'accommodation units'. I don't know how we are to sing our old song 'Home Sweet Home'. 'Accommodation Unit, Sweet Accommodation Unit, there's no place like our Accommodation Unit.' I hope to live to see the British democracy spit all this rubbish from their lips. Mr. Herbert Morrison made a complaint the other day. 'Socialized industries,' he said, 'are the subject of the most persistent misrepresentation, whereas the difficulties and deficiences of private industries are glossed over.' How does he mean, *glossed over*? If private enterprise fails the owners may find themselves in the bankruptcy court. Is that being glossed over?

It makes no material difference to the official bulk buyer or Government nominee on some Board of Control whether the business is solvent or sends in its bill to the Exchequer. So long as he does his duty in an honest way, attends punctually to his work and is respectful to the Socialist politicians who employ him, he is safe and secure. Whereas a private businessman may have everything to lose if his judgment is wrong or his administration wasteful. Thus you maintain the most searching process of natural selection, out of which the public gets increasingly good service and value for their money. Nationalized industries are monopolies in the worst sense of the word. If a private business should become a monopoly and abuse its position there is no difficulty in dealing with it. But a Government monopoly has behind it the whole strength of the Government and, under a Socialist Government, the Ministers themselves have a political interest in trying to bolster it up so as to justify their own policy and conduct. In this remark which I have quoted, Mr. Herbert Morrison shows how little he realizes the actual facts and processes which are at work in modern life. We have seen lately the extraordinary case of Lord Pakenham repudiating the report on a terrible aeroplane accident by an impartial committee which he himself had picked and set up, thus weakening confidence in the safety of British landing grounds among all other countries.

I remember in Victorian days anxious talks about 'the submerged tenth' (that part of our people who had not shared in the progress of the age) and then later on in the old Liberal period (the grand old Liberal period) we spoke of going back to bring the rearguard in. The main army we said had reached the camping ground in all its strength and victory, and we should now, in duty and compassion, go back to pick up the stragglers and those who had fallen by the way and bring them in.

That was the Liberal solution then. It is the policy of the Conservative and National Liberal parties now. But now, under the Socialists, it is no longer a question of bringing the rearguard in, but of bringing the whole army back. It is no longer the plan of helping the submerged tenth, but of submerging the other nine-tenths down to their level. This is what in fact is taking place day by day, as you can see in your own lives and homes as you look around you.

Mr. Morrison (I am so sorry to keep mentioning him. Perhaps we'll hear from Mr. Attlee. He is the Prime Minister, you know) said at Leeds the other day, 'We are leading the world.' So far as social services are concerned we have always led it. But as for leading the world in any other sense what nation is following the British Socialist Party? The Russian Soviet Government and its satellites claim to be going on ahead. They claim to lead. They call upon Socialists to come quicker. The rest of the world has turned decisively away from the Socialist theory. As a Socialist Prime Minister working for the establishment of a Socialist State, Mr. Attlee and his party are alone among the English-speaking peoples. The United States, at the head of the world today, vehemently repudiate the Socialist doctrine. Canada repudiates it. Australia and New Zealand, after a considerable trial of it in a very incomplete form, have just shaken themselves free. Remember also there is no Socialist Government in Europe outside the Iron Curtain and Scandinavia. It seems to me a very perilous path that we are asked to tread, and to tread alone among the free democracies of the West.

John T. Flynn
DEBTS AND DICTATORS

The presence of the problem of an economic system definitely out of repair did not impress itself on the consciousness of the American public until well after Mr. Roosevelt's administration had had its try at

From *As We Go Marching* by John T. Flynn, pp. 172–189. Copyright 1944 by John T. Flynn. Reprinted by permission of Doubleday & Company, Inc.

John T. Flynn (1882–   ) is an American journalist and writer on financial topics.

the situation for one term. After that the solemn truth settled only slowly upon our minds. By 1940 there were few who did not feel that there was something definitely out of joint.

However, as in Italy and Germany, our first attack upon our economic disorder, as it appeared in 1930, took the form of government spending and welfare. This was something quite new with us. Before 1914 public spending of borrowed money was a negligible feature of our economy. The expansion that astonished the world in America up to that time had been the product of private enterprise financed by private credit. In 1912, on the eve of World War I, after a century and a half of growth, the debts of our public bodies were as follows:

National	$1,028,564,000
States	345,942,000
Counties	371,528,000
Incorporated places	3,104,426,000
	$4,850,460,000[1]

Most of the national debt was a remnant of the Civil War. The bulk of these debts was municipal, incurred for building city utilities such as streets, water works, schools, hospitals, and such.

The war of 1917 marked the beginning of a new era of public spending and borrowing. With the coming of war we had three years of enormous deficits as follows:

1917	$ 853,357,000
1918	9,033,254,000
1919	13,370,638,000[2]

The history of the war measured in national debt may be stated as follows:

1914	$ 1,188,235,000
1919	25,482,000,000

State and local debts had risen from $3,821,896,000 in 1912 to $8,689,740,000 in 1922.[3]

This was due almost wholly to war. After that, however, in the period from 1922 to the depression of 1929, the federal government, instead of borrowing, annually reduced its debt. But the state and local authorities became heavy borrowers. However, no small part of the local

[1] *Statistical Abstract of the U.S.*, 1929, p. 220.
[2] *Statistical Abstract of the U.S.*, 1941, p. 178.
[3] *Ibid.*, pps. 230, 251.

debts was contracted for revenue-producing improvement and practically all of this debt was created with provisions for amortization. None of it was arranged as part of any scheme to produce national income, though it had that effect. It arose chiefly out of the demand of local communities for public utilities such as schools, education, health facilities, streets, and from the great demand for roads to make way for the stream of motorcars that poured from our factories. Whatever the purpose, however, the policy did accustom the public mind to public borrowing as a fixed policy of government.

The theory of public spending as an instrument of government to regulate the economic system first appeared in the early part of 1922. The theory was advanced by the Unemployment Conference of that year. Briefly stated, it held that during periods of prosperity, when private industry is supplying all the requirements of national income, the federal and local governments should go slowly on public-works expenditures. They should accumulate a reserve of necessary public-works plans to be put into execution when business activity shows signs of tapering off. However, it was not contemplated that the governments should go into debt for these purposes but should carry them out in accordance with the principles of traditional sound finance. This theory amounted merely to a plan to carry on public building and spending operations in periods of diminished private business activity rather than in time of prosperity.

When the depression appeared in 1929, therefore, Mr. Hoover, on December 4, 1929, sent a message to Congress proposing additional appropriations for public works. He asked an increase of $500,000,000 for public buildings, $75,000,000 for public roads, $150,000,000 for rivers and harbors, and $60,000,000 to dam the Colorado River.[4] He believed this could be done within the budget. Actually the Hoover administration provided $256,000,000 in 1929 and $569,970,000 in 1930 for agriculture, public works, and farm loans while at the same time reducing the public debt by $746,000,000.[5] The central theme of these proposals was to use public spending merely as a stabilizer. There was a pretty general agreement with the theory. But as the depression advanced there was a persisting failure of tax funds so that by 1931 there was a deficit of $901,-959,000 which increased the next year to nearly three billion dollars.[6] A part of this deficit resulted from the public-works expenditures but most of it was caused by a failure of tax revenues. Hoover, of course, never planned an unbalanced budget. However, so imbedded in the public consciousness was the aversion to national public debt that the Demo-

[4] *The Hoover Administration,* by Myers and Newton, Chas. Scribner, New York, 1936.
[5] *Ibid.* Also *Statistical Abstract of the U.S.,* 1941, p. 230.
[6] *Statistical Abstract of the U.S.,* 1941, p. 176.

crats in 1932 roundly denounced the Hoover administration for its
extravagances and its failure to balance the budget. The platform of June
1932 contained the following as its very first plank:

We advocate:

1. An immediate and drastic reduction of governmental expenditures by abolishing useless commissions and offices, consolidating
departments and bureaus and eliminating extravagance, to accomplish
a saving of not less than 25 per cent in the cost of the Federal
Government; and we call upon the Democratic party in the States to
make a zealous effort to achieve a proportionate result.

2. Maintenance of national credit by a *federal budget annually
balanced* on the basis of accurate executive estimates within revenues,
raised by a system of taxation levied on the principle of ability to
pay.

Mr. Roosevelt, the Democratic candidate, stood strongly behind
these declarations. He not only opposed heavy public spending but
public borrowing as well. He advised that a "government, like any family,
can for a year spend a little more than it earns, but you and I know that a
continuation of that means the poorhouse." He warned that "high-sound-
ing phrases cannot sugar-coat the pill" and begged the nation "to have
the courage to stop borrowing and meet the continuing deficits." Public
works "do not relieve the distress" and are only "a stopgap." And having
asked "very simply that the task of reducing annual operating expenses"
be assigned to him, he said he regarded it as a positive duty "to raise by
taxes whatever sum is necessary to keep them (the unemployed) from
starvation."[7]

The party itself plastered the nation with huge posters warning
that the Republican party had brought it to the verge of bankruptcy and
calling on the voters to "throw the spendthrifts out and put responsible
government in." The candidate and the party were quite sincere in these
declarations and promises. They were in accordance with the most
orthodox American convictions. But practical political leaders, in search
of power, besieged by resolute minorities with uncompromising demands
for results and bombarded by cocksure merchants of easy salvation, find
themselves forced along courses of action that do not square with their
public proclamations of principle. Just as Mussolini and Hitler denounced their predecessors for borrowing and spending and then yielded
to the imperious political necessity of doing the thing they denounced, so
the New Deal, once in power, confronted with a disintegrating economic
system and with no understanding of the phenomenon that was in erup-

[7] *Public Papers and Addresses of Franklin D. Roosevelt, 1928–36,* Random
House, New York, 1938.

tion before its eyes, turned to the very thing it denounced in Hoover. But there was a difference. Hoover's deficits were the result of failure of revenue and were unplanned. Mr. Roosevelt's *first deficit was a deliberately planned deficit.* Within a few months of his inauguration he approved a proposal for a $3,300,000,000 public-works expenditure with borrowed funds in the NRA Act of May 1933. He then turned in the following deficits: $3,255,000,000 in 1933–34; $3,782,000,000 in 1934–35; $4,782,000,000 in 1935–36; and $4,952,000,000 in 1936–37.

Nevertheless, despite this record, the administration persisted in its theory that budgets should be balanced. Its platform in 1936 said:

> We are determined to reduce the expenses of the government. . . . Our retrenchment, tax, and recovery program thus reflect our firm determination to achieve a balanced budget and the reduction of the national debt at the earliest possible moment.

In January 1937 the President triumphantly presented what looked like a balanced budget. He said:

> We shall soon be reaping the full benefits of those programs and shall have at the same time a balanced budget that will also include provisions for the reduction of the public debt. . . . Although we must continue to spend substantial sums to provide work for those whom industry has not yet absorbed, *the 1938 budget is in balance.*

The whole tone of this message was pitched on the growing importance of a balanced budget. Nevertheless, notwithstanding this amazing statement, the budget of that year was not in balance. It showed a deficit of $1,449,626,000. Immediately there was a tremendous drop in the rate of business activity. We began to have what was called a recession, while the President continued to talk about "the extreme importance of achieving a balance of actual income and outgo." I recall all this now in order to make clear that up to this time no party in this country seriously approved the practice of borrowing as a definite policy. I think it illustrates also with complete finality that the men who were guiding national policy knew nothing about the workings of our economic system. The President made it clear that he was spending and borrowing purely as an emergency device. As late as April 1937 he said:

> While I recognize many opportunities to improve social and economic conditions through federal action, I am convinced that the success of our whole program and the permanent security of our people demand that we adjust all expenditures within the limits of my budget estimate.

He then delivered himself of the following extraordinary opinion:

> It is a matter of common knowledge that the principal danger to modern civilization lies in those nations which largely because of an armament race are headed directly toward bankruptcy. In proportion to national budgets the United States is spending a far smaller proportion of government income for armaments than the nations to which I refer. It behooves us, therefore, to continue our efforts to make both ends of our economy meet.

Here was a clear recognition of the fact that in Europe for many decades governments had been doing what our government was then doing, spending great sums of money and going into debt for it, but doing it on armaments instead of on peacetime activities as Mr. Roosevelt was doing. But nations which borrow money and pile on vast national debts can go into bankruptcy whether the debts be for armaments or roads, parks and public buildings. European nations were far more deeply stricken in crisis and had been for years. The armaments had become an *economic* necessity to them. They were not to us. Our government was delivering lectures on sound fiscal policy, deploring the deficits, yet planning new and more extravagant means of spending money, soothing the Haves with promises of balanced budgets and lower taxes, and stimulating the Have-nots with promises of security and abundance. The government was doing, in fact, what Depretis was doing in Italy between 1876 and 1887. Let the reader turn back to the first part of this volume for a description of that record:

> He promised every sort of reform without regard to the contradictions among his promises. He promised to reduce taxation and increase public works. He promised greater social security and greater prosperity. When he came to power he had no program and no settled notion how he would redeem these pledges. His party was joined by recruits from every school of political thought. He found at his side the representatives of every kind of discontent and every organ of national salvation. The oppressed tenants along with the overworked and underpaid craftsmen of the towns crowded around him beside the most reactionary landowners and employers to demand the honoring of the many contradictory promissory notes he had issued on his way to office.

Depretis then, for lack of any other weapon, proceeded to do what he had denounced his conservative predecessors for doing—to spend borrowed money on an ever-larger scale. When he did *"every district wanted something in the way of money grants for schools and post offices or roads or agricultural benefits. These districts soon learned that the way to get a share of the public funds was to elect men who voted for Depretis. Men who aspired to office had to assure their constituencies that they could get grants for these constituencies from the Premier."* I quote again what the Encyclopaedia Britannica said of this episode:

> In their anxiety to remain in office, Depretis and the Finance Minister, Magliani, never hesitated to mortgage the financial future of the country. No concession could be denied to deputies, whose support was indispensable to the life of the cabinet, nor under such conditions was it possible to place any effective check upon administrative abuses in which politicians or their electors were interested.

Miss Margot Hentz, writing of the same episode, said:

> Pressure was brought to bear through the organs of local administration who were given to understand that "favorable" districts might expect new schools, public works, roads, canals, post and telegraph offices, etc.; while the "unfavorable" might find even existing institutions suppressed.

Depretis' policy was pursued on a larger scale by his successors, including Giolitti whose administration brought Italy to the eve of World War I and the threshold of bankruptcy. Those who have read the chapter in this volume on Germany will not fail to see the resemblance first on a small scale to the performances of the old imperial government and then on a larger scale to the policies of the republican government that preceded Hitler.

All this, however old, was a new chapter in American policy. When, therefore, these vast expenditures were made, the noblest and most heroic explanations were offered. Having denounced timid deficits, the administration embarked upon a program of huge deficits, but it did it in characteristic American fashion, with proclamations of righteousness as if America had suddenly discovered something new. In fact, it was called a *New Deal.* Actually, it was America dropping back into the old European procession.

The recession of 1937–38 marked a turning point of the greatest importance in American public policy. Up to this point spending had been done on the pump-priming theory. That is, public funds, flowing out into business, were expected to produce a resumption of business activity. But business utterly failed to respond to this treatment. Apparently the pump itself was seriously out of order. From this point on we hear no more about balanced budgets. We find the administration committed to the same policy that marked the fiscal programs of republican Germany. It turned to the device of public spending and borrowing as a continuing and permanent means of creating national income.

There was a renewal of depression, and the President himself had to admit in his 1939 message that his expectations of recovery when he reduced expenditures were overoptimistic. It had become plain to the political elements in the government that there was something wrong, that the idea of public works during an emergency, used even on an enormous scale, had not produced recovery and was merely a stopgap. The situation of the administration was critical in the highest degree. Almost all its plans had been discarded. The AAA was declared unconstitutional; the NRA was scrapped by the Supreme Court just as it was falling into utter chaos; the devaluation of the dollar and the idea of a managed currency, as well as the gold-buying plan, had proved ineffective; social security was an aid to the unfortunate but did nothing to make the economic system work. Apparently nothing was holding back a tidal wave of deeper depression save the spending and borrowing program which everyone had either denounced or apologized for. The public debt had risen as total depression deficits amounted to 19 billions. What possible avenue of escape opened for the government in the presence of rising unemployment, rising taxes at last, farmers, workers, the aged, investors all clamoring for swift and effective aid and the land filling up again with messiahs and their easy evangels?

About this time a group of young men published a little book— *An Economic Program for American Democracy* (Vanguard, 1938). It got little enough attention at the time. Its authors styled themselves Seven Harvard and Tufts Economists. It proclaimed boldly that the capitalist system as we have known it was done and that, instead of balancing budgets, the government should adopt the unbalanced budget as a permanent institution; that the only salvation of the nation was in a greater and ever-expanding program of national expenditures met with revenues raised by borrowing.

Completely unknown at the time, these men were actually announcing in this small book the theories that had been worked over by John Maynard Keynes in England and Dr. Alvin H. Hansen in this country. But they were by no means the inventors of them. They had already had a vogue in Germany under the republic, which indeed had been influenced by them in its fiscal policies.

Their theory, very briefly stated, is as follows:

The present capitalist system is no longer capable of functioning effectively. The reason for this are as follows:

The dynamic element in the capitalist system is investment. Since millions of people save billions of dollars annually, these billions must be brought back into the stream of spending. This can be done only through investment. When private investment · is either curtailed or halted, these savings remain sterilized or inert and the capitalist system goes into a depression. Nothing can produce a normal revival of the capitalist system save a revival of investment.

Private investment cannot be any longer revived on a scale sufficient to absorb the savings of the people. Hence recovery through private investment is hopeless.

Private investment cannot · be revived because there are no longer open to savers adequate opportunities for investment.

Opportunities for investment are not open any longer for three chief reasons: (1) because the frontier is gone, with its opportunities for territorial expansion and the discovery of new resources; (2) because population increase has slowed down to a snail's pace; (3) because technological development has matured. That is to say, there is no longer in sight any such great inventions as the railroads, the automobile, etc., which will change all the arrangements of our social life and call for huge money expenditures.

The present capitalist system is therefore incapable of recovering its energy. This is not a mere emergency condition but is a characteristic of the system which will continue indefinitely.

For this reason we must adopt a new type of economic organization. This new type is called the Dual System or the Dual Consumptive System. Under this system the government will become the borrower of those savings funds which private business will not take. It must then spend these funds putting them again into circulation. What we must look forward to, therefore, is a "long-range program of government projects financed by borrowed funds."

Of course such a program means borrowing perpetually by the government. It means that each year the government debt will increase. When the war ends we will owe not less than $300,000,000,000. Thoughtful men are gravely disturbed as to what course we shall pursue to mitigate the immense burden of this debt. These gentlemen say our course is clear—borrow more. Borrow endlessly. Never stop borrowing.

Of course one asks: What will be the end? How will we ever pay the debt? They reply: It is not necessary to pay public debts. As long as the bondholder gets his interest he is satisfied, and when he wants the principal he can sell his bond, which is all he asks. But how long will this ability to sell his bond last with a government that never stops borrowing and whose credit can become exhausted? This they say, despite all · the lessons of history, cannot happen because the more we borrow the higher we build our national income and hence the greater is our ability to borrow. But what about the interest? we ask. Will that not rise to appalling proportions? If our debt is $300,000,000,000 when the war ends, the interest, when we refund the debt, will be at least $9,000,000,000 a year. Before the depression this government never collected more than $3,500,-

000,000 in taxes. The greatest amount of taxes ever collected by the federal government in peacetime, even after we began to spend on war preparations, was $7,500,000,000 in 1941. But we will have to collect that much in taxes—and an additional $1,500,000,000—just to pay the interest on the national debt. Yet the advocates of this system say that when the war ends we must go on borrowing at the rate of 5 or 10 or even 20 billions a year. Mr. Tugwell estimated it must be around $12,000,000,000 a year in peacetime.

This theory has, in greater or less degree, been adopted by those most influential in the present government. It is not an idea that has infected a few choice spirits on the perimeter of the New Deal. It has become a part of the New Deal—indeed its most essential part. The evidence of this is that the job of planning for the post-war problems of America was taken over by the President himself, was not committed to any of the departmental bureaus, but was installed in his own executive office under his own eyes. For this purpose he organized as a department of his own office the National Resources Planning Board. The man who is the leading exponent of this theory, Dr. Alvin H. Hansen of Harvard, was brought to Washington as economic adviser of the Federal Reserve Board and installed as the chief adviser of the National Resources Planning Board. Six of the seven Harvard and Tufts economists who prepared the published plan were brought to Washington and made economic counsel of various important agencies. Mr. Richard V. Gilbert, one of them, and one of the most vocal apostles of this theory, is at the moment I write guiding the economic destinies of the OPA, which is supposed to be leading the battle against inflation. Most of the others have been given posts of importance in the government. Dr. Hansen has been described by such journals as the *New Republic* and *Fortune* as the man "whose fiscal thinking permeates the New Deal." The board has put out a series of pamphlets designed to outline its guiding ideas. The most important of these was written by Dr. Hansen. Everywhere in Washington, in the most important key positions, are men who have been indoctrinated with this theory.

It is interesting to note that as early as 1936 a little book appeared called *Uncommon Sense,* by David Cushman Coyle. The book, however, was circulated by the Democratic National Committee and one wonders if the hard-headed men who paid the bills realized what they were doing. It contained this amazing passage:

> There are two ways to get out of depression. One is for business to borrow ten or twenty billion dollars from investors and build a lot of new factories, loading itself with debts that the investor will be expected to pay. The other is for the Government to borrow money

and build public works, loading itself with debts that the investors will have to pay out of their surplus incomes. Some kind of taxpayer has to carry the debts either way. But business debts have to be paid mostly by the poorest taxpayers, whenever they go to the store to buy a cake of soap. Federal debts have to be paid by the people with better incomes who would not spend all their income anyway. That is why it is better for business and consumers if we get out of the depression by having the Government borrow than by having business do all the borrowing.

It is this incredible yet dangerous piece of nonsense which is at the bottom of the postwar plans that are being made in Washington. Recently Congress, to its amazement, became aware of these plans. It had provided funds for the National Resources Planning Board to work out a program for the postwar period. Of course everyone is in favor of that. It had been hearing about the "projects" which that board was blueprinting. It learned, finally, that the great project upon which the board was working was a project for recasting the whole economic and social system of America along the lines outlined here and based primarily upon a settled conviction that the capitalist system is dead. And it was doing this in the office of the President of the United States. It was the discovery of this fact which led to one of the first congressional revolts in 1943 and compelled the abolition of the National Resources Planning Board by Congress. The liquidation of this Board, however, does not in any particular alter the theories upon which the present government is proceeding. It is merely forced to transfer its revolutionary planning activities to other bureaus and departments.

All this is nothing more than a conscious imitation of the German experiment. Some of the political leaders, including the President, may not realize this, since they are not students. But the men who have been publicizing and promoting the program do. Thus, for instance, we find an article in *Harper's*[8] describing with a good deal of gusto the financial operations of the Hitler regime. We are told that we must not let the brutality of German political policy "divert our attention from the German financial program. *It is revolutionary and it is successful.*" The author then tells us that if we will look behind the dictatorship we may possibly find "clues to the nature of our own recent financial ills, indicating what has been wrong and *what can be done* to strengthen economic democracy now and in the future." The men who built this German system are called men of unquestioned genius. It is becoming clear that "Germany's internal financial program is removing the limitations of her financial environment on rates of productive activity. For years prior

[8] "The German Financial Revolution," by Dal Hitchcock, *Harper's Magazine*, Vol. 182, February 1941.

to the present war German industry operated at capacity. To do these things she is changing capitalism but she is not destroying it."

Of course there is nothing new about Hitler's financial operation. . . . It is merely the adoption by Hitler of the spending and borrowing tactics of his predecessors, whom he so roundly denounced. Hitler was doing little more than Mussolini was doing, than the republicans and Social Democrats did before him in Germany, and what the old Italian and German Ministers did before the last war. There has been altogether too much nonsense printed about the great financial wizardry of Schacht. Schacht did no more than any banker with his knowledge of modern banking might have done, caught in the same squeeze. Being an experienced financier and having seen one devastating inflation at work, Schacht introduced some clever devices to mitigate the effect of his fiscal policies. For instance, he arranged that when financial or industrial concerns of any category had accumulated large cash reserves, they were compelled to invest them in government bonds, thus relieving the government of the necessity of making inflationary bank loans. Better still, when the government decided that a new steel or munitions plant should be built, the operation would be carried on by a private corporation. It would issue its securities. In this country the government takes those securities through the Reconstruction Finance Corporation, buying them with funds raised by government borrowing on its own bonds or notes, thus plunging the government into debt. Schacht would force large financial institutions to take the securities of the private corporation directly, keeping the government completely out of the financial transaction. This was possible in Nazi Germany under a dictator. A dictator can order such things. A democratic government cannot. The author of the article from which I have quoted tops it off with the admiring observation that "the Nazis by experimentation were learning what to do while Keynes was discussing these theories in England." This is what is being offered to America. I quote once more:

> The irony of this financial revolution that has been unfolded in Germany lies in its implications for the future of economic democracy. What the Nazis have done, in essence, is to begin to chart the unknown realms of the dynamic use of government securities. Tragically for Germany and the whole world the brilliant contribution of her financial genius has been obscured by its diversion to the uses of tyranny and destruction. But can any of these financial methods be utilized so that a wise, self-governing people, determined to preserve individual freedom and anxious to make full use of individual initiative, could make private enterprise and capitalism better serve the purposes of economic democracy? If this is so—and I believe it is—we shall do well to examine the potentialities of this new arithmetic of

finance as carefully and dispassionately as we should study, let us say, those of a new German development in aircraft manufacture, and seize upon whatever we can use for our own democratic ends.

This was written in 1941. The author was painfully behind the times. For already in 1938 the administration had practically seized upon this theory of finance.

It is a little astonishing how far the parallel between our fiscal theories and those of Germany go and how, once adopted, quite without design, they led off into the same weird bypaths. For instance, Italy before World War I had already learned how to increase the charges of social security in order to provide the government with money, not for social security but for its regular expenditures, and the same thing appeared in Germany. The present administration did that here until it was stopped by Congress in 1938, and now it is energetically trying to do the same thing again. Recently the New York *Sun* reported that when auditors got into the books of Mussolini's treasury, after his fall, they discovered that a large part of his deficit was due to the paying out of huge sums in subsidies to conceal the rise in the cost of living—a plan industriously urged here by the Hansen group and adopted by the President but as yet resisted by Congress. It is a singular fact that at this moment the battle against inflation is in the hands of these Perpetual Debt economists who look upon government spending and borrowing—which are the cause of inflation—as things good and necessary, and who look upon the objections to huge government spending and deficits as "old-fashioned superstition."

How the funds will be spent or "invested" by the central government is a point upon which all the advocates of this system are by no means agreed. Generally they fall into three groups:

1. The first group insists that the government shall not engage in any activities that either compete with private industry or impinge on its province. The government should put out its funds upon projects outside the domain of the profit system—such as public roads, schools, eleemosynary institutions, playgrounds, public parks, health projects, recreational and cultural activities of all sorts. A possible exception might be the development of power across state boundaries. Another exception would be public housing or housing for the underprivileged, which would not actually compete with private industry since private investors never put any money into housing projects of this kind. They would leave the whole subject of producing and distributing goods to private enterprises.

2. Another group proposes to invest these government funds in the shares and bonds of private enterprises. An eligible list of public investments would be established. The government would thus become

the chief investor in private enterprise and in some cases—the railroads, for instance—the government might own all the bonds and perhaps much of the stock. Thus we would have a private corporation operating the utility in which much if not most of the funds would belong to the government. This plan, of course, would enable the general government, as the largest stockholder or holder of the mortgage, to exercise over properties a whole range of authority and power which it could not possibly exercise as a government *per se.*

3. A third plan is outlined by Mr. Mordecai Ezekiel, economic adviser of the Agricultural Department. He proposes an Industrial Adjustment Administration patterned on the lines of the Agricultural Adjustment Administration. It would work as follows: Industry, organized into local groups united by national councils, would plan each year not the amount of goods it could sell but the amount needed by the nation. This estimate, approved by the government, would be authorized as the production program of the year. Each region and each unit in the region would receive its allocation of what it might produce. Prices would be fixed and all the producing units would proceed to turn out their respective quotas. The government would guarantee the sale of everything produced, underwriting the whole program and taking off the hands of all producers their undisposable surpluses. The risks of business would be transferred almost entirely to the government.[9]

What is stewing in Washington is a potpourri of all these ideas. The National Resources Planning Board in its report to Congress did actually propose that the government should become a partner in railroads, shipping, busses, airlines, power, telephone, telegraph, radio, aluminum, and other basic industries. It proposed also government participation in the financing of industry without setting very much limitation on it. John Maynard Keynes—now Lord Keynes and a member of the Board of Governors of the Bank of England and the most distinguished English-speaking exponent of these theories—speaks of this as "a somewhat comprehensive *socialization of investment.*" By this he means to distinguish his plan from the *socialization of industry.* Industry would be operated by private groups but the *investment* in industry would be socialized. "It is not the ownership of the instruments of production which it is important for the state to assume. If the state is able to determine the aggregate amount of resources devoted to augmenting the instruments and the basic rate of reward to those who can own them it will have accomplished all that is necessary," says Lord Keynes. The government will interpose itself between the corporate enterprise and the investor. The government will sell its securities to the investor, and as

[9] *Jobs for All,* by Mordecai Ezekiel, Knopf, New York, 1939.

these will be guaranteed securities, the government can fix the rate of interest and therefore the rate of reward to the investor. The government will then invest these funds in industry. The industry is "owned" by a private corporation. But the government owns its bonds, perhaps much of its stock. Thus Lord Keynes thinks he avoids statism or government ownership of industry. What is perfectly obvious, however, is that in one form or another these men are attempting to fabricate a system that will not be communistic and will not involve state ownership but will put in the hands of the all-powerful state not only through institutions of public regulation but through financial investment complete control of the economic system, while at the same time running up vast debts against the government and utilizing the public credit to create employment.

Of course this is fascism. For this principle of the Dual Consumptive Economy, as Dr. Hansen calls it, or the principle of planned consumption, as the fascists call it, by whatever name it is called is in fact one of the ingredients of the fascist or national socialist system. And if we will add to it the other ingredients of fascism or national socialism, we will then have that baleful order in America.

Whether this is a sound system or not is a matter for discussion. But sound or not, as Mr. Dal Hitchcock points out, it is the Nazi system. Whether we shall adopt it or not is hardly any longer a question. We have adopted it. The question is, can we get rid of it, and how? And if we are to continue it, the next question is how can we do so while at the same time continuing to operate our society in accordance with the democratic processes? . . .

America has now stumbled through the same marshes as Italy and Germany—and most European countries. Her leaders had proclaimed their undying belief in sound finance and balanced budgets while they teetered timidly on unbalanced ones. The public clamor for benefits, the cries of insistent minorities for relief and work, the imperious demand of all for action, action in some direction against the pressure of the pitiless laws of nature—all this was far more potent in shaping the course of the administration's fiscal policy than any fixed convictions based on principle. An unbalanced budget, after all, is a more or less impersonal evil, not easily grasped by the masses; but an army of unemployed men and the painfully conspicuous spectacle of shrinking purchasing power are things that strike down sharply on their consciousness. It is not easy, perhaps, to eat one's words about balancing the budget. But it is easier than facing all these angry forces with no plan. It is easier to spend than not to spend. It is running with the tide, along the lines of least resistance. And hence Mr. Roosevelt did what the premiers of Europe had been doing for decades. Only he called it a *New* Deal.

Michael Harrington
THE NEW ECONOMIC MAN

Adam Smith had thought that the corporation was hopelessly medieval, since it represented the anonymous control of someone else's money, and this contradicted the spiritual essence and genius of capitalism. By the mid-twentieth century, the corporation was capitalism.

This developing new system created new kinds of people.

In *The Lonely Crowd*, David Riesman perceptively described the personality evoked by the old reality and ethic. The "inner-directed" entrepreneur lived on a social frontier between feudalism and capitalism. He therefore consciously chose his individualism and his values, operating on a sort of internal gyroscope. In the twentieth century, however, wealth had become a function of manipulation and organization. There appeared the "other-directed" man, the team player who needed radar rather than a gyroscope, who took his values from others—when he could find them.

C. A. R. Crosland described a similar change in England. "The old style capitalist was by instinct a tyrant and an aristocrat who cared for no one's approval. The new style executive prides himself on being a good committee man, and subconsciously longs for the approval of the sociologist." In France, Pierre Bauchet has documented the way in which the new directors, bureaucrats of capital rather than entrepreneurs, find it natural and useful to integrate their "private" activities into a state plan.

But perhaps the most poignant case in point came to light in William H. Whyte's study of *The Organization Man*. Whyte wrote his book while working for *Fortune*, a business magazine. Though honest about the reality of capitalism, he is hardly its ideological opponent, and this led him to a hopeless contradiction. Whyte candidly described the way in which the corporation was invading, and consciously rationalizing, the very lives of its employees. Even the romantic concept of marriage, one of the great moral accomplishments of capitalist civilization, is bureaucratized as the company calculates a man's wife along with the rest of the assets and liabilities.

Having described this relentless progress of the organization,

Whyte can recommend no resistance more profound than an interior aloofness. He counsels the young executive to be a sort of good business-man Schweik, defeating the system by disloyally playing its game. This individual act of disaffiliation is as far as Whyte can go, and thus the true believer in the individualistic truths of the old capitalist ethic becomes a fifth columnist within the actual capitalist economy.

In America, then, one can watch the cold decadence of capitalism as it transforms and collectivizes the executive personality. In Europe, however, these changes have become explicitly political.

France is the most illuminating example of this juridical denial of capitalist laws by capitalist economies. In the Paris of the early sixties, a conservative and nationalist general presided over the Fourth Plan and prepared the Fifth. His prime minister was a banker. They were both committed to a directed economy in which state planning is a means of mobilizing the entire society behind politically determined goals. They were also in favor of capitalism, or at least of extracting private profit from public effort. In this dual purpose of state plan and corporate gain, De Gaulle and Pompidou presented one of the most advanced instances of private collectivization.

The French Plan began immediately after the Second World War. In part, it was a culmination of the social consciousness of the Resistance; in part, it was a necessity imposed upon a war-torn nation which had to restore the very structure of its economy. By the mid-fifties, French planning had transcended both of the motives that presided over its birth. It had become conservative, or at least technocratic, rather than militant and plebian as in the Resistance ideal. And it was starting to plan in a context of relative affluence rather than that of poverty.

Even during the extreme parliamentary instability of the last days of the Fourth Republic, the French economy continued to register high rates of growth (annual increments of over 5 percent were common in the mid-fifties). When General de Gaulle took power, he inherited the accomplishments of the Plan and turned them into a vision of a paternal-istic, directed, and planned economy which would restore grandeur to the nation. (He also developed a curious thesis of a classless France in which workers, peasants, and the bourgeoisie would no longer contend among themselves but be tutored, on television, by the Leader.)

The Plan which was at the center of this philosophy does not in any way change the system of ownership or profit in France. It is "indica-tive" rather than compulsory, and the businessman is free to ignore its suggestions. Indeed, as critics of the Plan like Pierre Mendès-France have documented, even the nationalized enterprises, like Renault or the public banks, often violate the very guidelines of the Government which "owns" them. (In a society dominated by private corporations, public corporations absorb the former's methods, morality, and immorality.) Yet, the Government's control of 50 percent of new investment is a powerful lever with which to secure conformity to the Plan.

On paper, there is a wide participation of all classes in the society in the planning process (this is the basis for De Gaulle's claim to a classless, cooperative France). In fact, the Fourth Plan was elaborated by commissions which were weighted over 90 percent toward businessmen and state functionaries—the distinction between the two categories is not always clear—and about 8 percent for worker and peasant unionists. Still, even if there were numerical equality between corporate and popular representatives, the businessmen would be at an enormous advantage. They command professional, paid research staffs and are thus in a position to understand and shape the Plan. The unions, by virtue of the very income and power structure of the society, count for less in these deliberations, whatever the representational mathematics.

The chief concept of the French Plan was, and is, a denial of one of the basic propositions of capitalist economics. Rather than allowing the "invisible hand" of the marketplace to determine the allocation of resources and rewards, the planners make a conscious and political choice of a growth rate to be achieved over a period of several years. Supply and demand are then adjusted to this decision, rather than the other way around. The result was a more harmonious development of the entire economy and an increase in the profit of the corporations that now have the state as a center for market research. But, as Gilbert Mathieu, the economic correspondent of *Le Monde,* noted in 1963, the relative inequities of income distribution increased between 1956 and 1961.

Indeed, there is a sense in which this maldistribution of income under the Plan is inevitable. When the state intervenes in an economy in which rewards are still assigned on the basis of private profit, then an increase in the general integration and efficiency of the society will benefit the rich. This might be offset by a vigorous and progressive tax policy, but this is certainly not the case in France (which, if anything, provides more scope for tax avoidance by the wealthy than the United States). As it is, one comes up with a system that combines the collective mode of planning with the private appropriation of money, a hybrid that moves away from both capitalism and socialism. And in terms of the distribution of wealth, the effect is for the entire community to subsidize those who are best off.

In American discussions, the embarrassing French example is usually countered with the German "miracle." In that country, it is said, the "social market economy" has observed the classic rules and prospered accordingly. However, as *Business Week* noted in the early sixties, the reality is a little less Adam Smithian than the claim: 55 percent of all investment in plant, equipment, and construction was financed by the state, and more than 40 percent of aluminum and more than 40 percent of auto, lead, and zinc production were also statified. (According to a high official of the French Commissariat du Plan, conversations between French and German planners in 1963 indicated that the two nations had an equal government intervention, albeit in different forms.)

Given such facts, it becomes somewhat more understandable that the British Conservative Party, in the name of anti-socialism, should introduce national planning in their country. As George Lichtheim concluded from this case and others, the directed economies of Europe "may still be capitalist" but they "cannot any longer be described as bourgeois." Capitalism is destroying capitalist motivation, ideology, and even personality.

In the United States, however, this process has been somewhat more disguised than in Europe. In the absence of open government planning, America has preferred to carry out its collectivizations in the name of something called "free enterprise." Ironically, the French Commissariat du Plan sends a technician to America in order to learn planning methods from the corporations. For in this country, the exigencies of production demand planning as much as in Europe, only the piety of tradition will not allow the word to be spoken openly.

Even so, in the mid-sixties there were signs that American theory would at least begin to catch up with American practice. A majority report of the Senate Subcommittee on Employment and Manpower in 1964 urged conscious planning. And in the Housing Message of 1964, President Lyndon B. Johnson declared, "By 1970, we shall have to build at least two million new homes a year to keep up with the growth of our population. We will need many new classrooms, uncounted miles of new streets and utility lines, and an unprecedented volume of water and sewage facilities. We will need stores and churches and libraries, distribution systems for goods, transportation systems for people and communications systems for ideas. . . .

"Now is the time to direct the productive capacity of our home building industry to the great needs of the neglected segments of our population. . . . In the tradition of the long-established partnership between private industry and community development, the Federal Government should encourage and facilitate these new and desirable approaches."

Such a statement recognized that the housing needs of the nation were so complex and interrelated that they required both anticipation and planning. But, significantly, after the Federal Government had accomplished what the free market was once supposed to do—direct a broad allocation of resources—and after it had laid down the plans for the new communities and provided their infrastructure, they would be turned over to private builders for their profit. Here again, innovation is collectivized and profit privatized.

While the Europeans were carrying out frank social planning for private profit, America was doing the same thing shamefacedly. As a result, a conservative movement could arise in the United States and, in the logical name of all the hallowed truths, make the preposterous proposal to go back to *laissez faire*. And many of the wealthiest businessmen who supported this fantasy were themselves the most successful practitioners of the capitalist anticapitalism. The spectacle would be humorous were it not dangerous, yet clearly a society cannot long pay such an astronomical price for its rhetoric. Along with the old-fashioned virtues, the old-fashioned vocabulary will have to vanish.

In short, in the spiritual name of courageous, inventive, and risk-taking individuals, bureaucratized corporations, supported and subsidized by governments, were planning in increasing independence of the laws of supply and demand or the judgments of investors. Economic life was more and more dominated by anonymous collectivities, and a relatively few directors were making decisions that affected the existence of almost every citizen. The civilization of capitalism, its ethics, its morality, its philosophy, was being destroyed by the practice of capitalism.

And businessmen, without giving too much thought to the matter, were shaping new environments and new types of men.

10
Science and the Future

The revolutionary effects of science upon the life of the past century and the centuries to come have been implicit in the topics examined in the previous nine chapters. Some may argue that war and international relations have been the formative factors of our times, but the influence of science has been equally obvious.

Science is obvious as a presence, yes; beyond that, however, it is mysterious to all but its initiates and practitioners. Who but the high priests can understand the rituals of science? The modern man, like the modern soldier, is the fated target of distant and unseen forces, and this dilemma is in part a dilemma of education. It requires less knowledge to tremble before the threat of "the Bomb" than to fear devaluation or a gold outflow.

As brilliant an intellectual as Henry Adams felt that his formal education had prepared him for the eighteenth, not the nineteenth or twentieth centuries: lacking mathematics—the very language of the new world—he was an alien in the land of science. Adams was deeply concerned about his and his society's failure and described his life as an attempt at real education in science and in history.

Unlike Adams, twentieth century litterateurs glory in their ignorance of science and in their repudiation of the world of the future. C. P. (Sir Charles) Snow has coined the phrase "the two cultures" to represent this lack of communication and even hostility between scientists, on the one hand, and literary intellectuals on the other hand. Snow deplores the failure on the part of intellectuals and the culture that produces them to acknowledge the value of science.

Aldous Huxley, as befits the grandson of a famous scientist, attempted, like Snow himself, to refute this stereotype in his own person. But he pointed out that it is a difficult task for the artist of the future to build a bridge from myth to science. Huxley himself may be remembered primarily for his *Brave New World,* a satirical sketch of the horrible anti-Utopia that science could someday create.

Economist Robert L. Heilbroner tries to put the future of technology and automation in more precise and less emotional terms, though he too cannot be unaware of the "cold and depersonalizing tendencies of a scientifically organized world." His only hope is that science will open "larger possibilities for mankind."

For several centuries science has been the science of Bacon's *New Atlantis,* an instrument for the creation of Utopias. But P. B. Medawar calls our attention to the "bad biology" which has been applied to social problems and to the continuing tasks of human reason.

In Shaw's *Man and Superman,* "Life Worshipper" Don Juan argued with the Devil that the "brain is the organ by which nature strives to understand itself." Was this an anticipation of "good" biology? Can we understand the twentieth century from this bridge between the two cultures?

Henry Adams
THE NEW MULTIVERSE

The historian must not try to know what is truth, if he values his honesty; for, if he cares for his truths, he is certain to falsify his facts. The laws of history only repeat the lines of force or thought. Yet though his

From *The Education of Henry Adams,* published by Random House in 1918.

Henry Adams (1838–1918) was an American historian and philosopher. He won the Pulitzer Prize in 1919.

will be iron, he cannot help now and then resuming his humanity or simianity in face of a fear. The motion of thought had the same value as the motion of a cannon ball seen approaching the observer on a direct line through the air. One could watch its curve for five thousand years. Its first violent acceleration in historical times had ended in the catastrophe of 310. The next swerve of direction occurred towards 1500. Galileo and Bacon gave a still newer curve to it, which altered its values; but all these changes had never altered the continuity. Only in 1900, the continuity snapped.

Vaguely conscious of the cataclysm, the world sometimes dated it from 1893, by the Roentgen rays, or from 1898, by the Curies' radium; but in 1904, Arthur Balfour announced on the part of British science that the human race without exception had lived and died in a world of illusion until the last year of the century. The date was convenient, and convenience was truth.

The child born in 1900 would, then, be born into a new world which would not be a unity but a multiple. Adams tried to imagine it, and an education that would fit it. He found himself in a land where no one had ever penetrated before; where order was an accidental relation obnoxious to nature; artificial compulsion imposed on motion; against which every free energy of the universe revolted; and which, being merely occasional, resolved itself back into anarchy at last. He could not deny that the law of the new multiverse explained much that had been most obscure, especially the persistently fiendish treatment of man by man; the perpetual effort of society to establish law, and the perpetual revolt of society against the law it had established; the perpetual building up of authority by force, and the perpetual appeal to force to overthrow it; the perpetual symbolism of a higher law, and the perpetual relapse to a lower one; the perpetual victory of the principles of freedom, and their perpetual conversion into principles of power; but the staggering problem was the outlook ahead into the despotism of artificial order which nature abhorred. The physicists had a phrase for it, unintelligible to the vulgar: "All that we win is a battle—lost in advance—with the irreversible phenomena in the background of nature."

All that a historian won was a vehement wish to escape. He saw his education complete, and was sorry he ever began it. As a matter of taste, he greatly preferred his eighteenth-century education when God was a father and nature a mother, and all was for the best in a scientific universe. He repudiated all share in the world as it was to be, and yet he could not detect the point where his responsibility began or ended.

To educate—one's self to begin with—had been the effort of one's life for sixty years; and the difficulties of education had gone on doubling with the coal-output, until the prospect of waiting another ten years, in order to face a seventh doubling of complexities, allured one's imagination but slightly. The law of acceleration was definite, and did not require ten years more study except to show whether it held good. No scheme could be suggested to the new American, and no fault needed to be found, or complaint made; but the next great influx of new forces seemed near at hand, and its style of education promised to be violently coercive. The movement from unity into multiplicity, between 1200 and 1900, was unbroken in sequence, and rapid in acceleration. Prolonged one generation longer, it would require a new social mind. As though thought were common salt in indefinite solution it must enter a new phase subject to new laws. Thus far, since five or ten thousand years, the mind had successfully reacted, and nothing yet proved that it would fail to react—but it would need to jump.

C. P. Snow
THE TWO CULTURES

The statements in the lecture were as simple as I could make them. Any statements which have any reference to action must be simple. There is always something wrong, if one is straining to make the commonplace incomprehensible. I hedged the statements round with qualifications and I tried to illustrate some of them. I will now remove the qualifications and the pictures and rephrase the essence of the lecture as quietly as I can.

It is something like this. In our society (that is, advanced western society) we have lost even the pretence of a common culture. Persons educated with the greatest intensity we know can no longer communicate with each other on the plane of their major intellectual concern. This is serious for our creative, intellectual and, above all, our normal life. It is leading us to interpret the past wrongly, to misjudge the present, and to deny our hopes of the future. It is making it difficult or impossible for us to take good action.

I gave the most pointed example of this lack of communication in the shape of two groups of people, representing what I have christened 'the two cultures'. One of these contained the scientists, whose weight,

From *The Two Cultures and a Second Look* by C. P. Snow, pp. 60–65, 75–82. Reprinted by permission of Cambridge University Press.
C. P. Snow (1905–   ) is a British scientist and novelist.

achievement and influence did not need stressing. The other contained the literary intellectuals. I did not mean that literary intellectuals act as the main decision-makers of the western world. I meant that literary intellectuals represent, vocalise, and to some extent shape and predict the mood of the non-scientific culture: they do not make the decisions, but their words seep into the minds of those who do. Between these two groups—the scientists and the literary intellectuals—there is little communication and, instead of fellow-feeling, something like hostility.

This was intended as a description of, or a very crude first approximation to, our existing state of affairs. That it was a state of affairs I passionately disliked, I thought was made fairly clear. Curiously enough, some commentators have assumed that I approved of it; but at this I confess myself defeated, and take refuge in muttering Schiller's helpful line.

To finish this précis. There is, of course, no complete solution. In the conditions of our age, or any age which we can foresee, Renaissance man is not possible. But we can do something. The chief means open to us is education—education mainly in primary and secondary schools, but also in colleges and universities. There is no excuse for letting another generation be as vastly ignorant, or as devoid of understanding and sympathy, as we are ourselves.

From the beginning, the phrase 'the two cultures' evoked some protests. The word 'culture' or 'cultures' has been objected to: so, with much more substance, has the number two. (No one, I think, has yet complained about the definite article.)

I must have a word about these verbal points before I come to the more wide-reaching arguments. The term 'culture' in my title has two meanings, both of which are precisely applicable to the theme. First, 'culture' has the sense of the dictionary definition, 'intellectual development, development of the mind'. For many years this definition has carried overtones, often of a deep and ambiguous sort. It happens that few of us can help searching for a refined use of the word: if anyone asks, What is culture? Who is cultured? the needle points, by an extraordinary coincidence, in the direction of ourselves.

But that, though a pleasing example of human frailty, doesn't matter: what does matter is that any refined definition, from Coleridge onwards, applies at least as well (and also as imperfectly) to the development a scientist achieves *in the course of his professional vocation* as to the 'traditional' mental development or any of its offshoots. Coleridge said 'cultivation' where we should say 'culture'—and qualified it as 'the harmonious development of those qualities and faculties which characterise our humanity'. Well, none of us manages that; in plain truth, either of our cultures, whether literary or scientific, only deserves the name of sub-culture. *'Qualities and faculties which characterise our humanity.'*

Curiosity about the natural world, the use of symbolic systems of thought, are two of the most precious and the most specifically human of all human qualities. The traditional methods of mental development left them to be starved. So, in reverse, does scientific education starve our verbal faculties—the language of symbols is given splendid play, the language of words is not. On both sides we underestimate the spread of a human being's gifts.

But, if we are to use 'culture' in its refined sense at all, it is only lack of imagination, or possibly blank ignorance, which could deny it to scientists. There is no excuse for such ignorance. A whole body of literature has been built up over a generation, written, incidentally, in some of the most beautiful prose of our time, to demonstrate the intellectual, aesthetic and moral values inherent in the pursuit of science (compare A. N. Whitehead's *Science and the Modern World*, G. H. Hardy's *A Mathematician's Apology*, J. Bronowski's *Science and Human Values*). There are valuable insights scattered all over American and English writings of the last decade—Needham, Toulmin, Price, Piel, Newman, are only a few of the names that come to mind.

In the most lively of all contributions to this subject, a Third Programme feature not yet published, Bronowski deliberately avoided the word 'culture' for either side and chose as his title 'Dialogue between Two World Systems'. For myself, I believe the word is still appropriate and carries its proper meaning to sensible persons. But, while sticking to that word, I want to repeat what was intended to be my main message, but which has somehow got overlaid: that neither the scientific system of mental development, nor the traditional, is adequate for our potentialities, for the work we have in front of us, for the world in which we ought to begin to live.

The word 'culture' has a second and technical meaning, which I pointed out explicitly in the original lecture. It is used by anthropologists to denote a group of persons living in the same environment, linked by common habits, common assumptions, a common way of life. Thus one talks of a Neanderthal culture, a La Tène culture, a Trobriand Island culture: the term, which is a very useful one, has been applied to groups within our own societies. For me this was a very strong additional reason for selecting the word; it isn't often one gets a word which can be used in two senses, both of which one explicitly intends. For scientists on the one side, literary intellectuals on the other, do in fact exist as cultures within the anthropological scope. There are, as I said before, common attitudes, common standards and patterns of behaviour, common approaches and assumptions. This does not mean that a person within a culture loses his individuality and free will. It does mean that, without knowing it, we are more than we think children of our time, place and training. Let me take two trivial and non-controversial examples. The overwhelming majority of the scientific culture (that is, the group of scientists observed through anthropological eyes) would feel certain, without needing to cogitate or examine their souls, that research was the primary function of a university. This attitude is automatic, it is part of their culture: but it would not be the attitude of such a proportion in the literary culture. On the other hand, the overwhelming majority of the literary culture would feel just as certain that not the slightest censorship of the printed word is, in any circumstances, permissible. This position doesn't have to be reached by individual thought: again it is part of the culture. It is such an unquestioned part, in fact, that the literary intellectuals have got their way more absolutely than, thirty years ago, would have seemed conceivable. . . .

Major scientific breakthroughs, and in particular those as closely connected to human flesh and bone as this one in molecular biology, or even more, another which we may expect in the nature of the higher nervous system, are bound to touch both our hopes and our resignations. That is: ever since men began to think introspectively about themselves, they have made guesses, and sometimes had profound intuitions, about those parts of their own nature which seemed to be predestined. It is possible that within a generation some of these guesses will have been tested against exact knowledge. No one can predict what such an intellectual revolution will mean: but I believe that one of the consequences will be to make us feel not less but more responsible towards our brother men.

It was for this reason among others that, in the original lecture, I drew a distinction between the individual condition and the social condition. In doing so, I stressed the solitariness, the ultimate tragedy, at the core of each individual life; and this has worried a good many who found the rest of the statement acceptable. It is very hard, of course, to subdue the obsessions of one's own temperament; this specific note creeps into a good deal of what I have written, as Alfred Kazin has shrewdly pointed out: it is not an accident that my novel sequence is called *Strangers and Brothers*. Nevertheless, this distinction, however it is drawn, is imperative, unless we are going to sink into the facile social pessimism of our time, unless we are going to settle into our own egocentric chill.

So I will try to make the statement without much emphasis of my own. We should most of us agree, I think, that in the individual life of each of us there is much that, in the long run, one cannot do anything about. Death is a fact—one's own death, the deaths of those one loves. There is much that makes one suffer which is irremediable: one struggles against it all the way, but there is an irremediable residue left. These are facts: they will remain facts as long as man remains man. This is part of the individual condition: call it tragic, comic, absurd, or, like some of the best and bravest of people, shrug it off.

But it isn't all. One looks outside oneself to other lives, to which one is bound by love, affection, loyalty, obligation: each of those lives has the same irremediable components as one's own; but there are also components that one can help, or that can give one help. It is in this tiny extension of the personality, it is in this seizing on the possibilities of hope, that we become more fully human: it is a way to improve the quality of one's life: it is, for oneself, the beginning of the social condition.

Finally, one can try to understand the condition of lives, not close to one's own, which one cannot know face to face. Each of these lives—that is, the lives of one's fellow human beings—again has limits of irremediability like one's own. Each of them has needs, some of which can be met: the totality of all is the social condition.

We cannot know as much as we should about the social condition all over the world. But we can know, we do know, two most important things. First we can meet the harsh facts of the flesh, on the level where all of us are, or should be, one. We know that the vast majority, perhaps two-thirds, of our fellow men are living in the immediate presence of illness and premature death; their expectation of life is half of ours, most are under-nourished, many are near to starving, many starve. Each of these lives is afflicted by suffering, different from that which is intrinsic in the individual condition. But this suffering is unnecessary and can be lifted. This is the second important thing which we know—or, if we don't know it, there is no excuse or absolution for us.

We cannot avoid the realisation that applied science has made it possible to remove unnecessary suffering from a billion individual human lives—to remove suffering of a kind, which, in our own privileged society, we have largely forgotten, suffering so elementary that it is not genteel to mention it. For example, we *know* how to heal many of the sick: to prevent children dying in infancy and mothers in childbirth: to produce enough food to alleviate hunger: to throw up a minimum of shelter: to ensure that there aren't so many births that our other efforts are in vain. All this we *know* how to do.

It does not require one additional scientific discovery, though new scientific discoveries must help us. It depends on the spread of the scientific revolution all over the world. There is no other way. For most human beings, this is the point of hope. It will certainly happen. It may take longer than the poor will peacefully accept. How long it takes, and the fashion in which it is done, will be a reflex of the quality of our lives, especially of the lives of those of us born lucky: as most in the western world were born. When it is achieved, then our consciences will be a little cleaner; and those coming after us will at least be able to think that the elemental needs of others aren't a daily reproach to any sentient person, that for the first time some genuine dignity has come upon us all.

Man doesn't live by bread alone—yes, that has been said often enough in the course of these discussions. It has been said occasionally with a lack of imagination, a provincialism, that makes the mind boggle: for it is not a remark that one of us in the western world can casually address to most Asians, to most of our fellow human beings, in the world as it now exists. But we can, we should, say it to ourselves. For we know how, once the elemental needs are satisfied, we do not find it easy to do something worthy and satisfying with our lives. Probably it will never be easy. Conceivably men in the future, if they are as lucky as we are now, will struggle with our existential discontents, or new ones of their own. They may, like some of us, try—through sex or drink or drugs—to intensify the sensational life. Or they may try to improve the quality of their lives, through an extension of their responsibilities, a deepening of the affections and the spirit, in a fashion which, though we can aim at it for ourselves and our own societies, we can only dimly perceive.

But, though our perception may be dim, it isn't dim enough to obscure one truth: that one mustn't despise the elemental needs, when one has been granted them and others have not. To do so is not to display one's superior spirituality. It is simply to be inhuman, or more exactly anti-human.

Here, in fact, was what I intended to be the centre of the whole argument. Before I wrote the lecture I thought of calling it 'The Rich and the Poor', and I rather wish that I hadn't changed my mind.

The scientific revolution is the only method by which most people can gain the primal things (years of life, freedom from hunger, survival for children)—the primal things which we take for granted and which have in reality come to us through having had our own scientific revolution not so long ago. Most people want these primal things. Most people, wherever they are being given a chance, are rushing into the scientific revolution.

To misunderstand this position is to misunderstand both the present and the future. It simmers beneath the surface of world politics. Though the form of politics may look the same, its content is being altered as the scientific revolution pours in. We have not been as quick as we should to draw the right consequences, very largely because of the division of the cultures. It has been hard for politicians and administrators to grasp the practical truth of what scientists were telling them. But now it is beginning to be accepted. It is often accepted most easily by men of affairs, whatever their political sympathies, engineers, or priests, or doctors, all those who have a strong comradely physical sympathy for other humans. If others can get the primal things—yes, that is beyond argument; that is simply good.

Curiously enough, there are many who would call themselves

liberals and yet who are antipathetic to this change. Almost as though sleepwalking they drift into an attitude which, to the poor of the world, is a denial of all human hope. This attitude, which misinterprets both the present and the future, seems to be connected with a similar misinterpretation of the past. It is on this point that representatives of the putative third culture have been speaking with trenchancy.

The argument is about the first wave of the scientific revolution, the transformation which we call the industrial revolution, and it is occupied with questions about what, in the most elementary human terms, life was like in pre-industrial as compared with industrial society. We can gain some insights, of course, from the present world, which is a vast sociological laboratory in which one can observe all kinds of society from the neolithic to the advanced industrial. We are also now accumulating substantial evidence of our own past.

When I made some remark about the industrial revolution, I had imagined that the findings of recent research in social history were better known. Otherwise I should have documented what I said: but that seemed like documenting a platitude. Did anyone think that, in the primal terms in which I have just been discussing the poor countries of the present world, our ancestors' condition was so very different? Or that the industrial revolution had not brought us in three or four generations to a state entirely new in the harsh, unrecorded continuity of poor men's lives? I couldn't believe it. I knew, of course, the force of nostalgia, myth, and plain snobbery. In all families, at all times, there are stories of blessed existences, just before one's childhood: there were in my own. Myth—I ought to have remembered what Malinowski taught us, that people believe their myths as fact. I certainly ought to have remembered that, when anyone is asked what he would have been in a previous incarnation, he nominates—if he is modest—something like a Jacobean cleric or an eighteenth-century squire. He wouldn't have been any such thing. The overwhelming probability is that he would have been a peasant. If we want to talk about our ancestors, that is whence we came.

I was at fault, I suppose, in not trying to be more persuasive against these kinds of resistance. Anyway, there is no need for me to say much more. There are plenty of scholars professionally concerned with preindustrial social history. Now we know something of the elemental facts of the lives and deaths of peasants and agricultural labourers in seventeenth- and eighteenth-century England and France. They are not comfortable facts. J. H. Plumb, in one of his attacks on the teaching of a pretty-pretty past, has written: 'No one in his senses would choose to have been born in a previous age unless he could be certain that he would have been born into a prosperous family, that he would have enjoyed extremely good health, and that he could have accepted stoically the death of the majority of his children.'

Aldous Huxley
NEW BRIDGES, NEW GULFS

All our experiences are strictly private; but some experiences are less private than others. They are less private in the sense that, under similar conditions, most normal people will have similar experiences and, having had them, can be relied upon to interpret the spoken or written reports of such experiences in much the same way.

About the more private of our experiences no such statements can be made. For example, the visual, auditory and olfactory experiences of a group of people watching the burning of a house are likely to be similar. Similar, too, are the intellectual experiences of those members of the group who make the effort to think logically about the causes of this particular fire and, in the light of current knowledge, of combustion in general. In other words, sense impressions and the processes of rational thought are experiences whose privacy is not too extreme to make them unsharable. But now let us consider the emotional experiences of our fire watchers. One member of the group may feel sexual excitement, another aesthetic pleasure, another horror and yet others human sympathy or inhuman and malicious glee. Such experiences, it is obvious, are radically unlike one another. In this sense they are more private than sense experiences and the intellectual experiences of logical thought.

In the present context, science may be defined as a device for investigating, ordering and communicating the more public of human experiences. Less systematically, literature also deals with such public experiences. Its main concern, however, is with man's more private experiences, and with the interactions between the private worlds of sentient, self-conscious individuals and the public universes of "objective reality," logic, social conventions and the accumulated information currently available. . . .

In the hierarchy of the sciences, atomic physics is the most exact, the most completely expressible in terms of mathematics, and the most remote from immediate experience. For the writer, atomic physics is interesting, above all, for the way in which it illustrates the workings of the

From *Literature and Science* by Aldous Huxley, pp. 4–5, 75–76, 106–108, 111–112. Copyright © 1963 by Aldous Huxley. Reprinted by permission of Harper & Row, Publishers, Inc.
Aldous Huxley (1894–1963) was a British novelist and essayist. His book *Brave New World* is a satire on the technological world.

scientific mind as it moves from a set of sense perceptions to a set of unobservable, hypothetical entities and back again to another set of sense perceptions, in relation to which the concepts of the atomic hypothesis are operationally validated. In the words of an eminent physicist, Werner Heisenberg, "for the first time in history man, on this planet, is discovering that he is alone with himself, without a partner and without an adversary." To put it more picturesquely, man is in process of becoming his own Providence, his own Cataclysm, his own Saviour and his own invading horde of Martians. And in the realm of pure science the same discovery—that he is alone with himself—awaits him as he progressively refines his analysis of matter. "Modern science," says Heisenberg, "shows us that we can no longer regard the building blocks of matter, which were considered originally to be the ultimate objective reality, as being things 'in themselves' . . . Knowledge of atoms and their movements 'in themselves,' that is to say independent of our observation, is no longer the aim of research; rather we now find ourselves from the very start in the midst of a dialogue between nature and man, a dialogue of which science is only one part, so much so that the conventional division of the world into subject and object, into inner world and outer world, into body and soul, is no longer applicable and raises difficulties. For the sciences of nature, the subject matter of research is no longer nature in itself, but nature subjected to human questioning, and to this extent man, once again, meets only with himself."

To the literary artist who has been concerned with man's more private experiences, this talk about the inappropriateness of the conventional notions of objective and subjective, outer and inner, has a familiar ring. It reminds him of certain utterances of the poets and the mystics. Carried far enough, the analysis of man's public experiences comes, in theory at least, to the same conclusion as is reached existentially in the most private of all private experiences—infused contemplation, samadhi, satori. . . .

The hypotheses of modern science treat of a reality far subtler and more complex than the merely abstract, verbal world of theological and metaphysical notions. And, although a determinant of human nature and human behavior, this reality is nonhuman, essentially undramatic, completely lacking in the obvious attributes of the picturesque. For these reasons it will be difficult to incorporate the hypotheses of science into harmonious, moving and persuasive works of art—much more difficult, obviously, than it was to incorporate the notions of diabolic obsession or of a Lord of Power arbitrarily quickening and killing the souls of His creatures. But for any serious and gifted artist a difficulty is never an insurmountable obstacle; it is a challenge to intellectual combat, a spur to further achievement. The conceptual and linguistic weapons with which this particular combat must be waged have not yet been invented. We do not know and, until some great artist comes along and tells us what to do, we shall not know how the muddled words of the tribe and the too precise words of the textbooks should be poetically purified, so as to make them capable of harmonizing our private and unsharable experiences with the scientific hypotheses in terms of which they are explained. But sooner or later the necessary means will be discovered, the appropriate weapons will be forged, the long-awaited pioneer of genius will turn up and, quite casually, as though it were the most natural thing in the world, point out the way. What that way will be is of course completely unpredictable. To forecast what Shakespeare would do with the drama, an Elizabethan critic would have had to be another Shakespeare. In which case, needless to say, he would not have wasted his time talking about new kinds of literature; he would have made them. . . .

Science sometimes builds new bridges between universes of discourse and experience hitherto regarded as separate and heterogeneous. But science also breaks down old bridges and opens gulfs between universes that, traditionally, had been connected. Blake and Keats detested Sir Isaac Newton because he had cut the old connections between the stars and the heavenly host, between rainbows and Iris, and even between rainbows and Noah's Ark, rainbows and Jehovah—had cut the connections and so de-poetized man's world and robbed it of meaning. But in an age of science the world can no longer be looked at as a set of symbols, standing for things outside the world. *Alles Vergaengliche ist* NICHT *ein Gleichnis*. The world is poetical intrinsically and what it means is simply itself. Its significance is the enormous mystery of its existence and of our awareness of that existence. Wordsworth's "something far more deeply interfused, Whose dwelling is the light of setting suns, . . . and in the mind of man" is a deeper and more permanent foundation on which to build a life and a life-sustaining art than any traditional mythology. But the myths are still there, still make their appeal to something in the mind of man—something, it is true, considerably more shifting, considerably less deeply interfused than the great nameless Something of Wordsworth's poem, but still psychologically important. The contemporary man of letters finds himself confronted, as he prepares to write about Nature, by a fascinating problem—the problem of harmonizing, within a single work of art, the old, beloved raw materials, handed down to him by the myth makers of an earlier time, with the new findings and hypotheses now pouring in upon him from the sciences of his own day.

Robert L. Heilbroner
THE FUTURE OF CAPITALISM

This explosion of science and technology is often thought of as a product *of* capitalism, insofar as it arose in an age dominated by capitalism. Yet the association was far more one of coexistence than of causal interrelation. At best we can say that the secular air of bourgeois culture was compatible with, perhaps even conducive to, scientific investigation, but we can hardly credit the acceleration of scientific activities around the middle of the 19th century to the direct stimulus or patronage of capitalism itself.

Even scientific technology exhibits but little debt to the existence of capitalism. The technology on which capitalism began its long course of growth was strictly of a pragmatic, intuitive, pre-scientific kind. Watt, for example, invented the steam engine over fifty years before the basic formulation of the law of thermodynamics. The English textile, iron and steel, or chemical industries were founded and prospered with no "scientific" underpinnings at all. The same is true for the young railroad industry, for canal building, or road-laying. The deliberate employment of scientific investigation to create or refine the technology of production was considerably delayed in arriving. In this country the first private industrial laboratory was not built until 1900 by the General Electric company, and organized research and development on a large scale did not really get under way until 1913.

Thus, we find the flowering of science and the application of science to technology—the very hallmarks of the modern era—to be currents that arose *within* capitalism, but that do not owe their existence directly to capitalism. Rather, science and its technology emerge as a great underground river whose tortuous course has finally reached the surface during the age of capitalism, but which springs from far distant sources. Having now surfaced, that river must cut its own channels through the existing social landscape. Indeed, if we ask what force in our day might in time be strong enough to undercut the bastions of privilege

Condensation of pp. 114–134 of *The Limits of American Capitalism* by Robert L. Heilbroner. Copyright © 1966 by Robert L. Heilbroner. This is a portion of the article "The Future of American Capitalism" in *Commentary* (April 1966), and is reprinted by permission of Harper & Row, Publishers.

Robert L. Heilbroner (1919–   ) is an American economist.

of capitalism and to create its own institutions and social structures in their place, the answer must surely be the one force that dominates our age—the power of science and of scientific technology.

There is, I suspect, little to argue about as to the commanding pressure of science in modern times. What is likely to be a good deal less readily accepted, however, is the contention that this force will cause drastic modifications in, or even the eventual supersession of, capitalism. For at first glance this new current of history seems to have imparted an immense momentum to capitalism by providing it with a virtually inexhaustible source of invention and innovation to insure its economic growth. Merely to review in our minds the broad areas of investment and economic output that owe their existence *entirely* to the laboratory work of the last three decades—the nuclear and space establishments, electronics, the computerization of industry, the creation of new materials such as plastics—is to reveal the breadth of this new gulf stream of economic nourishment.

Yet, like the attractions of the cash market for the feudal lord, the near-term advantages of science and technology conceal long-term conflicts and incompatibilities between this new force of history and its host society. Indeed, the insinuation of science and technology into the interstices of business enterprise promises to alter the fundamental working arrangements of capitalism.

At least one of these alterations is already familiar to us. This is the tendency of technology to create social problems that require public controls to correct or forestall. In part, these agencies of control are contained and concealed *within* the centers of production themselves, where they show up as rising echelons of corporate administration and supervision. In part, the controls show up in the familiar bureaus of government that cope, with greater or lesser success, with the social repercussions of transportation, nuclear energy, drugs, air pollution, etc. In still a different aspect, the controls invade areas of social life rather than production, as in the astonishing network of government required solely to manage the automobile (an effort that requires the labor of one out of every ten persons employed by all state and local governments). Meanwhile, in the background of the social system the controls are manifest as the growing apparatus of regulation over wages and prices, and over the total flow of economic activity—all ultimately traceable to the need to intervene more closely into an economy of increasing technological disruption.

Not that the disruptive effect of technology is itself a new phenomenon. The dislocations of the technology of the pre-scientific age—say the spinning jenny—were quite as great as those of the modern age. The difference is that in an earlier age the repair of technological disturbances was largely consigned to the adaptive powers of the individual and his family, to the ameliorative efforts of small-scale local government, and to the annealing powers of the market itself. Today, however, these traditional agencies of social repair can no longer cope effectively with the entrance of technology. The individual, now typically a member of a small urban family rather than of a large extended rural family, is much less capable of withstanding economic displacement without external assistance. The local community, faced with large-scale problems of unemployment or ecological maladjustment brought about by technical change, has no recourse but to turn to the financial help and expertise available only from larger government units. The market, which no longer "clears" when the marketers are enormous firms rather than atomistic business units, also discovers that the only antidote to grave economic disjunction is the countervailing influence or *force majeur* of the central governing authority. In a word, technology seems to be exerting a steady push from many levels and areas of the economy in the direction of a society of *organization.*

To this well-known effect of technical progress we must now add another—the capacity of technology to render redundant the physical energies of man. That is, machines do man's work for him, thereby freeing him from the bonds of toil and, not less important in the context of our inquiry, from the hegemony of the market process.

We see this disemployment effect most dramatically in the case of agriculture. But equally startling is the labor-displacing effect of modern technology in that congeries of activities associated with the extraction of basic materials from nature and their fabrication, assembly, conversion, or transport to point of sale. Since 1900, science and technology have given us a stupendous array of new products, each requiring large quantities of human effort—the automobile, the whole range of consumer durables, the communications industry, office machinery, new metals, fabrics, and materials of all kinds, to name but a few. Yet at the end of that period, the total requirements on the labor force for all these goods-centered industries had risen by only *two percentage points.* During the era of the greatest increase in factory production ever known, virtually no increase in the distribution of labor in favor of the goods sector was needed—indeed, since the hours of work fell, there was actually a *relatively decreased* need for human effort in the output of these goods.

Today we stand at the threshold of a new stage in the application of scientific technology to human activities: automation. What is most threatening about this technology is that it has begun to invade a sanctuary of hitherto relatively unmechanized work—the vast numbers of jobs in the office, administrative, and service occupations. By 1960, more than half the labor force was in these jobs. And now, into this varied group of occupations, technology is starting to penetrate in the form of machines as complex as those that can read and sort checks, or as relatively simple as those that dispense coffee and sandwiches.

This is not to maintain that no new areas of employment exist. Certainly there remain very large and still untapped possibilities for work in the reconstruction of the cities; the provision of education; the improvement of health and recreation facilities; the counseling of the young and the care of the aged; the beautification of the environment. Provided only that demand can be marshaled for these activities, there is surely no dearth of job prospects for the coming generation.

But that is precisely the point. The incursion of technology has pushed the frontiers of work into a spectrum of jobs whose common denominator is that they require *public action and public funds* for their initiation and support. The employment-upsetting characteristics of technology thus act to speed capitalism along the general path of planning and control down which it is simultaneously impelled by the direct environment-upsetting impact of technological change.

If we look further ahead, the necessity for planning is apt to become still more pressing. The day of a "fully automated" society is by no means a fantasy, although its realization may well require another century, or more. That is to say, we can, without too much difficulty, imagine a time when as small a proportion of the labor force as now suffices to overprovide us with food, will serve to turn out the manufactured staples, the houses, the transportation, the retail services, even the governmental supervision that will be required.

What the leisured fraction of the population will then do with itself is an interesting and important question. It may possibly find avenues of remuneration that are resistive to mechanical duplication, so that instead of taking in one another's wash, we buy one another's paintings. But even in this best outcome, the underlying process of production, now enormously mechanized and intricately interconnected, would require some form of coordination other than the play of market forces. If we think of the network of controls over output and disposal that now characterize the agricultural sector, we catch some idea of the controls required to operate an economy where manpower requirements generally would have been reduced to a level comparable to that of farming today. And, if the leisured population does not find adequate remuneration in unmechanizable private employments, it will have to be given the direct right to share in society's output—another vital infringement on the market's function.

But the erosion of the market goes deeper yet. For the introduction of technology has one last effect whose ultimate implications for the metamorphosis of capitalism are perhaps greatest of all. This is the effect of technology in steadily raising the average level of well-being, thereby gradually bringing to an end the condition of material need as an effective stimulus for human behavior.

Everyone recognizes that the end to want would represent the passage over an historic watershed for mankind. But it must be equally clear that such a passage will also represent a basic revision of the existential situation that has hitherto provided the main impetus for work. As needs diminish, the traditional stimuli of capitalism begin to lose their force, occupations become valued for their intrinsic pleasures rather than for their extrinsic rewards. The very decision to work or not becomes a matter of personal preference rather than of economic necessity. More telling, the drive for profit—the nuclear core of capitalist energy—becomes blunted, as the purchasable distinctions of wealth decline. In a society of the imaginable wealth implicit in another hundred years of technical progress, who will wish to be the rich man's servant at any price?

All this is no doubt a gain in human dignity. But that is not an end to it. As a result of this inestimable gain in personal freedom, a fundamental assurance for social viability also vanishes, for the market stimuli that bring about social provisioning are no longer met with obedient responses. One has but to imagine employees in an industry of central importance going on strike, not with the slim backing of unemployment insurance and a small union supplement, as today, but with liquid assets sufficient to maintain them, if need be, for a year or more, to envisage the potential for social disorder inherent in the attainment of a genuinely widespread and substantial affluence.

Yet it is precisely such an affluence that is within clear sight, provided that the impetus of science and technology continue to propel the economy for another century. In this impasse there is but one possible solution. *Some authority other than the market must be entrusted with the allocation of men to the essential posts of society, should they lack for applicants.*

We have concerned ourselves so far only with the curious two-edged effect of science and technology on the functional aspects of capitalism. Now we must pay heed to a second and perhaps even more critical effect, the conquest of the capitalist imagination by science and scientific technology.

I think it is fair to say that capitalism as an *idea* has never garnered much enthusiasm. All efforts to raise money-making to the level of a positive virtue have failed. The self-interest of the butcher and the baker to which Adam Smith appealed in lieu of their benevolence may serve as powerful sources of social energy, but not as powerful avatars of the social imagination.

By way of contrast, I think it is also fair to say that science *is* the burning idea of the 20th century, comparable in its impact on men's minds to the flush of democratic enthusiasm of the late 18th century or to the political commitment won by Communism in the early 20th. The altruism of science, its "purity," the awesome vistas it opens and the venerable path it has followed, have won from all groups exactly that passionate interest and conviction that is so egregiously lacking to capitalism as a way of life.

It is not alone that science carries a near-religious ethos of conviction and even sacrifice. Within Communism as within capitalism, the new elites arising within the framework of the old society owe their ascendancy and their allegiance in large part to science. The scientific cadres proper, the social scientists, the government administrative personnel—even the military—look to science not merely as the vehicle of their expertise, but as the magnetic North of their compass of values. These new elites have not as yet divorced their social goals from those of the society to which they are still glad to pay allegiance, and no more than the 13th-century merchants huddled under the walls of a castle, do they see themselves as the potential architects and lords of a society built around their own functions. But as with the merchants, we can expect that such notions will in time emerge and assert their primacy over the aims of the existing order.

What sorts of notions are these apt to be?

One general direction of thought will surely be the primacy of scientific discovery as a central purpose of society, a *raison d'être* for its existence, perhaps even a vehicle for its religious impulses. No doubt the distribution of social resources and of privileges will reflect this basic orientation toward scientific exploration and application. Not less characteristic will be an emphasis on rational solutions to social problems. The key word of the new society is apt to be *control*. Not alone economic affairs (which should become a secondary importance), but the numbers and location of the population and its genetic quality, the manner of social domestication of children, the choice of life-work—even the very duration of life itself—are all apt to become subjects for scientific investigation and direction.

It is tempting, but idle, to venture beyond these few suggestions. What manner of life, what institutions, what ideologies may serve the purposes of a society dedicated to the accumulation of scientific knowledge and power, we cannot foretell; variations may well be as great as those observable in societies dedicated to the accumulation of material wealth. Nor does there seem to be much point in attempting to foresee by what precise stratagems the elites and ideas of the future may finally assert their claims. Historic projection is rarely, if ever, a matter of simple extrapolation from the present and recent past. Should there arise radical parties in America, broadly-based and aimed at a rational reorganization of economic affairs, the pace of transition would be quicker. Should there not, change will still occur, but more slowly. Veblen was too impatient for his engineers to take over; Schumpeter, more realistic when he advised the intelligentsia to be prepared to wait in the wings for possibly a century, a "short run" in affairs of this kind, he said.

So, too, the examples of the past discourage us from attempting to prophesy the manner of demise of the system to be superseded. The new protagonists of social and economic control will lack for some time an articulate conception of a purposively constituted and consciously directed social system. The old ideas of the proper primacy of economic aims will linger side-by-side with newer ideas of the priority of scientific interests. And no doubt the privileges of the older order will endure side-by-side with those of the new, just as titles of nobility exist to this very day. It is conceivable that violence may attend the transfer of power and responsibility from one elite to another, but more probably the transfer will be imperceptible; managed by the sons of the old elite entering the profession of the new.

All these are the merest speculations, difficult to avoid entirely, not to be taken too literally. Only one thing is certain. It is the profound incompatibility between the new idea of the active use of science within society and the idea of capitalism.

The conflict lies in the ideas that ultimately inform both worlds. The world of science as it is applied to society is committed to the idea of man as a being who shapes his collective destiny; the world of capitalism to an idea of man as one who permits his common social destination to take care of itself. The essential idea of a society built on scientific engineering is to impose human will on the social universe; that of capitalism to allow the social universe to unfold as if it were beyond human interference.

Before the activist philosophy of science as a social instrument, this inherent social passivity of capitalism becomes archaic, and eventually intolerable. The "self-regulating" economy that is its highest social achievement stands condemned by its absence of meaning and intelligence, and each small step taken to correct its deficiencies only advertises the inhibitions placed on the potential exercise of purposeful thought and action by its remaining barriers of ideology and privilege. In the end, capitalism is weighed in the scale of science and found wanting, not alone as a system but as a philosophy.

That an ascendant science, impatient to substitute reason for blind obedience, inquiry for ideology, represents a great step forward for mankind, I do not doubt. Yet it seems necessary to end on a cautionary note. Just as the prescient medievalist might have foreseen in capitalism the possibilities for the deformation of human life as well as for its immense improvement, so the approaching world of scientific predominance has its darker side. There lurks a dangerous collectivist tinge in the prospect of controls designed for the enlargement of man but inherently capable of his confinement as well. But beyond that, there is, in the vista of a scientific quest grimly pursued for its own sake, a chilling reminder of a world where economic gains are relentlessly pursued for their own sake. Science is a majestic driving force from which to draw social energy and inspiration, but its very impersonality, its "value-free" criteria, may make its tutelary elites as remote and unconcerned as the principles in whose name they govern.

Against these cold and depersonalizing tendencies of a scientifically organized world, humanity will have to struggle in the future, as it has had to contend against not dissimilar excesses of economic involvement in this painful—but also liberating—stage of human development. Thus, if the dawn of an age of science opens larger possibilities for mankind than it has enjoyed heretofore, it does not yet promise a society in which the overriding aim of mankind will be the cultivation and enrichment of all human beings, in all their diversity, complexity, and profundity. That is the struggle for the very distant future, which must be begun, nonetheless, today.

P. B. Medawar

THE FUTURE OF MAN

In this . . . lecture, I shall discuss the origin in human beings of a new, a non-genetical, system of heredity and evolution based upon certain properties and activities of the brain. The existence of this non-genetical system of heredity is something you are perfectly well aware of. It was not biologists who first revealed to an incredulous world that human beings have brains; that having brains makes a lot of difference; and that a man may influence posterity by other than genetic means. Yet

From *The Future of Man* by P. B. Medawar, Chapter 6, pp. 84–98. © 1959 by P. B. Medawar, Basic Books, Inc., Publishers, New York, 1960.

P. B. Medawar (1915–   ) is professor of zoology at the University of London.

much of what I have read in the writings of biologists seems to say no more than this. I feel a biologist should contribute something towards our *understanding* of the distant origins of human tradition and behaviour, and this is what I shall now attempt. The attempt must be based upon hard thinking, as opposed to soft thinking; I mean, it must be thinking that covers ground and is based upon particulars, as opposed to that which finds its outlet in the mopings or exaltations of poetistic prose.

It will make my argument clearer if I build it upon an analogy. I should like you to consider an important difference between a juke-box and a gramophone—or, if you like, between a barrel-organ and a tape-recorder. A juke-box is an instrument which contains one or more gramophone records, one of which will play whatever is recorded upon it if a particular button is pressed. The act of pressing the button I shall describe as the "stimulus." The stimulus is specific: to each button there corresponds one record, and *vice versa*, so that there is a one-to-one relationship between stimulus and response. By pressing a button—any button—I am, in a sense, instructing the juke-box to play music; by pressing this button and not that, I am instructing it to play one piece of music and not another. But—I am not giving the juke-box *musical* instructions. The musical instructions are inscribed upon records that are part of the juke-box, not part of its environment: what a juke-box or barrel-organ can play on any one occasion depends upon structural or inbuilt properties of its own. I shall follow Professor Joshua Lederberg in using the word "elective" to describe the relationship between what the juke-box plays and the stimulus that impinges upon it from the outside world.

Now contrast this with a gramophone or any other reproducing apparatus. I have a gramophone, and one or more records somewhere in the environment outside it. To hear a particular piece of music, I go through certain motions with switches, and put a gramophone record on. As with the juke-box I am, in a sense, instructing the gramophone to play music, and a particular piece of music. But I am doing more than that: I am giving it musical instructions, inscribed in the grooves of the record I make it play. The gramophone itself contains no source of musical information; it is the record that contains the information, but the record reached the gramophone from the outside world. My relationship to the gramophone—again following Lederberg—I shall describe as "instructive"; for, in a sense, I *taught* it what to play. With the juke-box, then—and the same goes for a musical-box or barrel-organ—the musical instructions are part of the system that responds to stimuli, and the stimuli are elective: they draw upon the inbuilt capabilities of the instrument. With a gramophone, and still more obviously with a tape recorder, the stimuli are instructive: they endow it with musical capabilities; they import into it musical information from the world outside.

It is we ourselves who have made juke-boxes and gramophones, and who decide what, if anything, they are to play. These facts are irrelevant to the analogy I have in mind, and can be forgotten from now on. Consider only the organism on the one hand—juke-box or gramophone; and, on the other hand, stimuli which impinge upon that organism from the world about it.

During the past ten years, biologists have come to realize that, by and large, organisms are very much more like juke-boxes than gramophones. Most of those reactions of organisms which we were formerly content to regard as instructive are in fact elective. The instructions an organism contains are not musical instructions inscribed in the grooves of a gramophone record, but *genetical* instructions embodied in chromosomes and nucleic acids. Let me give examples of what I mean.

The oldest example, and the most familiar, concerns the change that comes over a population of organisms when it undergoes an evolution. How should we classify the environmental stimuli that cause organisms to evolve? The Lamarckian theory, the theory that acquired characters can be inherited, is, in its most general form, an *instructive* theory of evolution. It declares that the environment can somehow issue genetical instructions to living organisms—instructions which, duly assimilated, can be passed on from one generation to the next. The blacksmith who is usually called upon to testify on these occasions gets mightily strong arms from forging; somehow this affects the cells that manufacture his spermatozoa, so that his children start life specially well able to develop strong arms. I have no time to explain our tremendous psychological inducement to believe in an instructive or Lamarckian theory of evolution, though in a somewhat more sophisticated form than this. I shall only say that every analysis of what has appeared to be a Lamarckian style of heredity has shown it to be *non*-Lamarckian. So far as we know, the relationship between organism and environment in the evolutionary process is an elective relationship. The environment does *not* imprint genetical instructions upon living things.

Another example: bacteriologists have known for years that if bacteria are forced to live upon some new unfamiliar kind of foodstuff or are exposed to the action of an anti-bacterial drug, they acquire the ability to make use of that new food, or to make the drug harmless to them by breaking it down. The treatment was at one time referred to as the *training* of bacteria—with the clear implication that the new food or drug *taught* the bacteria how to manufacture the new ferments upon which their new behaviour depends. But it turns out that the process of training belies its name: it is not instructive. A bacterium can synthesize only those ferments which it is genetically entitled to synthesize. The process of training merely brings out or exploits or develops an innate potentiality of the bacterial population, a potentiality underwritten or subsidized by the particular genetic make-up of one or another of its members.

The same argument probably applies to what goes on when animals develop. At one time there was great argument between "preformationists" and those who believed in epigenesis. The preformationists declared that all development was an unfolding of something already there; the older extremists, whom we now laugh at, believed that a sperm was simply a miniature man. The doctrine of epigenesis, in an equally extreme form, declared that all organisms begin in a homogeneous state, with no apparent or actual structure; and that the embryo is moulded into its adult form solely by stimuli impinging upon it from outside. The truth lies somewhere between these two extreme conceptions. The genetic instructions are preformed, in the sense that they are already there, but their fulfilment is epigenetic—an interpretation that comes close to an elective theory of embryonic development. The environment brings out potentialities present in the embryo in a way which (as with the buttons on a juke-box) is exact and discriminating and specific; but it does not *instruct* the developing embryo in the manufacture of its particular ferments or proteins or whatever else it is made of. Those instructions are already embodied in the embryo: the environment causes them to be carried out.

Until a year or two ago we all felt sure that *one* kind of behaviour indulged in by higher organisms did indeed depend upon the environment as a teacher or instructor. The entry or injection of a foreign substance into the tissues of an animal brings about an immunological reaction. The organism manufactures a specific protein, an "antibody," which reacts upon the foreign substance, often in such a way as to prevent its doing harm. The formation of antibodies has a great deal to do with resistance to infectious disease. The relationship between a foreign substance and the particular antibody it evokes is exquisitely discriminating and specific; one human being can manufacture hundreds—conceivably thousands—of distinguishable antibodies, even against substances which have only recently been invented, like some of the synthetic chemicals used in industry or in the home. Is the reaction instructive or elective?—*surely*, we all felt, instructive. The organism learns from the chemical pattern of the invading substance just how a particular antibody should be assembled in an appropriate and distinctive way. Self-evident though this interpretation seems, many students of the matter are beginning to doubt it. They hold that the process of forming antibodies is probably elective in character. The information which directs the synthesis of particular antibodies is part of the inbuilt genetical information of the cells that make them; the intruding foreign substance exploits that information and brings it out. It is the juke-box over again. I believe this theory is somewhere near the right one, though I do not accept some of the special constructions that have been put upon it.

So in spite of all will to believe otherwise, and for all that it seems to go against common sense, the picture we are forming of the organism is a juke-box picture—a juke-box containing genetical instructions inscribed upon chromosomes and nucleic acids in much the same kind of way as musical instructions are inscribed upon gramophone records. But what a triumph it would be if an organism could accept information from the environment—if the environment could be made to act in an instructive, not merely an elective, way! A few hundred million years ago a knowing visitor from another universe might have said: "It's a splendid idea, and I see the point of it perfectly: it would solve—or could solve—the problems of adaptation, and make it possible for organisms to evolve in a much more efficient way than by natural selection. But it's far too difficult: it simply can't be done."

But you know that it has been done, and that there is just one organ which can accept instruction from the environment: the brain. We know very little about it, but that in itself is evidence of how immensely complicated it is. The evolution of a brain was a feat of fantastic difficulty—the most spectacular enterprise since the origin of life itself. Yet the brain began, I suppose, as a device for responding to elective stimuli. *Instinctive* behaviour is behaviour in which the environment acts electively. If male sex hormones are deliberately injected into a hen, the hen will start behaving in male-like ways. The potentiality for behaving in a male-like manner must therefore have been present in the female; and by pressing (or, as students of behaviour usually say, "releasing") the right button the environment can bring it out. But the higher parts of the brain respond to instructive stimuli: we *learn*.

Now let me carry the argument forward. It was a splendid idea to evolve into the possession of an organ that can respond to instructive stimuli, but the idea does not go far enough. If that were the whole story, we human beings might indeed live more successfully than other animals; but when we died, a new generation would have to start again from scratch. Let us go back for a moment to genetical instructions. A child at conception receives certain genetical instructions from its parents about how its growth and development are to proceed. Among these instructions there must be some which provide for the issue of further instructions; I mean, a child grows up in such a way that it, too, can eventually have children, and convey genetical instructions to them in turn. We are dealing here with a very special system of communication: a *hereditary* system. There are many examples of systems of this kind. A chain letter is perhaps the simplest: we receive a letter from a correspondent who asks us to write to a third party, asking him in turn to write a letter of the same kind to a fourth, and so on—a hereditary system. The most complicated example is provided by the human brain itself; for it does indeed act as intermediary in a hereditary system of its own. We do more than learn: we teach and hand on; tradition accumulates; we record information and wisdom in books.

Just as a hereditary system is a special kind of system of communication—one in which the instructions provide for the issue of further instructions—so there is a specially important kind of hereditary system: one in which the instructions passed on from one individual to another change in some systematic way in the course of time. A hereditary system with this property may be said to be conducting or undergoing an *evolution*. Genetic systems of heredity often transact evolutionary changes; so also does the hereditary system that is mediated through the brain. I think it is most important to distinguish between four stages in the evolution of a brain. The nervous system began, perhaps, as an organ which responded only to elective stimuli from the environment; the animal that possessed it reacted instinctively or by rote, if at all. There then arose a brain which could begin to accept instructive stimuli from the outside world; the brain in this sense has dim and hesitant beginnings going far back in geological time. The third stage, entirely distinguishable, was the evolution of a non-genetical system of heredity, founded upon the fact that the most complicated brains can do more than merely receive instructions; in one way or another they make it possible for the instructions to be handed on. The existence of this system of heredity—of tradition, in its most general sense—is a defining characteristic of human beings, and it has been important for, perhaps, 500,000 years. In the fourth stage, not clearly distinguishable from the third, there came about a systematic change in the nature of the instructions passed on from generation to generation—an evolution, therefore, and one which has been going at a great pace in the past 200 years. I shall borrow two words used for a slightly different purpose by the great demographer Alfred Lotka to distinguish between the two systems of heredity enjoyed by man: *endosomatic* or internal heredity for the ordinary or genetical heredity we have in common with other animals; and *exosomatic* or external heredity for the non-genetic heredity that is peculiarly our own—the heredity that is mediated through tradition, by which I mean the transfer of information through non-genetic channels from one generation to the next.

I am, of course, saying something utterly obvious: society changes; we pass on knowledge and skills and understanding from one person to another and from one generation to the next; a man can indeed influence posterity by other than genetic means. But I wanted to put the matter in a way which shows that we must not distinguish a strictly biological evolution from a social, cultural, or technological evolution: *both* are biological evolutions: the distinction between them is that the one is genetical and the other is not.

What, then, is to be inferred from all this? What lessons are to be learned from the similarities and correspondences between the two systems of biological heredity possessed by human beings? The answer is important, and I shall now try to justify it: the answer, I believe, is almost none.

It is true that a number of amusing (but in one respect highly dangerous) parallels can be drawn between our two forms of heredity and evolution. Just as biologists speak in a kind of shorthand about the "evolution" of hearts or ears or legs—it is too clumsy and long-winded to say every time that these organs participate in evolution, or are outward expressions of the course of evolution—so we can speak of the evolution of bicycles or wireless sets or aircraft with the same qualification in mind: they do not really evolve, but they are appendages, exosomatic organs if you like, that evolve with us. And there are many correspondences between the two kinds of evolution. Both are gradual if we take the long view; but on closer inspection we shall find that novelties arise, not everywhere simultaneously—pneumatic tyres did not suddenly appear in the whole population of bicycles—but in a few members of the population: and if these novelties confer economic fitness, or fitness in some more ordinary and obvious sense, then the objects that possess them will spread through the population as a whole and become the prevailing types. In both styles of evolution we can witness an adaptive radiation, a deployment into different environments: there are wireless sets not only for the home, but for use in motor-cars or for carrying about. Some great dynasties die out—airships, for example, in common with the dinosaurs they were so often likened to; others become fixed and stable: toothbrushes retained the same design and constitution for more than a hundred years. And, no matter what the cause of it, we can see in our exosomatic appendages something equivalent to vestigial organs; how else should we describe those functionless buttons on the cuffs of men's coats?

All this sounds harmless enough: why should I have called it dangerous? The danger is that by calling attention to the similarities, which are not profound, we may forget the *differences* between our two styles of heredity and evolution; and the differences between them are indeed profound. In their hunger for synthesis and systematization, the evolutionary philosophers of the nineteenth century and some of their modern counterparts have missed the point: they thought that great lessons were to be learnt from similarities between Darwinian and social evolution; but it is from the differences that all the great lessons are to be learnt. For one thing, our newer style of evolution is Lamarckian in nature. The environment cannot imprint genetical information upon us, but it can and does imprint non-genetical information which we can and do pass on. Acquired characters are indeed inherited. The blacksmith was under an illusion if he supposed that his habits of life could impress themselves upon the genetic make-up of his children; but there is no doubting his ability to teach his children his trade, so that they can grow up to be as stalwart and skilful as himself. It is because this newer evolution is so obviously Lamarckian in character that we are under psychological pressure to believe that genetical evolution must be so too. But although one or two biologists are still feebly trying to graft a Lamarckian or instructive interpretation upon ordinary genetical evolution, they are not nearly so foolish or dangerous as those who have attempted to graft a Darwinian or purely elective interpretation upon the newer, non-genetical, evolution of mankind.

The conception I have just outlined is, I think, a liberating conception. It means that we can jettison all reasoning based upon the idea that changes in society happen in the style and under the pressures of ordinary genetic evolution; abandon any idea that the direction of social change is governed by laws other than laws which have at some time been the subject of human decisions or acts of mind. That competition between one man and another is a necessary part of the texture of society; that societies are organisms which grow and must inevitably die; that division of labour within a society is akin to what we can see in colonies of insects; that the laws of genetics have an overriding authority; that social evolution has a direction forcibly imposed upon it by agencies beyond man's control—all these are biological judgments; but, I do assure you, bad judgments based upon a bad biology. In these lectures you will have noticed that I advocate a "humane" solution of the problems of eugenics, particularly of the problems of those who have been handicapped by one or another manifestation of the ineptitude of nature. I have not claimed, and do not now claim, that humaneness is an attitude of mind enforced or authorized by some deep inner law of exosomatic heredity: there are technical reasons for supposing that no such laws can exist. I am not warning you against quack biology in order to set myself up as a rival pedlar of patent medicines. What I do say is that our policies and intentions are not to be based upon the supposition that nature knows best; that we are at the mercy of natural laws, and flout them at our peril.

It is a profound truth—realized in the nineteenth century by only a handful of astute biologists and by philosophers hardly at all (indeed, most of those who held any views on the matter held a contrary opinion)—a profound truth that nature does *not* know best; that genetical evolution, if we choose to look at it liverishly instead of with fatuous good humour, is a story of waste, makeshift, compromise, and blunder.

I could give a dozen illustrations of this judgment, but shall content myself with one. You will remember my referring to the immunological defences of the body, the reactions that are set in train by the invasion of the tissues by foreign substances. Reactions of this kind are more than important: they are essential. We can be sure of this because some unfortunate children almost completely lack the biochemical aptitude for making antibodies, the defensive substances upon which so much of resistance to infectious disease depends. Until a few years ago these children died, because only antibiotics like penicillin can keep them alive; for that reason, and because the chemical methods of identifying it have only recently been discovered, the disease I am referring to was only recognized in 1952. The existence of this disease confirms us in our belief that the immunological defences are vitally important; but this does not mean that they are wonders of adaptation, as they are so often supposed to be. Our immunological defences are also an important source of injury, even of mortal injury.

For example: vertebrate animals evolved into the possession of immunological defences long before the coming of mammals. Mammals are viviparous: the young are nourished for some time within the body of the mother: and this (in some ways) admirable device raised for the first time in evolution the possibility that a mother might react immunologically upon her unborn children—might treat them as foreign bodies or as foreign grafts. The haemolytic disease that occurs in about one newborn child in 150 is an error of judgment of just this kind: it is, in effect, an immunological repudiation by the mother of her unborn child. Thus the existence of immunological reactions has not been fully reconciled with viviparity; and this is a blunder—the kind of blunder which, in human affairs, calls forth a question in the House, or even a strongly worded letter to *The Times*.

But this is only a fraction of the tale of woe. Anaphylactic shock, allergy, and hypersensitivity are all aberrations or miscarriages of the immunological process. Some infectious diseases are dangerous to us not because the body fails to defend itself against them but—paradoxically—because it does defend itself: in a sense, the remedy *is* the disease. And within the past few years a new class of diseases has been identified, diseases which have it in common that the body can sometimes react upon its own constituents as if they were foreign to itself. Some diseases of the thyroid gland and some inflammatory diseases of nervous tissue belong to this category; rheumatoid arthritis, lupus erythematosus, and scleroderma may conceivably do so too. I say nothing about the accidents that used to occur in blood transfusions, immunological accidents; nor about the barriers, immunological barriers, that prevent our grafting skin from one person to another, useful though it would so often be; for transfusion and grafting are artificial processes, and, as I said in an earlier lecture, natural evolution cannot be reproached for failing to foresee what human beings might get up to. All I am concerned to show is that natural devices and dispositions are highly fallible. The immunological defences are dedicated to the proposition that anything foreign must be harmful; and this formula is ground out in a totally undiscriminating fashion with results that are sometimes irritating, sometimes harmful, and sometimes mortally harmful. It is far better to have immunological defences than not to have them; but this does not mean that we are to marvel at them as evidences of a high and wise design.

We can, then, improve upon nature; but the possibility of our doing so depends, very obviously, upon our continuing to explore into nature and to enlarge our knowledge and understanding of what is going on. If I were to argue the scientists' case, the case that exploration is a wise and sensible thing to do, I should try to convince you of it by particular reasoning and particular examples, each one of which could be discussed and weighed up; some, perhaps, to be found faulty. I should not say: Man is driven onwards by an exploratory instinct, and can only fulfil himself and his destiny by the ceaseless quest for Truth. As a matter of fact, animals do have what might be loosely called an inquisitiveness, an exploratory instinct; but even if it were highly developed and extremely powerful, it would still not be binding upon us. We should not be *driven* to explore.

Contrariwise, if someone were to plead the virtues of an intellectually pastoral existence, not merely quiet but acquiescent, and with no more than a pensive regret for not understanding what could have been understood; then I believe I could listen to his arguments and, if they were good ones, might even be convinced. But if he were to say that this course of action or inaction was the life that was authorized by Nature; that this was the life Nature provided for and intended us to lead; then I should tell him that he had no proper conception of Nature. People who brandish naturalistic principles at us are usually up to mischief. Think only of what we have suffered from a belief in the existence and over-riding authority of a fighting instinct; from the doctrines of racial superiority and the metaphysics of blood and soil; from the belief that warfare between men or classes of men or nations represents a fulfilment of historical laws. These are all excuses of one kind or another, and pretty thin excuses. The inference we can draw from an analytical study of the differences between ourselves and other animals is surely this: that the bells which toll for mankind are—most of them, anyway—like the bells on Alpine cattle; they are attached to our own necks, and it must be *our* fault if they do not make a cheerful and harmonious sound.

George Bernard Shaw
PROMETHEUS TO SUPERMAN

DON JUAN. Are we agreed that Life is a force which has made innumerable experiments in organizing itself; that the mammoth and the man, the mouse and the megatherium, the flies and the fleas and the Fathers of the Church, are all more or less successful attempts to build up that raw force into higher and higher individuals, the ideal individual being omnipotent, omniscient, infallible, and withal completely, unilludedly self-conscious: in short, a god?

THE DEVIL. I agree, for the sake of argument.

THE STATUE. I agree, for the sake of avoiding argument.

ANA. I most emphatically disagree as regards the Fathers of the Church; and I must beg you not to drag them into the argument.

DON JUAN. I did so purely for the sake of alliteration, Ana; and I shall make no further allusion to them. And now, since we are, with that exception, agreed so far, will you not agree with me further that Life has not measured the success of its attempts at godhead by the beauty or bodily perfection of the result, since in both these respects the birds, as our friend Aristophanes long ago pointed out, are so extraordinarily superior, with their power of flight and their lovely plumage, and, may I add, the touching poetry of their loves and nestings, that it is inconceivable that Life, having once produced them, should, if love and beauty were her object, start off on another line and labor at the clumsy elephant and the hideous ape, whose grandchildren we are?

ANA. Aristophanes was a heathen; and you, Juan, I am afraid, are very little better.

THE DEVIL. You conclude, then, that Life was driving at clumsiness and ugliness?

DON JUAN. No, perverse devil that you are, a thousand times no. Life was driving at brains—at its darling object: an organ by which it can attain not only self-consciousness but self-understanding. . . .

THE STATUE. Why should Life bother itself about getting a brain. Why should it want to understand itself? Why not be content to enjoy itself?

DON JUAN. Without a brain, Commander, you would enjoy yourself without knowing it, and so lose all the fun.

From *Man and Superman* by George Bernard Shaw. Reprinted by permission of The Public Trustee and The Society of Authors.

THE STATUE.   True, most true. But I am quite content with brain enough to know that I'm enjoying myself. I don't want to understand why. In fact, I'd rather not. My experience is that one's pleasures don't bear thinking about.

DON JUAN.   That is why intellect is so unpopular. But to Life, the force behind the Man, intellect is a necessity, because without it he blunders into death. Just as Life, after ages of struggle, evolved that wonderful bodily organ the eye, so that the living organism could see where it was going and what was coming to help or threaten it, and thus avoid a thousand dangers that formerly slew it, so it is evolving today a mind's eye that shall see, not the physical world, but the purpose of life, and thereby enable the individual to work for that purpose instead of thwarting and baffling it by setting up shortsighted personal aims as at present. . . . Has the colossal mechanism no purpose?

THE DEVIL.   None, my friend. You think, because you have a purpose, Nature must have one. You might as well expect it to have fingers and toes because you have them.

DON JUAN.   But I should not have them if they served no purpose. And I, my friend, am as much a part of Nature as my own finger is a part of me. If my finger is the organ by which I grasp the sword and the mandoline, my brain is the organ by which Nature strives to understand itself. My dog's brain serves only my dog's purposes; but my own brain labors at a knowledge which does nothing for me personally but make my body bitter to me and my decay and death a calamity. Were I not possessed with a purpose beyond my own I had better be a ploughman than a philosopher; for the ploughman lives as long as the philosopher, eats more, sleeps better, and rejoices in the wife of his bosom with less misgiving. This is because the philosopher is in the grip of the Life Force. This Life Force says to him "I have done a thousand wonderful things unconsciously by merely willing to live and following the line of least resistance: now I want to know myself and my destination, and choose my path; so I have made a special brain—a philosopher's brain—to grasp this knowledge for me as the husbandman's hand grasps the plough for me. And this" says the Life Force to the philosopher "must thou strive to do for me until thou diest, when I will make another brain and another philosopher to carry on the work."

THE DEVIL.   What is the use of knowing?

DON JUAN.   Why, to be able to choose the line of greatest advantage instead of yielding in the direction of the least resistance. Does a ship sail to its destination no better than a log drifts nowhither? The philosopher is Nature's pilot. And there you have our difference: to be in hell is to drift: to be in heaven is to steer.

THE DEVIL.   On the rocks, most likely.

DON JUAN.   Pooh! which ship goes oftenest on the rocks or to the bottom? the drifting ship or the ship with a pilot on board?

THE DEVIL.   Well, well, go your way, Señor Don Juan. I prefer to be my own master and not the tool of any blundering universal force. I know that beauty is good to look at; that music is good to hear; that love is good to feel; and that they are all good to think about and talk about. I know that to be well exercised in these sensations, emotions, and studies is to be a refined and cultivated being. Whatever they may say of me in churches on earth, I know that it is universally admitted in good society that the Prince of Darkness is a gentleman; and that is enough for me. As to your Life Force, which you think irresistible, it is the most resistible thing in the world for a person of any character. But if you are naturally vulgar and credulous, as all reformers are, it will thrust you first into religion, where you will sprinkle water on babies to save their souls from me; then it will drive you from religion into science, where you will snatch the babies from the water sprinkling and inoculate them with disease to save them from catching it accidentally; then you will take to politics, where you will become the catspaw of corrupt functionaries and the henchman of ambitious humbugs; and the end will be despair and decrepitude, broken nerve and shattered hopes, vain regrets for that worst and silliest of wastes and sacrifices, the waste and sacrifice of the power of enjoyment: in a word, the punishment of the fool who pursues the better before he has secured the good.

DON JUAN.   But at least I shall not be bored. The service of the Life Force has that advantage, at all events. So.fare you well, Señor Satan.

THE DEVIL [*amiably*].   Fare you well, Don Juan. I shall often think of our interesting chats about things in general. I wish you every happiness: heaven, as I said before, suits some people. But if you should change your mind, do not forget that the gates are always open here to the repentant prodigal. If you feel at any time that warmth of heart, sincere unforced affection, innocent enjoyment, and warm, breathing, palpitating reality—

DON JUAN.   Why not say flesh and blood at once, though we have left those two greasy commonplaces behind us?

THE DEVIL [*angrily*].   You throw my friendly farewell back in my teeth, then, Don Juan?

DON JUAN.   By no means. But though there is much to be learnt from a cynical devil, I really cannot stand a sentimental one. Señor Commander: you know the way to the frontier of hell and heaven. Be good enough to direct me.

THE STATUE. Oh, the frontier is only the difference between two ways of looking at things. Any road will take you across it if you really want to get there.

DON JUAN. Good. [*Saluting Doña Ana*] Señora: your servant.

ANA. But I am going with you.

DON JUAN. I can find my own way to heaven, Ana; not yours [*he vanishes*].

ANA. How annoying!

THE STATUE [*calling after him*]. Bon voyage, Juan! [*He wafts a final blast of his great rolling chords after him as a parting salute. A faint echo of the first ghostly melody comes back in acknowledgment*]. Ah! there he goes. [*Puffing a long breath out through his lips*] Whew! How he does talk! They'll never stand it in heaven.

THE DEVIL [*gloomily*]. His going is a political defeat. I cannot keep these Life Worshippers: they all go. This is the greatest loss I have had since that Dutch painter went: a fellow who would paint a hag of 70 with as much enjoyment as a Venus of 20.

THE STATUE. I remember: he came to heaven. Rembrandt.

THE DEVIL. Ay, Rembrandt. There is something unnatural about these fellows. Do not listen to their gospel, Señor Commander: it is dangerous. Beware of the pursuit of the Superhuman: it leads to an indiscriminate contempt for the Human. To a man, horses and dogs and cats are mere species, outside the moral world. Well, to the Superman, men and women are a mere species too, also outside the moral world. This Don Juan was kind to women and courteous to men as your daughter here was kind to her pet cats and dogs; but such kindness is a denial of the exclusively human character of the soul.

THE STATUE. And who the deuce is the Superman?

THE DEVIL. Oh, the latest fashion among the Life Force fanatics. Did you not meet in Heaven, among the new arrivals, that German Polish madman? what was his name? Nietzsche?

THE STATUE. Never heard of him.

THE DEVIL. Well, he came here first, before he recovered his wits. I had some hopes of him; but he was a confirmed Life Force worshipper. It was he who raked up the Superman, who is as old as Prometheus; and the 20th century will run after this newest of the old crazes when it gets tired of the world, the flesh, and your humble servant.